Law and Society in the South

NEW DIRECTIONS IN SOUTHERN HISTORY

Series Editors
Peter S. Carmichael, West Virginia University
Michele Gillespie, Wake Forest University
William A. Link, University of Florida

The Lost State of Franklin: America's First Secession
Kevin T. Barksdale

Bluecoats and Tar Heels:
Soldiers and Civilians in Reconstruction North Carolina
Mark L. Bradley

Becoming Bourgeois: Merchant Culture in the South, 1820–1865
Frank J. Byrne

Lum and Abner: Rural America and the Golden Age of Radio
Randal L. Hall

Entangled by White Supremacy:
Reform in World War I–era South Carolina
Janet G. Hudson

The View from the Ground: Experiences of Civil War Soldiers
edited by Aaron Sheehan-Dean

Southern Farmers and Their Stories:
Memory and Meaning in Oral History
Melissa Walker

Law and Society in the South

A History of North Carolina Court Cases

JOHN W. WERTHEIMER

THE UNIVERSITY PRESS OF KENTUCKY

Copyright © 2009 by The University Press of Kentucky
Paperback edition 2010

Scholarly publisher for the Commonwealth, serving Bellarmine University, Berea College, Centre College of Kentucky, Eastern Kentucky University, The Filson Historical Society, Georgetown College, Kentucky Historical Society, Kentucky State University, Morehead State University, Murray State University, Northern Kentucky University, Transylvania University, University of Kentucky, University of Louisville, and Western Kentucky University.
All rights reserved.

Editorial and Sales Offices: The University Press of Kentucky
663 South Limestone Street, Lexington, Kentucky 40508-4008
www.kentuckypress.com

The Library of Congress has cataloged the hardcover edition as follows:

Wertheimer, John, 1963–
  Law and society in the south : a history of North Carolina court cases / John Wertheimer.
    p. cm. — (New directions in southern history)
  Includes bibliographical references and index.
  ISBN 978-0-8131-2535-0 (hardcover : alk. paper)
   1. Law—Social aspects—North Carolina—History. 2. Race discrimination—Law and legislation—North Carolina—History. 3. African-Americans—Legal status, laws, etc.—North Carolina—History. I. Title.
  KFN7478.W47 2009
  340'.11509756—dc22   2009005659
  ISBN 978-0-8131-2615-9 (pbk. : alk. paper)

This book is printed on acid-free recycled paper meeting
the requirements of the American National Standard
for Permanence in Paper for Printed Library Materials.

Manufactured in the United States of America.

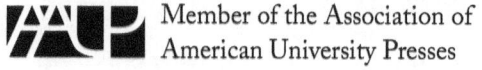

To my students

Student Contributors

The chapters in this book, excluding the introduction and conclusion, originated as research papers produced collaboratively by John W. Wertheimer and his students in "Law and Society in American History," an upper-level legal history seminar at Davidson College. The following students worked on these initial drafts:

Brook Andrews	Christine Larned
Kate Auletta	Brian Luskey
Patrick Baetjer	Rebecca MacLean
Hank Bahr	John Marshall
R. Stan Baker	Andrew Martin
Magdalena Barbosa	Laura McAlister
Louis Becker	J. J. McCarthy
Diana Bell	James McNab
John Bell	Dunn Mileham
Joshua Bennett	Josh Norris
Thomas Bevan	Lane Oatey
Eleanor Blackey	Chioma Ohanyerenwa
Jessica Bogo	Philip Osborne
Edward Bonapfel	Edward Page
Wilson Buntin	Ryan Patterson
Kelly Carraway	Emily Pesses
Timothy Cook	Chad Phillips
Michael E. Daly	Carrie Porath
Christian Deichert	Graham Powell
Andrew Devore	Thomas William Powell Jr.
David Dupee	Drew Prickett
Douglas Elkins	Mark Pustay
Maurice Falls	Charles Rayburn
Elizabeth Fleming	Shepherd Reynolds
William Fortune	David Rissing
Elizabeth Halligan Black	John Salter
Scott Herr	J. Matthew Strader
Andrew Holbrook	Elisabeth Summerlin Harper
Sarah House	Daniel Tedrick
Mark Jones	Robin Turley
Eugene Jung	Jamison G. White
Alison Kalett	David Wick
Erin Kane	Alan Williams
Michael Kaplan	Michael Wipfler
Nancy Kohler	Richard Wright
Andrew Lanoha	John Zidow

Contents

Preface ix
Introduction 1

Part I
Drawing Lines:
From Old South to Jim Crow

1. White Couples and "Mulatto" Babies:
   Jacksonian Age Divorce and Democratization 13
2. A Former Slave and His White Wife during Reconstruction:
   The Case of Pinkney and Sarah Ross 27
3. De Jure Housing Segregation in Progressive Era Winston-Salem:
   The Case of William Darnell 43

Part II
Modernity and Tradition:
Cultural Conflict between the World Wars

4. Evolution and Defamation:
   The Case of Reverend J. R. Pentuff 63
5. "Escape of the Match-Strikers":
   The Samarcand Arson Case of 1931 89
6. Padlocking Greenwich Village:
   Urbanization and Public Nuisance Law 107

Part III
Civil Rights:
The Paradigm Shifts, 1956–1980

7. Reading and the Right to Vote:
   James R. Walker Jr. and North Carolina's Literacy Test 127

8. Native Americans and School Desegregation:
   The *Chavis* Case in Robeson County   165

Conclusion   191
Notes   195
Index   267

Preface

I became a legal historian of the South quite by accident. My students made me do it. My conversion, like this book itself, began in "Law and Society in American History," a course I teach at Davidson College in North Carolina. Determined to expose my students to the joys of legal-historical research, I experimented with a format that, for me, was novel: collaborative scholarship. All of my seminar students and I would work together to produce a single research paper. I intended this effort to be a training device. The collaborative research exercise would, I hoped, teach students the techniques that they would need in order to write good individual papers at the end of the term.*

Immediately, however, the collaborative research project outgrew its role as a pedagogical means to an end and became an end in itself. Students loved working as a team and were passionate about their shared topic. When the time came to shift to individual papers, they pleaded for permission to continue with their group project. I granted their motion. The result, multiplied by eight, is now in your hands.

All eight chapters in this volume originated as group papers in my collaborative research seminar. In each case, additional research and writing followed the end of the seminar, resulting in the versions of the papers that appear here. All chapters concern the legal history of a single state: North Carolina. Because each seminar student must visit at least one research archive during the term and because I teach in North Carolina, a steady diet of home-state topics seemed a practical necessity. This necessity, however, quickly became a virtue. My students and I discovered that North Carolina has a fascinating but little studied legal history. Because all chapters concern law in a single state, common themes and characters recur, weaving the papers together into a single tome. And because North Carolina is a southern state, its history is rich

---

*See John W. Wertheimer, "The Collaborative Research Seminar," *Journal of American History* 88 (Mar. 2002): 1476–81.

with disputes concerning issues—race, religion, cultural values—that resonate powerfully to this day.

This book is collaborative in more than its classroom genesis. Many people helped bring it to fruition. Editors Michele Gillespie and William A. Link provided guidance and much-appreciated encouragement. To their credit, they viewed the project's unorthodox origins as a strength, not a weakness.

Several generous readers offered valuable feedback regarding one or more of the chapters. Eight of these readers were kind enough to make personal—and always productive—visits to my seminar over the years: Pamela Grundy, Suzanne Cooper Guasco, Nancy Hewitt, Martha Hodes, Stephen Kantrowitz, Brian Luskey, Rebecca Scott, and Richard Wertheimer.

Seven of my seminar students deserve special acknowledgment for continuing to work on their chapters after their seminars ended: Brian Luskey, Michael Daly, Mark Jones, Alison Kalett, Charles Rayburn, Elizabeth Halligan Black, and James McNab. Davidson College's generous support of student research made their work possible.

Three of the chapters have previously appeared in print, under slightly different titles. They are: Michael Daly et al., "*State v. William Darnell:* The Battle over De Jure Housing Segregation in Progressive Era Winston-Salem," in *Warm Ashes: Issues in Southern History at the Dawn of the Twenty-first Century,* edited by W. B. Moore et al. (Columbia: Univ. of South Carolina Press, 2003), 255–79; Mark Jones et al., "Pinkney and Sarah Ross: The Legal Journey of an Ex-Slave and His White Wife on the Carolina Borderlands during Reconstruction," *South Carolina Historical Magazine* 103 (Oct. 2002): 32–50; and Brian Luskey et al., "'Escape of the Match-Strikers': Disorderly North Carolina Women, the Legal System, and the Samarcand Arson Case of 1931," *North Carolina Historical Review* 75:4 (Oct. 1998): 435–60.

Davidson College promoted this project in additional ways. Grants from the college's George L. Abernethy Endowment and the office of the vice president for academic affairs provided financial support, the staff at Davidson's E. H. Little Library provided wonderful research support, and my colleagues in the Department of History provided my students and me with intellectual and moral support.

My greatest debt, however, is to the seventy-two students with whom I coauthored this book. Thank you for believing in this project and working so well with each other.

Introduction

Early in the twenty-first century, when many educated Americans can name all nine U.S. Supreme Court justices but struggle to identify even a single member of their home state's highest court, it may seem odd to devote an entire book to scenes from the legal history of a single state. But there are good reasons to do so.

Prior to the dramatic increase in the scope and power of federal law during the twentieth century, state law was prominent. As late as 1936, when Harvard Law School dean Roscoe Pound compiled a list of the ten top judges in American history, he included six judges who had served exclusively on state benches and another two whose careers included time on both state and federal benches. Only two of his top ten had served exclusively at the federal level.[1] As Pound's list suggests, the most prominent nineteenth-century state judges—James Kent of New York, Lemuel Shaw of Massachusetts, Thomas Ruffin of North Carolina—were once household names. Even somewhat less prominent occupants of nineteenth-century state benches, such as William Gaston and Leonard Henderson of North Carolina, were leading public figures. Indeed, I write these words just a short drive from both Gaston County and Henderson County, North Carolina. My neighbors and I may not pay much attention to state law, but our historical predecessors did. We should not antedate today's obsession with federal law.

Over the broad span of U.S. history, the day-to-day impact of state law on the lives of most Americans has arguably surpassed that of federal law. In part, this is because the sorts of issues handled in state courts (e.g., property law, contracts, marriage, divorce, and crime and punishment) have tended to touch American lives more directly than have the sorts of issues typically handled in federal courts throughout American history (e.g., admiralty law and patent law). The proximity of state law to people's lives eases one of the legal historian's central challenges: how to link law to society—that is, how to describe legal and social change in light of each other. This volume seeks to meet this challenge by carefully exploring several key episodes in the legal and social history of North Carolina.

In the spirit of Alexis de Tocqueville, who observed long ago that all American political questions eventually become legal questions, this book's eight chapters all concern disputes that began in North Carolina society and found their way into North Carolina courts. The time periods of these disputes and cases range from the 1830s to the 1980s. None of these cases previously has received careful scholarly attention.

This book takes an "external" approach to the study of legal history. It foregrounds the impact of extralegal factors—social, political, and economic—on legal development. It moves well beyond the question of doctrinal change to consider the many different ways in which law and society have been interwoven throughout North Carolina history. Its fine-grained, case-study approach reveals in sharp detail the rich textures of this historical interweaving. The resulting legal history is less about the law in books than about the law as lived in society. It is legal history with an emphasis on the latter. Rather than viewing the past only through the peepholes of reported appellate opinions, this book combines traditional legal research with a full range of archival, oral-history, and other sorts of historical research techniques, resulting in eight unusually detailed portraits of particular legal disputes, their factual contexts, and the social history surrounding the cases. The book's social-history emphasis casts legal disputes in a light that legal scholars do not regularly see; its legal emphasis, meanwhile, sheds new light on several standard themes of southern social history, including race relations, the role of religion in society, gender roles, and cultural mores.

As portrayed in these pages, the impact of North Carolina law could be felt well beyond courtroom doors. We find that it performed at least six distinct functions. First, it resolved particular disputes. Could African American tobacco worker William Darnell legally occupy a house that he owned, in defiance of a residential segregation ordinance in Winston? Could M. F. Boyles operate a risqué roadhouse in a quiet residential neighborhood, in defiance of his neighbors' wishes? In the 1870s, could Pinkney and Sarah Ross, an interracial couple, live as husband and wife in North Carolina, a state that barred interracial marriage? The North Carolina legal system answered these and other specific questions.

A second, and less tangible, function of state courts was to provide a high-profile forum in which North Carolinians debated fundamental values. Litigants frequently took culturally charged disputes to court in search of judicial validation. Lawyers translated their clients' cultural concerns into legal arguments. Judges, for their part, sometimes used particular legal disputes as occasions for airing their personal views on controversial issues.

Third, state litigation at times functioned in ways that might loosely be deemed "political." Litigants and lawyers went to state court in pursuit of political change that was unattainable through legislation. Additionally, some activist litigants and lawyers used state-court litigation to start grassroots movements. The publicity and fund-raising opportunities surrounding even doomed legal campaigns helped activists energize and expand their constituencies. The law's "political" function, as described here, became increasingly common during the twentieth century, as social-reform groups grew more sophisticated and as North Carolina's legal system became accessible to a wider array of individuals.

A fourth function of state courts was to provide a venue in which some North Carolinians might regain lost personal honor. Reverend James R. Pentuff, an anti-evolution crusader, used the courts in this way, as did Marville Scroggins, a white husband who charged that his white wife had humiliated him by giving birth to a "mulatto" baby. Scroggins sought a formal divorce not only to alter his legal status so he could remarry, and not only to negate any legal claim to his estate the wife might make after his death, but also to denounce his wife's misdeeds in a public forum and thereby regain personal honor. Concern with honor was not unique to the American South, but it did have special resonance there.[2]

The state courts' fifth function was to provide social therapy. Alienated and furious Native Americans in Robeson County found it at least somewhat curative to air their complaints about forced school desegregation before an attentive and respectful court. White members of the North Carolina bench and bar found it at least somewhat curative to listen.

This broad range of functions demonstrates the richness of state law as a historical subject. It also affirms the value of venturing beyond "book law" (contained in law reports) to "living law" (experienced in society). When we venture forth in this fashion, we can note a sixth function of the law: it serves, as Oliver Wendell Holmes Jr. noted, as a "magic mirror," wherein we see reflected not just our predecessors' lives but also our own.[3]

Three sorts of actors dominate the stage in the chapters that follow: litigants, judges, and lawyers. The litigants most purely represent the "society" aspect of the "law and society" phrase used in this book's title. Among them are men and women; youngsters and old-timers; blacks, whites, and Native Americans. A few were professionals, but most were workers or farmers. A few were economically comfortable, but most were lower middle class or poor. As a group, they were strikingly characteristic of North Carolina's population as a whole.

Some of the litigants were dragged into court against their will. Their only wish, once inside the legal system, was to get out and resume their lives. Other litigants, however, went to court intentionally. Some sought economic or other tangible gains. Litigation appealed to them because of the powerful remedies it offered victors. Others simply sought vindication. Litigation appealed to them because it was public, high profile, and authoritative. Some members of oppressed minority groups hoped that litigation, even if it failed in court, would expose injustice and provoke reform. Litigation appealed to them because, as minorities in a majority-rule democracy, they saw little hope of prevailing in other ways. All litigants benefited from the relatively open and accessible doors of the North Carolina courts. It was neither particularly difficult nor particularly expensive to have one's day in court.

The judges described in these pages best represent the "law" of the title. They were much less representative of the state's population than were the litigants. All of the judges described herein were white and male. Compared with state averages for personal wealth, particularly in the nineteenth century, judges were markedly well heeled.

These judges analyzed particular cases in light of two general considerations: established law and personal preference. Different judges weighed these two considerations differently. Their styles of writing opinions also varied. Some judges preached from the bench. They reached beyond the specifics of particular cases to hold forth about hot-button cultural matters. In 1832, Justice Thomas Ruffin used a divorce ruling as an occasion to lecture North Carolinians (and all others who would listen) on courtship and marriage. Chief Justice Walter Clark imaginatively invoked the English subjugation of the Irish and Russian anti-Semitism to caution Progressive Era North Carolinians not to treat African Americans too harshly. Justice Heriot Clarkson's rulings from the period between the world wars occasionally read like fire-and-brimstone sermons, heartfelt and faith based. At other times, however, judges, realizing that they were, in effect, untitled aristocrats in a democratic system, sought to mask rather than flaunt their power. They used carefully crafted written opinions and astutely calculated courtroom actions to placate the masses, not lecture them. On some occasions, this meant conveying respect for majority views. On other occasions, it meant conveying sympathy for potentially offended (and noisy) minority groups.

Mediating between litigants and judges, between social disputes and the legal system, between law and society, were the lawyers. The lawyers who people this book were marginally more diverse than the judges; not all of them, for instance, were white males. But like the judges, these lawyers almost uniformly had higher social status than the litigants they represented. The lawyers in these pages fall into three categories. Some were simply hired guns, or advocates, as most litigators are. They argued a particular position for a fee but would just as happily (and just as forcefully) have argued against that particular position. Other lawyers were paternalists—elite attorneys who agreed to help poor litigants, either out of compassion or conviction. These upper-class lawyers typically defended lower-class litigants against bullying from society's middle ranks. Finally, there were "movement lawyers," true believers in their clients' causes. These crusading attorneys shared their clients' ideological commitments and, in some cases, their social origins. The movement lawyers described in these pages ranged from the civil rights left to the anti-evolution right.

Both chronologically and thematically, the eight chapters of *Law and Society in the South* form three parts. Part I, "Drawing Lines," contains three chapters, each of which describes a "legal" effort to sharpen the demarcations of North Carolina's racial hierarchy. Each episode occurred during a different period of southern history: the slavery era, the Reconstruction era, and the Jim Crow era. Predictably, some of the whites discussed in part I's chapters sought to use the law to buttress their position of supremacy over nonwhites. Less predictably, their attempts at racial line-drawing were not particularly successful.

Chapter 1 details an attempt to etch racial lines into North Carolina divorce law. In 1832, two white husbands simultaneously sought divorces after their white wives gave birth to allegedly "mulatto" babies. Although the legal barriers to divorce were formidable at the time, the husbands claimed that the racial circumstances in their cases were so extreme that judges should open special "mulatto baby" loopholes through which they could escape their marriages.

Chapter 2 involves the racial lines inscribed in North Carolina's marriage laws. In 1873, a black man legally married a white woman in

South Carolina. Three years later, the couple, having moved to North Carolina, where interracial marriage was prohibited, was arrested for cohabiting without the benefit of marriage. Like twenty-first-century judges in cases involving out-of-state gay marriages, the judges in this case had to decide whether or not to recognize the legitimacy of a marriage that, though illegal in North Carolina, was lawfully performed in a different state.

Chapter 3 recounts an effort, spearheaded by white residents of Winston (soon to be Winston-Salem) to draw racial lines on the city's residential map. A municipal ordinance passed in 1912 made it a crime for people of one race to occupy residential property on a city block where people of another race predominated. William Darnell, an African American tobacco worker, was the first person arrested under this measure. His case, *State v. Darnell*, questioned the legitimacy of residential segregation ordinances in North Carolina.

Together, the three chapters of part I demonstrate the persistent obsession of some nineteenth- and early-twentieth-century whites with the "legal" drawing of racial lines, as well as the persistent determination of others, black and white, to blur or erase those lines. Part I demonstrates that the South's legalized racial hierarchy was affected not just by blockbuster statutes, constitutional amendments, and rulings by the Supreme Court of the United States but also by routine, state-level litigation.

The three chapters of part II, "Modernity and Tradition," explore cultural conflict between the world wars. During the 1920s and 1930s, industrial development, urbanization, scientific advances, and commercialized leisure produced widespread cultural tensions. Such tensions often generated litigation in state courts.

Chapter 4 details a North Carolina libel case that grew out of one of the hottest cultural debates in the South during the 1920s: whether or not to allow the teaching of Darwinian evolution in the public schools. In 1926, the *Raleigh Times* lampooned the "ignorance" of Reverend James R. Pentuff, a creationist preacher and one of the leading advocates of North Carolina's proposed ban on teaching evolution. Reverend Pentuff sued the *Raleigh Times* for libel, claiming, among other things, that members of the clergy deserved enhanced defamation protection, since they, in their professional capacities, were uniquely vulnerable to character assault. *Pentuff v. Park* contains some surprises for those whose knowledge of the day's evolution conflict begins and ends with the Scopes "monkey trial" in neighboring Tennessee.

Chapter 5 concerns North Carolina's legal response to the perceived delinquency of young white women in the age of textile-based industrialization and cultural modernism. The state sought to enforce traditional "womanly" behavior for white females through a mixture of legal chivalry (treating young white women with unique gentleness) and a harsh double standard (enforcing upon them a uniquely restrictive code of conduct). Errant young white women were "reformed" at the Samarcand Manor Industrial Training School, founded in 1918. By the early 1930s, conditions at Samarcand had grown so wretched that residents tried to burn it down to escape its horrors. The ensuing arson trial shows how the legal system both affected and was affected by these transgressive women.

Chapter 6 concerns another major cultural issue of the interwar years: alcohol prohibition. Reflecting the modern-day obsession with all things federal, conventional historical narratives assume that this issue evaporated, like so many droplets of spilled bathtub gin, following the repeal of national prohibition in 1933. But chapter 6 suggests that some local conflict over alcohol intensified following national repeal.

Together, the three chapters of part II suggest that interwar cultural traditionalists were quicker than their modernist rivals to invoke state law. Such hallmarks of cultural modernism as secularization and loosening sexual mores were organic responses to broad social forces. Their purveyors did not frequently resort to law. Those promoting traditional cultural ends, in contrast, were quick to employ novel legal means. They sought such legislation as alcohol prohibition and bans upon the teaching of evolutionary theory. They also creatively employed litigation, as these chapters demonstrate. Although these interwar cultural conservatives were notably quick on the legal draw, their record in courtroom showdowns was mixed. They fared better in state supreme courts, where elite religious conservatives predominated, than in trial courts, where popular juries, defying the "Bible Belt" stereotype of the culturally conservative southern populace, proved surprisingly unsympathetic to traditionalists' concerns.

Part III, "Civil Rights," ventures into the mid-twentieth century and explores two different sorts of civil rights activism by two different ethnic groups in two different parts of the state. The disputes described in chapter 7 took place in a region of northeastern North Carolina where the majority of the population was African American. There, from the mid-1950s through the early 1960s, James R. Walker Jr., a black attorney and political activist, led a surprisingly effective grassroots legal campaign for African American voting rights. The chapter reminds us that the history of African American civil rights litigation extends well beyond Thurgood Marshall and the National Association for the Advancement of Colored People (NAACP).

The case that is the focus of chapter 8 arose in the 1970s in Robeson County, a southeastern North Carolina county shared by three racial groups: whites, blacks, and Native Americans. Prior to *Brown v. Board of Education*, a three-way form of educational segregation prevailed in Robeson County. Each racial group attended its own public schools. Native Americans had developed a sense of ownership regarding their segregated schools, so when desegregation became law, some Native Americans protested. Their protests landed them in state court, where they argued that school desegregation laws should apply to blacks and whites but not to American Indians.

Taken together, parts I, II, and III reveal several trends. The book's chronologically arranged chapters trace the increasing institutional complexity of North Carolina life. The legal disputes described in part I all concerned the most basic of social institutions: the single-family household. The legal disputes in parts II and III involved larger and more complex institutions, both private and public. As North Carolina's social life became more complex, so did its legal history.

This book's chapters also serve to trace the state legal system's increasing openness to diverse voices. Ethnic minorities and women are important presences throughout the book, but their voices are almost never directly heard in the book's early chapters. Social hierarchy best explains this silence, but legal rules helped. In the 1830s, the decade in which chapter 1's case played out in court, the vast majority of African Americans in North Carolina were slaves. Although the state's legal system dealt extensively with slavery, it muzzled slave voices. Slaves, of course, could not serve as lawyers, much less judges. They also could not sue, and legal rules even barred them from testifying in court against whites. Women's participation in the legal system was minimized by similar, albeit much less severe, social and legal constraints. According to the doctrine of "coverture," for instance, the legal identity of a married woman, for many purposes, disappeared into that of her husband, leaving her, in the words of one North Carolina Supreme Court ruling, "under a personal incapacity to act."[4]

During the twentieth century, minority and female voices became much more audible within the state's legal system. As the book's later chapters show, twentieth-century representatives of these groups went to court to sue, argue, testify, and agitate. Several factors explain the enhanced ability of women and minorities to go to state court for relief. Some early twentieth-century women leveraged their domestic authority as wives and mothers to gain legal authority. Other women became lawyers and sought to defend women's rights through the legal system.

The legal experiences of African Americans were distinct but not entirely different from those of white women. The African Americans described in part I sought their desired legal ends by teaming with paternalistic (or self-interested) whites. Following World War II, a critical mass of African American lawyers emerged; these southern black lawyers played important (and still underappreciated) roles in the legal history of civil rights. In addition, national groups—from the Southern Conference Educational Fund to the American Friends Service Committee to the federal government itself—further enhanced the claims-making ability of local minority litigants. And by the 1970s, at least some white lawyers and judges listened to minority grievances with unprecedented—and unfeigned—interest.

This book also traces the increasing reach of federal law. The older North Carolina cases discussed herein had nothing to do with federal law. The more recent cases took place in the shadow of federal law. Although this trend reflects the themes of the cases involved (family law and civil rights, respectively), it also reflects the tremendous expansion of federal law during the twentieth century.

One final thought regarding federalism: when scholars discuss state law in the South, they often contrast it to federal law and portray it as almost uniformly antithetical to progress and change, especially in the area of race. This view is too simplistic. Admittedly, and unquestionably, law in North Carolina undergirded such oppressive institutions as slavery and Jim Crow segregation. *Law and Society in the South* contains ample evidence of this "legal" oppression. But the North Carolina courts acted in complex ways. The first three chapters, for instance, describe racist attempts to use North Carolina law to bolster the domination of whites over blacks. Each time, the North Carolina Supreme Court thwarted these politically popular attempts. Likewise, the book's later chapters show that the North Carolina courts became an important and often effective venue within which racial minorities in the twentieth century presented grievances in their own voices. This book suggests that the courts of North Carolina, and perhaps other southern states, played an underappreciated role in limiting the reach of white supremacy. Those who think that Alabama's conviction of the Scottsboro Boys in the 1930s or Mississippi's failure to convict Byron De La Beckwith in the 1960s says all that needs saying about law and society in the South might need to think again.

Part I

Drawing Lines: From Old South to Jim Crow

Chapter 1

White Couples and "Mulatto" Babies

Jacksonian Age Divorce and Democratization

For centuries, from the colonial period at least through the Jim Crow era, North Carolina law buttressed racial hierarchy. Elite whites, such as those who adopted North Carolina's slave codes, authored most of North Carolina's legalized racism. But the nature of Tar Heel democracy was such that even non-elite whites could attempt to inscribe racial distinctions into law. This chapter concerns two such attempts from the 1820s and 1830s, launched by two non-elite white men: Marville Scroggins and Jesse Barden.

Marville Scroggins was a white yeoman farmer in Buncombe County, North Carolina. Late in the 1820s, he came to a realization that allegedly "dissipated all hopes of happiness on this side of the grave." His white wife, he concluded, had given birth to a "mulatto" child. Scroggins sued for divorce.[1]

Jesse Barden, too, was a white yeoman Tar Heel. In the late 1820s, he also had a realization that "completely ruined his peace and happiness for life." He concluded, "to his utter horror and astonishment," that his white wife had birthed a "mulatto" child. Like Scroggins, he sued for divorce.[2]

Charles Rayburn, Patrick Baetjer, Diana Bell, Thomas Bevan, Jessica Bogo, Edward Bonapfel, Douglas Elkins, Erin Kane, Michael Kaplan, and Nancy Kohler contributed to this chapter.

Both men lost in superior court and appealed. During the North Carolina Supreme Court's term of December 1832, Justice Thomas Ruffin authored unanimous rulings in both cases. Strikingly, although the two men's claims were nearly identical, Marville Scroggins lost and Jesse Barden won.[3]

Scholars have uniformly explained this conspicuous divergence in terms of a presumed (and presumably racist) "public outcry." Historian Martha Hodes writes that a "public outcry" following Justice Ruffin's ruling in *Scroggins* "forced the court" to reverse direction in *Barden*. Legal historian Hendrik Hartog concurs. "Ruffin's opinion in *Scroggins*," Hartog states, "was reversed shortly thereafter because of a public outcry." Peter Bardaglio qualifies that assertion somewhat but nonetheless suggests an identical conclusion. "Apparently," Bardaglio carefully writes, "the public opposition generated by Ruffin's first opinion was enough to surmount the court's commitment to common-law tradition" of adherence to precedent. All three scholars suggest that Justice Ruffin's refusal to grant a "mulatto-baby divorce" in *Scroggins* provoked so much racist outrage that an intimidated court backed down in *Barden*.[4]

This chapter reaches a different conclusion: that Ruffin, having issued the strongly antidivorce ruling in *Scroggins*, did a superficial about-face. Bowing conspicuously to public opinion, he ruled weakly in favor of Jesse Barden—though in a way that invited future courts to ignore his reversal and abide by the powerful pro-marriage reasoning in *Scroggins*. By appearing to bend the formal law to the public will, Ruffin preempted popular outrage and inoculated his court against democratic reform. He used democratic language to preserve elite power.

In addition to presenting the argument outlined above, this chapter introduces several themes that are pervasive throughout the book. First, the state's legal system was accessible. To be sure, courthouse doors were all but sealed to many North Carolinians, most notably the one-third of the state's population who were slaves as of 1830. But the ability of decidedly non-elite white men such as Marville Scroggins and Jesse Barden to seek divorce in court is significant. Men of comparable social standing would not have been able to seek divorces in local English courts. In England, a private bill issued by Parliament was the only path to divorce; it was a narrow path, open only to the rich and well connected.[5] Divorce and many other legal remedies were comparatively accessible in North Carolina. Over the next century and a half, as future chapters will show, the state's legal system would grow even more accessible.

Second, in their divorce petitions, Scroggins and Barden urged judges to draw racial lines into state law. Justice Ruffin and his elite brethren, however, were reluctant to do so. Subsequent chapters describe similar efforts to persuade elite judges to inscribe white supremacy into law and similar judicial reluctance to do so, or to do so as fully as petitioners wished.

Finally, in *Scroggins* and *Barden*, we see how cultural conservatism—in particular, the elite judiciary's staunch opposition to divorce—entered North Carolina common law. In future chapters, cultural conservatism reappears in judicial responses to the theory of evolution, to religion, and to alcohol prohibition. Like racial hierarchy, cultural conservatism is an enduring theme of southern history. This chapter suggests that, like racial hierarchy, cultural conservatism traces at least part of its ancestry to the institution of slavery.

In analyzing the two nearly identical 1832 divorce appeals, we might first consider some alternate explanations for Scroggins's loss and Barden's victory. Class bias fails to explain Justice Ruffin's divergent opinions in the two cases, not because Ruffin was free of class bias but because both litigants came from the same social class: yeoman farmers. White yeoman farmers in the South at the time possessed modest amounts of land and owned no slaves or just a few (up to about ten). In the social order, they ranked above slaves, free blacks, and landless whites but below "planters," whose land and slave holdings vastly exceeded theirs. Unlike soft-handed planters, whose slave labor was sufficient to support their households, yeomen and their families had to labor in the fields themselves, whether or not they owned a few slaves. Yeomen were proud of their productive labor, their social superiority over the landless, and their presumed racial superiority over blacks.[6] In order to be granted a divorce, however, even the most self-reliant yeoman had to win the approval of the elite planters who dominated the state's legal machinery.

At the time of their marriage, Marville Scroggins and Lucretia Brigman belonged to the yeomanry, as did Jesse Barden and Ann Bradbury. The four future spouses and their families all occupied the more prosperous end of the yeoman category, some owning as many as eight slaves or as few as none. This relative wealth makes the later need for divorce logical in a social sense. The wealthier the couple, the greater the need to formalize a split through official divorce, in order to resolve property disputes. Poor couples, however incompatible, had both fewer means and less incentive to hire lawyers and prepare formal divorce petitions. As members of the middling yeomanry, Scroggins and Barden were financially comfortable, which explains their interest in filing—and ability to file—for divorce. It fails, however, to explain why Scroggins ultimately lost and Barden won.[7]

The lawyers who worked on the respective cases did not cause the divergent outcomes. Both litigants hired lawyers to prepare their initial divorce petitions. But whereas Scroggins hired a second lawyer to argue his appeal in the North Carolina Supreme Court, Barden sent his appeal to Raleigh without the benefit of counsel, a practice that, though not uncommon, was more risky. Yet it was the lawyer-less Barden who won.

A much more important distinction involves the timing of events described in the divorce petitions themselves. According to Marville Scroggins's allegations, his wife gave birth four and a half months after their wedding. Scroggins, thus, would not have seen the child until after saying "I do." Ann Barden, in contrast, gave birth prior to her marriage to Jesse Barden, meaning that the latter did have the opportunity to inspect the child before saying "I do." Scroggins's case for divorce thus seems much stronger. Yet it was Barden, not Scroggins, who won.[8]

Perhaps the explanation for the different results in each case lies inside the court itself. Justice Ruffin, who wrote both opinions, implied as much. "Upon the merits," he wrote in *Barden*, "I confess that, I am individually inclined" to rule against Jesse Barden "for the reasons upon which the [*Scroggins*] case . . . was decided. . . . But my brethren think there is a difference."[9]

Justice Ruffin's suggestion that his "brethren" strong-armed him into voting (and writing) in favor of Barden is unpersuasive. Ruffin, who already enjoyed a national reputation and who would later make Harvard Law School dean Roscoe Pound's 1936 list of the top ten judges in American history, was not easily strong-armed. He was reputed to have "dominated" his two "less-talented brother judges." Neither of his colleagues was in a strong position to challenge him. Joseph Daniel was at the very beginning of his judicial career. Chief Justice Leonard Henderson was at the very end and would die eight months after the *Barden* decision (Ruffin succeeded him as chief justice). More importantly, no evidence suggests that either Daniel or Henderson favored divorce liberalization. Neither, after all, had dissented in *Scroggins*. Indeed, both endorsed that decision. Subsequent to *Barden*, moreover, the court consensually reverted to its firm antidivorce stand. Ruffin's claim that his brethren imposed the *Barden* decision upon him is unconvincing.[10]

Thus, internal factors—social class, the merits of the petitions themselves, bench politics—fail to explain the *Scroggins-Barden* divergence. Perhaps the answer lies outside the court, in the realm of public opinion. Again, Justice Ruffin implied as much. At the end of his opinion in *Barden*, he provided the following explanation for his departure from the strongly antidivorce reasoning of *Scroggins*: "This is a concession to the deep rooted and virtuous prejudices of the community upon this subject."[11]

Previous scholars have uniformly concluded that *Scroggins* touched off a racist firestorm so fierce that the court backed down in *Barden*. "Ruffin's opinion in *Scroggins*," reads one typical analysis, "was reversed shortly thereafter because of a public outcry."[12] The "public outcry" hypothesis may be correct, but there are two serious problems with it. First, no scholar has yet produced any evidence that a public outcry occurred. Second, a "public outcry" explanation would require a substantial time gap between *Scroggins* and *Barden*, as follows: (1) the court rules on *Scroggins*, (2) news of the *Scroggins* ruling spreads, (3) an outcry materializes, (4) word of that outcry gets back to the court, and (5) the court factors the outcry into its *Barden* ruling.

But no such time gap existed. The North Carolina Supreme Court heard and decided both *Scroggins* and *Barden* in its term of December 1832, which lasted less than three months. In that brief span, the court issued eighty-eight written opinions. The written opinions in *Scroggins* and *Barden* seem to have been released consecutively, at about the same time. All surviving records of the court's business that term—newspaper reports, official case reports—list the two divorce rulings right next to each other, as the term's final two law cases. Surviving newspaper accounts did not report either ruling until both had been released. It is technically possible that the "public outcry" explanation could be correct, but it seems highly unlikely.[13]

This chapter's alternative hypothesis is that, while no public outcry occurred, Justice Ruffin used *Barden* to defuse the popular anger that he expected *Scroggins* to generate. Ruffin recognized that *Scroggins* would be controversial, in part because the case's central conflict—marital sanctity versus "racial" purity—divided antebellum whites along class lines. Ruffin and other planters tended to give higher priority to marital sanctity. Yeoman farmers, whose social status was less secure, tended to give higher priority to white supremacy. Because planters dominated the courts, they could render a decision that strongly bolstered marriage, hence the *Scroggins* decision. Recognizing, however, that yeomen might howl and might mobilize against continued elite control of the judiciary, Ruffin tossed them a legally insignificant (but politically effective) bone, hence the *Barden* decision. By appearing to bend to the public will, Ruffin averted an outcry and helped to deflect Jacksonian-type attempts to democratize the North Carolina Supreme Court.

Democratizing political trends associated with President Andrew Jackson provide an important context for the *Scroggins* and *Barden* decisions. In November 1832, just one month before Ruffin and his judicial brethren convened in Raleigh for the term that included the two divorce cases, President Jackson's powerful anti-elitist rhetoric propelled him to a decisive reelection victory. Ruffin and company were keenly aware of Old Hickory's popularity. In North Carolina, Jackson beat his nearest rival by roughly a 5-to-1 margin.[14]

Believing that, as the newly established *People's Press* of Wilmington, North Carolina, proclaimed on its masthead, "the People can do no wrong," the Jacksonians prescribed the same remedy for all public ills: democratization. They urged expanded white male suffrage and the conversion of as many public offices as possible from appointive to elective. Jackson and his followers believed that the spread of majority rule would break the elite's unearned monopoly on power, give virtuous farmers and mechanics the public voice they deserved, and create a fairer and better nation.[15]

Democratizers found an inviting target in the elite, unelected judiciary. President Jackson routinely thumbed his nose at the federal courts. He even proposed that federal judges should no longer be appointed for life; rather, they should be popularly elected for seven-year terms. Jacksonians were similarly critical of state judiciaries, since they, too, were unelected. State judges "should be made responsible to the people by periodical elections," demanded the Jacksonians, who wanted "no part of our government independent of the people." In 1832, just prior to the *Scroggins* and *Barden* appeals, Mississippi became the first state in the nation to require its judges to stand for election. Other states, including North Carolina, appeared poised to follow.[16]

In Raleigh, as the North Carolina Supreme Court convened for its December 1832 term, several propositions designed to clip the North Carolina judiciary's wings were in the legislative pipeline. One proposal would have slashed the salaries of state Supreme Court justices by 20 percent. Another sought to weaken the state bench's important power to impose punishments for contempt. A third bill proposed popular election of court clerks. "[I]f we adopt this system," one conservative critic sniffed, "our Judges will [soon] ascend to office through the portals of a grog shop." The law passed.[17]

A fourth bill, introduced just as Ruffin and his colleagues convened for their December 1832 term, was even more radical. It called for the abolition of the North Carolina Supreme Court. The bill would divide the state into seven judicial circuits. Judges would rotate around these circuits and would take turns serving on a supreme tribunal that would hear appeals. The existing judicial pyramid would flatten into seven swirling circuits. No judges would enjoy the permanent elevation that Ruffin and his two privileged brethren enjoyed. "Much to my astonishment," one conservative editor wrote after reporting on this bill's introduction, "I find it has many advocates, and doubts are seriously entertained whether it may not succeed." Although the bill fell two votes shy in the state senate, its message for Ruffin and company was clear: Public opinion has you in its crosshairs. Beware![18]

Scroggins and *Barden* were potential snares for the North Carolina Supreme Court because they pitted two of the day's top social values—marital sanctity and white supremacy—against each other. Denying the divorces would appear to give judicial sanction to mixed-race households and sex between black men and white women. Granting the divorces would weaken marriage by providing subsequent divorce seekers in North Carolina with legal precedent. The dilemma was especially tricky because Ruffin's strong preference for denying the divorces placed him at odds with the views of the state's mobilized democratizers.

Ruffin's elite social status was so firmly established that whiteness, as such, was of comparatively minor concern. A little blurring of racial lines among the lower orders was less threatening to him than it was to whites of lower social standing.[19] Marriage, on the other hand, was of central concern. As a judge, Ruffin knew of, and supported, the common law's longstanding presumption against divorce. Aware that legal loopholes have a tendency to grow, he was reluctant to create one for any class of divorce, even when so "odious" a circumstance as interracial infidelity was present. (Ruffin may have been aware of the situation in neighboring Virginia, where "mulatto baby divorces," having started as an exceptional loophole, had cleared a path for other sorts of divorces and remained, as of the 1830s, the single most common sort of divorce granted to Virginia husbands.)[20]

As a devout Christian, Ruffin believed that God was a "witness" to all proper marriages. He regarded the resulting marriage bonds between husband and wife to be unbreakable.[21] Moreover, his personal experiences as a plantation patriarch appear to have affected his views on family life, including divorce. In his well-known 1829 ruling in *State v. Mann*, Ruffin articulated a slavery-based understanding of domestic relations that accurately predicted his subsequent approach to divorce law. In *State v. Mann*, Ruffin argued that even well-intended state attempts to protect slaves from abuse (in this case, the state sought to punish a white master who had disciplined a female slave by shooting her) would ultimately be bad for masters and slaves alike. Slaves who knew that law courts were peering over their masters' shoulders would inevitably misbehave, prompting masters to "bloody vengeance." Judicial oversight of the master-slave relationship would thus intensify the very conflict that it sought to redress.[22]

Three years later, in *Scroggins v. Scroggins*, Ruffin transferred this slavery-based reasoning to divorce law. Just as slaves who thought that the courts would protect them would be more likely to misbehave and thus suffer at their masters' hands, Ruffin reasoned, spouses who knew that divorces were available would be less likely to make the sacrifices necessary to achieve happy, or at least tolerable, marriages.

Justice Ruffin, consistent with his class, ranked marital sanctity above racial purity and white supremacy. North Carolina yeomen did the reverse. Lacking both large plantations and formal legal training, yeomen cared relatively little about divided estates or common law proscription of divorce. An article in the anti-aristocratic *Greensborough Patriot* in 1832 suggests something of the day's relatively relaxed popular attitude toward divorce. The piece concerned a pair of modestly situated newlyweds who sought a divorce soon after their wedding. The local officer who had married them "until death [did they] part" agreed, for triple the marriage fee, to divorce them. He instructed the unhappy newlyweds to hold opposite ends of a cat, severed the animal with an ax, and proclaimed, "Death has now parted you!"[23]

Yeomen cared more about race than they did about the sanctity of marriage. Situated in the middle of the social hierarchy, yeomen sought to elevate themselves by suppressing blacks. In North Carolina, as elsewhere, the same anti-elitist, Jacksonian populists who sought to reduce social distinctions among different classes of whites sought to increase such distinctions between whites and others. In the year before the December 1832 term of the state's Supreme Court, North Carolina lawmakers, even as they democratized public life for whites, imposed new constraints upon nonwhites. New measures prohibited "free persons of color" from preaching in public, limited their ability to "hawk and peddle," and established exclusively for such persons a convict leasing system.[24]

To be sure, yeoman farmers were not the only North Carolinians who supported such racial measures. Indeed, in the aftermath of Nat Turner's slave rebellion in neighboring Virginia in 1831, these proposals enjoyed widespread white support. But yeoman farmers were the bone and muscle of a Jacksonian political movement that fought to elevate the political status of middling whites and to suppress the political status of free blacks. Amendments to the North Carolina constitution adopted between the mid-1830s and mid-1850s reflect the success of this movement. These "democratizing" constitutional revisions shifted political power from the state's planter-rich east toward its yeoman-rich west, expanded white male suffrage by removing property qualifications, and disfranchised blacks entirely. (North Carolina was not the only state during the Jacksonian age where suffrage barriers were lowered for whites but raised for free blacks.)[25]

Thus, Jacksonian democratizers sought, among other things, to sharpen racial distinctions. Mulatto babies in white families, in contrast, threatened to blur racial distinctions in ways that troubled the racist majority. One of the most significant privileges attached to white manhood, after all, was exclusive sexual access to white women.[26] Justice Ruffin apparently sensed that denial of "mulatto baby divorces" risked a political backlash. Neutralizing this delicate situation would require all of Ruffin's skills as a legal stylist and political strategist.

As an elite judge in a democratic age, Ruffin was careful. He deftly coated controversial legal rulings with a layer of political spin designed to immobilize potential critics. *State v. Mann* (1829) again proves instructive. John Mann, a slave renter, shot and wounded Elizabeth Jones, a rented slave, in the course of disciplining her. North Carolina convicted Mann of assault and battery. Ruffin overturned this conviction on the hard-hearted grounds that slave owners and renters needed "full dominion over . . . the slaves" in matters of discipline. Anticipating screams from the budding antislavery movement, however, Ruffin skillfully denied personal responsibility for his own ruling. As a compassionate *man*, he suggested in the decision's famous opening paragraph, he would like nothing better than to follow his "feelings" and give the brutal shooter his comeuppance. But as a *judge*, he could not do so. The law "impose[d]" a "severe" and "imperative duty" upon judges to follow rules, not emotions. Legal obligation "compelled" a "reluctan[t]" Ruffin to let John Mann go unpunished.[27]

This was not so, however. No law compelled Ruffin to overturn Mann's conviction. There was no controlling statute. There was no controlling case law. The decision was all Ruffin's. So effective was the opening disclaimer, however, that abolitionist author Harriet Beecher Stowe, though finding the result in *State v. Mann* "dreadful," had nothing but admiration for its author. "No one can read this decision," Stowe wrote, "without feeling at once deep respect for the man [Ruffin] and horror for the system."[28] Three years after *Mann*, Ruffin would utilize the same technique in his *Scroggins* and *Barden* opinions.

The hard core of Ruffin's ruling in *Scroggins v. Scroggins* was a powerful restatement of the legal argument against divorce. As in *State v. Mann*, however, Ruffin added a sort of Teflon coating, designed to deflect criticism. This time, Ruffin defensively pointed the finger not at the iron command of "the law" (as in *Mann*) but at the cowardice of the state legislature. At issue was an 1827 statute that empowered the North Carolina courts to grant divorces "whenever they may be satisfied of the justice" of doing so.[29] Unlike a previous statute, which specified impotence and adultery as the only allowable justifications for judicial divorce, the 1827 statute offered no explicit legislative guidance.

Although Ruffin, a great legal innovator, was perfectly comfortable exercising expansive discretionary power, he began his *Scroggins* opinion in apparent anguish. "This act," he wrote of the 1827 measure, "imposes a task of great difficulty on the courts, and one, perhaps less agreeable than any they can be called on to perform, that of acting upon a most important subject without a rule laid down for them by the legislature."

Judges such as himself, he claimed, are "lost in the mazes of discretion" and told by mush-brained legislators "to do what is right, but not told what they deem to be right." He advised would-be critics not to blame him or his judicial colleagues but to blame the state legislature instead.[30]

Ruffin's discussion of divorce began with an acknowledgment that many marriages were miserable. But if sympathetic judges terminated every marriage that turned unhappy, he reasoned, total unhappiness would increase, not decrease. Successful marriages were possible only if spouses "feel that they are ever to remain" married. Only that belief can "impress upon each, the necessity of mutual forbearance, of . . . overcoming antipathies and contributing to the enjoyments of each other." A liberal divorce policy might appear humane, but the "wiser, better, kinder" course was to declare marriages "insusceptible of modification."[31] This logic, which closely paralleled (and may have been derived from) Ruffin's views on slavery, would prevail in the *Scroggins* case.

Marville Scroggins's divorce petition claimed that Lucretia had committed premarital "fraud" by concealing the paternity of her unborn child. Justice Ruffin was skeptical. Concealment of defects prior to marriage is not fraud, he observed. It is courtship. Marville must have noticed that Lucretia was halfway to motherhood at the time of their marriage. The groom's failure to gauge the bride's character made him "criminally accessory to his own dishonor." Allow this divorce for "concealed paternity," Ruffin cautioned, and North Carolina would be on a slippery slope toward divorce for concealed "uncleanness . . . idleness, sluttishness, extravagance, [and] coldness." The only safe policy was "that persons who marry, agree to take each other *as they are.*" Buyer, beware. Inspect your betrothed thoroughly in advance, Ruffin cautioned; once you tie the knot, you may not untie it. "[N]othing could be more dangerous than to allow those who have agreed to take each other, in terms *for better, for worse,* to be permitted to say, that one of the parties is worse than was expected, and therefore, the contract ought to be no longer binding," Ruffin argued.[32] The Scrogginses would have to remain married.

Scroggins v. Scroggins reflected the deeply held antidivorce views of Ruffin and his colleagues. By employing powerful and easily generalized language, the court hoped to ensure that *Scroggins*, barring legislative revision to the state's divorce law, would influence judges and lawyers for years to come. But Ruffin was politically savvy enough to realize that the day's pervasive racism and burgeoning egalitarianism made *Scroggins* a ticking time bomb. He used a companion opinion, *Barden v. Barden*, to defuse this bomb.

Barden is a curious decision, and not just because it ran so counter to the recently decided *Scroggins* case. Other Ruffin opinions draped political wrappings around legal cores. *Barden*, in contrast, contained almost nothing inside its political cover. Legally, it was nearly hollow. Ruffin worked hard to ensure that future courts would ignore *Barden* in favor of *Scroggins*. He had peppered his *Scroggins* ruling with the sorts of pithy, quotable, general statements that make for powerful legal doctrine: "persons who marry, agree to take each other as they are"; "the wife may prove much better than the husband expected; so if she turn out worse, he must keep her because he chose her." The fact-specific *Barden* ruling contained no such "doctrine-able" lines. Furthermore, Ruffin plastered *Barden* with detour signs urging future jurists to ignore what they were reading and return to *Scroggins*. So tentative was Ruffin's voice in *Barden* that the law reporter who prepared the case's official headnotes took the highly unusual step of attributing the ruling to "Ruffin, J., hesitant."[33]

Ruffin's tone was hesitant from the outset. "Upon the merits," he wrote in the fourth sentence of *Barden*, "I confess that I am individually ... inclined to concur with the judge of the Superior Court [who had denied Jesse Barden's divorce petition], for the reasons upon which the case of *Scroggins v. Scroggins* was decided at this term. But my brethren think there is a difference." Ruffin began his explanation of this supposed difference by noting that the child was black, a fact "of deep die [dye]," in Ruffin's words. He then proceeded, weakly, to distinguish *Scroggins* from *Barden* and explain why the petitioner in the latter case, unlike the former, might deserve a divorce. If Jesse Barden had married *before* the child's birth, he would have run risks "and must patiently abide the results," as Marville Scroggins must do. But because Jesse waited until shortly after the child's birth before marrying Ann, "it is but reasonable to conclude, that the birth of the child and the belief that it was his own, constituted a prevailing ... motive" for Jesse's decision to go through with the marriage.[34]

Few jurists would have found this reasoning persuasive. By the tenets of caveat emptor (buyer beware), Jesse, who had the opportunity to inspect the goods before purchase, as it were, had a much *weaker* claim to divorce than did Marville, who could not inspect the child until after the marriage. Ruffin acknowledged as much. "The obstacle with me upon this part of the case," he wrote, is that "color is an object of the senses." Jesse had the opportunity to inspect the baby. Surely no man would marry a woman under these circumstances "without being drawn, even by curiosity, not to say, instinctive affection, to see the child itself." "But it may be," Ruffin speculated, "that in so young an infant, whose mother was white, it might not be in the power of an ordinary man, from inspection of the face and other uncovered parts of the body, to discover the tinge" of blackness. Thus, unlike Marville Scroggins, Jesse Barden, Ruffin unenthusiastically concluded, deserved a chance to return to superior court to petition anew for a divorce.[35]

Although the ruling guaranteed that Jesse Barden would have his day in superior court, it did not guarantee that Barden would prevail there. Indeed, Ruffin warned Barden that he had "many difficulties before him." In order to win his superior court case and secure his divorce, Barden would have to prove six things: that the child was "of mixed blood"; that Barden was white; that his wife Ann was white; that, at the time of the marriage, Barden believed that the newborn was white and was his; that these beliefs were "created by the . . . defendant" by "false representations and active means"; and that, as of the time of the marriage, Jesse "did not, and could not, from inspection, ascertain the truth" regarding the child's lineage—that is, Jesse would have to prove that "upon inspection at that time the real color was not so obvious as to be detected by the petitioner, or a person of ordinary diligence and intelligence, and not otherwise communicated to the petitioner."[36] Jesse Barden faced steep odds.

Ruffin's distinction between *Barden* and *Scroggins* was tortured. The point of *Barden*, however, was not legal analysis but political spin. Bowing extravagantly to public opinion, whose wrath he feared, Justice Ruffin, in the decision's final and only memorable line, stated that the *Barden* ruling was "a concession to the deep rooted and virtuous prejudices of the community." This brilliant bit of rhetoric implied two useful things: that the public had already voiced its disapproval of *Scroggins* (and thus no additional protests were necessary) and that the North Carolina Supreme Court respected public opinion (and thus no further judicial democratization was necessary).[37]

Ruffin's rulings had their desired legal effect. Future courts paid attention to *Scroggins*, not *Barden*. They also had their desired political effect.

Democratizing assaults on the North Carolina Supreme Court abated. North Carolina's constitutional revisions of 1835 called for the popular election of the state's governors but not its judges. Indeed, the North Carolina judiciary would not be elected directly by the people until after the Civil War. Scholars have attributed this delay largely to Ruffin's personal popularity. His political skill, in cases such as *Scroggins* and *Barden*, deserves greater appreciation.[38]

Regarding the relation between law and public opinion, we offer two final thoughts. First, public opinion may sometimes exert less of an impact on law than historians assume. Scholars have discussed *Scroggins* and *Barden* as cases in which public opinion forced judges to reverse themselves. We suggest, however, that in these cases elite judges created the illusion of public influence in order to prevent such influence from materializing. In other words, elite and unaccountable judges co-opted the language of democracy to mask—and thus bolster—their own power. Future scholars might profitably seek other examples of this phenomenon. Finally, just as historians should not exaggerate the influence of society upon law, legal scholars should not exaggerate the law's influence on society. Under North Carolina law, Marville Scroggins remained forever married to Lucretia Scroggins. But in a frontier nation, with a state-by-state system of family law, North Carolina Supreme Court decisions did not always prevail in practice. Marville and Lucretia Scroggins split. Marville moved to Alabama, married a South Carolina woman, and raised a new family, unconcerned that he was technically a bigamist. Perhaps this was the final accommodation: the elite would retain control of the book law, while the yeomanry would write their own living law. "Justice Ruffin has made his decision," Marville Scroggins seems to have said. "Now let us see him enforce it."[39]

Chapter 2

A Former Slave and His White Wife during Reconstruction

The Case of Pinkney and Sarah Ross

Two alleged sexual relationships between black men and white women played important off-stage roles in the previous chapter. In this chapter, another such relationship—a marriage, in fact—takes center stage. The setting is the 1870s, after the Civil War, by which time white opposition to intimate relationships between black men and white women was even more intense than it had been prior to emancipation. Some Reconstruction-era whites used mob violence to suppress interracial liaisons. Others, such as those described below, used the legal system.[1]

On 31 March 1873, "amidst the firing of guns, the ringing of bells, the waving of handkerchiefs and the shouting of the multitude," the first passenger train between Charlotte, North Carolina, and Spartanburg, South Carolina, pulled into the Spartanburg depot.[2] Its route through the Piedmont of North and South Carolina would become familiar to Pinkney and Sarah Ross, a couple who repeatedly shuttled back and forth across the state line during the 1870s. Pinkney Ross, a black South Carolinian, and Sarah, a white North Carolinian, courted in North Carolina, married in South Carolina in the spring of 1873, and settled

---

Mark Jones, Brook Andrews, Joshua Bennett, Elizabeth Fleming, William Fortune, Christine Larned, J. J. McCarthy, Edward Page, Michael Wipfler, and Richard Wright contributed to this chapter.

as newlyweds in North Carolina shortly thereafter. Three years later, North Carolina indicted them for "fornication and adultery." Following a trial in Charlotte and a state Supreme Court appeal in Raleigh, they moved back to South Carolina, where they lived out their days.

Interracial sex and marriage in the post–Civil War South have recently received considerable scholarly attention. Historians have documented both the "book law" and the "mob law" that combined to present increasingly formidable obstacles to interracial couples during these years, as whites sought new ways to enforce the old racial hierarchy following the end of slavery. Although this scholarship has cast clarifying light on a topic once shrouded in myth and denial, it has tended to be "top down" in nature. By emphasizing the actions of dominant groups—legislatures and lynch mobs—these works have tended to portray interracial couples themselves as passive victims who, in the face of overwhelming opposition, exercised little control over their destinies.[3]

In this chapter, we attempt a "bottom-up" history of one interracial couple from the era: Pinkney and Sarah Ross. One of the Rosses' principal assets, we find, was their mobility. Living on the border between the Carolinas, they were aware of the opportunities and risks that communities in each state offered at different times. Like many other interracial couples of the day, they moved from place to place as necessary to exploit opportunities and avoid risks. Their experience, therefore, was not consistent with the static "book law" of either state but was a dynamic lived legal experience of a borderland people.

Reflective of the "top-down" scholarship on interracial marriage generally, previous scholars who have studied *State v. Ross* have looked only at the North Carolina Supreme Court ruling.[4] But the Rosses' experience can teach us more. Pinkney and Sarah Ross were more than flat names on the pages of a court record. They were thinking, feeling people who made calculated decisions to protect themselves, as well as they could, from legal and social dangers. Perhaps surprisingly, they succeeded.

Justice Ruffin's previously discussed habit of wrapping legal decisions in a layer of political rhetoric shows one way in which law and politics can interact. The present chapter suggests two additional ways. First, and somewhat depressingly, it shows how political shifts in the ranks of public officials—caused, in this case, by the local victories of conservative Democrats over "Radical" Republicans toward the end of Reconstruction—can alter legal outcomes dramatically, even absent any formal changes in the written law. More encouragingly, this chapter also shows that legal analysis sometimes transcends politics. Twice during the Rosses' legal odyssey, judges overcame strongly held personal and social biases and enforced the law's dictates. The phrase "rule of law," we happily conclude, is not always empty.

The future Sarah Ross was born to Samuel and Harriet Spake in 1845, the second of eight children. During Sarah's youth, the Spakes, who were white, moved frequently as they struggled to wring a livelihood from the red clay soil of the western North Carolina Piedmont. By 1870, they had settled on a small Lincoln County farm, about twenty miles north of the South Carolina state line. Owning land, the Spakes were better off than some, but by no means were they wealthy. Their farm was one of the smallest in their relatively poor, rural community.[5]

According to a somewhat suspect family genealogy, young Sarah at some point married a white man, Perry Williams. Their marriage must have been brief, however, since Sarah was listed as single and living with her parents in both the 1860 census (when she was fifteen) and the 1870 census (when she was twenty-five). It seems likely that she and Perry married in the early 1860s and that he died soon thereafter, probably a Civil War casualty. With no husband and little money, Sarah returned home to her parents.[6]

As Sarah mourned the loss of her husband and helped her family eke out a living, Pinkney Ross (or "Pink," as he was commonly known) sought to take advantage of the new freedoms and mobility open to African Americans after the war. The son of Dock and Julia Ann Ross, Pink was born in Spartanburg County, South Carolina, around 1850. He almost certainly spent his childhood as a slave. The 1860 census reports that Spartanburg County contained 7,533 enslaved blacks but only twenty-six free blacks, making it extremely unlikely that Pink grew up free. Furthermore, if Pink's parents, who were also born in Spartanburg County, *had* been among the county's tiny group of free blacks, their names should have appeared in the South Carolina census's population schedules in the decades before emancipation, for these schedules listed free people, though not slaves, by name. Neither parent is listed in any population schedule between 1830 and 1860, reinforcing the likelihood that the Rosses were slaves. The northern Spartanburg County location, a surname in common, and sheer numbers suggest that Pink could well have belonged to D. B. Ross, who owned far more slaves than anyone else in the northern district of the county. (Among D. B. Ross's sixty-one slaves in 1860 was a ten-year-old boy. This may well have been Pink.)[7]

After emancipation, a teenaged Pink Ross left Spartanburg County, South Carolina, and headed across the state line to Cleveland County, North Carolina. He settled on John Byars's farm near Camp Creek, where he found work as a farm laborer.[8] By 1870, then, a twenty-year-old Pink Ross and a twenty-five-year-old Sarah Spake were living in the same state, less than twenty-five miles apart. Somehow, they came together. They may have met through an apparent link between their respective extended families. Sarah Spake's mother was a Dellinger. Several Lincoln County Dellingers had owned slaves, some of whom would likely have been named Dellinger, too. The 1870 census of Lincoln County lists a black Dellinger family living together with a black Ross family. Interestingly, this Ross family had a one-year-old son named Pink. This young boy could have been named after a relative, perhaps an uncle, perhaps Pink Ross of Spartanburg County, South Carolina. Had this Pink visited this Ross family, he could have run across nearby Sarah Spake.[9] Alternatively, Sarah may have gotten to know Pink while visiting relatives on her father's side in Cleveland County. The 1870 census lists two families of Spakes living in Camp Creek, close to John Byars's farm, where Pink lived and worked.[10]

However they met, Pink and Sarah took to each other, courted, and decided to marry. The decision to wed is always a big one, but it was especially momentous for these two, given that the state in which they lived barred people like them from marrying each other. Interracial marriage had been illegal in North Carolina since colonial times. In Pink and Sarah's day, the controlling law was the Marriage Act of 1838, which banned "all marriages . . . between a white person and a . . . person of color to the third generation." Violators risked fines and imprisonment for up to ten years.[11]

Often harsher than the formal law was the court of public opinion. Interracial couples risked injury or death at the hands of lawless whites. The danger was particularly pronounced for couples like Pink and Sarah, a black man and a white woman. "If the negro [man] marries an outcast white woman—of course no white woman who is not an outcast of the worst possible sort would ever think of marrying him," thundered one white North Carolina man in 1867, "both he and she ought to be hung."[12]

Extralegal threats of this sort existed throughout the Carolinas. Legal barriers to interracial marriage, however, existed only north of the shared Carolina state line. Perhaps aware that some interracial couples had gotten into legal trouble when they risked marriage in North Carolina, and perhaps aware that other interracial couples had avoided legal trouble by heading south of the state line to celebrate their nuptials, Pink and Sarah opted for a South Carolina wedding.[13]

In May 1873, only a month after that first Charlotte train reached Spartanburg, South Carolina, the Ross-Spake wedding party arrived there. Although tradition dictated marriage on the bride's home turf, not the groom's, a Spartanburg wedding was prudent for this couple. Pink had family in the area. Spartanburg apparently was a good place for quick and easy marriages. Most importantly, in Spartanburg an interracial marriage was legal.[14]

Before the Civil War, when interracial marriage bans were common elsewhere, South Carolina had none; its social taboos against interracial marriage were so strong that none seemed necessary. But in 1865, South Carolina's white leaders, frightened by the end of slavery, passed a series of measures designed to maintain a lower-caste status for African Americans. Among these measures was an interracial marriage ban. It did not last long. Within a few years, a majority-black Republican government won control of the state legislature. At no other time in the history of South Carolina—a state where blacks outnumbered whites almost three to two—had the government been so representative of its constituents. In 1868, the state legislature repealed South Carolina's ban on interracial marriages.[15]

After legalization, interracial marriages did not proliferate in South Carolina, but their tiny numbers did increase. Some of this increase had in-state origins. The war had taken the lives of approximately one-third of the state's white men of military age. Tens of thousands of white South Carolina women lost husbands or suitors. A few of these women married black men.[16]

Decriminalization also attracted mixed couples from other states. Exploiting their freedom of movement—and demonstrating legal savvy—interracial couples trickled into South Carolina after the 1868 repeal. Most migrants appear to have settled just inside South Carolina's boundaries. For instance, according to the 1880 census, Fort Mill, South Carolina—just across the state line from North Carolina—

contained fifteen times as many interracial couples as did Broad River, a community of roughly similar size and demographics in the middle of the state. The majority of Fort Mill's interracial couples had migrated there from North Carolina.[17]

Thus, when Pink Ross and Sarah Spake chose to wed in South Carolina, just across the North Carolina line, they were part of a broader movement. Their moving, however, would continue. Conditions in the Palmetto State, where war and Reconstruction had exacted a heavy toll, apparently discouraged the newlyweds from staying there long. Deeply in debt, South Carolina had raised taxes to burdensome levels. Locally, midwestern grain, shipped cheaply on new rail lines, had undermined Spartanburg's corn-based economy. Pink, a farm laborer, could well have found himself without work. Equally troubling to the Rosses may have been the gruesome prevalence of Ku Klux Klan activity that appeared to accompany the collapse of the local corn economy. Spartanburg, in other words, was a great place in which to marry but a poor place for the Rosses to live. In August 1873, three months after their marriage, Pink and Sarah headed northeast to the bustling border town of Charlotte, North Carolina.[18]

Interracial marriages were just as illegal in North Carolina in August 1873 as they had been in May. But having been married legally and having lived for three months elsewhere, Pink and Sarah may have believed that their legal risks had been reduced, that their South Carolina marriage was transferable to North Carolina.

In any event, Charlotte's call must have been hard to resist. The town, which had escaped damage during the Civil War and which benefited from a postwar cotton boom, was flourishing. Its position at the junction of multiple rail lines had made it a regional trading center and had transformed it from an "unpretending village" in 1850 into the economic "'hub' of this whole region." "A new era has dawned for this town," one observer gushed early in 1874. "[S]he will speedily be transformed into a full fledged city, ambitious of being second to none of the interior ones in the South." Charlotte's population quadrupled between 1850 and 1870 and experienced another burst of growth in the 1870s.[19]

As of 1873, the year of the Rosses' move to Charlotte, Republicans still controlled much of the local government. Consequently, legal risks in the Ninth Judicial District seemed modest. Republican solicitor

W. P. Bynum did not prosecute interracial couples aggressively. Republican superior court judge George Logan had a reputation for leniency. That reputation seems well deserved. In *State v. Reinhardt and Love* (1869), Alexander Reinhardt, a "person of color," and Alice Love, a white woman, had married in North Carolina, notwithstanding the Marriage Act of 1838. Although the violation seemed clear, Judge Logan ordered a verdict of "not guilty." Conservatives were outraged but not surprised, for they regarded Judge Logan as a Radical Republican who, as one Democratic newspaper put it, "would decide in favor of the negro everytime."[20]

In the elections of 1874, anti-Reconstruction Democrats set their sights on pro-Reconstruction Republicans in the Ninth Judicial District and across the state. For the office of solicitor, local Democrats nominated W. J. Montgomery, a Confederate veteran and a loyal party man. To challenge Judge Logan, the Democrats nominated David Schenck, a promising young attorney and a former Ku Klux Klan chief. Just three years previously, a federal grand jury had indicted Schenck on charges of "Ku Kluxing" in Lincoln County, where Sarah Spake lived before marrying Pink Ross. Schenck's legal prowess, his KKK connections, and his conviction that African Americans were "poor, deluded, ignorant creatures" apparently made him an attractive judicial candidate to the Democrats. "Logan is the representative of the negro party," the local Democratic press blared, and "Schenck is the representative of the white man."[21]

The politics of race proved successful for the Democrats. Montgomery and Schenck swept to victory in the Ninth Judicial District, just as their fellow Democrats did across the state. In words that must have made the Rosses shudder, Charlotte Democrats applauded the 1874 election returns: "all white men who are in favor of a white man's Government, achieved a great victory."[22]

North Carolina Democrats, in step with resurgent Democrats elsewhere in the former Confederacy, exploited their electoral momentum the following year by calling a state constitutional convention. Their goal was to do away with the "Reconstruction Constitution" of 1868, an instrument that, Democrats insisted, had been imposed on an unwilling people. One proposed change was the addition of an interracial marriage ban. Although this provision would not alter the state's criminal law—interracial marriages were already illegal—it would shine a political spotlight on the issue of interracial marriage. Charlotte Democrats considered the interracial marriage amendment to be one of the new constitution's "important features" and cited it as one of a handful of reasons why "every honest white man" should support the new constitution.[23]

The new constitution went into effect in 1876, the same year in which Democrats completed their political sweep of North Carolina by retaking the office of governor. For the Rosses, the Democratic triumph was ominous news. Although local Democrats insisted that their leadership would benefit black and white residents alike, they made clear their intention to impose specific boundaries that blacks would not be allowed to cross. The *Charlotte Democrat* explained: "While white men intend to rule in the county and State Governments, and do not want any negro office-holders, they ... intend to accord to the negro all rights in law and equity. But imprudence and social equality will never be tolerated or permitted." In Democratic eyes, few instances of "imprudence and social equality" could have been less tolerable than marriages between black men and white women.[24]

In the summer of 1876, Solicitor Montgomery brought record numbers of fornication and adultery (F&A) cases against interracial couples. Previous solicitors had prosecuted F&A cases, but only occasionally. In 1873, the year before Montgomery's election, F&A prosecutions accounted for between 1 and 2 percent of the criminal cases heard in the Mecklenburg County superior court. In contrast, fully 10 percent (12 out of 120) of the criminal cases that Montgomery brought in the same court in the August 1876 term were for F&A.[25]

Besides increasing the quantity of F&A prosecutions, Solicitor Montgomery also changed their nature. Previous solicitors had generally invoked the charge against unmarried, same-race cohabitors. During the spring 1872 term of the Mecklenburg County superior court, for instance, the state tried William Bryan and Mary Blythe for F&A. Bryan and Blythe were an unmarried, same-race, cohabiting couple. The 1870 census lists them as sharing a household, their last names suggest that they were not married to each other, and the census categorized both as "white."[26] The Democratic solicitor Montgomery, in contrast, systematically targeted interracial couples for F&A prosecution. We have positively identified the races of six out of the twelve couples tried for F&A in August 1876. All six couples consisted of black men paired with white women. Among these were Pink and Sarah Ross.[27]

Two days before hearing *State v. Ross*, superior court judge Schenck heard another F&A prosecution: *State v. Isaac Kennedy and Mag Kennedy*. Since the Kennedys' story resembled the Rosses', their case was highly relevant. Isaac Kennedy, a black North Carolina man, and Mag Dulin, a white North Carolina woman, had joined the first wave of post-repeal migrants by traveling to South Carolina in 1869 to get married. Immediately after their wedding, the Kennedys returned to Charlotte, North Carolina, where they lived as husband and wife for seven years, until their indictment for F&A in 1876.[28]

The Kennedy case raised what the *Charlotte Observer* termed a "very interesting and novel" legal question: would North Carolina, which barred in-state interracial marriages, recognize the legitimacy of out-of-state interracial marriages? Because the North Carolina Supreme Court had not yet ruled on this issue, lawyers on both sides agreed that the Kennedys would be tried by "special verdict." This meant that a jury would find the facts and then Judge Schenck, based on those facts, would pronounce the Kennedys either "guilty" or "not guilty." In his jury charge, Judge Schenck formulated a legal rule to govern couples who, like the Kennedys, sought to circumvent North Carolina's interracial marriage ban by marrying out of state. Schenck declared that North Carolina residents could not evade North Carolina marriage law simply by going to another jurisdiction to marry and then returning to live in North Carolina. The marriage law of another state would apply, Schenck ruled, only if defendants could prove that they were both residents of that other state at the time of their marriage. Isaac and Mag Kennedy could make no such claim. The jury found that they were both North Carolinians at the time of their marriage and that they never intended to move to South Carolina. Based on the jury's finding of fact, Judge Schenck found the Kennedys guilty and sent them to jail.[29]

The jailing of the Kennedys boded ill for the Rosses. Judge Schenck's jury charge, however, opened a legal loophole for them. In order to slip through this loophole, the Rosses sensed, they would need legal help. Many other criminal defendants of the day, including some interracial marriage defendants, opted to appear without the benefit of legal counsel. The Rosses took no such chance. They prudently hired the same lawyers who had represented the Kennedys: William Shipp and William Bailey.[30]

Both Shipp and Bailey were top-drawer lawyers. Their law office's tony address, one block from "The Square" in downtown Charlotte, bespoke their professional prominence. Shipp had served as superior court judge in the Ninth Judicial District until 1868, when the Republican, Logan, defeated him. Between 1870 and 1872, Shipp was North Carolina's attorney general. He then practiced law in Charlotte for several years, gaining a reputation as one of the "best-informed lawyers in the State." In 1881, when Judge Schenck retired from the Ninth Judicial District bench, Shipp replaced him.[31]

William Bailey's legal résumé was equally impressive. Like Shipp, he had once served as North Carolina's attorney general. He also had written several law books and had distinguished himself as a law professor. Judge Schenck considered Bailey "perhaps the most learned lawyer in the Circuit."[32]

The touchy politics of the Ross case fazed neither Shipp nor Bailey, for both were, from a political standpoint, fairly independent. Shipp was a Democrat, but not a militant one. Prior to the Civil War, indeed, he had been a "staunch Whig." His postwar embrace of the Democratic Party was sufficiently loose to enable him to become "the only Democrat on the ticket" elected in 1870, the year he won the race for attorney general. Bailey was even more independent politically. Judge Schenck privately characterized him as a former Democrat who, during Reconstruction, had "drifted with Radicalism and in all elections lends his talents with negros to defeat his own race." Observers of Bailey's subsequent stint in the state legislature during the 1880s noted that, while he generally voted with the Democrats, he was "very liberal and independent."[33]

Professionally successful and politically independent, the Shipp & Bailey law partnership could afford, both financially and politically, to represent clients such as the Rosses. The lawyers' appellate caseload in 1876, the year of the Ross trial, is instructive on this point. The partners, despite working 170 miles away from the state capital, argued an impressive twenty cases before the North Carolina Supreme Court that year. Seventeen of these twenty Supreme Court appeals were civil cases—typically property and contract disputes, many of which involved large sums. With remunerative cases such as these (and deep-pocketed clients such as the Salisbury Building and Loan Association), Shipp & Bailey could afford to take on a few controversial and nonremunerative criminal cases. *State v. Neely* (1876), in which they defended an African American man accused of "assault with intent to commit rape" on a white woman, was one such case. *State v. Kennedy* and *State v. Ross* were others.[34]

The Shipp & Bailey partnership was especially well suited to defend the Rosses, having represented Isaac and Mag Kennedy just two days previously. The Kennedy trial had taught the lawyers that interracial couples who left North Carolina to get married and then returned right away stood no chance in Judge Schenck's court. Based on this knowledge, the lawyers and their clients prepared an effective trial defense.

On 30 August 1876, Pinkney and Sarah Ross rose as Judge Schenck entered the Mecklenburg County superior court. Solicitor Montgomery read the charges against them. According to local press reports, Montgomery could "read a bill of indictment heavier than anyone.... [W]hen he reads it the jury is sure to convict." Montgomery charged the Rosses with "bed[ding] and cohabit[ing] together, without being lawfully married," contrary to North Carolina law.[35]

Shipp and Bailey admitted that the Rosses had "bedded and cohabited together" but insisted that the couple was lawfully married at the time. To establish the legitimacy of the Rosses' marriage, the lawyers presented two arguments. First, they contended that the right of persons to marry, regardless of color, is "one of the guarantees of American citizenship" and as such was protected by the Fourteenth Amendment of the U.S. Constitution. In *Loving v. Virginia* (1967), such an argument prevailed. Shipp and Bailey, however, were a century too early. Both on trial and on appeal, their Fourteenth Amendment argument failed, perhaps because it involved what was then understood to be a social right, not a civil right. At the time of the Rosses' case, most American courts interpreted the Fourteenth Amendment as having no application to social rights such as marriage, as long as marriage laws, including bans on interracial marriage, applied "equally" to all racial groups.[36]

The defense lawyers' second argument had more promise. Shipp and Bailey sought to establish that, at the time of the marriage, the Rosses were "domiciled" in South Carolina and, therefore, governed by that state's marriage law. For this argument to succeed, they would have to convince jurors that Pink Ross was a resident of his native South Carolina at the time of the marriage. If the lawyers could accomplish this, they could then invoke the doctrine of coverture to argue that Sarah Ross, as a wife, had adopted her husband's domicile at the moment of marriage.[37]

There was just one problem with the facts that the defense sought to establish: they were not exactly factual. As the attentive reader will recall, Pink Ross was living in North Carolina, not South Carolina, at the time of the 1870 census. While it is theoretically possible that he stayed only a short time in North Carolina—perhaps but a single day, the day the census was recorded—it seems much more plausible that Pink lived in North Carolina for an extended period. How else would he and Sarah have courted and decided to marry?[38]

Nevertheless, the testimony and arguments offered on the Rosses' behalf convinced jurors that Pink and Sarah, prior to their marriage, had always resided in different states. This implausible finding, as recorded in the "special verdict," read as follows: "Pink Ross is a native of South Carolina, *and resided there until August, 1873* [three months after the marriage took place]. Sarah Ross was a resident and citizen of North Carolina up to the time of the marriage [emphasis added]."[39]

Based on this finding of fact, Judge Schenck had little choice but to rule for the defendants. He found that Pink was a South Carolinian; that Sarah, upon marriage, became a South Carolinian, too; that their marriage under South Carolina law was bona fide; and that, therefore, the prosecution's "fornication" charge had no merit.

The Rosses walked away from Judge Schenck's courtroom with their marriage intact, but their legal troubles were not over. Their trial, like that of the Kennedys, had employed the "special verdict" form, meaning that the jury had found the facts in their case, but Judge Schenck had ruled the couple not guilty. At trial, this procedure had worked to the Rosses' advantage. Schenck, despite his Klan background, had respected the legal rule that he had devised in the Kennedy case and found the Rosses not guilty. The couple may not have been as lucky with the jury.[40]

Although the special verdict procedure was advantageous to the Rosses at trial, it became a liability thereafter. The state could not appeal jury acquittals, but it could appeal special verdict acquittals, "double jeopardy" protections notwithstanding. Indeed, one of the purposes of employing the special verdict form in criminal cases was to enable appellate courts to clarify murky areas of the law, whatever the trial verdict. As the North Carolina Supreme Court explained in an 1847 ruling, a conviction *or acquittal* by special verdict "leaves the matter of law distinctly open to review in a higher Court. It is for this reason, principally, that special verdicts are given in criminal cases; so that the State, as well as the prisoner, can have the matter of law solemnly decided" on appeal.[41]

There would be an appeal in *State v. Ross*, however, only if North Carolina's attorney general decided to file one. Again, political changes affected the Rosses. When Pink and Sarah married in 1873, North Carolina's attorney general was a Republican. In the election of 1876, however, Democrat Thomas Kenan captured the office. One of Kenan's first official acts was to appeal *State v. Ross*.[42]

The *Ross* appeal reached the North Carolina Supreme Court in January 1877. Once again, Shipp and Bailey represented the couple. As at trial, they argued the "general rule" that a valid home-state marriage was valid everywhere. Attorney General Kenan countered that this "general rule" had exceptions that were "as well established as the rule itself." He noted that incestuous and polygamous marriages—unions that may have been legal elsewhere—were invalid in North Carolina, notwithstanding the "general rule" relied upon by the Rosses. Asserting that an interracial marriage was "as unnatural and as revolting as an incestuous one," Kenan argued that the Rosses' marriage was not valid under North Carolina law.[43]

The North Carolina Supreme Court shared the attorney general's abhorrence of interracial marriage. Justice William Rodman wrote in his majority opinion, "The State of North Carolina . . . has declared its conviction that marriages between [the races] are immoral and opposed to public policy. . . . It is needless to say that the members of this court share that opinion." Fortunately for Pink and Sarah, however, the justices' personal views on interracial marriage would yield to the jury's findings of fact and to the rule of law. "[W]e must suppose," Justice Rodman wrote, with a hint of suspicion, "that [Pinkney's] domicile was *bona fide* in South Carolina" as of the wedding day. And when Sarah married Pinkney, he wrote, "the domicile of her husband became hers." Thus, Rodman analyzed the case "as if both parties had been domiciled in South Carolina at the time of the marriage."[44]

Justice Rodman then addressed the "general rule" that a valid home-state marriage was valid everywhere. He acknowledged that polygamy and incest were exceptions to this rule but concluded that interracial marriage was not. Whereas incest and polygamy were outlawed almost everywhere, he noted, comparatively few societies prohibited interracial marriage. "However revolting to us . . . such a marriage may appear,

[this] . . . cannot be said to be the common sentiment of the civilized and Christian world." Rodman's conclusion that miscegenation did not qualify as an exception to the general rule that valid home-state marriages were valid everywhere would not long stand. In subsequent years—indeed, up until 1967, when the U.S. Supreme Court voided interracial marriage bans—miscegenation was *the* great exception to this rule. But this exception had not yet crystallized at the time of *State v. Ross*.[45] Thus, a reluctant majority of the North Carolina Supreme Court felt "compelled" to rule in the Rosses' favor. Two justices dissented, arguing that interracial marriage, like smallpox, was an "evil" against which the state had every right to shut the door. But Justice Rodman's reasoning prevailed. One can only imagine the relief that Pink and Sarah must have felt. They were free.[46]

Credit for the Rosses' victory must be shared. The couple's lawyers contributed greatly. Given the time and place, their willingness to defend clients such as the Rosses—and to do so as effectively as they did—was exemplary. So was the professionalism of the trial and appellate judges. From all indications, Judge David Schenck and Justice William Rodman despised the thought of black men marrying white women. Nonetheless, when they saw the balance of legal argument tip in Pink and Sarah's favor, they refrained from pressing racist thumbs on the other side. And Pink and Sarah deserve recognition for making some shrewd decisions. Taking advantage of the relative freedom of movement that the post-emancipation South afforded, they wisely joined other interracial couples of the day in locating their wedding in South Carolina, where such marriages were legal. Their decision to remain in South Carolina for three months after their wedding also helped their cause. After their 1876 arrest, they prudently secured the services of good lawyers. Working with these lawyers, they managed to convince jurors of an implausible set of facts. The Rosses' story suggests that at least some interracial couples in the post–Civil War South had more control over their fates than is generally imagined.

Following their escape from legal danger, the Rosses left North Carolina, the state that had sought to take away their freedom, and returned to South Carolina, settling just a few miles inside the state line. If their hope in moving was to secure the comfort of a state that allowed interracial marriages, their respite was brief. In 1879, South Carolina Democrats, having recaptured power, reinstituted the state's ban on interracial marriage. Again, the Rosses found themselves living in a state that outlawed marriages such as theirs.[47]

In the following year, 1880, a U.S. Census worker in Spartanburg County, South Carolina, found Pink and Sarah Ross living together as husband and wife on a farm in Limestone Springs Township. Pink had made something of himself. In 1870, he could neither read nor write; ten years later he could do both. In 1870, he had been a "farm laborer" on someone else's land; a decade later he was listed as "farmer." In other words, unlike many of his neighbors whose 1880 occupation was described as "works on farm," Pink had been able to acquire land.[48]

Sarah's transformation was equally dramatic. In the 1870 census, and all previous censuses, she had been white; in 1880, she was listed as black. Three possible explanations might account for Sarah's official racial conversion. First, it might have resulted from a deliberate decision made by a racist census taker. That official might have resolved that Sarah Ross, having married a black man, had sacrificed her claim to whiteness. Second, and less conspiratorially, Sarah's being listed as "black" might simply have resulted from the carelessness of an overworked census taker who simply assumed, rather than determined, Sarah's race.[49] More plausible, however, is a third possibility: that Sarah's racial conversion, like so many previous events in the Rosses' lives, resulted from the purposeful calculation of Pink and Sarah themselves. After all, if South Carolina census takers in 1880 had stripped whiteness from intermarried wives as a matter of course, no interracial couples should appear in that year's record. Yet, as previously discussed, the 1880 South Carolina census is peppered with biracial household listings, especially in border communities such as Fort Mill. Furthermore, if Sarah's 1880 listing as "black" resulted from a simple recording error, subsequent reports should have corrected that error. Yet the 1900 census, the only other one taken before Sarah's death (other than the 1890 census, which was destroyed by fire), also lists Sarah as "black," despite being compiled twenty years later by a different "enumerator."[50]

One other bit of evidence suggests that the Rosses may have self-identified as an African American couple. Mike's Creek Baptist Church was an African American place of worship established in northern Spartanburg County in 1865. Among the ministers who served there during the 1880s was "Rev. Pinckney Ross." Although Pink's service as minister falls short as definitive proof of Sarah's private or public racial identification, it does suggest the possibility that Sarah, as the wife of a prominent member of the African American community's leading institution, may also have come to identify herself with that community.[51]

It thus seems reasonable to suspect that the Rosses consciously chose to present themselves (to census takers and perhaps to others) as an African American couple. No longer able to reduce legal risks by crossing geographical borders, the couple resorted to crossing racial borders. Apparently, they succeeded. Cultivating a shared life as black farmers in upstate South Carolina, they appear to have faced no further legal troubles.

The Rosses never produced children, but they did stay together until death parted them. Sarah died first. By the time of the 1910 census, she was gone and Pink was listed as a widower. Following Sarah's death, Pink moved in with relatives. He died of pneumonia in 1925. Fittingly, he was buried about a mile from the state line—the line that he and Sarah had crossed so many times, when they were young and free.[52]

Chapter 3

De Jure Housing Segregation in Progressive Era Winston-Salem

The Case of William Darnell

The instances of legal "line-drawing" discussed in the two previous chapters concerned the most basic of social institutions: the nuclear family. The present chapter suggests that, as North Carolina society grew more complex, attempts to inscribe racial lines into North Carolina law grew more complex, too. This chapter concerns a residential segregation ordinance adopted by the city of Winston, North Carolina, in the second decade of the twentieth century. The story reflects the tangible impact on North Carolina life and law of such broad social forces as industrialization, urbanization, Progressive Era "reform," and the era's highly contagious impulse to separate the races.

At the corner of Eleventh Street and Highland Avenue in what is now called Winston-Salem, a swing set stands sentinel over land that was once the center of an important legal controversy. A tobacco worker named William Darnell attempted, in 1913, to move into a house that he had recently purchased on this site. For this act, and this act alone, he was arrested. A city ordinance passed in 1912 forbade people from moving onto blocks where they would be in the racial minority. The block's other residents were white; William Darnell was black. Darnell's

---

Michael E. Daly, R. Stan Baker, John Bell, Wilson Buntin, Scott Herr, Andrew Holbrook, Sarah House, and J. Matthew Strader contributed to this chapter.

arrest initiated a chain of legal events that, given the time and place, had a surprising result: the North Carolina Supreme Court overturned his conviction and invalidated the segregation ordinance.

Other than the case that bears his name, William Darnell left but a scant paper trail. He was born in 1859, in Guilford County (not far from Winston-Salem), making him in all likelihood a slave at birth. As a middle-aged man, he moved to Winston-Salem to take up tobacco work. He died of stomach problems in his ninetieth year and was buried in an unmarked grave in Winston-Salem's Evergreen Cemetery. We know little else about him. (Even his surname remains unclear; different records and directories referred to him variously as Darnell, Donnell, Donald, and Daniel. Like the law reporter in his case, we will refer to him as Darnell.)[1]

As for his lawsuit, it has yet to receive the in-depth scholarly treatment that it deserves. That a Progressive Era southern court invalidated a Jim Crow measure in itself justifies greater attention. In addition, the case highlights a fascinating New South drama performed by an unlikely cast against a backdrop of social change, political conflict, and racial tension.

Because *State v. Darnell* resulted in a defeat for de jure segregation, it raises an important historical question: what prevented Jim Crow's "strange career" from advancing even further than it did?[2] Some scholars, perhaps mindful of the NAACP's dramatic victory in *Brown v. Board of Education*, have emphasized the important role played by African Americans in resisting—and ultimately reversing—the segregationist tide. One such scholar attributed "nearly every major [pre-*Brown*] courtroom triumph" over Jim Crow, including *State v. Darnell*, to the efforts of African American civil rights crusaders.[3] In this vein, scholars have described *Darnell* as "a victory for Winston-Salem blacks," an inspiring case in which the city's African American community "challenged Winston-Salem's housing segregation ordinance and won."[4]

Other scholars have credited "the powerful American commitment to economic *laissez-faire*" with the setting of outer limits on legalized racial segregation, especially when private property was at issue, as it was in *Darnell*. The willingness of Progressive Era judges to strike down residential segregation ordinances convinces these scholars that "*laissez-faire* jurisprudence*," though typically criticized for favoring the privileged over the oppressed, in fact "had positive effects on the welfare of African-Americans."[5]

Neither explanation—not "African American resistance" or "*laissez-faire* jurisprudence"—fully accords with the facts in *State v. Darnell*. Although William Darnell, an African American, clearly played a role in his lawsuit, he was but one member of a diverse ensemble. A small-time white realtor and two prominent, elderly, and paternalistic lawyers played crucial (and heretofore unappreciated) roles. So, too, did a judge who, far from being a conservative proponent of laissez faire, advocated greater governmental activism and marched in the progressive vanguard of his day.[6] In *State v. Darnell*, the efforts of this varied group combined to set an outer limit to Jim Crow's distressing reach in one southern state.

Like the first two chapters, then, this one concerns the drawing of racial lines in North Carolina law. It is set in another critical era of southern race relations. Chapter 1 concerned the Old South, chapter 2 concerned Reconstruction, and this chapter deals with the period famously (though debatably) dubbed the "nadir" of African American history: the Jim Crow era.

Viewed from a distance, the plot here is a familiar one. The central conflict once again pitted elite whites and downtrodden minorities against the social middle. As before, prominent members of bench and bar used the judicial system to frustrate the legislatively achieved racist designs of middling whites. Upon closer inspection, however, these broad outlines blur. Some middling whites fought against segregation. Some elite whites—and some prominent blacks—did not. These variations add intrigue.

In 1910, Baltimore, Maryland, became the nation's first city to adopt a residential segregation ordinance. Towns in Virginia, Kentucky, South Carolina, Georgia, Oklahoma, Missouri, and Louisiana soon followed. Winston, North Carolina, passed such an ordinance in 1912. Winston, which would merge with neighboring Salem one year later, was then a booming New South city—North Carolina's largest and fastest growing. Its meteoric rise reflected the growth of its powerful tobacco industry.[7]

By no mere happenstance did North Carolina's first residential segregation ordinance appear in a tobacco town. Like textiles—the region's other major industrial employer—tobacco work attracted waves of rural migrants. But unlike the textile mills, which tended to have their own villages and employ mostly whites, Winston-Salem's tobacco factories clustered downtown and employed mostly African Americans.

R. J. Reynolds, Winston-Salem's leading tobacco mogul, was particularly dependent on black labor. Reynolds sent special trains to South Carolina and eastern North Carolina to recruit African American workers. The new arrivals settled primarily in the eastern part of Winston, near the tobacco factories that clustered around the railway lines on that side of town. It was in this area of Winston that pressure for a residential segregation ordinance built.[8]

The push there toward de jure housing segregation had three sources. First, Winston-Salem's breakneck growth created a red-hot real estate market. In 1890, the city had only three real estate agents; by 1910, it had twenty-four. Similar increases occurred in contractors and building and loan associations. The housing market's explosiveness pleased builders and real estate agents but unnerved some local whites, who feared an influx of black tobacco workers into their neighborhoods. Concerned whites initially sought racial stability through "restrictive covenants"—clauses written into property deeds beginning in 1890, if not before, prohibiting buyers from selling or renting to African Americans for specified periods of time, usually five or ten years. By around 1910, however, these private contractual devices had clearly failed to prevent the movement of African Americans into neighborhoods where whites did not want them. Disgruntled whites searched for stronger alternatives.[9]

Second, segregation in general was on the rise. Jim Crowism came relatively late to the Tar Heel State. Railroad segregation and African American disfranchisement both arrived around 1900, a decade after their implementation in Mississippi. But once it arrived, segregation swept through North Carolina's public and private life. Around the time that Winston adopted its residential segregation ordinance, it already had racially separate annual fairs, YMCAs, Women's Civic Leagues, insurance firms, and hospitals, to name but a few examples. Segregation of residential neighborhoods—by government decree, if necessary—might well have seemed a logical next step.[10]

Third, Winston-Salem's city government, in step with Progressive Era trends elsewhere, was growing more active every year. At the time of the debate over residential segregation, the city government was busily building regulatory muscle. It adopted a new traffic ordinance, imposed speed limits, and hired a milk and meat inspector. In 1912, a supportive local editor effectively captured the progressive spirit that underlay such initiatives: "The citizens of Winston . . . now have an opportunity of taking a long step forward that will put their city in the forefront of Progressive cities of the South. . . . If we fail to provide for municipal improvements . . . to make life pleasant and living convenient . . . it cannot but mean that our growth will be stopped."[11]

In 1912, the racially volatile housing market, the general urge to segregate, and the Progressive Era trend toward governmental solutions for perceived social problems converged in a proposal for a residential segregation ordinance. The initial push came from white residents living on or around East Fourth Street, a major east-west corridor onto which some African Americans had recently moved. Fourth Street ran from the overwhelmingly white residential districts on the west side of town, through the city center, to a "stable white residential area" in the east. In between these two white residential areas, and just to the east of downtown, was a low-lying, north-south strip of soggy creek beds and noisy rail lines where African Americans traditionally lived. Housing here was cheap, owing to the absence of paved roads, sewage lines, or street lights and to the presence of occasional flooding, not to mention rats, snakes, bugs, and factory-and-rail-yard-related noises and smells. Poor tobacco workers could not afford to be picky, however. Their turn-of-the-century influx swelled this African American strip in an arc to the northeast and southeast. By 1912, African American residences surrounded predominantly white east Winston on three sides. (The remaining side was the city's uninhabited eastern edge.)[12]

Increasingly cut off from whites elsewhere in the city and threatened by what they saw as black encroachment, East Fourth Street whites grew desperate. They turned to a governmental cure and sought to draw racial lines into the law. Their "Movement to Oust Negroes" (as the press labeled it) advanced along two different legal paths. First, a white plaintiff named J. W. Carter sued a white defendant named James Timble for violating a restrictive covenant. Carter had sold an East Fourth Street house to Timble with a racist string attached to the deed: Timble was never to sell or rent the property to any "colored people." When Timble violated this restriction by selling to a "colored person," Carter contended that the property should rightly revert to him. The press predicted that a victory by Carter would inspire waves of copycat suits, potentially causing "scores of lots in this section [to] change hands." The case, however, apparently went nowhere.[13]

The second legal path explored by nervous East Fourth Street whites appeared more promising: they petitioned the Winston Board of Aldermen for legal relief. On 13 June 1912, at a special session of the Board of Aldermen, more than two hundred citizens packed the meeting to express their concerns. Not a single African American was in attendance.[14]

The petitioners' arguments revealed their anxieties. Some criticized real estate agents for "robbing the white people" of east Winston by "selling them land at exorbitant prices, all the time holding over [them] the threat that they will sell it to the negroes." Others complained about East Fourth Street whites who breached their restrictive covenants by selling to African Americans. Still others, in line with the Progressive Era ethos of technocratic solutions to social problems, contended that a segregation ordinance would reduce "friction of the races."[15]

Swayed by these arguments, the Board of Aldermen adopted a residential segregation ordinance. The measure, enacted on 13 June 1912, the very day of the protest meeting, was narrowly tailored to meet the East Fourth Street neighborhood's concerns. It prohibited "any colored person to own or occupy any dwelling fronting on East Fourth Street, between Depot Street [near downtown] and the city limits on the east." The measure also banned white people from residing on specified sections of Third and Depot streets—sections already wholly settled by African Americans. The ordinance called for racial treatment that was separate and *unequal*. It forbade African Americans from owning or occupying specified dwellings, but forbade whites from occupying (but allowed them to own) specified dwellings. This distinction benefited white landlords by allowing them to own houses in "colored" sections, as long as they rented to "colored" tenants. In the age of "separate but equal," this disparity exposed the ordinance to constitutional challenge. Recognizing the ordinance's legal vulnerability, proponents of segregation urged a revision.[16]

On 1 July 1912, the Board of Aldermen revised the ordinance. Henceforth, it would be illegal throughout Winston for any black person to occupy a residence on a majority-white block, and it would be illegal for any white person to occupy a residence on a majority-black block. Violators faced up to fifty dollars in fines and thirty days in prison for each offense, with each day in violation constituting a separate offense.[17]

In order to avoid rupturing relations between black domestic workers and their white employers, the ordinance exempted "servants or employees" who occupied residences on blocks where they worked. The ordinance was not retroactive. It applied only to residents who moved into dwellings after 1 July 1912. Its principal goal was to prevent any additional racial "tipping" of existing housing stock, while imposing controls on the racial composition of all future housing stock. (Builders of new residences on previously uninhabited blocks had to state in their building permit applications whether future occupants were to be "white" or "colored.")[18]

The African American response to the revised ordinance was subdued, especially when contrasted with the uproar from that community a year later when the city sought to move a segregated black public school to a less desirable location. (Irate African Americans then sent a protest letter to the Board of Aldermen. The letter opposed the move and expressed mock gratitude—"We thank you for the crumbs from the table"—for the $20,000 that the city spent each year on black schools, as opposed to the $150,000 spent for white schools. African Americans also published a protest letter in a local newspaper and secured legal representation to make their case before the Board of Aldermen.)[19]

The residential segregation ordinance of 1912 provoked no such outcry. In an era of racial violence, black opponents of segregation held their tongues. Some issues—for example, where to locate a segregated black school or even how generously to fund black versus white public schools—were fair game. Blacks could debate them vigorously without challenging the central premises of white supremacy, but the residential segregation ordinance was not one of these safe issues. Even staunchly opposed blacks kept quiet.[20]

There is also evidence that not all blacks were staunchly opposed to residential segregation. A local white newspaper reported that "there was no opposition [to the segregation scheme] ... and it is understood that many of the better class of colored people look with favor upon the ordinance." There is reason to be skeptical of the white press during this era, but this particular assertion may not have been groundless. Simon G. Atkins, the city's most prominent black leader, did endorse voluntary segregation. Like his role model, Booker T. Washington, Atkins had struck a tacit bargain with powerful local whites: Atkins would support segregation, and white patrons would support Atkins. Indeed, Atkins's views on segregation must have been conflicted. He must have loathed the racial inferiority that it implied. Yet segregation was, in some ways, the foundation of his power. He was president of the Slater Industrial Academy (today's Winston-Salem State University), an all-black school.

He was the founder of Columbia Heights, a fashionable all-black Winston suburb. Integration might have threatened Atkins's power more than segregation did.[21]

The housing ordinance had a relatively uneventful first year. In the spring of 1913, however, some whites began to grumble about lax enforcement. One incident involved an African American grocer, George W. Penn. Penn sought a building permit for a lot on a majority-white stretch of Twelfth Street in east Winston. Under pressure from white Twelfth Street residents, Board of Aldermen secretary William Holcomb refused Penn's request, citing the ordinance. Penn hired a prominent white attorney and appealed. Penn's lawyer admitted that the particular block in question was mostly white but noted that the surrounding area was predominantly black. The board agreed to a compromise: Penn could build on the lot, but he could not move in. He would have to sell or rent to a white person.[22]

Although this result does not seem like much of a victory for Penn, segregationists viewed it as a setback for their side. They urged stiffer enforcement of the ordinance. In response, city leaders reaffirmed their support for segregation and warned transgressors that the police would soon act against them.[23] The police soon acted. On 10 June 1913, they arrested their first suspected segregation violator: William Darnell.

In 1906, a forty-seven-year-old William Darnell came to east Winston to work in a tobacco factory. At first, he and his wife, Lillie, lived in the southeast part of Winston, in an inexpensive Johnson Avenue home that was too often flooded by nearby creeks and too often rattled by nearby railroad yards. By 1913, the Darnells had saved enough money to move to a more expensive home. They sold their Johnson Avenue house for $450 and looked forward to a more comfortable life in a home worth twice that amount on Highland Avenue in northeast Winston. Northeast Winston was in a state of flux.[24] Above Seventh Street, the neighborhood was predominantly black. Highland Avenue, however, was something of an anomaly. It retained a substantial white presence well north of Seventh. Prior to the Darnells' arrival, the east side of Highland between Eleventh and Twelfth was exclusively white.

The Darnells purchased "lot 169" on Highland Avenue from a white man named Francis M. Sledge, who had owned the property for only a month. Sledge was a small-time real estate broker who rented and sold properties in all parts of the city to customers white and black. Sledge's actions in the Darnell case betray a strong dislike for the housing ordinance, perhaps because it reduced the market for any given property by at least 40 percent. (Winston-Salem was then about 40 percent African American.)[25]

Sledge took three steps to defy and invalidate the ordinance. First, he approached the other property owners on the block, all of whom were white, with a striking proposal. "We, the undersigned citizens owning property on the East side of Highland Avenue between Eleventh and Twelfth streets," the document read, "do hereby agree to sell our property to colored people." Only one inhabitant of the all-white block failed to sign.[26]

Second, Sledge sold lot 169 to William Darnell, an African American. By 10 June 1913, just five days after Sledge signed his covenant, Darnell had purchased the property and had been arrested. A municipal court judge found that Darnell had violated the ordinance and fined him five dollars plus court costs. At the time, more than 90 percent of litigants who lost in Winston's municipal court accepted their fate. Darnell was not among them. He appealed for a new trial in superior court.[27]

Third, pending the superior court retrial, Sledge paid Darnell's twenty-five-dollar bail bond. He then appeared in court with Darnell in August, November, and December 1913 to confirm that Darnell would be present for his superior court retrial. Sledge's continued involvement with Darnell after "flipping" the property to him reinforces suspicion that this was a test case engineered to challenge the segregation ordinance.[28]

At the time of Darnell's trial and retrial, Winston-Salem had three practicing African American attorneys. None of them worked on Darnell's case, and we do not know why. In this racist era, however, even the city's leading black attorney, John Fitts, made it a point to appear in superior court only as the associate of a white lawyer, to avoid damaging his clients' fortunes with potentially racist jurors and judges. Prudence suggested the use of white counsel for Darnell.[29]

Even so, the firm that represented Darnell—Watson, Buxton & Watson—catches the eye, much as Shipp & Bailey did on behalf of Pink and Sarah Ross in the previous chapter. North Carolina observers considered Watson, Buxton & Watson to be "one of the very strongest [law firms] in the state." Cyrus B. Watson was one of Winston-Salem's most distinguished citizens. After fighting with the Confederate Army, he served terms in both houses of the North Carolina legislature. He was the Democratic nominee for governor in 1896. In court, he had few peers. Some considered him the greatest criminal lawyer in his state's history to that point. When Watson died, in 1916, the chief justice of the North Carolina Supreme Court proclaimed him "the uncrowned king of the North Carolina bar."[30] Watson's law partner, John C. Buxton, also had an impressive record. He had served as mayor of Winston and as a state senator, and for twenty-six years he chaired the city's school board. Like Watson, Buxton had a "splendid" courtroom reputation.[31]

What motivated these two prominent Democrats to represent a black tobacco worker in a modest criminal appeal? It is possible that Watson and Buxton took Darnell's case simply because it was offered to them, because their representation of Darnell would create no conflict of interest, and because the fee for their services would be paid. Paternalism may also have played a part. Watson and Buxton represented a class of elderly, elite southern whites whose sense of noblesse oblige drove them to seek at least some justice for African Americans. Both lawyers were in their sixties, members of a pre–Civil War generation of whites that was less captivated by Jim Crowism than younger generations were. Both lawyers were privileged enough to be immune to status anxiety; both lived in Winston's West End, far from tobacco factories and their workers. Both had histories of paternalistic concern. In 1893, Watson drafted and fought for an anti-lynching bill in the state legislature. Buxton, for his part, frequently provided legal services to African Americans, especially those charged with crimes. (It was he who represented George W. Penn, the black grocer who in May 1913 sought permission to build on a street with a white majority.)[32]

In addition, the two lawyers may have had financial incentives to oppose the Winston ordinance. Both had longstanding real estate interests in the city. They often served as "trustees" on deeds securing mortgage loans. It was they, in fact, who secured the loan that Sledge took out on lot 169, prior to selling it to Darnell. The mortgage itself came from the Winston-Salem Building and Loan Association, whose president was none other than J. C. Buxton.[33]

The opposing counsel was Winston-Salem solicitor Gilbert T. Stephenson. He was of a different generation—just twenty-nine at the time of the trial. Besides being a respected lawyer, Stephenson was "perhaps the country's foremost" scholar of racial segregation law. In an important treatise published in 1910, Stephenson separated race *distinctions* ("separate but equal" measures) from race *discriminations* (measures affording blacks inferior legal treatment). "The welfare of both races," he argued, "requires the recognition of race distinctions and the obliteration of race discriminations." Stephenson considered Winston's "separate but equal" housing ordinance to be a legitimate race "distinction."[34]

Darnell's superior court retrial was originally scheduled for 3 October 1913 but was postponed pending the outcome of a Maryland case involving similar issues. The delay confirms that the residential segregation debate was a national one, and North Carolina judges knew it. On 7 October 1913, the Maryland Supreme Court struck down Baltimore's pathbreaking residential segregation ordinance because it applied retroactively. Winston's ordinance was not retroactive, so Darnell's trial would proceed.[35]

It did so in January 1914. Stephenson's case for the prosecution was straightforward. He offered testimony from a white man, V. E. Barnes, who lived just around the corner from lot 169. Prior to Darnell's arrest, Barnes had petitioned the Board of Aldermen for stiffer enforcement of the segregation ordinance. He testified that there were "four white families and no colored ones" living on the block at the time of Darnell's purchase. J. D. Welch, the man who sold lot 169 to Sledge in May 1913, confirmed the existence of a white majority on the block in question. The state rested.[36]

Watson and Buxton were more creative. They had to be. Both the facts and the law were against them. First, they raised the sorts of technical objections to the ordinance that lawyers routinely raise and judges routinely reject. They argued, for instance, that the ordinance was not submitted in writing to the Board of Aldermen before it was passed, in violation of city rules. Judge W. A. Devin rejected these arguments.[37] Second, they argued that the ordinance was unconstitutional because it "deprive[d] the defendant of his property without the due process of law." Judge Devin was not persuaded. He instructed the jury to consider the ordinance to be constitutional and valid.[38] Third, they sought to demonstrate that African Americans dominated surrounding blocks, albeit not Darnell's immediate block, at the time of the purchase. The state, noting that the ordinance explicitly concerned the racial composition of individual blocks, not surrounding blocks, objected to all defense questions regarding the racial composition of surrounding blocks. Judge Devin sustained the state's objections.[39] Fourth, Watson and Buxton offered testimony from F. M. Sledge. Sledge sought to introduce the document wherein he and the block's other white property owners had agreed to sell to African Americans. The trial judge ruled this evidence inadmissible.[40]

After deliberating for thirty minutes, the jury returned a verdict of guilty. Perhaps hoping to discourage an appeal, the court lowered Darnell's fine from five dollars to one dollar and costs. Nonetheless, Watson and Buxton promptly announced their intent to appeal to the state Supreme Court. Pending that appeal, Sledge again posted Darnell's bond, this time for forty dollars.[41]

Local interest in the trial was intense. "Perhaps no case tried" in superior court that term, the *Twin-City Daily Sentinel* of Winston-Salem reported, "was of greater local interest than that of William Darnell." The white press loudly applauded the guilty verdict. Another city newspaper, the *Journal*, reported that the *Darnell* jurors, like most jurors, had "decide[d] things right, because they are on the ground." The editors worried, however, that the North Carolina Supreme Court might use Darnell's appeal to strike down the ordinance. They warned Darnell that "the best thing this colored citizen can do is to abide by the law of the city without getting the Supreme Court mixed up in the affair at all."[42]

Darnell and his backers, however, did not drop their appeal; nor would the social forces that underlay the dispute await the case's resolution. As the lawyers prepared their Supreme Court briefs, two additional African Americans—George Crews and Dr. Edward Smith—were arrested under the segregation ordinance. Strikingly, both cases arose in the 1100 block of Highland Avenue—Darnell's block. Crews's new house was two lots to the north of Darnell's; Dr. Smith's new house was one lot to the south. The vendors of both properties were signatories of Sledge's document.[43]

In April 1914, the North Carolina Supreme Court heard arguments in *State v. Darnell*, a case "awaited with interest from every section of the state." The justices pressed Stephenson about Winston's authority to adopt the ordinance. The solicitor pointed to the "general welfare" clause in the city's charter, which provided that the aldermen "may pass any ordinance which they deem wise and proper for the good order, good government, or general welfare of the city, provided it does not contravene the laws and Constitution of the State." Stephenson insisted that the ordinance indeed provided for the welfare of city residents, be they black or white. "Wherever there is indiscriminate residence," he argued, "there is irritation, constant irritation, and it always works hardship upon the negro. He gets the worst of every clash. It [the ordinance] will be a protector to him. It will help the weaker race."[44]

On behalf of Darnell, Watson and Buxton reiterated the arguments they had used in superior court. Their principal focus was an attack on the constitutionality of the segregation measure. Citing the "due process" clauses of both the state and the national constitutions, they argued that the ordinance abridged Darnell's inalienable right to own and occupy property. The government "cannot deprive one of the right to live in his own house," they insisted.[45]

The North Carolina Supreme Court decided *State v. Darnell* on 8 April 1914. The author of the unanimous ruling, Chief Justice Walter Clark, was no civil rights crusader. Clark grew up on a large Virginia plantation. His family owned many slaves. After the Civil War, in which he fought for the Confederacy, he advocated *white* labor for the South on the grounds that freedmen could not "live among us in the present state of things." Later, Clark employed the language of white supremacy in championing women's suffrage. North Carolina's fifty thousand white women, he noted enthusiastically, outnumbered—and thus could outvote—the state's black women and black men, combined.[46]

Clark's long judicial record—he served on the North Carolina Supreme Court from 1889 until his death in 1924—offered the Darnell camp additional cause for pessimism. He was a progressive judge. In classic progressive fashion, he favored measures—for example, an elected federal judiciary and the direct election of U.S. senators—that would amplify the will of the people in government. He also favored laws—such as labor laws and railroad regulation—that would enhance the role of government in society. He was outspoken in opposition to judicial review, the practice whereby judges nullified legislation on constitutional grounds. "If a legislature should not observe the Constitution," he argued, "the supervision lies with the people in electing another legislature." Clark's respect for the popular will, his preference for active government, and his hostility to judicial review did not bode well for Darnell and his lawyers, who challenged the constitutionality of a popularly enacted governmental regulation.[47]

But there was another side to Chief Justice Clark. He was an elite and elderly (upper sixties) paternalist. Like Darnell's attorney C. B. Watson, one of Clark's "closest friends," Clark saw himself as a benevolent guardian of African Americans. During the Civil War, when Clark's slave Neverson sought to accompany his master to the front, Clark reputedly insisted that he stay back, out of danger. Throughout Clark's thirty-five years on the state bench, a former slave named Alston attended him daily at work and at home. Given this history of close (though clearly hierarchical) relationships with African Americans, Clark may have had doubts concerning the wisdom of governmentally enforced housing segregation. In short, Clark's progressivism inclined him to the state's arguments, but his paternalism favored Darnell's.[48]

Clark's divided leanings mirrored divided precedents from other state courts that heard similar cases in the second decade of the twentieth century. Courts in Maryland and Georgia invalidated residential segregation ordinances as unconstitutional infringements on the vested rights of property owners. In contrast, two other state courts deemed such measures to be constitutional attempts to reduce race friction.[49]

Clark forged a distinctive path. He found a way to rule in favor of Darnell but not on the constitutional grounds that Darnell's lawyers (and other state courts) had emphasized. He managed this trick by finding the Winston ordinance to be unauthorized, not unconstitutional. He began by invoking "Dillon's Rule." Dillon's Rule held that local governments, such as Winston's, could exercise only those powers that were expressly granted or necessarily implied in their legislative charters. Invoking Dillon's Rule, Clark found that Winston's charter did not empower it to pass the ordinance in question. Clark admitted that the city's charter authorized it to provide for the "general welfare" of its inhabitants. But to uphold the segregation ordinance under this "general welfare" provision would, in Clark's words, "give to the words 'general welfare' an extended and wholly unrestricted scope" far beyond the state legislature's intent.[50]

Clark's opinion in *Darnell* highlights a curious feature of Dillon's Rule. That rule, which constrained the powers of local (city and county) governments, enjoyed its fullest flowering in the South. In other words, the southern states were both the nation's most vigilant defenders of local rule in the form of "states' rights" and the nation's least vigilant defenders of local rule in the form of municipal governments, even though these were arguably even closer to "the people." Clark's ruling also put an intriguing twist on the relationship between "states' rights" and white supremacy, two bedrock concepts of southern history. From slavery through civil rights, southern defenders of white supremacy steadily beat the drum of "states' rights" against federal "intrusion." In *Darnell*, in contrast, Clark invoked the language of states' rights to *nullify* a white supremacy measure. Clark argued that Winston's residential segregation ordinance threatened states' rights, as it were, from below.[51]

By relying on Dillon's Rule rather than the constitutional provisions that Darnell's lawyers had stressed, Clark was able to side with Darnell without violating his own longstanding opposition to judicial review. Dillon's Rule, however, was less absolute than Clark's opinion implied. Indeed, the North Carolina Supreme Court's application of it had been uneven. The court had applied the rule most rigidly (that is, had circumscribed local governments' powers most tightly) when local governments had sought to impose taxes or fees without express legislative authorization. The court had granted somewhat more leeway to local governments that sought to provide public services (sewage systems, fireworks shows, and the like) that legislative charters did not expressly authorize. The court's application of Dillon's Rule was looser still when local governments exercised regulatory powers, as in *Darnell*. In *Small v. Edenton*, a regulatory case heard just six years prior to *Darnell*, the court had upheld the authority of a city to compel local property owners to remove a particular sort of street awning. "[L]ocal matters," Clark himself wrote for the majority in that 1908 case, "are properly left to the people of a self-governing community, to be decided and determined by them for themselves, and not by a judge or court for them."[52]

Clark bolstered his Dillon's Rule reasoning in two ways. First, he mentioned property rights—in particular, the right of property owners to dispose of their property. The Winston ordinance, he wrote, forbade the owner of property "to sell or lease it to whomsoever he sees fit." This was problematic because the right of disposing of property had, in Clark's words, "always been held one of the inalienable rights incident to the ownership of property." This emphasis on property rights may have held special appeal to Clark's conservative brethren, especially Associate Justice George H. Brown, an avowed defender of property rights and vested interests. Three years after *Darnell*, a comparatively conservative U.S. Supreme Court emphasized property rights while holding, in *Buchanan v. Warley* (1917), that a residential segregation ordinance from Louisville, Kentucky, was unconstitutional.[53]

The second way in which Clark reinforced his Dillon's Rule reasoning was to emphasize the racially discriminatory aspect of the ordinance.

In classic "slippery slope" antidiscrimination language, he reasoned that if Winston could, without express legislative authorization, separate black and white residences, it could also "require Republicans to live on certain streets and Democrats on others; or that Protestants shall reside only in certain parts of the town and Catholics in another," and so forth.[54]

Concern with the effects of racial discrimination also underlay a digression in which Clark discussed North Carolina legislation regarding out-of-state "labor agents." In the late nineteenth century, northern labor agents had traveled south to recruit cheap black labor. Fearing an exodus of black agricultural workers—and a threat to the local racial caste system—North Carolina had adopted statutes requiring labor agents to pay steep licensing fees. By enacting these measures, Clark concluded, the state had made clear its interest in preventing black workers from leaving the state. Winston's discriminatory ordinance, however, would likely encourage black workers to leave the state by restricting their housing options. That exodus would contradict the state's demonstrated preference for maintaining its black workforce.[55]

To demonstrate the ordinance's likely effect, Clark discussed the effect of ethnic discrimination in European history. "In Ireland there were years ago limits prescribed beyond which the native Irish or Celtic population could not reside," he wrote. One of the long-term results of this unhappy policy was "continued disorder and unrest in that unhappy island" that contributed to the departure of more than half of the Irish population. Similarly, in Russia, "to this day, there are certain districts to which the Jews are restricted, with the result that vast numbers of them are emigrating." Reasoning that Winston's ordinance would have similar demographic effects—that is, would encourage productive African American workers to leave the state—Clark concluded that the Winston measure was contrary to the state's legislative will, as expressed in the "labor agent" laws. Based on this reasoning, Clark nullified the ordinance and voided Darnell's conviction.[56]

The white press received Clark's "anxiously awaited" decision with immense disappointment. "We lament, of course, along with most of the best citizens of this city, that the court could not . . . uphold the Winston-Salem segregation ordinance," the local *Journal* editorialized. "There is no doubt in our minds but that segregation of the races in the cities is the best policy. In fact, we believe that experience will prove that it is the only way to maintain peace in the community." The editors noted happily, however, that segregation was proceeding steadily throughout the region "without a law requiring it."[57]

The reaction was scarcely more positive in the nation's law reviews. The *University of Pennsylvania Law Review* objected to Clark's "time worn sophistry" about segregation's dangers and criticized him for ignoring *Plessy v. Ferguson*. Similar complaints about Clark's "rather obscurely reasoned opinion" appeared in the *Virginia Law Review*.[58] In contrast, the NAACP applauded *Darnell* and printed favorable, "gratifying comment" on the decision from select northern newspapers.[59]

State v. Darnell probably prevented other North Carolina cities from adopting residential segregation ordinances. It may also have discouraged the state legislature from adopting a similar measure on a statewide basis, although nothing in the ruling expressly barred statewide legislative action. *Darnell* did not, however, end housing segregation in Winston-Salem. Indeed, because the ordinance had sought to freeze residential patterns as of 1912, a year of relatively integrated housing by twentieth-century standards, Chief Justice Clark's decision had the practical effect of clearing the way for continued "blockbusting" and increased housing segregation. In subsequent years, blacks flowed into east Winston, and whites flowed out. By 1960, east Winston was 84 percent African American. By 1970, Winston-Salem was the second most segregated city in the United States.[60]

At first blush, it is tempting to view *State v. Darnell* as a straightforward African American triumph, a case in which Winston-Salem blacks "directly initiated reform."[61] Deeper investigation forces a different conclusion. In *Darnell*, we submit, three groups crossed racial and class lines to oppose Jim Crow: (1) black property owners, both professionals (Dr. Smith) and workers (Darnell), who sought the right to live where they chose; (2) small business owners, both black (Penn) and white (Sledge), who had at least one eye on the bottom line; and (3) elite, elderly white members of the North Carolina bar and bench (Watson, Buxton, Clark), who mixed paternalistic, economic, and professional motivations. In the courts, if not on the streets, their combined efforts prevailed over the nervous white homeowners and "progressive" city leaders who favored de jure housing segregation.

State v. Darnell challenges preconceptions. Here, a southern court during Jim Crow's heyday voided a segregation measure. A "progressive" judge, an outspoken champion of majority rule and active government, nullified a popularly enacted social regulation. The language of states' rights, forged in racist state capitals as a shield against federal attack, was recast as a sword with which to strike down a racist local measure. Former slave owners and former slaves collaborated on the segregation ordinance's demise. The perverse result of their triumph was increased, not decreased, segregation.

There was one final result. Following his Supreme Court victory, William Darnell moved back into his house at 1105 Highland Avenue. This time, he was not arrested.

Part II

Modernity and Tradition: Cultural Conflict between the World Wars

Chapter 4

Evolution and Defamation
The Case of Reverend J. R. Pentuff

"Probably never before in the history of Charlotte," that city's *Observer* reported in 1922, "has there been such a surprise as was experienced by the congregation of Calvary Methodist church Sunday night." The surprise came when three men, "robed in the costume of the Ku Klux Klan," approached Reverend J. A. Sharp during a service, handed him a letter, and silently departed. The Klan's letter commended Reverend Sharp for persistently preaching against "all forms of vice and immorality." Sharp frequently sermonized, as he had that Sunday, against "local vice and immoral conduct, including dancing to jazz music, drinking, licentiousness and the laws against the teaching of the Bible" in public schools. The Klan thanked Sharp for his efforts and promised him "the hearty and earnest co-operation of its hundreds of members."[1]

The KKK's visit to Calvary Methodist captured, in microcosm, the widespread cultural tensions that pitted modernists against traditionalists during the so-called Jazz Age following World War I. North Carolina's distinctively "New South" version of this nationwide drama reflected the state's volatile combination of strong religiosity and rapid economic modernization. Pious Tar Heel traditionalists found in the word *jazz* a useful metaphor for everything modern and troubling. Just as jazz music represented, in the words of the *Charlotte Observer*, the "defiance of all musical law," the term *jazz* as a general concept captured the disturbing modern tendency to "defy recognized law and established conventions" of all sorts. Jazz dance, for instance, threatened

---

James McNab, Timothy Cook, David Dupee, John Marshall, Thomas William Powell Jr., and Drew Prickett contributed to this chapter.

to replace time-honored "dancing ethics and dancing law"—so "refined and graceful"—with "disorderly movements, irregular and irrational, often obscene." Even more distressing was the generalized spirit of jazz elsewhere in society, a spirit "that would defy law and authority . . . that would overthrow all traditions, that would make a clean sweep of all things that have hitherto been regarded as fundamental."[2]

Traditionalists sought to use the law to combat the perceived threats posed by this "jazz" spirit, broadly understood. This chapter and the two that follow explore three such culturally charged legal cases from North Carolina in the 1920s and 1930s. All three chapters touch on issues that Reverend Sharp included in his KKK-approved sermon. The present chapter concerns debates about Darwinian evolution and the proper place of religion in society. Chapter 5 deals with the unruly behavior of young women. Chapter 6 touches on illegal alcohol, jazz music and dance, and what Reverend Sharp referred to as "licentiousness." On the whole, the traditionalists described in these chapters were quicker than their modernist counterparts to litigate and more creative in their use of the legal system. Modernists, however, held their own in court. We begin with a controversy about the teaching of Darwinism in public schools.

Prior to the 1960s, when the Supreme Court of the United States, during the tenure of Chief Justice Earl Warren, struck down state bans on the teaching of evolution in public schools, only two evolution-in-the-schools disputes had produced appellate cases in the United States. The first of these cases, *Scopes v. State* (Tennessee, 1925), is world famous. The second, *Pentuff v. Park* (North Carolina, 1927), is utterly obscure, perhaps because it was a libel suit filed against a journalist, not a *Scopes*-style criminal prosecution of a biology teacher. *Pentuff* is worth exploring, however, because it invites reconsideration of several popular assumptions. These popular assumptions, based on the universally known *Scopes* model, portray the evolution debate of the 1920s as pitting South against North, religion against science, and rural values against urban ones.[3]

Pentuff v. Park calls these notions into question. The case grew out of an evolution debate that was strictly intraregional; all major disputants were Tar Heels. The supposed "religion-versus-science" dichotomy was tangled and messy in North Carolina. Tar Heel evolutionists blended religion with science. Their opponents did likewise. Many of

North Carolina's anti-evolutionists were as urban as their adversaries. And state legislators in Raleigh, unlike those in Nashville, rejected a proposed ban on teaching evolution in the public schools.

Absent any statewide ban, the legal history of anti-evolutionism in North Carolina was distinctive. Private law, not criminal or constitutional law, predominated. *Pentuff v. Park* was a libel case, brought by a Concord, North Carolina, creationist preacher named James Pentuff against a Raleigh newspaper that had lampooned his "ignorant" views on evolution. Among other things, Pentuff's suit claimed that members of the clergy deserved enhanced libel protection, since they, in their professional capacities, were uniquely vulnerable to character assault. The case raised questions about evolution, expressive freedom, and the proper place of religion in society.

Pentuff v. Park is a drama in two acts. Act I features a heated argument about evolution between two colorful North Carolinians: William Poteat and James Pentuff. Their debate sets the stage for act II, in which Pentuff sues the *Raleigh Times* and its editor, O. J. Coffin, for libel.

In 1925, the Scopes "monkey trial" in Tennessee produced what some scholars consider to be the most famous scene in American legal history: defense attorney Clarence Darrow's theological interrogation of opposing counsel William Jennings Bryan. Historians love this scene both for its high drama and because its celebrity protagonists seem so perfectly to embody the opposing sides in the day's broader evolution debate. As reported then and since, it was not merely Darrow versus Bryan. It was "scientific secularism" versus "traditional evangelical faith." It was "admitted agnosticism" versus "unwavering fundamentalism." It was science versus religion.[4]

But the Bryan-Darrow showdown, despite its undeniably high drama, did not accurately reflect the broader evolution debate. Few Americans were as fervently fundamentalist as Bryan. Fewer still were as agnostic as Darrow. Indeed, notwithstanding the either-or hype surrounding *Scopes,* the vast majority of Americans at the time believed deeply in both science *and* religion. In this sense, Tennessee's mainstage production of the drama that might be titled *The Evolution Controversy* makes for gripping theater but misleading history. A truer, albeit less glitzy, production of the same drama took place on a side stage in neighboring North Carolina. That drama began with a debate between a Christian evolutionist and a scientific creationist.

The Christian evolutionist was Wake Forest University president William Poteat. Like Darrow, Poteat believed deeply in science. Indeed, he was an eminent biologist. Unlike the agnostic Darrow, however, Poteat was deeply religious. He was an influential lay leader of North Carolina's largest religious denomination, the Baptists. Two lines from Poteat's résumé utterly confound the "science versus religion" formula derived from *Scopes:* Poteat had led both the Baptist State Convention and the North Carolina Academy of Science. He was a Southern Baptist biologist.[5]

Science and religion blended as harmoniously in Poteat's mind as on his résumé. He criticized both "extreme Modernists," who embraced science but rejected religion, and "extreme Fundamentalists," who did the reverse.[6] He firmly believed that science and religion were "bound together in the relation of positive friendship." When science solved natural mysteries, it glorified God, the Creator. And when science failed to solve eternal mysteries, as it inevitably would, scientists could and should dig "over the fence in the theological preserve." Poteat poetically mused, "I think of Science as passing to and fro in God's garden, busy with its forms of beauty, its fruits and flowers, its creeping thing[s], its beast[s] and bird[s], the crystal shut in its stones . . . and coming now at length in the cool of the long day upon God Himself walking in His garden."[7]

When it came to evolution, Poteat saw little room for debate. Although specialists admittedly still disagreed about details, as Poteat hoped they always would, he believed that all responsible biologists fully accepted the central principles of evolution. Poteat observed in 1925 that evolution, like Copernican astronomy or the germ theory of infectious disease, had become deeply "embedded in the texture of the intellectual life of today." Indeed, evolutionary thinking was so fundamental to "well-nigh all fields of inquiry" that Poteat had trouble believing that anti-evolutionists actually envisioned its suppression. "One wonders," he wrote in the year of the *Scopes* trial, "whether the proposal to disentangle and expunge it [evolutionary thought] by . . . legislative enactment can . . . really be serious."[8]

Poteat's belief in evolution, however, did nothing to erode his faith in the Bible. He had no patience with fundamentalists who, with small-minded literalism, believed "everything in the Bible from cover to cover, including the covers." Rather than taking the Bible's creation story literally, he read it as divinely inspired poetry—as, he believed, it was intended to be read. To Poteat, the central message of Genesis was unmistakable: God was the creator of all things. The "pictorial details" adorning this message were but "incidental." By reading in this way, Poteat found the Bible's creation account to be "in remarkable accord with modern science." Genesis provided no dates "and so allows for the antiquity of the earth demonstrated by geology." The Bible recognized, as did modern biologists, that the creation of life occurred in stages (poetic "days"), not all at once. The Good Book's silence on the precise method of life's unfolding was "a challenge to human wit to discover it." Now that science had determined that evolution was "the method which God use[d] in creation," modern Christians could "return to [the Bible] . . . with a new reverence for its inspiration." Poteat concluded, "To the catechism question, 'Who made you?' we may still reply, 'God made me,' although we now know how."[9]

Poteat's top adversary in the North Carolina evolution debate of the mid-1920s was James R. Pentuff, a Baptist minister. Like William Jennings Bryan, Pentuff was a religious fundamentalist. Unlike Bryan, however, Pentuff was not ignorant of science. Indeed, he fancied himself a scientific creationist. Pentuff's story challenges both the narrow stereotype of "creationist as scientific illiterate" and the broader stereotype of "creationist as uneducated rube."

Like Poteat, Pentuff blended science and religion throughout his training and career. He was born in Rutherford County, North Carolina, in 1864. When he was seventeen, his family moved to South Carolina, where he attended Furman University, a Baptist institution. Pentuff's college studies were "mainly scientific." Beyond the classroom, his pursuits were mainly religious. He preached at a nearby country church throughout his college years.[10]

Pentuff's studies did not end with his graduation from Furman in 1891. He subsequently earned a master's degree in theology and a doctorate in philosophy. After working as a minister for a time, he returned to academia as professor, dean, and president of schools and colleges in Iowa, Missouri, Texas, and West Virginia. All the while, he continued preaching. And he continued studying science on his own.[11]

Evolutionary theory was Pentuff's scientific passion. He was an outspoken critic of Darwin's theories. In 1925, he wrote a one-hundred page rebuttal of William Poteat's pro-evolution writings. Pentuff's fundamentalism was on clear display in this work. "The doctrine of Creation is true," Pentuff argued, "and if it be true, Evolution is false."[12]

One of the most striking features of Pentuff's anti-evolutionism was its extensive invocation of science, which took several forms. One was his habitual scientific résumé-thumping. The "Rev. Prof. J. R. Pentuff, Ph.D., D.D.," as he liked to be called, made it clear that, for "the last twenty-five years," he had "made a thorough study" of evolutionary science. He had "kept abreast . . . of the different . . . books that have come out on science," was familiar with the latest "theories about evolution," and had even conducted "independent research" on the topic using "[h]igh powered microscopes."[13]

Pentuff emphasized that his disagreement was with Darwinian theory, not science or the scientific method. Indeed, he cited science books, quoted scientists, and employed scientific jargon at every opportunity. In one typical passage, he ostentatiously quoted a prominent British botanist to bolster his argument that different life forms could not be proven to have evolved out of each other. Pentuff wrote, "It is impossible to trace one phylum from another. Rather it is said: 'We know nothing whatever of the angiospermous families.' Prof. D. H. Scott." Pentuff finished the paragraph with attributed quotations from two additional scientists.[14]

Pentuff's point here was not just that the Bible trumped science but also that creationist science trumped what he called evolutionary "pseudo-science." In support of this argument, he repeatedly cited "the evidences" found in "the physical universe." "The facts are against Evolution," he insisted. Creationism satisfied "the Bible and also science"; evolutionism satisfied neither.[15]

Take geology, he argued. The "geological record as we now know it" gave "no support to the fantastic, speculative, artificial arrangement of the fossils by evolutionists." But that record was in "perfect agreement" with biblical accounts of creation and the deluge. Charles Darwin's ignorance of these geological "facts" was a "fatal blunder" recently repeated by Professor Poteat of Wake Forest. Pentuff described this supposed blunder in his typical style: Darwin and Poteat had inadvisably swallowed "Lyell's geology, based on Werner, Smith, and Buffon," even though "[n]ot one of them knew much about geology as we now know it." In short, Pentuff believed evolution was a "false conception." For him, it did not qualify as legitimate science.[16]

Science was as prominent in Pentuff's oratory as it was in his writing. An "absorbing address on evolution" that he delivered at Charlotte's First Baptist Church in February 1925 is illustrative. Publicity for the event stressed Pentuff's academic credentials and scientific approach.

"Dr. Pentuff, former president of the Baptist College for Women in Missouri, will discuss the subject [of evolution] scientifically and relate it to the Bible and Christianity," the *Charlotte Observer* announced on the morning of the event, adding that Pentuff had "made a thorough study of evolution." The next day's headlines summarized the central message of Reverend Pentuff's talk: "Organic Evolution Theory of Darwin Is Unscientific." Pentuff listed several ways in which "recent investigations of scientists" had supposedly disproved evolution. He closed by stating that he "would like to see the state ban the teaching of evolution in the public schools." Charlotte's First Baptist Church, crowded upstairs and down, burst into applause.[17]

Thus, both of North Carolina's principal antagonists in the evolution debate blended science and religion. They invoked both when challenged. Poteat, the evolutionist, faced attacks from fundamentalists, who sought to remove him from the presidency of Wake Forest. Poteat responded by testifying to the depth of his Christian faith. (Once, he literally held up a copy of the Bible at the podium, as if it were a shield.) The biologist's Christian testimony was always so heartfelt that it assuaged fundamentalist critics.[18]

Reverend Pentuff faced different sorts of attacks. Opponents, President Poteat among them, challenged his scientific credentials. Poteat wrote to the president of Furman University and others, asking skeptical questions about Pentuff's educational record. Had Pentuff really graduated from Furman? What school had granted "Dr. Pentuff" his much-trumpeted PhD? Had he really been a college president? Although Pentuff's educational claims held up, the skepticism of his critics reinforced his compulsion to prove his scientific bona fides.[19]

Thus, in the evolution debates of the 1920s, perceived expertise in both science and religion mattered. In no other state did such expertise matter more than in North Carolina, where educational leaders—including Poteat and Pentuff—were uniquely central to the debate. To call a North Carolina disputant "ignorant" was to invite a fight. In 1926, a Raleigh newspaper invited a fight. It accused Pentuff of ignorance on the subject of evolution. Pentuff countered with a libel suit seeking twenty-five thousand dollars.[20]

The series of events that produced *Pentuff v. Park* began early in 1925, when Rep. David Poole introduced an anti-evolution bill in the North Carolina House of Representatives. The Poole Bill—or the "Resolution

Restricting the Teaching of Darwinism in the State Schools of North Carolina"—harmonized with three national trends: the legislation of morality, most famously illustrated by the prohibition of alcohol; the general politicization of the schools, as exemplified by the World War I–era flag salute and English-only instruction mandates; and the particular urge to suppress Darwinism, as demonstrated by the introduction of thirty-seven anti-evolution bills in twenty state legislatures during the 1920s.[21]

The Poole Bill declared it the "sense of the General Assembly of North Carolina that it is injurious to the welfare of the people . . . for any . . . teacher in the State, paid wholly or in part by taxation, to teach . . . as a fact . . . any . . . evolutionary hypothesis that links man in blood relationship with any lower form of life." This resolution was not as restrictive as it could have been. It established no criminal penalties. Its ban on teaching Darwinism "as a fact" implied that instructors might acceptably teach Darwinism as a *theory*. Its particular focus on hypotheses linking humans to lower forms of life suggested that nonhuman evolution might be taught without objection. Such nuances, however, were absent from public debate. As far as the attentive public was concerned, the Poole Bill quite simply would "prohibit the teaching of evolution in the public schools of North Carolina."[22]

The Poole Bill debate raged across the state. It generated so many letters to the *Raleigh News and Observer* that the editor, having "printed an equal number on both sides" and still having "a pack on each side" left over, took the unusual step of calling a "moratorium on communications on evolution." When the Poole Bill came up for debate in the House Committee on Education on 10 February 1925, an "enormous crowd" gathered in Raleigh to witness the proceedings.[23]

The "chief spokesman" in favor of the bill, the man who "carried the burden of battle" for his side, was Reverend Professor James R. Pentuff, PhD, DD. Pentuff consumed fifty of the sixty minutes allotted for debate in favor of the measure. His arguments were his usual ones. He insisted that evolution should be banished from the public schools "because it isn't science and, therefore, the State has no right to teach it." Recent scientific findings, he testified, had thoroughly debunked Darwin's theories. Yet because North Carolina educators were lamentably unwilling to "keep up with the newer sciences," Darwin's "discarded theories" were still taught in tax-funded schools throughout the state.[24]

Among the "great crowd" listening to Pentuff's presentation that day was William Poteat. Twice, according to press reports, supporters urged the Wake Forest president to speak against the bill, "each time his name being greeted with long cheering and much handclapping." But because the Poole Bill concerned only tax-supported schools, Poteat, who led a private school, thought it best to leave the fighting to representatives of public institutions. University of North Carolina president Harry Woodburn Chase was among the representatives of tax-supported schools who spoke against the resolution. The anti–Poole Bill remarks of Bertram Wells, a botanist from North Carolina State College, were Poteat-esque. Wells testified that his belief in Darwinian evolution had made him more, not less, of a Christian.[25]

During the trial arising from Pentuff's libel suit the following year, his behavior at this legislative hearing in 1925 was an issue. The allegedly libelous editorial accused Pentuff of being so "unmannerly" and "discourteous" during this hearing that the committee chair "suppressed" him. The facts are murky. As reported at the time of the 1925 hearing, Pentuff responded to some of the Poole Bill's critics by rhetorically asking when Darwinism had become accepted as fact. The committee chair told him that he could not "quiz the whole house." He had to address his question to particular persons. "I will ask . . . some of my monkey brethren," Pentuff quipped. With a tap of his gavel, the committee chair silenced the pastor. "The gentleman will observe the amenities of debate," he said. Despite close coverage of the hearing, few North Carolina newspapers saw anything newsworthy in this exchange. Only later, at Pentuff's trial, did the incident attract scrutiny.[26]

Following what the press called "the first big fight of the [1925 legislative] session," the North Carolina House of Representatives rejected the Poole Bill, 67 to 46. The bill's opponents exhaled. "[W]e have had . . . few if any exhibitions in North Carolina worse than this one, few more depressing spectacles," wrote journalist Nell Battle Lewis (whom we shall meet again in chapter 5). "I thank God with all my heart that it's over."[27]

But it was not over. Far from surrendering, anti-evolutionists redoubled their efforts. Setting their sights on the 1926 elections, they urged North Carolinians to return a General Assembly that would be more sympathetic to "Christian" concerns than its predecessor had been—sympathetic enough, they hoped, to pass a new and stronger version of the Poole Bill, since the original bill was, in their view, "[g]ood as far as it went, but did not go far enough."[28]

In the meantime, individuals in various localities took up the fight, led by anti-evolutionists in Mecklenburg County. Mecklenburg was the nerve center of anti-evolutionism in North Carolina. Immediately after the Poole Bill's defeat, Mecklenburg citizens sent anti-evolution petitions to state legislators and to public school officials. An association of Mecklenburg County ministers adopted and published a series of anti-evolutionist resolutions. Around the same time, the Mecklenburg County Board of Education passed a resolution opposing the teaching of evolution in its public schools "and the teaching of anything that brings in question the truth of the Bible or any part therein." The board of education also gave the superintendent and his assistant the power to censor public school libraries to keep out "any books on evolution or any books that question the truth of the Bible." Some other counties soon followed Mecklenburg's lead.[29]

Mecklenburg County's heavy concentration of Presbyterians helps explain its leadership in the North Carolina anti-evolution movement. Presbyterians were the state's third-largest denomination, behind Baptists and Methodists, but were second to none in anti-evolution zeal. Two of the nation's most prominent anti-evolutionists, evangelical preacher Billy Sunday and William Jennings Bryan, were Presbyterians. So was North Carolina's David Poole, author of the Poole Bill. Mecklenburg was the only North Carolina county in which Presbyterians were the most prevalent denomination. Mecklenburg County contained almost three times the Presbyterian population of any other North Carolina county.[30]

Mecklenburg County's vigorous anti-evolutionism challenges the textbook truism that the 1920s evolution debate was a rural-versus-urban affair, with "urban" on the side of evolution. Mecklenburg was one of the most densely populated counties in the state. Only four of North Carolina's one hundred counties were more densely populated. Mecklenburg County's dominant city, Charlotte, ran neck-and-neck with Winston-Salem as the state's largest. Mecklenburg was, in short, one of North Carolina's most urban counties, yet it was also the hub of North Carolina anti-evolutionism. Contemporaries traced the Poole Bill's origins to Charlotte.[31]

Following the Poole Bill's defeat in 1925, Pentuff redoubled his anti-evolution efforts. Much of his work was organizational. He was one of the "moving spirits" behind the creation of the "Committee of 100," a group of anti-evolutionist ministers and laypersons formed in Charlotte (Mecklenburg County) in the spring of 1926. This group vowed to fight in all one hundred North Carolina counties to remove "un-Christian doctrines" from the public schools.[32]

Pentuff also worked solo. In February 1926, a year after his Poole Bill testimony, Pentuff took his anti-evolution message to Fuquay Springs, a small town near Raleigh. The press labeled Pentuff's Fuquay Springs visit the "opening gun" of a much-anticipated drive to elect a new General Assembly that would ban evolution from North Carolina's schools. This electoral drive was to begin that June, in North Carolina's Democratic primaries.[33]

Pentuff delivered two anti-evolution lectures in Fuquay Springs. True to form, the first concerned science and the second concerned religion. Large crowds attended both. The press quoted one "prominent Fuquay Springs citizen" who was dazzled by the preacher's performance. "The remarkable thing about Dr. Pentuff's lectures," this sympathetic listener remarked, "is that he is so full of his subject that he can deliver one lecture after another without any notes and quote authorities and give the book and page number, and those who have heard him deliver these lectures at different times say that he never gives the same lecture twice." At the end of Pentuff's second Fuquay Springs address, the crowd unanimously pledged to support candidates who opposed the teaching of evolution.[34]

A few days later, the *Raleigh Times* published a stinging editorial about the Fuquay Springs rally. In Pentuff's view, the piece was so defamatory, so false, and so malicious that only a transfer of twenty-five thousand dollars from newspaper to pastor could return the scales of justice to equilibrium.

The author of the offending piece was *Raleigh Times* editor Oscar J. Coffin. Coffin was a liberal southern journalist, one of a group that would achieve renown during the century's middle decades for its comparatively progressive views on the issue of race. In the 1920s, however, they wrote much less about race than about the need to defend intellectual and cultural liberty in the South against homegrown intolerance. O. J. Coffin, like other liberal southern editors of the 1920s, sought to enlighten the "benighted South," one witty editorial at a time. During an age of widespread Ku Klux Klan activity, prevalent anti-Catholicism, and pervasive attempts to legislate morality, Coffin used his editorials to criticize Klan intolerance, speak kindly of "our Catholic friends and neighbors," and ridicule the overzealousness of moralizing "uplifters," whose incessant attempts to "bolster up the public morals" inevitably backfired.[35]

With regard to the "fundamentalists" and their obsession with evolution, Coffin's views closely resembled those of William Poteat, whom Coffin held in "high and lively regard." Like Poteat, Coffin was neither anticlerical nor antireligion. He was a liberal Protestant who perceived no tension between religion and science. Evolution, Coffin wrote, was but "God Almighty's program of progress." The Poole Bill, that "viciously self-righteous" attempt to "enjoin intelligence," struck Coffin as a futile and absurd attempt to "[pass] a law for the protection" of God. God, Coffin assured readers, needed no such assistance. Coffin also feared that passage of such a backward measure as the Poole Bill would render North Carolina's legislature "nationally ridiculous."[36]

Coffin found Reverend Pentuff, the Poole Bill's top supporter, to be an irresistible target. The editor first noticed Pentuff during the hearing on the Poole Bill in 1925. Coffin conceded Pentuff's "painful earnestness" but pointed out that honesty of purpose was "not sufficient grounds for the enactment of statutes; there must be intelligence coupled with it." Alas, intelligence was in short supply among such "pseudo-scientists as the preacher person Mr. Pentupp [sic] from Concord," whose presentation was marked by "crass ignorance." Coffin had a clear message for Pentuff and his ilk: "[n]atural law cannot be repealed at will by the [North Carolina] House of Representatives, the Senate concurring."[37]

When Pentuff reentered the fray the following year, so did Coffin. "We see," Coffin wrote, "that Fuquay Springs under the leadership of one Pentuff of Concord has declared war against what it is pleased to term evolution." Coffin hoped that the good people of Fuquay Springs had other sources of information on the topic. If they relied on Pentuff, they were in trouble. "For Pentuff, if our memory does not play us false," Coffin continued, "is the same chap who tried to tell the legislative committee on education all about evolution at the last session of the General Assembly." In Coffin's view, Pentuff's testimony had left evolution in the dark, illuminating only Pentuff's own arrogance and ignorance. "Beyond stating categorically that he had been president of a college or two of which nobody in the audience had ever heard," Coffin wrote, and beyond insisting that "science had disproved something that he called 'evolution' but had evidently never met," Pentuff's testimony had contributed nothing to the legislative debate.[38]

As if egotism and ignorance were not bad enough, Coffin further charged Pentuff with incivility. Pentuff was, "indeed, so unmannerly in his approach to the matter before the House, so discourteous to those whom he deemed to be in disagreement with him," Coffin wrote, "that the chairman of the committee . . . suppressed him." Coffin followed these sharp jabs with a roundhouse punch:

> There has not to our knowledge appeared in public within the memory of the present generation of North Carolinians a more ignorant man than Pentuff, or one less charitable toward men who might honestly disagree with him. If Fuquay Springs will insist on taking the word of an immigrant ignoramus against that of men of proven character and intelligence such as Drs. [Richard] Vann [former president of Meredith College] and Poteat, whom it has known all their lives, we suppose there is nothing that can be done about it. But it does the intelligence of the people of . . . [Fuquay Springs] scant credit.[39]

In March 1926, shortly after the publication of the *Raleigh Times* editorial containing these statements, Pentuff filed his libel suit against Coffin, *Raleigh Times* publisher John A. Park, and the Times Publishing Company, demanding twenty-five thousand dollars.

Pentuff's complaint charged that Coffin's piece had maliciously sought to defame him as an individual, as an educator, and as "a minister of the gospel." Pentuff claimed that the article had disgraced him among "members of all the churches of the Baptist denomination in the . . . State of North Carolina." Thanks to the editorial, Pentuff alleged, people—especially Baptists—would wrongly conclude that he had been "unmannerly" and "discourteous" in legislative debate; that he was an "'uncharitable' minister of the gospel"; that he was ignorant on the topic of evolution; and that he was, in general, an "ignoramus." Pentuff also charged that Coffin's slurs had caused him "great mental anguish," both personally "and in contemplation of the pain and suffering" that the article had caused his wife. Adding this anguish to the aforementioned injury, Pentuff calculated that the editorial had damaged him "in the sum of twenty-five thousand dollars."[40]

The defendants denied having libeled the plaintiff. Their published assertion that Pentuff was an unmannerly ignoramus was not libelous, they explained, because it was absolutely true.[41] The defendants' hard line was no surprise. Since the episode began, they had been utterly unrepentant. North Carolina law provided that plaintiffs who sued periodicals for libel had to provide defendants with at least five days' advance warning before they sued. Defendants then had ten days in which to print apologies and retractions. Doing so would shield them from both punitive damages and pain-and-suffering awards, limiting their liability to actual damages only. On 4 March 1926, a week and a half after Coffin's editorial appeared, Pentuff, in accordance with North Carolina law, warned the *Times* that he intended to sue. But the newspaper published no retraction.

Ten days passed, then nineteen. Pentuff filed suit. The very next day, the *Times* broadcast its lack of repentance. In an article about Pentuff's newly filed lawsuit, the newspaper refused to back down in any way. "[T]here is no desire or intention on the part of *The Times* to subtract anything," the piece declared. "In our opinion, J. R. Pentuff is ignorant, he is unmannerly in debate and he is uncharitable in his dealings with good and intelligent men of even his own denomination"—a veiled reference to Poteat. "If that be 'false and defamatory,' let him make the most of it."[42]

Even though the *Times* was a Raleigh newspaper, Pentuff filed suit 150 miles to the west, in Concord, where he lived and preached. He would enjoy home court advantage in Concord. In addition, since Concord was a much smaller town than Raleigh, Pentuff and his lawyers may have hoped that jurors there—like the ones in Dayton, Tennessee, who had recently convicted John Scopes—would be comparatively receptive to their arguments.

At trial, Pentuff bore the burden of proving defamation. He sought to refute Coffin's editorial of 23 February point by point. Coffin had claimed that Pentuff was so "unmannerly" and "discourteous" before the Education Committee that the chair had "suppressed" him. Depositions from plaintiff's witnesses stated otherwise. They affirmed that Pentuff was perfectly courteous that day and that the chair did not suppress him. Pentuff's oral testimony concurred: "[During the Poole Bill hearing, I] conducted myself as a gentleman, as if I had been in the pulpit preaching the gospel. I do not recall any act of discourtesy or breach of good manners on my part."[43]

Coffin's editorial had also accused Pentuff of being an "immigrant ignoramus." Pentuff denied both elements of this charge. By "immigrant," Coffin had not meant that Pentuff was from a foreign country.

He had meant that Pentuff was not a North Carolina native. Under oath, Pentuff countered that he was a third-generation North Carolinian who had lived in the state for his first seventeen years. Although he admittedly left thereafter to study, preach, and teach elsewhere and did not "c[o]me back home" until "three or four years" before the libel trial, he insisted that he was, by any reasonable measure, a native North Carolinian.[44]

Pentuff strove even harder to refute Coffin's charge that he was an "ignoramus." The bulk of his direct testimony concerned his educational credentials. He showed the court a catalog from the San Marcos Academy in Texas, where he had worked as dean. The catalog "contains a history of the faculty and a picture of me," he pointed out. Plaintiff's evidence also included a deposition from the president of Furman University, confirming Furman's conferral upon Pentuff of a bachelor's degree in 1891 and an honorary doctorate nine years later. Plaintiff's exhibit E was a diploma certifying Pentuff's master's degree from the Southern Baptist Theological Seminary. Exhibit F was an old catalog from Stephens College, a women's school in Missouri for which Pentuff had served as dean and president.[45]

Lastly, Pentuff testified that the *Times* editorial had done him real harm. The piece "caused me mental anguish and humiliation," he said. "I have a wife and three children. I am dependent upon my education and reputation as a teacher and minister of the gospel for my living for myself and children." Coffin's "attack on my character and reputation has given me a great deal of concern about my future employment."[46]

Then came the cross-examination. Defense lawyers were extremely well prepared. Acting more like private investigators than attorneys, they had dug up huge amounts of dirt on the Baptist preacher. On the stand, they forced Pentuff to admit—often after uncomfortable pauses—a series of embarrassments. Most were financial. He was briefly jailed in Yancey County, North Carolina, for debt. (Pentuff tried to mitigate the damage by relating how he had led other prisoners in Bible study.) More than once he had passed bad checks. He had engaged in a shady stock-selling scheme. As pastor over the years, he had borrowed money from multiple church members, many of whom still awaited repayment. "How much other money do you owe?" defense lawyers asked at one point. Pentuff sheepishly replied, "More than I can pay."[47]

Defense lawyers also asked about Miss Twitty, a hen belonging to the Pentuff family. (In *Scopes* trial terms, this was as close as the Pentuff trial got to a "Jonah and the Whale" moment.) Even though hens lay no more than one egg per day, the Pentuffs claimed that Miss Twitty could lay two or three times that number—up to seventeen eggs in one five-day stretch. (When a skeptical neighbor visited one day to witness the bird's prowess, Miss Twitty produced but a single egg.) Seeking to capitalize on the local notoriety that they had created for their hen, the Pentuffs advertised in a local newspaper that they were selling "[eggs] laid by Miss Twitty, who laid twice a day." Defense lawyers questioned Miss Twitty's astonishing productivity and suggested that the Pentuffs had fabricated the story in order to make a quick buck selling eggs. Pentuff denied the charge and mocked both the line of questioning and the theory of evolution. A rooster shared Miss Twitty's enclosure, Pentuff noted. Perhaps *he* had laid some of the eggs. "If he is an evolution rooster he would lay eggs," Pentuff quipped. Miss Twitty was unlikely to be an evolution hen, however, "because she didn't hatch out any goose eggs or duck eggs."[48]

Pentuff's cross-examination helped the defense in several ways. It impeached Pentuff's credibility as a witness. It suggested that sordid financial motives, not legitimate concern about reputation, might have motivated his libel suit. Perhaps most importantly, it destroyed Pentuff's claim to a pristine pre-editorial reputation.

Pentuff v. Park had been the most eagerly anticipated Cabarrus County superior court case that term. Thus far, during the plaintiff's case, spectators—especially voyeuristic ones who enjoyed watching people forced to admit embarrassing things about themselves—had seen a pretty good show. Then, suddenly, the trial ended, without a second part, that being the evidence for the defense. As soon as counsel for the plaintiff rested, counsel for the defendants asked the judge to terminate ("non-suit") the trial and declare immediate victory for the defense, on the grounds that Pentuff had failed to establish a legitimate cause of action. The defendants' side argued that Coffin's allegedly libelous editorial was not "actionable per se." Nothing in the article, in other words, warranted a jury trial. For instance, the editorial did not impute to Pentuff an infamous crime or a contagious disease. Most importantly, the piece never mentioned that Pentuff was a minister and therefore did not explicitly derogate him "in respect to his profession or calling." Even if all of Pentuff's allegations were true, defense lawyers maintained, there was no reason to continue with the trial, for none of his allegations was "actionable."[49]

Those raised exclusively on *Scopes* might guess that the Cabarrus County superior court, sitting in a small southern town not unlike Dayton, Tennessee, would deny this defense motion. But Judge A. M. Stack granted it and dismissed the complaint. To call a minister an ignoramus, Judge Stack explained, was not defamatory, particularly when evolution was involved. "When we get to talking about evolution," the trial judge said, displaying very un-Bryan-esque doubt, "we are all ignoramuses."[50]

Pentuff immediately appealed to the North Carolina Supreme Court. The only question on appeal was whether Coffin's editorial of 23 February was "actionable per se," meaning automatically deserving of a full jury trial. If the Supreme Court agreed with Pentuff that the article *was* actionable per se, it would order a new trial. Otherwise, the non-suit would stand and the case would end.

Lawyers for both sides addressed Pentuff's job as a minister. Pentuff's vocation mattered because of the Anglo-American common law precept that people have a right to the fruits of their industry. An entire branch of defamation law derives from that precept. As an influential legal treatise explained in 1924, the law of defamation enabled a "man" to seek monetary compensation when defamatory words damaged his "fair reputation and character *in his particular business* [emphasis added]." For instance, if Jones falsely wrote that Smith, a merchant, was bankrupt, Smith could sue for libel on grounds that Jones's published assertion was economically damaging. In this respect, a preacher was no different than a merchant, a dentist, or a manual laborer. In each case, "words which slander a man in his trade" were "actionable per se."[51]

Among the "trades," however, "ministers of the gospel" enjoyed longstanding and special privileges. As explained in an early nineteenth-century precedent from Pennsylvania, a given set of barbed words, though having no effect upon a layperson's professional prospects, might deprive a clergyman of "that respect, veneration, and confidence, without which he can expect no hearers as a minister of the gospel." Ministers deserved special legal protection, another nineteenth-century precedent held, because they are "teachers and exemplars of moral and Christian duty; and a pure and even unsuspected moral character [is] necessary to their usefulness in the community." A Minnesota case from 1910 stated that a clergyman "must, if he is to be successful in the practice of his profession, maintain a spotless reputation." Reducing the issue to "a mere matter of dollars and cents," an Ohio court reasoned that "the purity, the integrity, the uprightness of a minister's life is his capital in this world's business." By the time of the Pentuff appeal, legal scholars had surveyed the case law and concluded that words could often be actionable "when spoken of clergymen which would not be so if spoken of others."[52]

Reverend Pentuff sought to invoke this doctrine. Confronting him, however, was an inconvenient factual obstacle: the *Raleigh Times* editorial upon which his suit was based never mentioned that he was a pastor. Authorities split on whether he could still claim special clergymen's prerogatives. Precedents in some states held that, as far as libel law was concerned, members of the clergy never went off duty. "[A] minister being both a teacher and an exemplar of morality," a Kentucky case held in 1921, "[i]t is not possible . . . to draw a line of demarcation between his conduct as a minister and his conduct as a man. . . . Destroy the people's confidence in his morality . . . and you end his career as a minister."[53]

North Carolina precedents, however, were not helpful to Pentuff. The leading case was *McDowell v. Bowles* (1860). McDowell was a Baptist minister and self-described "clear blooded white man." He sued Bowles for slander after Bowles verbally alleged that Reverend McDowell was actually a "free negro" and therefore ineligible to vote. As in *Pentuff,* the trial judge non-suited the plaintiff. McDowell appealed. The North Carolina Supreme Court upheld the non-suit on grounds that the words in question made no mention of plaintiff's trade. The "sacred character" of McDowell's profession, the court elaborated, was irrelevant unless the alleged defamation concerned him "in his capacity of minister." This precedent appeared to bode ill for Pentuff, since the editorial of 23 February neither mentioned Pentuff's trade nor obviously concerned him "in his capacity of minister."[54]

Pentuff's appellate briefs contended—weakly—that *McDowell* should not apply since it involved spoken defamation (slander) rather than written defamation (libel). With more force, Pentuff's lawyers urged the court to reject the *McDowell* doctrine, since it would have the absurd consequence of allowing publishers to dodge liability merely by avoiding explicit mention of their victims' lines of work. "If this be the law," they argued, newspapers could "falsely and maliciously" print horrible things about any well-known minister, teacher, or lawyer "and escape liability therefore simply by calling the proper *name* of said minister, teacher or lawyer, without adding the term minister, teacher or lawyer ... when every reader of said ... publication knows that the person referred to is in fact a minister, teacher or lawyer."[55]

Defense attorneys countered that Coffin's editorial, like the alleged slander in *McDowell*, was utterly unrelated to the plaintiff's profession. "There is nothing in the entire article which would even tend to intimate that the plaintiff was remotely connected with ministerial work," they argued. The editorial was merely "an attack on the plaintiff's knowledge of evolution, a knowledge which he, by making a public address on the subject, held himself out as having." To say that a minister would suffer professional embarrassment when charged with ignorance of evolution made no more sense than to say that a lawyer would suffer professionally if charged with ignorance of Einstein's theory of relativity.[56]

On this point, and on all others, the North Carolina Supreme Court held for Pentuff. Its 1927 opinion, by Justice Heriot Clarkson, found that Coffin's editorial was indeed "actionable per se." Justice Clarkson wrote that the editorial *was* "calculated to injure [Pentuff] in his vocation or calling as a minister of the Gospel," even though it nowhere mentioned Pentuff's profession. Clarkson marshaled three underwhelming arguments in defense of this proposition. First, Clarkson found a passage in the Coffin editorial that, in his judgment, *implicitly* referred to Pentuff as a minister. This was the passage in which Coffin wrote, "If Fuquay Springs will insist on taking the word of an immigrant ignoramus [Pentuff] against that of men of proven character and intelligence, such as Drs. Vann and Poteat, whom it has known all their lives, we suppose there is nothing that can be done about it." Justice Clarkson wrote that this passage "compared [Pentuff] with two well-known ministers"—Vann and Poteat—and therefore indirectly "referr[ed] to plaintiff in his calling." Even though the editorial did not state that Vann and Poteat were ministers, Clarkson suggested, their fame as ministers was such that any comparison with them would imply to readers that Pentuff was also a minister.[57]

This analysis would have been questionable even had it been factually accurate, but it was not factually accurate. Vann and Poteat were principally known as educators, not ministers. (Coffin's editorial suggested as much by referring to them as "Drs.," not "Reverends.") Vann, it is true, was ordained in the Baptist Church and had worked in the late nineteenth century as a pastor. Since the turn of the century, however, he had focused primarily on his "life's great work": education. His greatest fame derived from his high-profile presidency of Meredith College, a Baptist school for women. The "minister" label fit Poteat even more poorly. Poteat was a biologist and a college president. Although he was also a Baptist lay leader, he was not a member of the clergy. Clarkson was simply wrong on the facts.[58]

For his second argument, Clarkson pointed out that the follow-up editorial that the *Raleigh Times* published on 24 March in response to Pentuff's decision to sue *did* explicitly name Pentuff's profession. This editorial mentioned "one J. R. Pentuff of Concord, by profession a preacher." Pentuff's libel suit, however, concerned the editorial of 23 February, not 24 March. By 24 March, Pentuff had already filed his libel suit.[59]

In his final argument, Clarkson quoted approvingly from treatises and out-of-state precedents regarding the legal preferences that clergymen enjoyed as plaintiffs in defamation cases. "Though a charge of immorality . . . is not actionable per se," one of these passages read, "there is an exception in the case of clergyman or priest." Clarkson also quoted a passage asserting that ministers, "being teachers and exemplars of moral and Christian duty," carried with them "constantly, whether in or out of the pulpit, superior obligations to exhibit in [their] whole deportment the purity of that religion which [they profess] to teach."[60]

Clarkson's review of precedents was notably selective. Conspicuously absent was *McDowell v. Bowles* (1860), the presumably controlling in-state precedent in which the North Carolina Supreme Court had upheld the non-suit of a minister's defamation case because the alleged defamation—Bowles's allegation that McDowell was a "free negro"—had failed to touch the plaintiff "in his capacity of minister." Although appellate briefs for both sides had extensively discussed *McDowell*, Clarkson did not mention it.[61]

To understand Clarkson's ruling fully, we must move beyond black-letter law and consider the black-robed lawmaker. Everything in Clarkson's past predisposed him to side with Pentuff. Like Pentuff, Justice Clarkson was a self-described religious fundamentalist and a cultural traditionalist. He did not hesitate to incorporate his religious faith into his legal opinions. He peppered his legal rulings with quotations from biblical passages and citations to scriptural authority. "It may be well for us to hark back to the Mosaic law," he once explained in a usury case, before quoting from Leviticus. Off the bench, Clarkson was a lifelong and influential advocate of alcohol prohibition. Anti-evolutionism closely resembled the alcohol prohibition movement, which also was church based and sought to marshal state power against a cultural influence that many fundamentalists perceived as corrosive. Moreover, Clarkson was a longtime resident of Charlotte, the center of North Carolina anti-evolutionism.[62]

Clarkson's Supreme Court colleagues probably offered little resistance to his pro-clerical views. Chief Justice Walter Stacy, for instance, was active in Christian groups and was a Methodist minister's son. Associate Justice George Connor prepared for college by studying under the tutorship of an Episcopal priest and remained a devout Episcopalian thereafter. Clarkson was no outlier.[63]

Clarkson's background and values affected his *Pentuff* ruling. Recall the defendants' argument that knowledge of evolution was as irrelevant to a minister's job as knowledge of physics was to a lawyer's. Clarkson's experiences as a churchgoer impelled him to disagree. Evolution, he wrote in his decision, absolutely *was* "discussed by clergymen in their vocation or calling." To ridicule Pentuff's views on evolution, therefore, *was* to touch him professionally. This made the editorial actionable per se.[64]

Clarkson's pro-clerical ruling gave voice to the widely held, culturally conservative fear that public esteem for religious leaders had eroded dangerously. During the "Roaring Twenties," when middle-class flouting of the church-backed Prohibition law was rampant and when popular works such as Sinclair Lewis's *Elmer Gantry* (published just months before Clarkson's *Pentuff* ruling) openly mocked organized religion and attacked the clergy, traditionalists such as Clarkson worried that American religion was under siege. On the very day that Clarkson's *Pentuff* ruling appeared, one Tar Heel traditionalist lamented in the press that Americans one generation earlier had "accepted . . . what they heard from the pulpit." But in the 1920s, "no institution is more slandered than the church and no men more [slandered] than Christian ministers." In *Pentuff*, Clarkson sought to combat this trend by granting members of the clergy special legal protection.[65]

Liberal journalists objected to the North Carolina Supreme Court's ruling. They found the "clerical license" (to quote one Raleigh headline) that Clarkson granted in *Pentuff* to be deeply troubling. The *Raleigh Times* (no longer edited by Coffin) bemoaned the "perilous . . . implications" of Clarkson's holding that the offending editorial was actionable just "because the plaintiff happened to be . . . a minister." The debate between Justice Clarkson and his liberal detractors mirrored the day's larger debates between traditionalists and modernists over the proper role of religion in society.[66]

Clarkson's North Carolina Supreme Court decision appeared to bring *Pentuff v. Park* to a *Scopes*-like conclusion. It appeared that, in the North Carolina courts, creationism and the clergy had won, while evolution and free speech had lost. Scholars have characterized *Pentuff v. Park* in this way.[67]

Clarkson's ruling, however, did not end the case. There remained the retrial back in Concord. All of the advantages appeared to favor Pentuff. As in the first trial, the suit would be heard in his hometown, before a jury of churchgoers, "most" of whom (according to the press) were farmers. Moreover, Pentuff now enjoyed several new advantages. Perhaps most importantly, his claims now carried the powerful imprimatur of the North Carolina Supreme Court. Justice Clarkson could have ruled simply that the non-suit was flawed and that Pentuff deserved a jury trial. But Clarkson appeared to go much further, suggesting not just that Pentuff deserved a full trial but also that he deserved to win that trial. The defendants *had* referred to Pentuff in his calling, Clarkson declared. Their libel *had* exposed Pentuff to contempt and ridicule. The editorial *was* "libelous *per se*." The new judge and jury in Concord would have to consider the case in the strongly pro-Pentuff light emanating from the state's highest court.[68]

Pentuff's lawyers also had strengthened their arguments. Their original libel claim had focused exclusively on Coffin's editorial of 23 February. When the case returned to Concord for retrial, Pentuff's lawyers renewed their twenty-five-thousand-dollar claim based on the 23 February article and added a new thirty-five-thousand-dollar claim, based on the 24 March follow-up article. Because the March piece, unlike its predecessor, mentioned Pentuff's profession, the new claim improved Pentuff's odds of prevailing. It also increased the total libel claim to sixty thousand dollars—twenty-four times the pastor's annual salary.[69]

Pentuff also had fresh evidence of damage. In October 1926, around the time of the first trial, Pentuff had resigned from Concord's McGill Street Baptist Church. Thereafter, Pentuff alleged, Coffin's libels had prevented him from obtaining new work. Pentuff claimed that he "had always been able to secure employment." After the editorials appeared, however, "I have tried to get positions and have not been able." No

Baptist congregation in eastern North Carolina, where the *Raleigh Times* circulated, would hire him. A Piedmont congregation considered employing him until "what they had seen in the newspapers" changed their mind. "It grew out of that editorial," Pentuff told the jury. "I have gone hungry when I needed food as a direct result of these publications." Too much worry and too little food had hurt his health and caused him to lose twenty-five pounds over nine months.[70]

At the retrial, however, none of these advantages—not the home court, not the Supreme Court seal of approval, not the inclusion of the March editorial, and not the new evidence of damage—was enough. Pentuff lost. The jury, mostly farmers, was out for less than two hours—including a forty-minute supper break—before delivering a "complete victory" to O. J. Coffin and the *Raleigh Times*. Pentuff had sought sixty thousand dollars. The jury awarded him nothing.[71]

The jury did not explain its verdict, of course. Juries never officially do. Guided by newspaper commentary of the time, however, we can speculate about why the jury may have ruled as it did. First, the jury's verdict for the *Raleigh Times* may have been a simple expression of support for free speech. Ever since the trial of John Peter Zenger in 1735, American juries have often rejected the attempts of public figures to use the law to stifle criticism. Thin-skinned, pretentious plaintiffs have fared especially poorly. At trial, Pentuff may have cut just such a figure.[72] Free speech was the preferred explanation of cultural conservatives, who preferred not to consider the verdict's other implications. Newspapers published in the anti-evolution hotbed of Mecklenburg County ascribed the *Pentuff* verdict to free speech. The *Charlotte News* said nothing about the case's broader political context, reporting only that the jury had upheld the "right of *The Raleigh Times* . . . to call Dr. James R. Pentuff . . . an 'immigrant ignoramus.'" Similarly, the *Charlotte Observer* downplayed the evolution angle and highlighted the verdict's apparent insistence that "a newspaper has a right to express itself freely."[73]

Jurors also may have been motivated by an aversion to Justice Clarkson's belief that members of the clergy deserved special legal advantages. Clarkson had ruled that some things could be actionable if said of "clergymen" that would not be actionable if said of others. Jurors may have bristled at this attempt to establish a two-tiered system of justice in North Carolina. Some liberal pundits were convinced that the jury's verdict was at least partly a protest against Clarkson's excessive proclericalism. Although the *Raleigh Times* found the case's free-speech angle to be important, it found the jury's courageous refusal, "in the face of a Supreme Court opinion," to grant the plaintiff a preferred position "by reason of his calling" to be even more important. "[N]ot even a Supreme Court opinion," the newspaper reporter marveled, could make jurors accept "the class distinction" favoring clergymen that Clarkson's opinion had attempted to write into North Carolina law.[74]

Finally, the jury verdict might be understood as a clear defeat for anti-evolutionism. Note the new trial judge's charge to the jury, when, at trial's end, he reiterated Pentuff's twin allegations: that the editorials were "slanderous" and that they were "false." Because the North Carolina Supreme Court had already confirmed that the editorials were "slanderous," the trial judge explained, the only remaining issue was whether they were "false." The trial judge, therefore, instructed jurors to consider three questions: Were the charges contained in the first editorial true? Were the charges contained in the second editorial true? If the jury answered "no" to either or both of these questions, it would consider a third one: "What damage, if any, is the plaintiff entitled to recover?"[75]

Quickly and unanimously, the twelve-man jury found the two editorials to be "true." Was it "true" that Professor Pentuff spoke of evolution as if he had "evidently never met" it? The jury thought so. Was it "true" that Pentuff, one of the state's top anti-evolution authorities, was an "ignoramus"? Yes, it was. Was it "true" that no public North Carolinian within memory was "more ignorant . . . than Pentuff"? Yes. If any of the jurors had shared Pentuff's views on evolution, the jury surely would have had trouble answering these questions so quickly in the affirmative.

Anti–Poole Bill commentators were quick to embrace this final analysis. They giddily viewed *Pentuff* as a "decisive licking" for anti-evolutionists in North Carolina. For the first time, one widely reprinted analysis noted, evolution had come directly before the "so[v]ran pee-pul"—a twelve-person jury—rather than an elite group, such as the General Assembly. And these twelve citizens, "with no evolutionists to 'gog and magog'" them, "let the verdict speak the truth. . . . [They] have said that they do not care to have the subject of biology made a political issue in North Carolina."[76]

The jury's striking willingness to defy Justice Clarkson's Supreme Court ruling recalls the story of Marville Scroggins, related in chapter 1. When Scroggins sought a divorce, Justice Thomas Ruffin, an elite defender of traditional values, used the North Carolina high bench as a pulpit from which to preach the sanctity of marriage. A century later, Justice Clarkson, another elite defender of traditional values, similarly used *Pentuff* to preach respect for members of the clergy. Neither ruling appears to have gained much traction with North Carolina's ordinary citizens. Marville Scroggins defiantly moved out of state and remarried, even though Justice Ruffin had refused to allow his divorce. A century later, Cabarrus County jurors likewise thumbed their noses at Justice Clarkson. Historians should think twice before treating elite (and easy-to-research) opinion makers such as Ruffin and Clarkson as spokespeople for their respective ages.

Pentuff v. Park should prompt rethinking of many *Scopes*-based assumptions. The evolution debate in *Pentuff* did not pit North against South, city against country, or, in any simple way, religion against science. Pentuff's litigation involved civil law, not criminal law. And the trial verdict resulted in a loss, not a victory, for anti-evolution forces. Historical discussion of Darwinism in the 1920s will probably always begin with *Scopes*, but it should not end there.

The *Pentuff* verdict brought a symbolic end to the 1920s evolution conflict in North Carolina. According to the local press, Pentuff's defeat represented "the last and the [most] grandiose effort to agitate among the untutored" of the state on behalf of anti-evolution.[77]

The *Pentuff* imbroglio did not damage O. J. Coffin's journalistic career. In the year of the first trial, he joined the prestigious faculty of the University of North Carolina as a journalism professor. Subsequently, when the university created a separate journalism school, Coffin was its inaugural dean.[78]

William Poteat retired from Wake Forest University in 1927. He remained engaged in public affairs and continued to mix science with religion, as when he advocated eugenics, a popular "reform" concept during the interwar period.[79]

Justice Heriot Clarkson served on the North Carolina Supreme Court until the early 1940s. As chapter 6 will show, his legal decisions continued to cite both law books and the "Good Book."

James Pentuff did not prosper. The libel suit that he initiated to burnish his reputation wound up soiling it. "If Mr. Pentuff had said nothing about [the alleged libel]," the *Raleigh Times* accurately observed in 1926, "only that part of [this newspaper's readership] who turn to the editorial page would ever have known that we had termed him an 'immigrant ignoramus' and they would have soon forgot it." Instead, Pentuff's shortcomings were broadcast statewide. Following his courtroom loss, a still-unemployed Pentuff moved, fittingly, to Mecklenburg County, North Carolina's anti-evolution hub. He died in 1942, too early to witness the anti-evolutionist revival that continues to this day, a revival in which we hear more than a faint echo of Pentuff-esque "creation science."[80]

Chapter 5

"Escape of the Match-Strikers"
The Samarcand Arson Case of 1931

In his KKK-approved sermon to Charlotte's Calvary Methodist Church in 1922, Reverend J. A. Sharp foreshadowed the previous chapter by urging that there be more God and less atheism in the public schools. He also foreshadowed the present chapter by lamenting modernity's effect on young women. In the Jazz Age, Reverend Sharp lamented, young women "park their corsets on the outside of the pavilion and throw decency to the wind, exclaiming: 'Come on, boys, the sky is the limit.'"[1]

Reverend Sharp's concerns reflected fundamental transformations in what it meant to be a young woman, including an unruly young woman, in the South. Wage labor in textiles and other industries, commercialized leisure, the enhanced power of the state, the perceived fraying of rural communities, new sexual mores, and other features of cultural modernity did not *create* the unruly southern white woman (for she had long existed) but did affect debates about her proper treatment. One result was the creation of state-run "training schools," whose purpose was to reform wayward young white women. North Carolina opened such an institution, the Samarcand Manor Industrial Training School, in 1918. Thirteen years later, a suspected case of arson at this all-white facility transfixed the region and reignited debates about the state's treatment of disorderly women.

On the afternoon of 12 March 1931, in rural Moore County, administrators at the Samarcand Manor "training school" for delinquent white

---

Brian Luskey, Christian Deichert, Eugene Jung, Rebecca MacLean, Dunn Mileham, Josh Norris, Ryan Patterson, Graham Powell, John Salter, Daniel Tedrick, Jamison G. White, and David Wick contributed to this chapter.

girls heard screams and saw smoke rising from Bicket Hall. By the time fire trucks barreled past the "NO TRESPASSING" signs at the facility's gate, it was too late. Bicket was destroyed. Among the anxious onlookers was a young resident of nearby Chamberlain Hall, Margaret Pridgen. Pridgen, a week shy of fifteen, typified Samarcand's inmate population. Her father had committed her to the institution not for any criminal or violent behavior but for "being mean & running around" with men. Nearly two years after her arrival, Pridgen remained in Samarcand, subject to a staff notorious for administering harsh punishments for even trivial offenses.[2]

The fire that destroyed Bicket Hall surprised administrators but not residents familiar with the recent gossip that some inmates were willing to burn Samarcand down in order to escape its torments. Margaret Pridgen had heard this gossip. That evening, when some girls were in bed and others were undressing in nearby Chamberlain Hall, Pridgen entered a closet, set a match to some paper, and burned the building down.[3]

The Samarcand blaze of 1931 illuminates a little-seen corner of Depression-era southern history: the interaction between the legal system and young, white, working-class women. It also casts light on a contentious issue: how the American legal system has treated disorderly women. Some scholars maintain that the legal system applied a harsh double standard that punished women for behavior tolerated in men. Others conclude the reverse: that the legal system, in the tradition of patronizing chivalry, historically treated women with unique lenience and gentleness.[4]

In the Samarcand case, this chapter suggests, North Carolina employed both a harsh double standard *and* legal chivalry to enforce prevailing standards of white, female propriety. The state enforced a code of acceptable behavior that was, in many ways, especially rigid for young white women. But when excessive rigor provoked Samarcand's inmates to acts of violence and destruction, the state, proclaiming chivalrous intent, treated the young white female lawbreakers with special leniency.

The first part of this chapter shows how North Carolina, through Samarcand Manor, sought to force conventional behavioral norms on southern white women. Promiscuous, cigarette-smoking, young white females were just as troubling to moralists in the textile-producing South as they were to moralists in the Jazz Age North. As in the previous chapter, where the subject was evolution, traditionalists, troubled by modern trends, looked to the government for redress. The Samarcand Manor Industrial Training School was one innovative legal response.

The second part of the chapter argues that the legal system, in addition to affecting the behavior of transgressive women, was affected by that behavior. The Samarcand arson case horrified North Carolinians. At a time of penal reform nationally, the press and the public were quick to hold reformatories accountable for inmates' misdeeds. This was especially so with Samarcand, where the unruly inmates were white women, a group assumed to be naturally disinclined to disorderly behavior. The arson case convinced people that reform was necessary, for only a grave institutional failure could have produced such a troubling breakdown of white femininity. Thus, the Samarcand women's destructiveness, having been provoked by their harsh treatment at the hands of the legal system, in turn provoked reform of that system.

The Samarcand Manor Industrial Training School was a product of the "rehabilitative ideal" prevalent in the first two decades of the twentieth century. When applied to juvenile justice, the "rehabilitative ideal" sought not so much to punish delinquent children as to reshape them into respectable future adults. A keystone of juvenile rehabilitation was the "training school," an institution dedicated to the vocational, academic, physical, and moral education of wayward youth.[5]

Like many other southern states, North Carolina was comparatively late in establishing its juvenile institutional program. It did not open its first training school for girls, Samarcand Manor, until 1918. Built in rural Eagle Springs, amid the pine forests and sandhills of south-central North Carolina, Samarcand eventually sprouted many buildings, including a small hospital, a chapel, and seven multilevel residence halls, each of which housed about forty inmates. The typical Samarcand resident was in her teens and came from a poor, often farming or mill-working family.[6]

Samarcand's mission statement, written by R. Eugene Brown, the assistant commissioner of the state's Department of Welfare, embodied the reformist sentiment of the Progressive Era: "The fundamental idea of Samarcand Manor is that every girl upon entering leaves her past behind her and begins life anew. The underlying principles of her training are the preparation of the girl for a useful life."[7]

North Carolina's system of training schools illustrates just how salient the distinctions of race and sex were in the first third of the twentieth century. The state maintained separate and unequal training schools for white boys, white girls, black boys, and black girls, respectively. Stonewall Jackson Training School (established 1907) and the Eastern Carolina Industrial Training School (1923) served white males; Samarcand (1918) served white females; the Morrison Training School for Negro Boys (1921) and the Efland Home (privately founded in 1921 and given some state support starting in 1927) received at least some state money and served African American youth. Each quadrant had its own ideology.

North Carolina's training schools treated errant white boys quite differently than errant white girls. For instance, white teenage boys were sent to Stonewall Jackson only by state officials (usually judges) and only when found guilty of specific criminal infractions. Jackson boys were committed for the following sorts of offenses: larceny (the most common offense), trespassing, housebreaking, storebreaking, breaking into freight cars, violating Prohibition laws, and manslaughter.[8] White teenage girls, on the other hand, could be sent to Samarcand (if approved by the facility's board of directors) by family members as well as by courts and could be sent upon the mere suspicion that they were in danger of straying down unladylike paths. To be sure, some Samarcand inmates had been convicted of such misdemeanors as vagrancy, public drunkenness, and prostitution. Other inmates, however, had not been convicted of any offense. "[Maybe] the girl herself hasn't done anything [wrong]," one approving reporter noted of Samarcand's admissions policies in 1931. "Perhaps her home simply isn't and can't be made a fit place for her to grow up in." In 1929, a Wake County juvenile court ordered Mary Jones to Samarcand not for violating any law but rather for living "in such environments that she was likely to develop into an immoral" woman. An aunt committed one of the young arson suspects because she would not stay home.[9]

The typical Samarcand inmate was committed for promiscuity, for "being in danger of prostitution," for "running around," for drinking, for disobeying her parents, or for refusing to attend school. As this list suggests, girls often were incarcerated for conduct that would have been deemed unremarkable, and no basis for commitment, in boys.[10]

Not surprisingly, the "training" offered by the two institutions also differed. Jackson boys supplemented their book learning with instruction in plumbing, carpentry, masonry, electrical work, metal work, dairying, poultry husbandry, printing, shoe-making, woodworking, and auto mechanics. Samarcand girls supplemented their academic and religious studies with instruction in arts and crafts, weaving, cooking, sewing, housekeeping, gardening, and fruit and vegetable canning.[11]

Samarcand inmates had fewer rights and more restrictions than their male counterparts at Jackson. Their curfew was earlier, for instance. Unlike Jackson boys over fifteen years of age, they were not permitted to smoke cigarettes. Even the disciplinary humiliations meted out at the two facilities reinforced prevailing gender roles. Jackson boys who misbehaved were sometimes "made to wear dresses." If a Samarcand girl was caught attempting to run away, one inmate reported, "they cut your hair."[12]

Subtle differences also distinguished the ways in which the two institutions released their charges. Both Jackson and Samarcand monitored the progress of inmates and discharged only those deemed fit. But because Jackson boys were committed for specific crimes, their sentences, though extremely flexible in practice, nonetheless technically resembled traditional penal sentences. The file of one Jackson boy, for instance, reports his being "sentenced to serve sixty days for larceny."[13]

In contrast, the law establishing Samarcand specified that "[n]o commitment shall be for any definite term." Samarcand girls served until the institution's trustees discharged them or until they turned twenty-one. By the time of the arson case, Samarcand inmates had grown deeply resentful of their indefinite sentences. As one girl complained in a letter to the girls' defense lawyer, residents "could not understand why some girls could come and stay only a few months while others who had already spent . . . [more than] two years were not allowed to leave."[14]

In the world of North Carolina training schools, distinctions of race were just as pronounced as distinctions of sex. Samarcand, unlike many comparable institutions for young women in the North, was for whites only. For years, North Carolina offered nothing comparable for blacks. Lacking the in-between "training-school" option that Samarcand offered whites, young African American women were either sent to prison or were entirely outside of the correctional system. This was both blatantly discriminatory and insulting. The state's racist policy implied that straying white girls could be nudged back onto the path of respectability but that straying black girls were a lost cause, not worth the effort to try to "train" back to virtue.[15]

In the early-1920s, Charlotte Hawkins Brown, an African American philanthropist from North Carolina, demanded that the state redress this inequity. When the state dragged its feet, Brown's group, the Federation of Colored Women's Clubs, pooled $30,000 in private money to establish a modest "training school" in Efland, North Carolina. North Carolina finally agreed to provide the Efland Home with some public funding by the end of the 1920s, but only a pittance. Annual appropriations at decade's end were about $150,000 for Jackson, $100,000 for Samarcand, and $2,000 for Efland.[16]

Although Efland served young women, many of its policies more closely resembled Jackson's than Samarcand's. Like Jackson boys, for instance, Efland girls were admitted only by judicial order and only after committing crimes. The many discrepancies between Efland and Samarcand suggest that the powerful "southern cult of ladyhood" was closed to blacks, notwithstanding the best efforts of African American "uplifters" such as Charlotte Hawkins Brown.[17]

In its early years, Samarcand achieved a reputation as, in the words of one journalist, "heaven on earth" for its growing population of fallen white angels. Newspapers portrayed Samarcand as a "moral life-saving station," a veritable "model for institutions of its character."[18] In the late 1920s, however, conditions at Samarcand deteriorated. Many attributed Samarcand's problems to the failed leadership of Superintendent Agnes McNaughton. As superintendent, McNaughton enjoyed (in the words of the *North Carolina Code*) "the same power [over her] inmates as keepers of jails and other penal institutions possess as to persons committed to their custody." The immigrant Scot exercised this power freely, provoking the enmity of employees and inmates alike. Staff members constantly feared losing their positions. One instructor later recalled that "no one ever knew when they got up in the morning whether they would be fired before nightfall." From January 1929 through March 1931, there were ninety-eight personnel changes at Samarcand, an annual turnover rate of 114 percent.[19]

By the early 1930s, complaints about McNaughton's leadership abounded. Samarcand's physician compared the facility to "a ship without a rudder" and advised that the "school will do better under a new head and new management." The superintendent of a nearby public school system remarked that, thanks to McNaughton's mismanagement, "these girls have not had the care and guidance that should be guaranteed to every girl."[20]

For Samarcand inmates, however, a more pressing concern than the lack of "care and guidance" was the dreadful catalog of punishments that they had to endure whenever they broke one of the institution's many rules. According to the defendants in the 1931 arson case, inmates guilty of even first-time, insignificant offenses were subject to being held facedown while McNaughton ordered staff members—or other inmates—to beat them with switches, sticks, or leather straps. Accused arsonist Margaret Pridgen reported being flogged in this manner once as punishment for bringing dessert to a girl in solitary confinement. Some beatings were so severe that staffers would "put water in [the beaten girls'] faces to keep them from fainting." Other beatings sent inmates to Samarcand's small "hospital," where McNaughton occasionally irritated nurses by interfering with treatment. Solitary confinement in small, bug-infested rooms for weeks or months with scratchy blankets and no sheets was another common punishment (never mind that the North Carolina state penitentiary, home to hardened felons, had abolished both flogging and the "dark cell" in 1923). Sixteen-year-old Mary Lee Bronson succinctly summarized conditions at Samarcand as of 1931: "They treated you like a dog." It is little wonder that many inmates contemplated arson.[21]

On 12 March 1931, fire, in the words of the press's breathless reports, "totally destroyed" two Samarcand residence halls. The *New York Times* estimated the damages at $100,000; the *News and Observer* of Raleigh guessed twice that amount. Both estimates exceeded Samarcand's total annual appropriations at the time: about $90,000. Making matters worse, insurance on the two buildings totaled less than $30,000.[22]

After the fires were extinguished and the eighty or so Bicket and Chamberlain girls resettled among the institution's remaining (and already overcrowded) buildings, the administration, suspecting an inside case of arson, ordered staff members to investigate. They moved quickly. Within a day, police had arrested sixteen inmates for arson in the first degree. The punishment facing "any person" convicted of this crime was death.[23]

Not one of the "Samarcand 16" had been violent before arriving in Eagle Springs. Like most inmates, they had been sent to the institution for running away, running around, refusing to obey parents, refusing to attend school, or committing any of the sexual offenses that ranged from "immoral conduct" to "promiscuity" to "prostitution." One of the suspects, Margaret Abernethy, had never been in trouble before moving to Samarcand. She was sent to the institution because of "mistreatment by father"—incest—that began when she was but ten years of age.[24]

What provoked these sixteen young women, none of whom had previously been destructive, to arson? Paradoxically, it was Samarcand itself. The press reported that the inmates set the blaze to protest foul conditions, including the cracker-and-water diets that they routinely suffered for rules infractions. Margaret Pridgen later explained that Samarcand made her "just feel mean." She and the others hoped that their desperate act would force administrators to "send them home."[25] The fire did free the sixteen young defendants from Samarcand, but it did not "send them home." Instead, it landed them in jails around the state. Despite Pridgen's attempt to take full responsibility, the state filed preliminary charges of first-degree arson against all sixteen girls, each allegedly having "admitted some part in firing the buildings." So in jail they remained, awaiting a "trial for [their] lives" that was scheduled for May.[26]

More disorder followed. On 15 April 1931, after about a month in custody, six of the "Samarcand 16" rioted at the Robeson County Jail in Lumberton. Using matches apparently collected (along with cigarettes) from sympathetic visitors, the girls started what was called "the worst insurrection in the history of this section" of the jail by setting their bunks on fire. The jailer to whose "fatherly guidance" (as the press phrased it) the young women had been entrusted saw the smoke and feared that it would choke the young women. He removed the group from danger by unlocking their cell and turning them out into an adjoining common-area "run around." According to press reports, the Samarcand group responded by dashing to the windows, "tearing out panes of glass and sash," and attacking a jailer with the shards, "cutting one finger almost off and filling his face with glass." When Robeson County sheriff P. S. Kornegay and the Lumberton fire department arrived, they met the same treatment. Glass flew and the girls' profanity "rent the air." Sheriff Kornegay finally restored order with physical force. After moving the girls to a cell from which every piece of furniture had been removed, officials arranged their transfer to the Moore County Jail, near Samarcand.[27]

Two weeks later, Moore County Jail officials learned "just how much of a rampage five little girls can kick up when they really go 'on the prod.'" Though held in a supposedly "fire-proof cell," the five riotous transfers from Lumberton (the sixth being hospitalized with appendicitis at the time) again set fire to their bunks. The flames were extinguished quickly, but jailers again released the girls from their smoke-filled cell into a corridor. "All seemed quiet" again, but not for long.[28]

Within minutes, the Samarcand rioters set another fire, this one reportedly of "some proportions." As the flames spread, the young rebels kicked out "all window panes they could reach," both in the corridor and in their unlocked, smoky cell. They also swiped pocketknives from a hallway container of prisoners' personal belongings. When firefighters arrived, the young women met them with "vulgarities, curses and imprecations." "[M]ostly pretty, [faces] distorted with rage, ... hair awry and eyes gleaming," they seemed angered to the point of explosion. Some reports even had them romping through the halls naked. Finally, Sheriff C. J. McDonald ordered a fire hose turned on the rioters. Clint McCaskill, a twenty-five-year-old volunteer firefighter, hauled his hose into position. Just then, when the excitement "was at fever heat," the crowd outside was "horror-struck to hear" that the girls had cornered young Clint "and were slashing him to ribbons with their knives." This was an exaggeration; they only stabbed him in the arm. A dazed McCaskill recalled this as "his most harrowing experience" and admitted that "he thought his time had come."[29]

The Samarcand arsonists had been victims of a harsh double standard in the reasons for their incarceration in the training school and the treatment they received while incarcerated. Now, as criminal defendants, these young women would benefit from "legal chivalry." The sheriff of Moore County sounded the prevalent tone in response to the riot that wracked his jail. "[I]f they were men," Sheriff McDonald said, "we would know how to deal with them." They being women, however, "we cannot be rough with them."[30]

The "Samarcand 16" were aware of such sentiments and exploited them. From jail, a week after the Moore County riot and eleven days before the trial date, Pearl Stiles, one of the accused, wrote to Governor O. Max Gardner. Seeking clemency, she appealed to the governor's sense of chivalry: "Dearest Governor Gardner, will you please help us ... girls in this case of trouble? ... Mr. Gardner the way we were treated is terrible. We were locked, beat, and fed on bread and water most of the time. ... Please pardon us.... If you only help us out of this trouble we will be happy." Trashing state facilities was not proper behavior for a southern white girl, but appealing humbly to the protective reflexes of powerful men was. Stiles closed with a distinctly feminine flourish: "Well all the girls said to give you their love for them. Will close with good heart. . . . answer at once." Governor Gardner neither answered at once nor granted clemency, but the dynamic of chivalry would persist.[31]

The task of defending the accused fell officially to George McNeill, a public defender. The "brunt of the defense" work, however, was borne by Nell Battle Lewis, a young attorney and gifted columnist for Raleigh's *News and Observer* whom McNeill enlisted to help with this unusual case. As a female lawyer and a southern feminist in 1931, Lewis was an unusual case herself. Only about 2 percent of the nation's lawyers at that time were women.[32]

Although Lewis became rather conservative following World War II, she was, at the time of the Samarcand trial, an outspoken social reformer. Her newspaper columns advocated penal reform and railed against the unfairness of the double standard that treated men and women differently. The Samarcand case provided an ideal vehicle for her advocacy of penal reform because the training schools' failings were obvious and dramatic.

When it came to the double standard, however, the case presented complications. Lewis favored equal legal treatment of men and women. It would have violated her principles to ask the court for leniency simply because her clients were female. On the other hand, Lewis was professionally obliged to provide the best legal defense possible; a "chivalric" defense could be her most effective, especially since there was so much evidence proving the participation of the defendants in the burnings. Lewis settled on a defense strategy that emphasized the traumas suffered by the girls before and, especially, after admission to Samarcand, thus evoking the sympathies of a paternalistic court without explicitly requesting favoritism for females.[33]

On 19 May 1931, the Samarcand defendants—now numbering fourteen, the state having declined to prosecute the remaining two—filed into a packed Moore County superior court to be tried for first-degree arson before Judge Michael Schenck. "Looking much the same as any group of teen age girls, attractively dressed in silk and cotton dresses," the defendants, who, according to press reports, "appeared awed" by the solemn atmosphere and by the realization that their lives were on the line because of the first-degree arson charges, gave "no indication of the spirit" shown during their recent jailhouse riots.[34]

Solicitor F. D. Phillips, representing the state of North Carolina, concentrated on proving that the young women had indeed committed the acts for which they were charged. He called to the witness stand, for instance, Estelle Stott, secretary to Samarcand superintendent Agnes McNaughton. Stott testified that school officials had questioned each of the defendants and that they all "had admitted taking part in the burning of the buildings."[35]

Unsurprisingly, defense attorney Nell Battle Lewis took a different approach. She sought to shift attention from Samarcand's cinders to its sins, recasting her clients as victims, not perpetrators. Under her cross-examination, Samarcand officials admitted that whippings and beatings were regular occurrences at the institution. Lewis then called eight of the defendants to the stand for moving testimony about abuses they had suffered. For instance, Margaret Abernethy testified that, after experiencing childhood abuse at the hands of a father now jailed for incest, she arrived at Samarcand only to have the nightmare continue. Her Samarcand experiences included repeated whippings for offenses like "being rude to a teacher," as well as confinement for three months in a locked room in Chamberlain Hall in which the infestation of bedbugs made sleep "next to impossible." Abernethy testified that she had helped to set the fire out of a desire to "get away from Samarcand."[36]

To establish the traumatized states of the defendants, Lewis called to the stand Dr. Harry W. Crane, an "expert and specialist in P[s]ychology, Hygiene, and the treatment of mental diseases." Dr. Crane, a professor at the University of North Carolina and director of the state's Bureau of Mental Health and Hygiene, testified to the psychological troubles he had noted while evaluating several of the defendants. He testified that the "mental ages" of some of the Samarcand girls were substantially below their actual ages. Lewis used this testimony not only to suggest that her clients were, as Dr. Crane concluded, incapable of understanding the nature of their actions but also to portray the girls as, in her phrase, unfortunate "victims of state neglect."[37]

At this point, Solicitor Phillips, uneasy about the prospect of seeking capital punishment for a group of young women, proposed a plea bargain. He offered to drop the first-degree arson charges, which carried the death penalty, in exchange for guilty pleas to the lesser charge of "attempting to commit arson," which carried the more palatable maximum sentence of ten years' imprisonment. Nell Battle Lewis and her clients accepted.[38]

Legal chivalry was evident in the sentencing proceeding that followed. Solicitor Phillips argued that the defendants, who had violated state law, destroyed state property, and endangered many lives, had to be punished. But he made it clear to Judge Schenck that he had "no desire to see them dealt with harshly."[39]

Nell Battle Lewis appealed for leniency. In the emotional high point of the trial, she invited sympathy for the defendants and reminded listeners of the unpardonable crimes committed against them by state and society. "Two indictments are brought here today," she said. "One, the formal, legal indictment brought by the solicitor—the other less tangible but no less real against society for the presence of these children in a criminal court room. These children, like all others, are the products of their environment, heredity, and the pressure that society has brought to bear on them." Lewis excoriated the state for claiming children as wards and then abusing them so. "[H]alf-grown girls in a civilized community," she insisted, "should not be laid on a whipping carpet." As Lewis spoke, eyes misted and handkerchiefs bloomed around the courtroom. Even several of the defendants, heretofore stoically unmoved by the proceedings, broke down and wept.[40]

The following day, Judge Schenck reconvened his court. In the "slow, firm voice" of a stern but compassionate paternalist, he summoned the convicts for sentencing. "Now young women," he said, "I want to talk to you." All was silent. "[Y]ou could have been tried for your lives," he paused, "and sent to the electric chair. The state did not want to send you to the electric chair. You could be sent to the penitentiary for ten years"—another pause—"I do not want to do that." Instead, Judge Schenck, explaining that as an officer of the law he "had to send them to prison," imposed a range of sentences, the harshest and most common of which was eighteen months to five years in the state penitentiary. He hinted strongly that, if the young women behaved themselves, they would serve their minimum sentences and little more. (Fifteen-year-old Margaret Pridgen had her one-to-three-year sentence suspended.)[41]

The *Charlotte Observer* called this outcome the "escape of the matchstrikers." The plea bargain, the editorial noted approvingly, "rescued the State from what might have proved an embarrassing prospect": putting a large number of "girls to death in the electric chair." The *Observer* also approved of the convicts' ladylike responses to their sentences: they wept. (The editors were silent about the defendant who, as some of her colleagues cried on the way to the prison bus, was busy lighting up a cigarette.)[42]

One final instance of legal chivalry: North Carolina chose not to prosecute any of the Samarcand defendants for their highly illegal actions during the two jailhouse riots.

The founders of Samarcand Manor hoped that the facility would help inmates to "leave their pasts behind" and prepare for "useful" lives. Instead, the institution turned a group of troubled but nonviolent young women into riotous arsonists. This institutional failing was sufficiently troubling to North Carolinians of 1931 to generate calls for reform.[43]

Press reports of the Samarcand case immediately stimulated talk of change. The prevailing sentiment was that the Samarcand fires were but "smoke signals" that called attention to the institution's shortcomings. "It's a case of [the girls] being more sinned against than sinning," one report noted. "This is the most serious indictment of North Carolina's correctional system that has ever been made," the *Rocky Mount Telegram* reported. The *Greensboro News* even suggested that the case be retried with the State of North Carolina as defendant. "Enough has been brought out," the newspaper editorialized, "to demand a searching inquiry and corrective steps."[44]

What explains this impulse to sympathize with the arsonists and to damn the state institution that they torched? The first explanation involves some history, in particular, a wave of penal reform that swept the county in the early 1930s. The rehabilitative spirit that gave rise to Samarcand Manor during the Progressive Era had dissipated rapidly following World War I. By the middle of the jazz-and-gangster 1920s, as crime rates rose and moral strictures loosened, sympathy for penal reform evaporated. "For the past ten or fifteen years," wrote one exasperated Jazz Age observer, "we [Americans] have been engaged in alleviating the lot of inmates of our prisons, making life more and more comfortable for them." As a consequence, "the country is in danger of being overwhelmed by a rising tide of crime." Public officials agreed. One New York judge observed in 1925 that the "principal cause [of crime] was the pampering of prisoners by sentimental reformers." Also in 1925, Charles Evans Hughes lamented "the terrible advances crime makes, because our people do not seem intelligent enough to ... punish the guilty."[45]

Samarcand burned in the 1930s, however, not the mid-1920s, and this made a huge difference. As the Depression descended, the nation reevaluated its penal system with reawakened concern for the downtrodden caught therein. By 1931, there was a consensus that the stern backlash of the 1920s had gone too far. "Long sentences are killing hope and breeding recklessness and despair," reported the National Committee on Prisons in 1931. The "get-tough" measures of the 1920s had backfired, the committee concluded, for the "efforts of law enforcement agencies to reduce crime on the outside are being nullified to a great extent by conditions in the prison." Another reformer noted that the inmate was expected to "rebuild his character and . . . become a worthy member of society." Given the horrid conditions and "official stupidity" of American corrections, however, "what chance has he?"[46]

National support for penal reform grew. Public officials responded. In one revealing case from 1931 (all but unimaginable during most other eras of U.S. history), New York City's commissioner of corrections offered cash prizes to the inmates who submitted the best criticisms of the prison system in which they were held. The grand prize winner walked away, so to speak, with fifty dollars for suggesting, among other things, that New York lock-ups serve less boiled and more roasted food.[47]

In the same spirit, former U.S. attorney general George Wickersham headed a blue-ribbon presidential commission that studied more than three thousand federal and state correctional institutions. The commission's 1931 report found corrections in the United States to be "a failure so complete that a new type of penal system must be developed." The report described overcrowding, rundown facilities, and inhumane punishments for trivial offenses. And what was true of prisons in general was equally true of the typical juvenile facility. Boys and girls under eighteen endured "filth and misery impossible to convey. Discipline," the report added, "is often brutal."[48]

Such authoritative findings reduced public tolerance for harsh corrections officials and provided powerful rhetorical ammunition to reformers like Nell Battle Lewis. Lewis took full advantage. Assembling evidentiary ammunition, she saved newspaper clippings regarding the Wickersham Commission and other penal reform movements. In her column three days after the Samarcand fire, she applauded Governor Gardner for naming his own commission to study North Carolina's penal system.[49]

The years surrounding the Samarcand blaze also saw a national epidemic of prison fires and riots, accompanied by general public sympathy for the responsible inmates. The most horrific incident was a riot and fire in 1930 at the state penitentiary in Columbus, Ohio, which resulted in the deaths of 319 inmates. The press dubbed the Ohio fire "the most terrible prison catastrophe the United States has ever seen." Yet, although rioting prisoners had set the flames and cut fire hoses, the public outcry revealingly targeted the officials who oversaw the wretched facility, not the inmates who burned it down.[50]

Reformers nationwide saw the cycle of prison uprisings as an indictment of American corrections. Sanford Bates, superintendent of federal prisons, described the rash of uprisings as "the culminating answer of the criminal population to the campaign of force which society has carried on against it." So widespread was public support for suffering inmates that, the very week of the Samarcand fire, a warden at the Illinois state penitentiary at Joliet attributed an eleven-hundred-inmate riot to "a feeling among the prisoners that the public sympathy was with them."[51]

The Samarcand arsonists may or may not have been aware of previous fires at other correctional facilities and the public compassion they inspired. Well-informed North Carolinians, however, were likely to appraise the Samarcand fire in a sympathetic context. They had read repeatedly of prison failings and the resulting uprisings; they were familiar with the day's "entire cycle" of hard-hitting prison films (including 1931's *Ladies of the Big House*); and they had heard commission after commission plead for reform, as did the National Committee on Prisons in a report released the week of the Samarcand trial: "The call today—and never before has it sounded so clearly and so strongly," the committee wrote, "is for the great forces in the community . . . to [mobilize] . . . so that from the ashes of burning buildings, from the bloodshed and riot of the past year will grow rapidly and surely [a] . . . new and better system."[52]

Thus, at least in part, the Samarcand affair unfolded as it did because it unfolded *when* it did. The early 1930s was a time of widespread penal reform nationally. The Samarcand affair also produced reform because of who was involved and where the incident occurred. These were white women in the American South. The threshold for acceptable misbehavior in North Carolina was higher for white men and black men and women than it was for white women. Because white females were thought to possess the least unruly nature of any of the state's major social groups, violence at a training school for white females was most likely to win attention and provoke institutional reform.

An experimental "control" is conveniently available. During the very week that Samarcand burned, arsonists set fire to three cottages at the Jackson school for white boys. After severe whippings at the hands of Jackson staffers, two teenaged residents confessed that they were the culprits. The legal system actually treated these two suspects with comparative leniency. One pleaded guilty and received a one-year penitentiary sentence. The other pleaded not guilty and was acquitted. (Recall that most of the Samarcand defendants received eighteen months to five years.) But whereas the Samarcand fires sparked institutional reform, the Jackson fires did not. Even though the whipping of young inmates received substantial attention at both well-publicized arson trials, posttrial reforms halted whippings at Samarcand but not at Jackson. Apparently, misbehavior by Jackson boys, unlike misbehavior by Samarcand girls, did not signal an institutional breakdown.[53]

The rebellion of the white girls of Samarcand in the spring of 1931 convinced many North Carolinians that something at the facility had gone terribly wrong and that changes had to be made. "Something made these girls come to the point of revolt and frenzy," the *Chapel Hill Weekly* reported in the weeks following the trial. "It must have been something extraordinary to have raised such a spirit of rebellion in such a type of girls." "All of which," the newspaper concluded, "demands a full and unsparing investigation of the whole Samarcand project."[54]

A "full and unsparing" investigation was forthcoming. In the aftermath of the arson trial, R. Eugene Brown, assistant commissioner of the state's Department of Welfare and author of Samarcand's original mission statement, launched an official study of conditions at the facility. His 1932 report contained detailed recommendations that tacitly admitted Samarcand's guilt as charged by Nell Battle Lewis. Brown's report called for administrative changes to reduce Superintendent McNaughton's power, closer state supervision, improved staff training, construction of new buildings to alleviate overcrowding, and improved medical care for all inmates. The report also discouraged corporal punishment and suggested many alternative correctional techniques. Finally, Brown recommended that Samarcand officials, in the name of accountability and oversight, henceforth file written reports of all disciplinary actions.[55]

Samarcand's board of directors approved all of Brown's recommendations. Haltingly, reform began, but the slow pace of change frustrated Brown. Upon visiting Samarcand in 1934, he wrote that "the institution needs to be thoroughly reorganized with a person of ability and experience at the head." Before the year was out, Agnes McNaughton departed for a "six-month leave." She did not return.[56]

Samarcand changed. By 1939, the *Charlotte Observer*, an open critic of the institution during the trial, reported that "Samarcand stands as testimony to the warm, helpful, kindly heart of a great commonwealth." (Never mind that brutal conditions persisted for the young African American women at Efland. In the mid-1930s, one staffer punished an inmate by choking her "until she foamed at the mouth." In 1939, Efland shut its doors for lack of support, the "warm, helpful, kindly heart of a great commonwealth" notwithstanding.)[57]

Samarcand's ultimate vindication came from Nell Battle Lewis herself. In a newspaper column written in 1945, she recalled that, at the time of the trial, she had wondered why the girls "hadn't burned the whole place to the ground," but she now recognized that a "general cleanup of administration" had taken place. "I'm reliably informed," she remarked, "that Samarcand at present is a very well-run institution."[58]

By the end of World War II, extensive reform had restored Samarcand's image of white, womanly propriety. Gone were the "unattractive buildings," the "matrons with harsh manners," and the window-smashing firebugs of yesteryear. In their place, at least in the public mind, were shiny new facilities, supportive teachers, and happy inmates. Once again, observers portrayed inmates as veritable models of southern white femininity, "dressed in white, flowers in their hair."[59]

Chapter 6

Padlocking Greenwich Village
Urbanization and Public Nuisance Law

The KKK-approved sermon that Reverend J. A. Sharp delivered in 1922 condemned jazz, drinking, and "licentiousness." Historians of this period regularly situate such sentiments within a "rural-versus-urban" framework. "Rural America and urban America had eyed each other warily since the nineteenth century," reads one typical survey of American history. Following the Great War, "suspicion turned to outright hostility.... In the eyes of many country folk, the cities stood for everything that rural areas stood against.... Increasingly, the nation divided along the line drawn between the country and the city."[1]

Like most bits of conventional wisdom, this one contains much truth. But it is a static description of a dynamic age. It fails to capture the extent to which local squabbles over drinking, dancing, and other aspects of Jazz Age culture were provoked by urbanization—the spread of cities into the surrounding hinterland. Just as the Civil War between North and South was sparked in important ways by debates over the future of the West, so too were at least some interwar cultural clashes spurred by debates over the future of fast-spreading urban outskirts.

This chapter explores dancing, sex, and bootleg booze in Greenwich Village. This sounds typical enough for an interwar cultural clash until we learn that the Greenwich Village at issue was not the bohemian New York neighborhood that symbolized modern culture in the 1920s but rather a roadhouse on a recently built highway just west of Charlotte, North Carolina. In this chapter, as in the previous two, it was

---

Alison Kalett, Magdalena Barbosa, Andrew Lanoha, Chad Phillips, Carrie Porath, David Rissing, Elisabeth Summerlin Harper, Robin Turley, and John Zidow contributed to this chapter.

traditionalists who initiated legal processes. They did so with customary creativity, imaginatively invoking a long-dormant "public nuisance" statute against the roadhouse. Thereafter, public nuisance cases of this sort proliferated. Along with such better-known legal devices as zoning ordinances and restrictive covenants, public nuisance litigation facilitated the "sorting out" of New South cities.

Dr. Memory Ford Boyles, the Greenwich Village roadhouse's quirky proprietor, embodied interwar cultural modernism. Although he was born in 1893 in Lincoln County, North Carolina, not too far from the future location of his roadhouse, he moved frequently around the United States. By the time he settled down in Charlotte in his fortieth year, Boyles had already lived in New York, California, Virginia, Pennsylvania, Georgia, several different North Carolina cities, and possibly Minnesota and Wisconsin. Boyles's peripatetic ways exposed him to diverse cultures. They also seem to have diluted tradition's hold on him. When the time came to name his Charlotte-area roadhouse, his urban, modernist sensibilities showed. He dubbed it "Greenwich Village," a name that recalled the spiritual home of American cultural modernism.[2]

Boyles studied medicine and became a doctor but was hardly a distinguished professional. In 1925, federal agents arrested him and his brother Alphonso, a North Carolina dentist, for running what the press called a "dope ring" in the Carolina Piedmont. The ensuing federal trial revealed that, while living in New York, Memory Ford Boyles (also known as M. F.) had informed his brother that "he could supply the 'Boston baked beans'"—that is, the narcotics—"in most any quantity," at a pricey fifty dollars per can. The Boyles brothers and a third conspirator moved enough "beans" to become the "largest importers and distributors of narcotics" in North Carolina. Doctor and dentist pleaded guilty and were sent to federal prison to serve sentences of eighteen months and one year, respectively.[3]

The political connections that Boyles exploited to win parole were, typically for him, atypical. Boyles was one of the more exotic birds in the day's political aviary: a southern white Republican. Being a Republican in the 1920s was a liability in North Carolina, but it opened doors in Calvin Coolidge's Washington. Fortuitously for Boyles, narcotics dealing was a *federal* crime. He was out in seven months.[4]

Boyles's defiance of convention continued after his move to Charlotte in 1933. He explored different parts of the city before settling into an apartment at 115 West Hill Street. Although Boyles and the other residents of his eight-unit complex were white, the surrounding neighborhood was entirely African American. Boyles chose to live among African Americans in one of America's most segregated cities.[5]

Boyles's apparent lack of interest in organized religion also was distinctive. Mid-1930s Charlotte had more than one hundred churches. Boyles apparently joined none of them.[6]

The average age of marriage for men of Boyles's generation was twenty-four. Boyles did not wed until 1936, his forty-third year.[7] The woman he married was nearly as unconventional as he. Mary Springs Harkey was from Mount Holly, a small town in Gaston County, North Carolina. Perhaps yearning for greater opportunities and excitement, Mary moved to Charlotte in 1927, her twentieth year. She found work as a clerk for Southern Bell Telephone and Telegraph. After several years with Southern Bell, she landed a bookkeeping job with the *Charlotte Observer*. With the exception of two years spent with siblings, Mary lived on her own in Charlotte.[8] In 1936, Mary married M. F. Boyles. She was twenty-nine at the time, fourteen years younger than her husband, but still well above the average marrying age for women. In further defiance of traditional family patterns, Mary Harkey Boyles bore no children and continued working outside the home throughout her marriage.[9]

Greenwich Village's proprietor, thus, was relatively rootless, had a checkered past, and was comfortable with African Americans, liberated women, and things unconventional. The staff whom he hired to work at Greenwich Village reflected these characteristics. Many Greenwich Village employees had lived in distant states. Some had had previous run-ins with the law. Some were African American. And some Greenwich Village workers were women (there was trial testimony that "you could buy [illegal] whiskey from the waitresses").[10]

Nobody personified the tradition-defying Greenwich Village spirit more than filling station employee Velma Webb. Like Dr. Boyles, Webb was footloose. She was from Florida; her ex-husband (whom she hoped never to see again) was in New Jersey; her father was in New York; she herself, though just twenty-two, had already seen "38 states and Old Mexico." A licensed pilot, she had been "with an air circus for a long time, stunting . . . and doing parachute jumps." She partied hard. (At one hotel bash, she overdid it and fell out of a third-story window, breaking both legs.) After moving to Mecklenburg County, but before landing the Greenwich Village job (and, presumably, before breaking both legs), she did a tap-dance routine at a club on Concord Road. Like Greenwich Village's proprietor, she had, in her own words, "been around."[11]

For three years prior to his marriage, M. F. Boyles had run an apparently legitimate pharmacy in Charlotte. He closed this downtown pharmacy and opened the outlying roadhouse in the year of his marriage, 1936. It seems unlikely that he would have done this without at least tacit approval from his wife. Mary's involvement seems all the more plausible given that fully half of Mecklenburg County's other known roadhouses at the time were run either by husband-and-wife teams or by women alone.[12]

Boyles began work on his roadhouse in March 1936, when he bought two lots on Wilkinson Boulevard, three miles west of the Charlotte city limit. Seven months, six additional lots, and twenty-six-thousand dollars later, he completed "one of the largest roadhouses in the county." On 18 October 1936, Greenwich Village, at 2912 Wilkinson Boulevard, opened for business.[13]

To daytime visitors, Greenwich Village appeared to be an innocuous "tourist camp," a place where travelers could pull off the highway, refuel, eat, and spend the night. The main building contained a dining room, a kitchen, and Boyles's office. Out front was a filling station, which Boyles leased to the Standard Oil Company. Out back were two parking lots and twelve tourist cottages, each equipped with a bed, a dresser, a table, chairs, running water, and electricity.[14]

Greenwich Village was part of a national tourist camp explosion. Increases in both auto sales and rural highway construction during the 1920s sparked the boom. Nationally, automobile registrations increased from about 9 million in 1920 to more than 23 million in 1929. In Charlotte, car ownership increased from under two thousand to more than twenty thousand between 1917 and 1925. Charlotte soon trailed only Atlanta among major centers of automobile ownership in the South.[15]

With automobiles came highways. In 1921, under Cameron Morrison, the "Good Roads Governor," North Carolina issued a $50 million bond to fund construction of an intercity web of paved highways. By the mid-1920s, North Carolina led the South in the construction of paved roads.[16]

Dowd Road, where Greenwich Village would be built, was a product of the highway program. It was the state's first paved intercity highway and would remain the primary route between Charlotte and Gastonia into the 1960s. By 1926, when it was renamed Wilkinson Boulevard after prominent mill owner William Wilkinson, it was the most traveled road in the state.[17]

The highway programs of the 1920s sparked the tourist camp boom; the Great Depression of the 1930s intensified it. Millions of cash-starved Americans looked to auto travel and tourist camps as inexpensive and convenient alternatives to train travel and downtown hotels. Sensing this demand, many farmers whose land abutted rural highways opened tourist camps. Nonfarmer proprietors, including Dr. Boyles, also sought economic opportunity in tourist camps set in rural or semirural locations. Of the twelve known tourist camps in Mecklenburg County between 1937 and 1942, ten, including Greenwich Village, were located beyond city limits.[18] The combined effect of more autos, more highways, and less money during the 1930s was dramatic. In 1926, there were an estimated two thousand tourist camps nationally. By 1940, there were an estimated thirty-five thousand.[19]

Greenwich Village, however, was not merely a refuge for weary highway travelers. Its main building contained a physician-and-surgeon's office (reflecting Boyles's professional background), a drugstore (which reputedly sold illegal alcohol and contraceptives, along with patent medicine and toothpaste), a jukebox, and a dance floor. The illegal liquor sales and the dance floor suggest a nocturnal clientele that was local, pleasure seeking, and willing to defy the law. This was not unusual. FBI chief J. Edgar Hoover, noting the tendency of tourist camps to cultivate prostitution, narcotics, and other mischief, dubbed them "camps of crime."[20]

Charlotteans from their mid-teens to their mid-twenties frequented Greenwich Village. Cars had revolutionized their social lives. Automobiles had moved courtship and socializing away from home and, in many cases, toward roadhouses. As the *Mecklenburg Times* lamented in September 1937, "Our youth which [in the past] found contentment and diversion and wholesome pleasure in the Christian activities of the churches . . . are today finding greater satisfaction and influence in the roadhouses."[21]

On a typical night, these young men and women would either drive themselves or pay ten cents for a Yellow Cab or Blue Bird taxi to drive them out Wilkinson Boulevard to Greenwich Village. Witnesses reported some patrons "going into the cabins, staying 30 to 45 minutes, just a boy and a girl." Other patrons bought and drank illegal alcohol, fought, and generally caused commotion. "I have seen drunk people hollering and screaming," one witness testified, "and drunk men and women urinating out the window." Still another neighbor recalled, "I have heard and seen drunk men and women there nude. They would come from behind the cabins drunk and urinate behind there."[22]

At the Greenwich Village trial, Dr. Boyles would protest that his business neither sold illegal booze nor rented cabins to unmarried couples. However, overwhelming evidence substantiates accusations that Greenwich Village violated alcohol prohibition and anti-prostitution laws.[23]

Dr. Boyles chose a good location for Greenwich Village. The Wilkinson Boulevard lots were far enough away from Charlotte to be affordable, yet close enough to be within taxi range of downtown. And since Wilkinson Boulevard was the main highway linking Charlotte to all points west, the roadhouse could attract long-distance travelers as well as local pleasure seekers. Moreover, law enforcement was less strict outside than inside Charlotte city limits. The rural police, in whose jurisdiction the roadhouse fell, were almost comically lax. In Boyles's line of work, that was a plus.[24]

In other respects, however, Greenwich Village's location posed serious problems. The doctor had built his new, automobile-dependent roadhouse in the middle of a new, automobile-dependent suburban development. Greenwich Village occupied one corner—and about one-eighth of the total acreage—of a six-block residential subdivision called Dowd Manor. Dowd Manor's 18.5 acres were originally farmland. During World War I, the property was used for military training as part of Camp Greene. After the war, the acreage changed hands a couple of times, finally reaching the McNeely Land Company, a Charlotte-based firm that specialized in carving up and selling off land. "Let McNeely Land Company subdivide and sell your city and suburban property at auction," their ads proclaimed. "We know how."[25]

On the Fourth of July, 1925, to the strains of a brass band, the McNeely Land Company began auctioning off Dowd Manor, lot by lot. At least some initial purchasers had to accept three conditions: structures built on the property had to be built "30 feet from front property line"; "no building might be erected on said property, except it be a residence"; and said residences had to "be occupied by white people." Dowd Manor was an American suburb.[26]

American suburbs swelled during the 1920s. In Charlotte, the proliferation of cars and highways combined with the widespread availability of electricity and plumbing to make suburban life more attractive than ever. "The tendency on the part of those who have lived all of their lives right in the heart of things here to get out and enjoy more spatial areas is spreading," noted the *Charlotte News* in 1925. "[T]hose who are wise can easily see coming . . . a tremendous spreading out of . . . this community in all directions."[27] Much of this spreading occurred along Wilkinson Boulevard, west of town. City View Heights, Gilreath Park, Marsh Estates, West View, and West Highland all sprouted along the new highway within a year of Dowd Manor's founding.[28]

Charlotte's suburban pioneers of the 1890s and 1900s had been an elite, white-collar bunch; Wilkinson Boulevard suburbanites of the 1920s and 1930s were not. Charlotte's 1940 city directory confirms that residents of the western suburbs were white, family oriented, and lower middle class. Roughly a third of the adults whose occupations are listed worked in auto-related jobs (truck or bus drivers, mechanics, filling station workers). About a quarter worked as skilled laborers (machinists, plumbers, electricians, carpenters, chemical plant workers). Another quarter or so were clerks. Five percent held managerial positions in grocery stores or factories. Another 5 percent were cooks or waiters. Less than 4 percent were professionals such as insurance agents. Only three women were employed. No one in the area was a farmer or a textile worker.[29] Most residents were recent arrivals. Eighty percent of the families living on or near Wilkinson Boulevard in 1940 had owned their homes for a period of ten years or less.[30]

Thus, the Greenwich Village roadhouse disturbed a new and rapidly evolving suburban area inhabited by lower-middle-class white families whose claims to suburban respectability were tenuous. Conflict was inevitable.

On 15 September 1937, at 5:15 P.M., two Mecklenburg County sheriff's deputies padlocked Greenwich Village and posted a summons ordering Boyles to appear in court the next month. This was not a unique event. The sound of many such padlocks snapping shut echoed across Mecklenburg County that fall. Just twelve days before closing Greenwich Village, the authorities shut down Major's Place, also on Wilkinson

Boulevard. Over the next couple of months, at least six other area roadhouses met a similar fate.[31]

The county-wide—indeed, statewide—crackdown on roadhouses reflected not only the conflict with the new residential suburbs. It also reflected a little-known portion of Prohibition history in the United States. Conventional wisdom holds that, once the Great Depression hit, Americans lost interest in their neighbors' drinking habits and abandoned the "Noble Experiment." This explanation is plausible at the national level but not in North Carolina and some other states, in which public debate over alcohol continued long after 1933. Indeed, national repeal, far from cooling alcohol prohibition debates in these states, may have intensified them, for what had been a distant federal dispute devolved into state and local fights in which neighbors and friends slugged it out.[32]

Federal repeal in 1933 left North Carolina legally dry, as it had been since 1909. In 1935, however, the state's General Assembly, in a victory for "wets," voted to allow each of the state's one hundred counties to choose independently whether or not to allow county-operated liquor stores. Mecklenburg's "local option" vote occurred in June 1937. It stirred the area's "bitterest prohibition fight in years."[33]

Mecklenburg County wets argued that county-operated liquor stores would generate urgently needed public revenue. Local bootleggers, operating "under the guise of dine-and-dance emporiums, . . . filling stations, and so forth," reputedly pulled in $2.5 million a year. Wets viewed legalization as a way to divert this robust revenue stream to public coffers while simultaneously increasing public control over the flow of alcohol.[34]

"Drys" disagreed. Pledging to "re-consecrate Prohibition," Mecklenburg County drys argued that the government should continue "confiscating liquor instead of selling it." Allowing county liquor stores would be penny-wise but pound foolish, they contended, since any increases in local revenue would be more than offset by the local government's responsibility for "[t]he poverty, the drunks, the debauched, the maimed, the orphaned, the insane, the crime, and the other human wreckage" that legal liquor would leave in its wake. Their conclusion was clear: "We do not want whisky back."[35]

The drys prevailed in Mecklenburg County's local option vote in June 1937.[36] According to press reports, triumphant local prohibitionists then sought to use their electoral mandate to challenge Mecklenburg's reputation as "the driest voting, wettest drinking" county in the state. They would "see that [the prohibition] laws are enforced."[37]

Several factors, however, complicated the drys' efforts to enforce prohibition in Mecklenburg County. First, the rural police, whose jurisdiction included Charlotte's periphery, home to many roadhouses, were utterly ineffective and reputedly in league with the liquor dealers. The county formally investigated the department in the spring of 1937 on charges of "direct and indirect connection with illicit liquor selling." During the investigation into "laxity in the enforcement of liquor laws," rural police chief Vic Fesperman, accused of "participation in the local liquor racket," broke down and cried on the witness stand. (Chief Fesperman denied the charges but did admit his son-in-law's reputation as a bootlegger.)[38]

Another factor complicating prohibition enforcement was the failure of old criminal laws to keep pace with new roadhouses. Note the case of Noah Wilson. In the 1880s, before automobiles and paved highways, Wilson kept an old-fashioned "disorderly house" along a mule-and-wagon way. "[S]piritous liquors were sold and drunk" there; fighting and "lewd behavior" occurred. As soon as the state arrested Wilson, however, the nuisance ended.[39]

Roadhouse nuisances of the 1930s were not so easily controlled. In February 1937, the state highway patrol sought to do what the county's rural police force would not. The highway patrol raided Greenwich Village one night and made an arrest. But unlike their nineteenth-century predecessors, who shut down Noah Wilson's place with a single arrest of the live-in proprietor, the highway patrol netted only a small fry: Greenwich Village filling station employee James Lanier. Lanier pleaded guilty and lost his job. Meanwhile, Dr. Boyles slept soundly back home in Charlotte, and the Greenwich Village nuisance continued unabated. New legal remedies were necessary.[40]

The criminal law, wielded by state authorities, had failed to stop the Greenwich Village nuisance. A civil statute, wielded by local residents, would succeed. The civil public nuisance statute that the neighbors used was a Progressive Era measure designed, like so many other statutes of its day, to prevent the "degrading of morals." It defined a public nuisance as the use of any building for "the purpose of lewdness, assignation, prostitution, gambling or illegal sale of whiskey." Upon suspicion that such a nuisance existed, any prosecutor, solicitor, or even private citizen could sue in the name of the state. The statute had sharp teeth. Should the suit succeed (a likely prospect, given that "general reputation" constituted sufficient proof), the establishment could immediately be padlocked. All "fixtures, furniture, musical instruments, or moveable property used in conducting the nuisance" could be removed and sold.[41] For years after its 1919 passage, however, the civil public nuisance statute was a dead letter. Not a single Mecklenburg County civil plaintiff invoked it prior to 1937, the year of the Greenwich Village dispute.[42]

The idea of using the padlocking provision of the old nuisance statute against Mecklenburg County roadhouses may have originated with Wilson Warlick, an avid prohibitionist and a superior court judge. (Warlick would ultimately preside at the Greenwich Village trial.) In July 1937, Warlick declared that "padlocking ought to be employed to close the numerous bootlegging places in the county." The press picked up on Warlick's suggestion and asked Mecklenburg County solicitor John Carpenter (whom we shall meet again) if he planned to do some padlocking. Carpenter explained that, since padlocking was "a civil matter, not criminal," he could not initiate these cases. But padlocking was a good idea, he said, "if we can get folks to complain."[43]

Some women who lived close to Greenwich Village did complain. Sallie Randall and Mason McGinnis spearheaded the community campaign. Both were white and had husbands and children. Both had lived on Wilkinson Boulevard since the 1920s.[44] Both had openly opposed Greenwich Village since its opening in October 1936. Just two weeks after the roadhouse began business, Randall paid an indignant 4:00 A.M. visit. "My children have been woke up continually for a week or more," she fumed. The nuisance persisted. On another occasion, Randall asked an unruly Greenwich Village patron to be quiet. The patron cursed her, and the nuisance persisted. Randall later testified against Chief Fesperman in hearings regarding the rural police force's notorious laxity in prohibition enforcement. Still, the nuisance persisted.[45]

Finally, Randall and McGinnis sought legal help from Charlotte attorney Ralph Kidd. In Kidd's office, the two women executed affidavits against Greenwich Village and its proprietor, Dr. Boyles. The women listed many abuses and accused Boyles of running his roadhouse "in such as way as to constitute a public nuisance and an affront to public morals."[46]

With these affidavits, the swift and powerful padlocking statute shook off its rust and sprang into motion. Attorney Kidd prepared a formal complaint, attached the affidavits, and moved for an injunction to shut down Greenwich Village. He took his papers to solicitor John Carpenter. Carpenter, an avid "dry," endorsed the complaint and whisked it to superior court judge Wilson Warlick. Judge Warlick, also an avid dry, immediately and without the benefit of any hearing issued a temporary restraining order. About "fifteen minutes after Judge Warlick signed the order," a padlock snapped shut on Greenwich Village.[47]

Randall and McGinnis had taken the initiative. In the 1930s tradition of collective action, however, the two women explained their behavior in communal, not individual, terms. McGinnis later testified at trial that the two women believed that their affidavits "were the sentiment of the whole community, not just Mrs. Randall and me."[48] Quite a large community agreed with the two plaintiffs. Dr. Boyles asked Judge Warlick for permission to reopen his roadhouse under bond until a trial could be held. In angry response, "[a]bout 100 Mecklenburg county residents" crammed Warlick's courtroom. When attorney Kidd asked for witnesses to speak against the roadhouse and in defense of the preliminary injunction, "50 or more [volunteers] rose from their seats." In addition, a total of eighty-two people—white, lower-middle-class, family-oriented men and women who had moved to the Wilkinson Boulevard area within the past ten years—signed petitions urging Judge Warlick to "save our neighborhood" by keeping Greenwich Village locked. "Our conviction in the matter is that it [the roadhouse] should not be reopened at all," the petition read, "and we would be glad to see this place, together with all of its kind, entirely outside of our community." The injunction remained in effect until the trial.[49]

On 11 October 1937, an all-male Mecklenburg County jury heard opening arguments in *State of North Carolina, on the relation of John G. Carpenter, Solicitor, versus Dr. M. F. Boyles, Trading and Doing Business as "Greenwich Village."* The community turned out in force. According to newspaper reports, "more than a score of witnesses," almost all from nearby homes, testified against Boyles.[50] The neighborhood witnesses cared little about alcohol prohibition, the issue that the case's legal elites cared about most. Indeed, several plaintiffs' witnesses admitted having purchased alcohol at Greenwich Village. What they did care about was the unseemly conduct at Greenwich Village to which their families were exposed.[51]

Although both male and female witnesses testified to Greenwich Village's bad reputation, the most effective testimony came from women. The men's accounts were relatively dry and factual; the women's accounts had drama and passion. Female witnesses successfully employed the traditional language of motherhood to substantiate their pathbreaking legal attack. Rare was the witness who moralized abstractly, as did Clara Thompson, who, despite having "not observed anything [at Greenwich Village] myself," opposed the roadhouse "because I am a Christian and belong to a church." Much more common and effective were the women who presented themselves as wives and mothers seeking to defend their families. Mason McGinnis's vivid description of an inebriated Greenwich Village patron stumbling over her children's playthings, "so drunk it frightened them," was typical. There was testimony about the roadhouse unruliness that had "continually" awakened sleeping children; the roadhouse's "drunk men and women," sometimes nude, who had engaged in "roughness, yelling, ... [and] profanity"; the half-hour cabin rentals; the fighting; the "dancing at all hours"; and the various stances and locations employed for public urination at Greenwich Village.[52]

Dr. Boyles offered a meager defense. His case consisted of two character witnesses who scarcely knew him; several employees who would lose their jobs if the padlock remained in place; a representative of a vending machine company whose cigarettes would go stale inside the roadhouse machine if the injunction continued; and Boyles himself, a felon who had been convicted on narcotics charges. Boyles's lawyer was probably not an asset in Judge Warlick's courtroom. He was Tom Jimmison, an outspoken supporter of labor unions, a view that placed him on the fringe in the South. Jimmison had also served time for liquor offenses.[53]

After two days of testimony, Judge Warlick submitted to the jury a single question: "Has Greenwich Village been operated in such a way as to ... constitute a public nuisance?" The jury unanimously said yes. The temporary injunction became permanent. Greenwich Village would remain closed, and a public auction would dispose of its fixtures.[54]

Neither side, however, holstered its weapons. Solicitor Carpenter, attorney Kidd, and residents of suburban communities all around Charlotte declared "padlock warfare" against what the press called "highway 'hot spots.'" Meanwhile, Dr. Boyles appealed his trial loss to the North Carolina Supreme Court.[55] His legal appeal would not be frivolous; a great deal of tainted evidence had been admitted at trial. More importantly, the constitutionality of North Carolina's public nuisance statute had never been tested and was an open question. The draconian procedure of padlocking prior to trial, without a hearing, seemed particularly vulnerable to a charge of lack of "due process."[56]

Sitting on the North Carolina Supreme Court, however, was a man who, as one admirer put it, "marches in morality," a man for whom "the desire to eradicate the evils of liquor . . . was always an overwhelming passion": Mecklenburg County's own Heriot Clarkson. We first met Clarkson in chapter 4, when he ruled in favor of creationist preacher J. R. Pentuff. Clarkson fully embodied the cultural traditionalism of his day. Both his conservative public commitments and his conventional private life contrasted tellingly with the modernism of M. F. Boyles.[57]

The son of a Confederate officer, Clarkson was born in South Carolina in 1863. The Civil War destroyed the Clarksons' plantation, and in 1873, the family, like Pinkney and Sarah Ross and many other South Carolinians that year, moved to Charlotte. Unlike the peripatetic Dr. Boyles, however, Heriot Clarkson would never leave.[58]

Clarkson graduated from the Carolina Military Institute, clerked at a law firm, studied law at Chapel Hill (graduating first in his class), and practiced law. For him, the law was more than a profession. It was a means to further his social values, the deepest of which emanated from his religious faith. "For my guidance through life I prefer to get my marching orders from that blessed Book—the Bible—the God of books," wrote Clarkson, a passionate Episcopalian, in 1940. "I am a fundamentalist. I was taught at my mother's knee to revere the teachings of the Bible . . . to guide our footpaths along life's highway from the cradle to the grave."[59]

Like most white southerners of the time (but unlike Dr. Boyles), Clarkson was a Democrat. Memories of Reconstruction, which he referred to as those "eleven long years" following the Civil War when "the Republican Party kept its heel on the neck of the citizens of the South," cemented his party loyalty. Like many southern Democrats, Clarkson enthusiastically supported disfranchisement and Jim Crow. In 1896, he helped organize the state's first "white supremacy club." That same year, he drafted a resolution declaring that "white supremacy, through white men[,] shall rule and control in North Carolina." The state's Democratic convention in 1896 adopted this resolution. Years later, Clarkson recalled that he was "strongly in favor of the elimination of the Negro in politics" and "did all [he] could" to make disfranchisement a reality. (See chapter 7 for much more on disfranchisement.)[60]

It was the prohibition of alcohol, however, that best defined Clarkson's public life. "My strongest ambition as a boy," he later recalled, "was to see the saloons abolished." He worked tirelessly to achieve that goal. In 1903, he organized Charlotte's Anti-Saloon League. The following year, Charlotte, largely as a result of Clarkson's efforts, became the largest city in the country to vote out the saloon. He then focused his formidable energies on a campaign to secure a statewide ban on alcohol. On New Year's Day, 1909, North Carolina's governor signed a statewide prohibition law. He sent Clarkson the pen.[61]

Between 1919 and 1933, national alcohol prohibition came and went; Clarkson's zeal remained. He chaired a committee that drafted the Turlington Act of 1923, a state law designed to bolster national alcohol prohibition. (According to one observer, North Carolina's Turlington Act "out-volstead[ed the national] Volstead" Act in regard to alcohol suppression.) After the Twenty-first Amendment repealed the Eighteenth in 1933, Clarkson organized the United Dry Forces in North Carolina and vigorously opposed state-level repeal. Clarkson's record of combating what he termed "the drink evil" contrasts starkly with Dr. Boyles's record of selling controlled substances.[62]

Clarkson's private life, like his public life, distinguished him from the modernist Boyles. Unlike Boyles, who left no evidence of church membership, Clarkson was active in one Charlotte church and founded another. Unlike Boyles, who defied convention by remaining a bachelor into his forties, Clarkson married in 1889, at age twenty-six. At the time, the average age for men at marriage was twenty-six. Clarkson's bride, Charlotte native Mary Lloyd Osborne, was twenty-two; the average age for women at marriage at the time was twenty-two. Boyles's wife, Mary, worked outside the home before and during marriage; Clarkson's wife, also named Mary, did not work outside the home, though she was active in the women's auxiliary of her church and the United Daughters of the Confederacy. Unlike the childless Boyleses, the Clarksons had four surviving children. (The national statistical average at the time was 3.5.) Unlike the Boyleses, the Clarksons lived in an exclusive, all-white Charlotte neighborhood and rarely traveled out of state.[63]

By the time of the Greenwich Village appeal, Heriot Clarkson had sat on the North Carolina Supreme Court bench for almost fifteen years. A court leader, he had already written more than a thousand majority opinions, many of which reflected his conviction that his judicial duty included an obligation to, as he put it, "fight [against] . . . the deterioration of morals." (Dr. Boyles's conduct in the medical profession reflected no similar notion.)[64]

Two of the arguments that Boyles made in his legal appeal held considerable importance for the future of public nuisance law in North Carolina. First, Boyles challenged Judge Warlick's decision not to require a prosecution bond—a monetary security provided by the plaintiff to cover the defendant's costs and damages should the defendant subsequently win the case. There was an apparent conflict between two bond provisions in North Carolina's Consolidated Statutes. Judge Warlick, the trial judge, had relied on section 3181, the nuisance law, which authorized the trial judge to "allow a temporary writ of injunction *without* bond [emphasis added]," if satisfied, through affidavits, that a nuisance likely existed. On appeal, Boyles argued that section 493 controlled, not section 3181. Section 493 stated that plaintiffs in civil actions *must* provide prosecution bonds.[65]

The state's Supreme Court affirmed Judge Warlick's reliance on section 3181. This ruling was significant. Had the high court resolved the statutory conflict in favor of section 493's authority and had it required prosecution bonds in nuisance cases, future communities seeking action against alleged nuisances would have faced a riskier, slower, and more expensive process.[66]

Boyles's second substantive contention was that the nuisance statute was unconstitutional. The measure empowered judges to shut down establishments upon mere allegations that they constituted public nuisances and without any hearing or other opportunity for the defendant to respond. Immediately upon receiving solicitor Carpenter's complaint, Judge Warlick had ordered Greenwich Village closed. Fifteen minutes later, Boyles's business—his livelihood—was padlocked, even though he had neither heard the allegations against him nor been given an opportunity to rebut them. Boyles argued on appeal that this procedure violated both the state constitution and the U.S. Constitution by depriving him of his liberty and property "without due process of law."[67]

Clarkson disagreed and rejected the constitutional challenge. The single precedent he cited was a 1905 North Carolina opinion upholding the state's authority to ban fishing in certain waters and to confiscate the fishing equipment of violators without hearing.[68] Clarkson's unanimous opinion upheld the nuisance statute and Judge Warlick's application of it.

Clarkson's opinion concluded with vintage hellfire and brimstone preaching:

> Centuries ago the Almighty entered a judgment, "destruction by fire," against two cities in the plain of Jordan. Today the fire of the law must sometimes be applied by upright citizens to the Sodoms and Gomorrahs that have sprung up along our highways, creating nuisances against public morals. In an age when the respect for law and order has well-nigh withered away ... it is encouraging to find patient and long-forbearing, but upright, citizens aroused against cancerous growths on our social body. They will find the processes of the law ever ready and adequate for such social surgery, all too often necessary to the wholesome health of society.[69]

This sermon resonated in Mecklenburg County. The day after the decision was issued, both the *Charlotte News* and the *Charlotte Observer* reprinted the fiery concluding passage. In fact, the *News*, in a single article, reproduced the entire homily, twice.[70]

The state Supreme Court's decision in *Carpenter v. Boyles* validated the 1937 padlockings and invited more. Mecklenburgers took the hint. Within a month of the May 1938 ruling, two more outlying roadhouses, Sportland and the Oyster Bar, were shut down. Padlockings continued steadily thereafter, even following the passage of a 1939 law requiring state licensing of roadhouses. Once redisovered, the long-dormant public nuisance law proved to be a popular legal tool.[71]

Although the revolution in civil liberties law initiated by the Warren Court would somewhat limit the reach of public nuisance padlocking statutes, both the padlocking remedy and the *Boyles* precedent remained important. Through the end of the century, the section of *West's North Carolina Digest* dealing with public nuisance law referenced *Boyles* more frequently than any other case.[72]

The Greenwich Village case illustrates, in miniature, the social tensions over land use that resulted from the proliferation of automobiles and rural highways during the interwar years. It highlights the post-1933 persistence of intense state-level debates about alcoholic beverages. It highlights a Depression-era legal culture that stressed communal action (in this case, communal litigation). The dispute suggests that public nuisance litigation, initiated by local communities, should join zoning ordinances and restrictive covenants on the list of legal devices used to shape the development of American suburbia.

The Greenwich Village case also illuminates the increasingly active public role played by mid-twentieth-century women. Neighborhood women led the anti–Greenwich Village campaign. Indeed, women, often invoking the powerful language of motherhood, appear to have initiated the vast majority of North Carolina's public nuisance cases during this period. One former sheriff estimates that, in his jurisdiction, during the public nuisance law's mid-twentieth-century heyday, more than 90 percent of padlocking cases were initiated by women. Historians who confine their attention to the male city leaders who adopted zoning ordinances, the male real estate developers who drafted restrictive covenants, or the male loan officers who engaged in redlining miss this instance of female agency.[73]

Finally, the Greenwich Village case casts new light on the origins of interwar cultural tensions in the South. The standard "rural traditionalism" versus "urban modernism" template is of limited use here. It was the rural police force, after all, that failed to close Greenwich Village and did not seem to mind bootlegging. And it was Justice Clarkson, a big-city judge, who administered the coup de grace to Greenwich Village and preached against "demon rum." The rapid spread of southern cities, this case suggests, sparked cultural clashes.

Heriot Clarkson remained on the North Carolina Supreme Court until his death in 1942. He continued to urge temperance, occasionally with speeches that quoted his fiery diatribe at the end of the *Boyles* opinion. To this day, the University of North Carolina law student who earns the highest grade in "professional responsibility" receives the Judge Heriot Clarkson Award.[74]

Memory F. Boyles remained in Mecklenburg County until his death in 1948. Twelve years later, the City of Charlotte annexed Dowd Manor. Greenwich Village, meanwhile, met a fitting end: it reopened, with the court's blessing, as an automobile dealership.[75]

Part III

Civil Rights: The Paradigm Shifts, 1956–1980

Chapter 7

Reading and the Right to Vote

James R. Walker Jr. and North Carolina's Literacy Test

The social and ideological changes sparked by America's involvement in World War II breathed new life into the struggle for African American civil rights. This book's final two chapters explore two central themes of the resulting civil rights movement: voting rights (this chapter) and school desegregation (the following chapter). Both chapters explore the mix of "bottom-up" and "top-down" factors that characterized the era's rich legal history. The national government looms much larger in these chapters than in previous ones. Partly as a result, nonwhite North Carolinians were able to exert unprecedented agency within the state's legal system. We begin with voting rights.

In the spring of 1956, Louise Lassiter, a forty-one-year-old African American woman from Northampton County, North Carolina, decided that the time had come for her to vote. "If more people vote," she reasoned, "I think we'll have more freedom. . . . It would cause the white people to pay more attention to the rights of the colored." Alone but determined, Lassiter entered the country store that doubled as the local registrar's office. Helen H. Taylor was the registrar and administered the state's literacy test. Although Lassiter read the text placed before her, Taylor, invoking the wide discretion available to registrars, deemed Lassiter illiterate and therefore ineligible to vote. The applicant's alleged shortcoming was mispronouncing a few words in the state's constitution.[1]

James McNab, Louis Becker, Eleanor Blackey, Andrew Martin, Chioma Ohanyerenwa, Philip Osborne, and Shepherd Reynolds contributed to this chapter.

The following year, Lassiter reappeared. This time, however, she was not alone. She came with a lawyer, James R. Walker Jr., a northeastern North Carolinian who was in the process of mounting what would become a formidable grassroots legal attack on the state's literacy test. Walker would take Lassiter's case from that country store to the Supreme Court of the United States.

Walker's story highlights an underappreciated aspect of civil rights during the 1950s and 1960s: grassroots litigation—that is, locally based efforts to achieve legal change through test cases in appellate courts. Considered separately, of course, both "grassroots" and "litigation" represent well-established aspects of civil rights history. Grassroots movements such as bus boycotts and lunch-counter sit-ins are renowned, as are litigation campaigns, most famously the one that produced *Brown v. Board of Education*. When these aspects are combined to form the concept of grassroots litigation, however, the phrase prompts less recognition. Grassroots protesters in the South typically worked outside the legal system, violating unjust laws on the streets, perhaps, but not themselves challenging these laws in appellate courts. Litigation, meanwhile, was famously orchestrated by distant, national organizations—most importantly, the New York–based National Association for the Advancement of Colored People (NAACP).

From the mid-1950s to the early 1960s in northeastern North Carolina, James R. Walker Jr. led a surprisingly successful grassroots litigation campaign against the state's literacy test. Historians have paid insufficient attention to Walker and other grassroots litigators. Social historians of civil rights have undertaken a "view from the trenches," to appreciate the crucial contributions of local activists, but legal historians have been less inclined to do so. This is unfortunate, for grassroots litigation was an important part of the legal challenge to white supremacy in the decades following World War II.[2]

This chapter describes the actions of one grassroots litigator. It explores what enabled Walker to wage his litigation campaign, what his legal strategy was, and what he achieved. It argues that Walker's personal background as a child of African American professionals in the Jim Crow South, combined with such historical events as World War II and the expanded reach of federal civil rights law, facilitated his career as a local civil rights organizer and grassroots litigator. Walker's energetic advocacy put a public spotlight on egregious voting rights problems and provoked legislative and judicial change. Considering the humble scale of his operations, his achievements were striking.

North Carolina adopted its literacy test around the turn of the twentieth century, at the dawn of the Jim Crow era. The weakening of the Republican Party in the South, the reduction in the national government's protection of African American rights, and a widespread belief among southern whites that the Fifteenth Amendment was illegitimate all facilitated the spread of disfranchisement schemes across the South. In North Carolina, as elsewhere, the legislators who adopted the literacy test generated their "electoral reform" program by mixing ostensible good-government concern about electoral corruption with white supremacist hysteria about "Negro domination." The resulting legal program, which swept the region in the two decades bracketing 1900, included poll taxes, all-white primaries, grandfather clauses, and literacy tests. Florida and Tennessee initiated the "reform" in 1889 by instituting poll taxes. Other states across the South soon followed with other measures. (Not included in the program of restrictive legislation, of course, were the unofficial but very real racial violence and intimidation that often confronted blacks who sought to exercise their political rights.)[3]

North Carolina's literacy test arose out of the threat that "Fusion" politics posed to the state's conservative Democratic Party. The "Fusion" was a biracial coalition of members from the Populist and Republican parties. In 1894, Populists and Republicans wrested control of North Carolina's legislature from the Democrats. Two years later, Republican Daniel Russell became the first non-Democrat to win the North Carolina governorship since Reconstruction, and George Henry White, an African American Republican from northeastern North Carolina, won election to the U.S. House of Representatives.[4]

Notwithstanding these political changes, black office-holding in North Carolina remained modest. Governor Russell estimated that his 818 appointments to state office included just eight African Americans. In counties across the state, only about ten black persons on average held any kind of public office between 1895 and 1900. Even in majority-black northeastern counties, the number of African Americans holding public office never matched—and generally fell far short of—their proportion of the population. Nonetheless, Democrats screamed "Negro domination" and launched what they openly called a "white supremacy" campaign to remove blacks from political life. Violence and intimidation were central to this plan, as demonstrated most graphically in the brutal Wilmington Massacre of 1898, in which white Democrats violently overthrew that city's interracial government, killed about a dozen African Americans, and took power themselves.[5]

Also fundamental to this white supremacy campaign was an 1899 proposal to add a poll tax, a grandfather clause, and a literacy test to the North Carolina constitution. The Democratic-sponsored amendment, which was modeled on disfranchising laws recently adopted by other southern states, passed and went into effect in North Carolina in 1901. It did the trick. By the 1904 elections, virtually no African Americans were able to vote in the state. Disfranchisement solidified the political dominance of North Carolina Democrats and whites for generations. After Russell, no Republican would be elected governor until 1972. After White, no African American would represent the state in the U.S. Congress until 1992.[6]

On its face, North Carolina's literacy test did not violate the U.S. Constitution's Fifteenth Amendment, which barred suffrage restrictions based on "race, color, or previous condition of servitude." The literacy test, like the poll tax, theoretically applied equally to all citizens, regardless of race. Test supporters, however, candidly stated that it would, in the words of one Democrat, "exclude a very large percentage of the negroes from the ballot box"—a felicitous result, he thought, since "negroes . . . are ignorant and have, neither by acquisition nor inheritance, the capacity to vote intelligently."[7] Another supporter contended that the black man's "unfitness and total incompetence to participate in[,] much less administer[,] the affairs of government" justified the new suffrage restrictions.[8]

White newspapers cheered disfranchisement. Raleigh's influential—and enthusiastically white supremacist—*News and Observer* reported in 1899 that the state's newspapers were "practically unanimous in favor of submitting an amendment that will take from the ignorant negro the power to dominate the legislation of the Commonwealth." Reasoning in 1900 that "the greatest folly and crime in our national history was the establishment of negro suffrage immediately after the war," the newspaper clearly voiced the Democratic Party's logic of white supremacy: "White man, you are worthy to vote; although poor and illiterate, you have the character, the manhood, the practical education, the intelligence and the political knowledge requisite to make a good voter.

Nigger-man, you have not the knowledge, nor the intelligence, nor the character, nor the manhood, nor the practical education requisite to vote. Step aside and let the white man vote."[9] Thus, although the letter of the new voting law may not have violated the Fifteenth Amendment, its spirit unquestionably did.

The North Carolina literacy test went into effect in 1901. Even if implemented in a racially neutral manner, it would have had a devastating effect on African American suffrage. At the time, more than 50 percent of black southerners were illiterate, as opposed to fewer than 20 percent of white southerners.[10] The implementation of North Carolina's literacy test, however, was never racially neutral. A grandfather clause exempted almost all white persons from having to take the test. "[N]o male person, who was, on January 1, 1867, or at any time prior thereto, entitled to vote under the laws of any State in the United States . . . and no lineal descendant of any such person," the clause read, "shall be denied the right to register and vote at any election in this State by reason of his failure to possess the educational qualifications herein prescribed." Although the U.S. Supreme Court declared grandfather clauses unconstitutional in 1915, North Carolina's version remained on the books for decades thereafter.[11]

Even without the grandfather clause, however, the very language of the literacy test invited biased implementation, for it granted almost limitless discretion to local registrars. "Every person presenting himself for registration," the provision read, "shall be able to read and write any section of the Constitution in the English language, and shall show *to the satisfaction of the registrar* his ability to read and write any such section when he applies for registration [emphasis added]." All too often, as Louise Lassiter and countless other black North Carolinians would learn, local registrars, not "literacy," determined voter eligibility in North Carolina.[12]

North Carolina's literacy test would remain on the books until federal law voided it in stages beginning in 1965. Until then, its only serious legal challenge came from James R. Walker Jr.

Several factors explain Walker's willingness and ability to challenge the North Carolina literacy test through grassroots litigation. Part of the reason Walker cared so much about civil rights in northeastern North Carolina was because he was a native son. He was born in the small Hertford County town of Ahoskie, on 2 February 1924, the first of James and Ethel Walker's eight children. Hertford County, like several others in northeastern North Carolina, was poor and rural, and the majority of its residents were black. African Americans faced harsher denials of political rights in this part of the state than in any other.[13]

Walker's regional roots affected his litigation campaign in a variety of ways. Having grown up in the area, he had firsthand knowledge of its system of white supremacy. He had local friends and relations upon whom he could call for help. He had an emotional attachment to the region that drew him home years after leaving to pursue opportunities elsewhere. He was drawn back not so much by nostalgia for the past as by a commitment to create a better future.

Walker's family prepared him for civil rights leadership. "It wasn't anything unusual for me to take an interest in social welfare and [to] fight social injustice," he reflected years later. "It was more or less a family tradition on both sides." Members of his family had long been leaders of important African American institutions. They taught him racial pride. ("I didn't come up in the white folks' kitchen," he proudly remarked.) They taught him an ethos of service and the importance of fighting for civil rights. When he grew up and joined the struggle, his family was supportive. Walker Sr. apparently suffered economic retribution as a result of his son's activism, but the son remembered the father saying, "Go ahead, son . . . fight the problem. We'll survive." His family imparted a sense of justice that served him well in the legal profession. "I was always legal minded," he told an interviewer. "I practiced my own law before I got into law school. There were certain instinctive things I had about justice and so forth that I had been practicing all my life." His family deserved much credit.[14]

Both of Walker's parents, unlike most African Americans in the region, were highly educated professionals. James R. Walker Sr. was the valedictorian of his class at the Hampton Institute, a historically African American school in Virginia that was a leading center of higher education in the "industrial" style of the era. Both Walker Sr. and his wife, Ethel, had long careers as educators in North Carolina's segregated public school system. This professional experience made them natural leaders of the black community, especially given the high rates of illiteracy among black residents of rural northeastern North Carolina. "Whatever 'Professor Walker' said" carried weight among blacks, the civil rights attorney recalled, "because he could read and write and interpret things to people." The example set by Walker's parents inspired his own educational and professional aspirations. Their relative affluence made such aspirations attainable.[15]

Another influential member of Walker's family was his maternal grandfather, Reverend Sander Dockery, a preacher and school administrator in Statesville, North Carolina. In his spare time, Reverend Dockery pursued civil rights. He was an early member of the North Carolina branch of the NAACP, and his civil rights activism inspired his grandson. "He preached against oppression for years, and I sat under him," recalled Walker. Reverend Dockery also influenced his grandson's career. According to one relative, it was Dockery who urged his grandson to become a lawyer. The minister's example also inspired Walker to become a preacher. "I have a double profession," the attorney later explained. "I . . . consider things from a religious standpoint from my church and I consider [them] from a civic standpoint though the law." Walker's civil rights activism benefited greatly from his twin professions. Being, as he put it, "ministerially inclined," he could visit black churches to recruit support for his civil rights efforts. Once there, he "could not only speak like a lawyer" but also like a preacher. "I knew the Bible and I knew biblical stories to illustrate what I wanted," he explained. "I knew how to interpret things to these people in terms of their religious concepts. I could be the minister motivating his people" as well as the lawyer defending them in court.[16]

Another gift Reverend Dockery gave to his grandson was physical distance from Hertford County. Statesville, where Dockery lived, lies in the North Carolina Piedmont, some 250 miles to the west-southwest of Ahoskie. In general, the Piedmont was more affluent and more urban than the northeastern part of the state. It also had a larger white population. The political disabilities facing African Americans were somewhat less severe there. The substantial time that Walker spent in Statesville throughout his life enabled him to view Ahoskie from a distance.[17]

In 1944, at the age of twenty, Walker got to see Ahoskie from a much greater distance. He went to war. World War II was a crucial experience for Walker, as it was for many other African Americans. The ideological opposition to fascism that flourished on the home front during the war years opened many eyes to the inequities of Jim Crow. Given this ideological context, the discrimination that Walker and other blacks faced in the armed services was especially galling. One of Walker's bitterest wartime memories involved his service assignment. Upon being drafted in 1944, he applied for Officer Candidate School. As a college senior whose liberal arts training included instruction in German, geography, and history, he felt well qualified to lead troops in Germany. The army, however, rejected his application summarily. Walker later reported that the army "threw my application in the trash can ... according to a corporal who was in the administrative office" at the time. Army leaders, Walker concluded, "weren't interested in having black officers." They assigned him to a segregated unit and sent him to Germany under the command of a white officer—a former soda jerk with no college training. It stung.[18]

Walker also was indignant about the army's habitual exclusion of blacks from the infantry. According to Walker, army leaders did this because they "didn't want it to get back that [African Americans had] died serving their country." In fact, Walker reported, plenty of black soldiers who were officially assigned to low-prestige support roles were transferred into infantry units in Europe to replace fallen white soldiers. When these black soldiers subsequently died in combat, Walker angrily recalled, the army reported them as having served in mundane support units, not in the infantry.[19]

The discrimination that Walker experienced in the armed services did not surprise him. "Being a history major, I knew all that," he said, but the ideological hypocrisy of the war effort left him in a fighting mood. "We were supposed to be fighting for the Four Freedoms," he later noted. "I had never seen any of them." His overseas service convinced him that more fighting was needed at home; it also prepared him to wage that fight. Asked years later to account for his extraordinary acceptance of personal risk during the civil rights struggle, Walker responded, "I was an army man. Had been to the front. . . . I was three years in the service. I wasn't scared of nothing." Walker was not the only one to link his war service to his civil rights work. When an African American newspaper reported enthusiastically on Walker's voting rights efforts in the late 1950s, editors ran an old photograph of Walker in his army uniform. "His Big Battles," the caption read, "Were to Come Later."[20]

Walker's military service helped prepare him for civil rights combat in another important way, thanks to the G.I. Bill. Upon returning from war, Walker—along with 700,000 other African American veterans, including many future civil rights leaders—used the G.I. Bill to pursue higher education. Walker completed his undergraduate degree at North

Carolina College for Negroes in Durham, now North Carolina Central University.[21] Then he turned his sights on law school. In 1949, he applied to the prestigious—and all-white—University of North Carolina School of Law. He qualified for admission in every way but one: he was black. So the school rejected him.[22]

Reluctantly, Walker enrolled in the law school at North Carolina College for Negroes, a separate (and unequal) facility for African Americans. The state had established it in 1939, one year after the U.S. Supreme Court ruled that states offering public legal education to whites must also offer public legal education to blacks. Rather than integrate the all-white law school in Chapel Hill, North Carolina established a separate law school for blacks in Durham.[23]

Walker, however, would not accept segregation—especially of the "separate and unequal" variety. In 1949, when Walker enrolled, the North Carolina College School of Law was "poorly equipped" and "barely making ends meet." It also was, in Walker's words, "not on anybody's list." "I didn't want to go to an unaccredited law school," he explained. "I . . . wanted to go to a law school [such as UNC,] where I could take the bar and practice anywhere in the United States." More importantly, Walker's native sense of justice convinced him that he simply "had a right to go" to the law school in Chapel Hill.[24]

Walker withdrew from the North Carolina College School of Law "to keep from graduating." He did so in order to preserve his legal standing to sue for admission to UNC. "If I had graduated from the black law school," he reasoned, "I would no longer be a student eligible to raise the question" of equal access to the state's flagship university. His eyes still set on Chapel Hill, Walker left Durham and transferred to the law school at Boston University, the same majority-white private university at which Martin Luther King Jr. would soon earn his doctorate. Walker was at BU when, in 1950, the U.S. Supreme Court heard *Sweatt v. Painter*. In its ruling, a victory for the NAACP and its top legal counsel, Thurgood Marshall, the Supreme Court ordered the integration of the all-white University of Texas School of Law. Texas, like North Carolina, had tried to preserve the all-white nature of its flagship public law school by establishing a separate public law school for African Americans. In *Sweatt*, however, a unanimous U.S. Supreme Court ruled that the educational and professional opportunities available at the new and unknown Texas State University for Negroes were in no way "equal" to those available at the prestigious University of Texas School of Law. As a practical matter, *Sweatt* meant that public law schools could no longer exclude applicants on the basis of race.[25]

Sweatt demonstrated to Walker in the most tangible way the impact that appellate litigation could have. It also reignited Walker's crusade to gain admittance to the law school in Chapel Hill. After some further stonewalling, and after an additional push from the federal courts, the University of North Carolina grudgingly cracked opened its doors to Walker and a handful of other qualified black students. In 1952, Walker and one other African American graduated from the law school, becoming the first blacks ever to receive University of North Carolina diplomas.[26]

Walker's attitude in law school was hardly typical. He rejected the reverence for legal precedent that lay at the heart of legal pedagogy. Law professors, Walker later recalled, trained their students to apply existing legal doctrines. Walker resisted. "I never was a student who accepted [established law] decisions as being sacred," he explained. "I was a student who found what was wrong with [the] decisions that everybody else was praising." His adversarial approach to legal precedent hurt his law school grades but helped make him an imaginative civil rights litigator after graduation.[27]

Outside the UNC classroom, Walker insisted upon equal treatment. In one widely publicized incident in the fall of 1951, Walker refused to accept free tickets to watch Tar Heel football games because they were for the Jim Crow (all-black) section, not the (all-white) student section. "I am a part of the student body," he declared, "and want to cheer and express school spirit as part of the student body and not be set apart down behind the goal posts in an undignified and humiliating manner."[28]

UNC chancellor Robert House was unmoved. He distinguished sharply between what he called "education services" on the one hand and "social recognition" on the other. Although federal law compelled the university to grant blacks equal education services, he reasoned, nothing compelled the school to grant blacks equal social recognition. Because football was "social," not "educational," university officials believed that they could discriminate on Saturday afternoons. Chancellor House further noted that white students were charged through tuition for football tickets. African Americans were not; their section "K" tickets were free.[29]

Walker did not back down. He and four black classmates sent a telegram to North Carolina governor Kerr Scott, requesting a legal opinion on the matter from North Carolina attorney general Harry McMullen. Governor Scott did nothing. When Walker threatened litigation, however, the university capitulated. By the end of the 1951 football season, Chapel Hill had opened the student section to Walker and other black students.[30]

The football incident and others like it taught Walker several important lessons: North Carolina's assertions of racial progressiveness were often hollow; litigation—or even its threat—could be a powerful weapon; and, on a personal level, civil rights activism was deeply satisfying. After graduating, he would put these lessons to use as a grassroots civil rights litigator.[31]

The North Carolina that Walker confronted, law degree in hand, was relatively liberal for a southern state at the time. A 1958 survey, taken a few years after Walker's law school graduation, estimated that 31 percent of potential black voters in North Carolina were registered. This compared favorably to, for example, Louisiana's 14 percent or South Carolina's 11 percent.[32] But 31 percent black registration was dwarfed by 84 percent white registration in the state. Moreover, statewide figures masked pockets within North Carolina where disfranchisement was as pronounced as anywhere in the South. These pockets were concentrated in Walker's native northeast.[33]

Corrupt application of the literacy test was just one of many factors limiting the black vote there. Genuine illiteracy did exist. A 1961 study pegged the number of illiterate and "functionally illiterate" North Carolinians at 425,000, or almost 10 percent of the state's total population of 4.5 million. This report estimated that 75,000 people in the state were totally illiterate and another 350,000 people were functionally illiterate. African Americans probably accounted for a disproportionate share of this figure, since 7.5 percent of blacks were illiterate nationally in 1959, compared to 1.6 percent of whites. Black illiteracy was probably highest in areas such as northeastern North Carolina, where poverty abounded and educational opportunities did not.[34]

Apathy and hopelessness among potential African American voters further suppressed registration. Some blacks were so disillusioned with the political process, and so cynical about the prospect of change, that they did not even seek to register. This frustrated those black leaders who believed that the vote could achieve positive change. One aggravated black southerner perhaps exaggerated a bit in 1956 when lamenting, "You can't get most Negroes to talk to you about voting. . . . Some say their votes don't count; some say they [whites] would elect whom they want anyway, others think [voting] is a good thing if somebody else does it." James R. Walker Jr. himself later remarked that one of his biggest challenges in the 1950s was "undoing some notions that blacks had . . . that voting was all white folks' business." Another black activist conceded that "lethargy among [African American] people themselves" did suppress black registration and voting but rightly noted that the many "hurdles placed between the eligible voters and the ballot box" had a lot to do with the creation of this lethargy.[35]

Another factor suppressing black registration and voting was white intimidation. Some blacks who contemplated electoral participation faced quiet but menacing pressures. Examples included pressures applied by school boards on black teachers, by white landowners on black farm workers; and by white merchants on black debtors. Other techniques were less subtle. Whites in majority-black Bertie County positioned German shepherds in front of the Perrytown precinct station; they restrained the snarling dogs when whites approached but loosed them when African Americans sought to register.[36]

Beyond intimidation lay violence. Blacks who led voter registration efforts in Georgia in 1957 had their cars bombed and their front porches blown up. A married couple who led a Florida voter registration drive died when a bomb exploded in their home on Christmas Eve. Indeed, voter registration drives between the mid-1950s and mid-1960s left numerous martyrs, the most famous of whom were Medgar Evers, James Chaney, Andrew Goodman, and Michael Schwerner. All too often, especially in majority-black areas, intimidation and violence kept even unquestionably literate blacks off the voting rolls.[37]

The literacy test, locally administered, made matters worse. Despite its infamy, the test has been subject to surprisingly little close scholarly scrutiny. Historical studies tend to include it in general discussions of voting rights and to focus on national developments, such as the Voting Rights Act of 1965. But real voting rights history, at least prior to 1965, occurred at the county and precinct level. As the United States Commission on Civil Rights recognized in a 1961 report, it was local registrars in individual precincts who "wield[ed] the real power affecting suffrage" in the United States.[38]

North Carolina electoral law gave local registrars expansive discretionary powers. A federal study of North Carolina voting rights in 1960 found that the "procedures followed by registrars to determine literacy var[ied] widely from registrar to registrar, and from county to county." Some registrars asked applicants to read passages from the North Carolina constitution; others used the U.S. Constitution. Some registrars asked applicants to read aloud; others read aloud and asked potential registrants to transcribe their dictation. A few registrars did not ask voters to prove literacy at all.[39]

Grading standards varied even more than testing formats. Potential voters had to prove their literacy "to the satisfaction of the registrar." Not surprisingly, judgments about what constituted "satisfactory" literacy varied widely from registrar to registrar—and applicant to applicant. Moreover, some counties gave registrars the additional power to reject potential voters not of "good mind." Thus, racist registrars could easily discriminate against African Americans. As the federal Commission on Civil Rights observed in 1959, North Carolina's low nonwhite voter registration was due largely to "varying practices in administering the State's literacy requirement."[40]

In general, the fairness of the literacy test as administered in North Carolina was inversely proportional to the percentage of African Americans in the local population. Where black populations were sparse, black voting rights tended to be robust, and black registration figures approximated those of whites. For example, in Burke County, in western North Carolina, blacks accounted for about 7 percent of the 1960 population. Officials there claimed to administer suffrage tests with an absolutely even hand, and registration figures substantiate their boasts. About 82 percent of Burke County nonwhites were registered to vote in 1958. This was almost identical to the statewide figure for whites. In mountainous Macon County, located even farther west, blacks accounted for less than 2 percent of the population. Macon County officials reportedly did not even bother to administer the literacy test.[41]

As one moved eastward and the concentration of blacks increased, nonwhite voter registration fell. This was no coincidence. Whites in majority-black eastern counties feared that true democracy would destroy their dominance. They did whatever was necessary to limit the black vote. "It is in this [eastern] section of the state," lamented one African American in 1950, "that Negroes are kept from voting and intimidated if they even try to register to vote."[42]

The counties of northeastern North Carolina had the state's highest percentage of African American residents and the state's lowest percentage of registered African American voters. In 1960, eleven of North Carolina's one hundred counties had populations that were predominantly nonwhite. Eight of these eleven counties formed a contiguous cluster in the state's northeastern area. Although civil rights scholars have largely overlooked this region in favor of the Deep South, which it in many ways resembled, it was, in the words of one civil rights leader of the day, "one of the most repressive areas in the South." By 1960, nonwhite voter registration in these eleven counties averaged 16.4 percent. Although this level was higher than it had been just a few years previously, it was less than half the statewide average for nonwhites. It was also woefully behind the statewide average for white citizens in that year: 92.8 percent.[43]

Because North Carolina had no poll tax, the literacy test was the principal legal device for maintaining white electoral dominance. A fair application of the test would have disfranchised more blacks than whites, since illiteracy was higher among blacks. But the application of the test was not at all fair. Asked in 1961 if he had ever seen a white person fail the literacy test, a registrar in Bertie County in northeastern North Carolina was honest enough to admit, "No. I mean I didn't have any to try it." The African American press reported in the mid-1950s that it was an "age-old complaint amongst the colored people" of North Carolina "that registrars abuse their discretion and pull all kinds of tricks on the 'reading' requirements" in order to "keep colored people from registering."[44]

On paper, the state's registration requirements were few and straightforward. Registrants had to be citizens of nation and state; they had to be at least twenty-one years of age; they had to be residents of North Carolina and of their voting precincts; and they had to be able to read and write any section of the state constitution in English, to the satisfaction of the registrar. But many registrars were not "satisfied" with black applicants. Some registrars found literate blacks to be illiterate. Others required blacks who read and wrote successfully to interpret murky constitutional passages. Still others followed reading and writing tests with tricky questions about government and history.

A registrar in Enfield Township of Halifax County in northeastern North Carolina asked a black applicant to transcribe a dictated section of the state constitution. The applicant did so. The registrar asked the applicant to read back the dictation. He did so. The registrar then asked a series of questions about state government, including, "Which has the most force, the militia or the General Assembly?" The applicant aced all questions except for this one. He was not registered. Other unfair questions reportedly asked by registrars of blacks included, "Who is your congressman?" "How many electoral votes does North Carolina have?" "How many rooms are in the county courthouse?" "What is habeas corpus?" "Name the signers of the Declaration of Independence," and, "If the NAACP attacked the U.S. government, on which side would you fight?"[45]

One black columnist fumed that "registrars in the eastern part of the state" were so "malicious in their anxiety to keep colored people from registering" that they kept raising the bar as high as necessary to trip up qualified blacks. No evidence suggests that white applicants were similarly tested.[46] James R. Walker Jr. vowed to end such abuse.

Following his graduation from UNC in 1952, Walker "built up a little law practice" in his grandfather's hometown of Statesville, North Carolina. His subsequent career as a civil rights activist benefited from the failure of this law practice to be emotionally rewarding.[47]

Walker did not find his true calling until 1955, when he accompanied his father on a book tour. The elder Walker had retired from the Statesville school system in 1953 and turned to poetry. Two years later, he published an original collection, *Be Firm My Hope* (1955). Reviewers praised the collection as "reflecting genuine emotion and deep religious conviction." Indeed, religious devotion was the book's overriding theme. But social justice and racial discrimination—treated in such poems as "Race Relations," "Separate but Equal," and "Slavery"—were powerful subthemes. The elder Walker may have had his son's World War II service in mind when writing,

> May all who've in her [America's] battles fought,
> Enjoy what life and blood have bought;
> It matters not if black or white,
> For man is man and right is right.

Another poem concerned voting:

> It matters not about your hue,
> Nor what you have to eat or wear;
> It matters not who scorns at you,
> The ballot's yours, go do and dare.

According to subsequent press accounts, the senior Walker's poetry inspired "much" of his son's "devotion to action in civil rights."[48]

The book tour took the Walkers to northeastern North Carolina. Tiring of the school libraries where his father promoted his books, the young lawyer took to visiting surrounding communities. He soon realized that the poor, rural, majority-black northeastern part of the state desperately needed legal advocacy of the sort that he could provide. Local leaders in the Halifax County town of Weldon implored him to lend them a hand: "With a guy like you, what we could do here," they said. In exchange, "we ought to be able to provide a [rent-free] place for you to stay and an office place," though no salary was offered. Father and son returned to Statesville at the end of the book tour, but the younger Walker soon traveled east on his own "to explore further . . . what I might be able to do back in the area where I was born." Interviewed in Weldon decades later, Walker explained his decision to relocate: "I figured I could be of more service over here than over there." He was home.[49]

Black lawyers were then in short supply in North Carolina. According to the 1950 Census, compiled five years before Walker's trip east, there were 2,279 members of the legal profession in North Carolina, of whom just 26 were African American. Thus, the state contained one white lawyer for every 1,300 white residents and one black lawyer for every 40,000 black residents. To be sure, white lawyers often represented African American clients. But in politically explosive matters such as voting rights cases, which threatened the foundations of the racial caste system, local white lawyers willing to litigate aggressively for black clients were scarce. Walker found it moving to see "so many people without legal counsel or guidance of the type they wanted." Desperate African Americans "besieged" him "with requests for legal aid." He answered their call.[50]

When Walker moved east, he became the only African American lawyer in a six-county area of northeastern North Carolina. He immediately joined the leadership of the local civil rights movement. His background and training had prepared him to lead. He was also free of familial and professional commitments. Unlike nine in ten American men of Walker's age at this time, Walker was unmarried. Without a family to support, Walker was freer than were most beginning attorneys to concentrate on non-revenue-generating cases such as voting rights disputes. He was also free of the indirect threats against spouses and children that hate groups sometimes employed against civil rights leaders. Likewise, Walker had no law firm, law partners, or law office to protect. He worked in Weldon, in office space donated by the African American supporters who had invited him east. His opponents could not easily threaten professional reprisal.[51]

Walker joined the legal battle for voting rights at a critical moment. The social and intellectual changes wrought by World War II had sparked a dramatic, though temporary, increase in southern black voting. Black registration in the South rose from 3 percent in 1940 to 20 percent in 1952. The white southern backlash against *Brown v. Board of Education* (1954), however, slowed and, in places, reversed this progress. Black voter registration in Mississippi fell by more than half between 1954 and 1956; Virginia, Georgia, and Alabama adopted new laws that made voter registration more difficult. In the post-*Brown* South, white tolerance of black voting decreased, even as black electoral aspirations rose. Conflict was inevitable. "Register and Vote" meetings in North Carolina and elsewhere inspired unprecedented numbers of blacks to visit registration offices. As often as not, they confronted registrars newly recommitted to white supremacy. Unjustly rejected black voter applicants needed legal representation.[52]

For years, the NAACP had led the struggle for African American voting rights. Its greatest achievement in this field was *Smith v. Allwright* (1944), a wartime case in which the Supreme Court of the United States struck down the whites-only Democratic primary in Texas. In the early 1950s, however, the NAACP turned away from voting rights litigation in favor of alternatives that seemed more promising. Between 1955 and 1961, just as voting rights disputes intensified, the drop in NAACP voting rights litigation became precipitous, owing largely to the many nuisance suits that southern states filed against the civil rights group during these years. The nuisance suits failed in the courts but put the NAACP on the defensive.[53] It was precisely at this critical moment that Walker and other grassroots litigators stepped in and took up the slack.

In recent decades, scholars have worked hard to explain the civil rights litigation strategies of the NAACP and its most famous attorney, Thurgood Marshall. The legal strategies of James R. Walker Jr. and other grassroots litigators also deserve attention. Walker experimented with a variety of legal approaches. He probed the political foundations of white supremacy, seeking soft spots. Although he lacked the NAACP's resources and personnel, he did surprisingly well.[54]

One of Walker's techniques was to litigate in his own name. This enabled him to avoid the ethical and practical complications of using surrogate clients. In June 1956, he challenged in his own name the legitimacy of a "single-shot" voting law that applied to local elections in Halifax County, his home county. The previous year, largely in response to *Brown v. Board of Education,* North Carolina, like several other southern states, had prohibited "single-shot" voting in many local elections. North Carolina's anti–single-shot law, which applied in select "at-large" local elections, including many school board elections, required voters to cast as many votes as there were seats to fill.

The unstated purpose of this 1955 law was to minimize African American voting strength, at a time when black voting, especially in cities, was moving from "negligible" to "measurable" and when black candidates for local office were appearing for the first time in decades. No African American had held elective office in Halifax County since 1898, yet three black candidates for local positions ran in the Democratic primary in the spring of 1956. (Walker, incidentally, managed all three campaigns, none of which resulted in victory.) One of these African American candidates was Dr. Salter J. Cochran, a physician and "decorated war hero" who sought at-large election to the Halifax County Board of Education. His prospects for victory were greatest if his supporters, who were overwhelmingly—perhaps exclusively—African American, could vote for him alone, without also having to vote for any of his rivals, all of whom were white. The "single-shot" law prohibited such voting by requiring full slates from each voter. (In some counties, indeed, voting machines were literally returned to factories to be "one-shotted," guaranteeing that they would accept only full slates in at-large elections.) Given the day's political realities, the single-shot measure decreased the likelihood that black candidates would prevail in at-large elections.[55]

Acting as both plaintiff and plaintiff's counsel, Walker sued the Halifax County Board of Elections for "throwing out his ballot on which he had voted [for] only one candidate in a race in which seven out of eight were to be elected." Walker sought to strike down the "single-shot" voting law. The state legislature, however, deftly mooted his lawsuit in the spring of 1957 by converting board of education positions from elective to appointive. North Carolina's "single-shot" ban persisted until voided by federal judges early in the 1970s.[56]

Walker could attack the single-shot rule in his own name because the law affected him personally. He was, after all, a registered voter. Precisely for that reason, however, he could *not* attack the literacy test in his own name. That law had not prevented him from registering or voting. In order to challenge the literacy test in court, he would need to find clients who had fallen victim to the literacy test. Challenging the literacy test and finding affected clients necessitated organization.

As he planned his strategy for attacking the literacy test, Walker's first impulse was not to establish an independent, grassroots organization but to work through the NAACP. He was already a dues-paying member. He attended local meetings and was a regular at the annual state conference. Soon after settling into Halifax County, he "tried to make the NAACP work." Doing so, he later explained, "would have saved me the trouble of setting up something independent." But the lawyer and the organization were mismatched. As of 1955, Walker's eyes were locked on voting rights; the NAACP, in contrast, focused largely on implementing the recent *Brown* ruling. Walker considered the NAACP's narrow focus on school integration to be badly "out of step" with local African American concerns and needs.[57]

Walker's eagerness for direct action also clashed with the NAACP's instinctive moderation. "I was too aggressive for them," Walker later told an interviewer. "I couldn't get them to get up and fight any issues that needed to be fought. . . . They weren't ready for that type of action."[58]

Speed was also a divisive issue. With registration for the 1956 elections fast approaching, Walker itched for action. The NAACP's deliberate procedures were not designed for speed. "At the state conference [of the NAACP]," he later complained, "you would never get anything [done] for the next year or two." He elaborated: "I had just come out of Carolina [the newly integrated state law school]. . . . I was already out from under any yoke of segregation myself. I'm trying to free other people. And I'm impatient." Walker conceded that the NAACP, given its nature, may have had no choice but to "go through the state conference and do this, that, and the other." But he was not so encumbered. "I was going to file my suits and do whatever I was going to do before they got an answer from anybody. I was a punch man. I hit now."[59]

Perhaps most importantly, the NAACP demanded closer supervision and control than Walker was prepared to cede. According to Walker, "I didn't want it [the NAACP] to tell me what to challenge or what not to challenge or how to practice my law. I used my legal profession to raise and fight ... legal issues as I saw them." The result was predictable: the NAACP "wouldn't give me any money" and "would not take the cases I was handling." Walker realized that, in order to advance, "I *had* to have something else."[60]

Concluding that the NAACP "just didn't meet the local needs," Walker founded an independent group to support his grassroots litigation campaign: the Eastern Council on Community Affairs (ECCA). Widespread suffrage abuses and a local tradition of black mobilization made organizing easy. "[T]here was a big need for the [ECCA] before we got it set up," Walker recalled. With elections drawing near, the organization "built up out of necessity." "I didn't have any problem organizing blacks over here," Walker explained. "They were willing and ready."[61]

The ECCA covered twenty-five counties in eastern North Carolina, with special focus on the majority-black northeast. Walker appointed representatives in each county, being sure to name people whose leadership in other organizations was likely to make them well known in their communities. The group had a newsletter, occasional meetings, and little else. Primarily, it served as a communications network. Blacks who were unjustly denied suffrage in any of the covered counties were urged to contact their local ECCA representatives, who would forward the news to Walker in Weldon. "[W]ithin twenty-four hours after they got turned down," Walker claimed, "I would know it through the network we had had set up."[62]

Walker's first impulse was to respond to a voting rights denial with direct action. "See, I didn't start in court," he recalled. "I went straight in and handled the thing direct. Direct action and civil protest ... I did that so many times. I'd get a number of people to protest ... just go on down and push for something." One of the first voting rights complaints that Walker received came from the Halifax County town of Enfield, where a local voting registrar, under suspicious circumstances, had rejected the applications of several African Americans. Walker visited Enfield and "asked for the registrar's resignation for being so arbitrary and unfair." Instead of getting rid of the registrar, Enfield got rid of Walker. The police ordered him to leave town, and Walker recalled that they "tried to bring some charges against me."[63]

Walker learned from the experience. In the future, although he would not abandon what he called "civic action," he would combine it with litigation. If direct action did not work, he said, "I'd come back with a [law]suit."⁶⁴

In those lawsuits, statistics demonstrating that the literacy test, as applied, had a racially discriminatory effect would have been most persuasive. Statistical evidence of this sort would later become a standard feature of employment discrimination cases. In 1956, however, statewide voter registration statistics simply did not exist in North Carolina. Compiling them would have required two things that Walker did not have: the cooperation of county- and precinct-level electoral officials and the money to hire statisticians. Instead, Walker employed other legal techniques. A series of cases from his busiest period of grassroots litigation, 1956–1961, illustrates these techniques and highlights his creativity, resolve, and flexibility in light of changing legal circumstances.

The first and simplest of Walker's legal techniques was to sue unjust registrars personally. In 1956, Walker initiated a civil suit on behalf of Ernest Ivey, a sixty-two-year-old African American preacher. Three times Ivey had tried but failed to register in Halifax County's Littleton precinct before the Democratic primary in May 1956. His problem was not illiteracy. Walker alleged that Ivey had "the equivalent of a high school education and ha[d] done academic work in extension classes in the Ministry." He was "well able to read, write and understand any non-technical matter in the English language and is for all purposes a literate person." Ivey could pass any fair literacy test. But he could not pass an unfair "literacy" test administered by registrar T. W. Cole. Cole administered an "academic test ... on matters pertaining to the Constitution of the United States and United States history and government." Questions included "On what date each year does [the U.S.] Congress convene?" and "What would be the total vote of two-thirds of the [U.S.] House and Senate?" This test was neither improvised nor clandestine. A typewritten version of it appears as exhibit A in the *Ivey v. Cole* case file. Walker reminded the court that North Carolina required only that voters be able to "read and write." Cole's civics test, he argued, was "not even a token attempt at compliance" with state law.⁶⁵

Ivey's complaint, filed in federal district court in Raleigh, alleged that Cole's "literacy" test was malicious, arbitrary, and unlawful and that, among other things, it violated Ivey's rights under the Fourteenth and Fifteenth Amendments to the U.S. Constitution. It alleged that Cole administered his "humiliating, harassing, degrading and unlawful" test "only to applicants of . . . the Negro race" and that "persons of . . . the white race . . . are registered without" having to take it. Ivey claimed to know "many other persons of his race who were denied registration by the defendant solely . . . because of the academic test" and further alleged that Cole "ha[d] not denied registration to any white person by reason of the academic test." Ivey sued Cole for five thousand dollars in compensatory and punitive damages.[66]

It was no accident that Ivey sued in federal court, not state court. Civil rights litigators in the South during this period uniformly preferred federal to state courts. Segregationists preferred state courts. As one African American noted in 1957, opponents of African American civil rights sought "to avoid federal courts whenever possible."[67]

The U.S. District Court in Raleigh was a comparatively congenial venue in which to present civil rights claims. Raleigh was a Piedmont city; civil rights generally fared better in the cities than in the countryside and generally fared better in North Carolina's Piedmont than in its northeastern counties. Raleigh was also home to Samuel S. Mitchell and Herman Taylor, two black lawyers whom Walker had met during the battle to integrate UNC's law school. Both Raleigh lawyers were impressive. Mitchell had been a top student at Howard University Law School, where Thurgood Marshall had studied. Taylor's résumé showed stints with the NAACP Legal Defense Fund and the North Carolina College for Negroes Law School faculty. When the two formed a law partnership in Raleigh in 1952, they quickly became the state's leading civil rights attorneys. Their willingness to collaborate on civil rights cases would prove extremely helpful to Walker over the next few years. As Walker fondly recalled, "I would hold conferences with them as though we were getting ten thousand dollars for a case. And it wasn't ten cents." The Raleigh lawyers also generously donated the services of their legal secretaries, providing Walker with needed administrative support.[68]

Ivey's suit sought monetary damages from the registrar. Similar suits had succeeded elsewhere in the South in the 1940s and early 1950s. Such suits had some advantages. Even before reaching court, they could attract media attention and publicize voting rights abuses. Courtroom victories, or out-of-court settlements, would produce much-needed money for reinvestment in the struggle. Here, a victory would force a racist registrar to pay five thousand dollars for his misdeeds, a sum hefty enough to make other racist registrars think twice before abusing their authority.[69]

Individual suits for damages, however, also had disadvantages. *Ivey v. Cole* did not directly challenge the literacy test as an institution or seek to enjoin the use of Cole's civics test. Even a favorable result would have left intact all of North Carolina's voting laws. Follow-up litigation, seeking monetary damages on a registrar-by-registrar, precinct-by-precinct, county-by-county basis was simply not affordable or feasible. Furthermore, civil lawsuits for money damages and no injunctive relief can drag on in the courts for years.

That is indeed what happened. The defense managed to deny justice by delaying it, again and again. In July 1963, a full seven years after it began, *Ivey v. Cole* was dismissed.[70]

In the second front that Walker opened in his legal war, he challenged the literacy test directly rather than challenging the registrar who administered it. His attack began in Northampton County, a northeastern county where whites accounted for about 36 percent of the population but where registered whites, as late as 1960, outnumbered registered nonwhites by more than a 5-to-1 ratio.[71] In the weeks preceding the Democratic primary on 26 May 1956, numerous Northampton County blacks contacted Walker with voter registration complaints. Several law cases resulted.

One of these cases featured an unexpected criminal defendant: Walker himself.

On 12 May 1956, two African Americans—a female nurse and a male college student—tried to register at the Seaboard precinct in Northampton County. After the registrar, Helen Taylor, rejected their applications, these two would-be voters contacted Walker, who accompanied them to the general store where the registrar conducted her official business. Taylor told Walker that she had not registered his clients because they had not satisfactorily answered her questions regarding the constitution. Walker protested that those questions were illegitimate and insisted that Taylor register the two applicants. The registrar asked him to leave. Walker pressed his registration arguments, underscoring his points with decisive hand motions. At that juncture, Walker later recalled, W. H. Taylor, the registrar's husband and the proprietor of the general store, called the police. Walker was arrested on two charges: disorderly conduct and trespassing.[72]

In Northampton County Recorder's Court, Walker's lawyer argued that the prosecution had failed to prove either of the charges. Walker had done nothing more "disorderly" than point his finger during an argument. Regarding trespassing, the defense contended that a voter registration office, even when located in a privately owned store, is inherently a public place. Walker had every right to be there.[73]

Trial judge Ballard S. Gay found Walker guilty as charged. Since Walker lived out of district and was not a potential voter in the Seaboard precinct, Judge Gay reasoned, he had no right to be in the registrar's office. "When outsiders start to interfere with the affairs of Northampton County," Gay declared from the bench, "we are not going to stand for it." He sentenced Walker to ninety days at hard labor on the roads and a one-hundred-dollar fine.[74]

Walker appealed for a *de novo* jury trial. When he got to superior court, he found that his criminal charge had mutated from "trespassing and disorderly conduct" to "assaulting a female." The evidence remained the same. Registrar Taylor testified that Walker had "sh[aken] his finger as he pointed across the desk." The jury found Walker guilty of "assaulting a female." Although Walker attempted to appeal once again, the North Carolina Supreme Court ruled that the deadline for filing an appeal had passed. Walker was fined five hundred dollars (plus court costs) and sent briefly to jail.[75]

Still the state did not rest. Citing the very same incident, prosecutors charged Walker with yet another crime: "disturbing an elections registrar in the performance of h[er] duties." Walker again was found guilty, briefly jailed, and fined again. Over the next couple of years, he was also arrested for property tax evasion in Halifax County, notwithstanding his protests that he owned no property there, and the seats and upholstery of his fifteen-year-old car were slashed beyond repair. Local whites, Walker declared, "don't intend to have any Negro lawyers practice in this section. They threw the book at me to try to cripple me and to drive me out. They used the criminal law to interfere with my practice of the law and as a psychological weapon to scare away clients and keep me broke." But Walker's grassroots litigation campaign continued.[76]

On 5 May 1956, one Saturday prior to the finger-shaking incident, Louise Lassiter entered the same W. H. Taylor general store in the Seaboard precinct of Northampton County and attempted to register to vote. She did so, she said, because she wished to help create a freer and fairer world for her three children. She had been inspired by the example of her husband, Lloyd, a local civil rights activist who had been registered to vote since 1950. Lloyd and Louise Lassiter were not wealthy. (The U.S. Supreme Court would later grant Louise "pauper" status, which Walker had requested so that the government would waive the printing costs associated with her federal appeal.) The Lassiters, however, were not the poorest of the poor. Indeed, they owned a farm, albeit a small one, near Seaboard. About three out of every four Northampton County black men worked on farms; relatively few blacks, however, owned the land they worked. Land ownership protected the Lassiters from economic intimidation. As Walker explained, "A lot of persons were denied [voter registration] but did not want their names attached [to test cases] for they were tenant farmers . . . or something." The Lassiters, in contrast, "had a little twenty-five-acre farm" and vowed to "fight it all the way."[77]

Between "farm wife" Louise Lassiter (as the press called her) and the ballot box, however, stood the registrar, Helen Taylor, who deemed Lassiter illiterate and refused to register her. Lassiter was not illiterate. She had completed a year of high school, which meant that she had more formal education than 70 percent of Northampton County adults at that time. Later, she was said to be able to read the U.S. Supreme Court opinion in her own case. Her alleged failing in Taylor's store was to mispronounce a few words from the North Carolina constitution, including the word *indictment*.[78]

Walker filed a lawsuit on behalf of Louise Lassiter against the Northampton County Board of Elections challenging the constitutionality of North Carolina's literacy test. Lassiter was not Walker's first choice for a test-case plaintiff, however. He preferred and had first sued on behalf of Alexander Faison, one of the two African Americans whose registration denial on 12 May had provoked Walker's finger-shaking argument with Helen Taylor. Faison's educational qualifications were less assailable than Lassiter's. She had finished just one year of high school; he was an undergraduate at the North Carolina College for Negroes, Walker's alma mater. Faison had the additional advantage of being a U.S. Air Force veteran, a credential that may have sat well with patriotic judges and jurors. But Faison's case tripped on a technicality. He apparently lived on the wrong side of a road and thus was ineligible to register in the Seaboard precinct. By March 1957, this defect had surfaced, the Faison case had collapsed, and Walker, along with his

Raleigh collaborators Taylor and Mitchell, had filed *Louise Lassiter v. Northampton County Board of Elections* in federal district court.[79]

Although Lassiter was not Walker's top choice, he had reasons to select this "farm wife" from the "churchfull of folks" in Northampton County who might have served as a test-case client. She was willing. She was poised enough to make a good witness. And, as Walker later noted, she "was a mother" who was "typical enough" to be effective in the national court of public opinion. (Although Walker acted locally, he thought nationally.)[80]

Walker hoped that the *Lassiter* challenge to the constitutionality of the literacy test would induce federal judges to rewrite North Carolina's electoral law. One week before *Lassiter* was to be heard by a three-judge federal court, however, the case induced state legislators to do some rewriting. On 12 April 1957, the North Carolina General Assembly, fearing that Walker might well prevail in court, removed some of the most obviously unfair elements from the state's literacy test. Prior to the 1957 revision, would-be registrants had to demonstrate literacy "to the satisfaction" of registrars. Rejected applicants had no recourse other than civil court appeal—a cumbersome procedure that could rarely provide relief before election day. The 1957 revision deleted the phrase "to the satisfaction of the registrar." It also opened new avenues for appeal. The rejected applicant now had rapid recourse to the local board of elections and, if still unsatisfied, to the local superior court. Both county-level bodies could reverse the local registrar's decision. The 1957 revision also deleted North Carolina's grandfather clause, which had remained on the books even though the U.S. Supreme Court had ruled grandfather clauses unconstitutional in 1915.[81]

For Walker, the 1957 revision was a mixed result. On the positive side, the revision appeared to reduce the discretionary authority of registrars and to facilitate timely literacy test appeals. In the future, blacks would sometimes win these appeals, both in local boards of election and in the North Carolina Supreme Court. Although Walker hoped that *Lassiter* would ultimately achieve much more, he could rightly have felt proud that, even before a court hearing, his grassroots litigation campaign had achieved tangible results.[82] On the negative side, however, the 1957 revision offered a deeply flawed remedy to persons denied the right to register to vote. According to the new measure, a person denied the right to register could appeal to the local board of elections but had to initiate this procedure "by 5:00 P.M. on the day following the day of denial"—an extraordinarily short period of time. Would-be voters who missed this deadline apparently would lose the right to appeal.[83] In addition, the 1957 revision made it much less likely that Lassiter would win her test case. The measure was clearly a preemptive response to Walker's litigation. Legislative supporters of the revision warned that, unless the bill passed, the state's literacy test "would likely be declared unconstitutional" in *Lassiter*. After passage of the revised law, the state's attorney general observed that the measure would "strengthen the hand" of the defense (the board of elections) in *Lassiter*. He was right.[84]

Lassiter resumed. The ideal test case, from Walker's perspective, would presumably have featured a diabolically racist registrar and a perfectly literate applicant. In Helen Taylor and Louise Lassiter, Walker had neither. When a defense lawyer at the federal court hearing asked Taylor if she gave "everyone—white, black and Indian—the literacy test," the "stout smiling registrar" replied, "Yes sir." Two white defense witnesses from the Seaboard precinct testified that Taylor had indeed made them take the literacy test. Taylor even recalled rejecting an illiterate white registrant back in 1952. Walker did not challenge this evidence.[85]

Doubts also emerged regarding Louise Lassiter's literacy. On the stand, she was asked to read part of the state's constitution. She did so, but "somewhat haltingly." A demeaning spelling quiz followed. Lassiter answered "c-h-a-r-t-y" for "charity" and declined to attempt some more difficult words.[86]

It is possible that the evidentiary weaknesses in *Lassiter* reflect Walker's inexperience and lack of resources. He was new to civil rights litigation and was learning on the job. He lacked the time and staff needed to sift through the "hundreds" of possible test cases open to him, looking for the perfect one.[87] Perhaps, however, the evidentiary weaknesses in *Lassiter* were deliberate. After all, much stronger fact situations existed, as Walker well knew. The Ernest Ivey case discussed previously featured a more literate plaintiff and, in the absurd civics exam, a far more abusive application of the literacy test than was evident in *Lassiter*. Yet when Walker sought a test case for his constitutional challenge, he chose Lassiter, not Ivey. For Walker, the danger of too strong a fact situation was that it could divert attention from the larger issue: the inherent injustice, and unconstitutionality, of the literacy test. If Ivey had been his client, Walker could have won the case on the facts but still lost his bid to strike down the literacy test as a matter of law.

Walker's decision to downplay the particular abuses suffered by Louise Lassiter arguably mirrored the NAACP's approach in *Brown v. Board of Education*. In that case, civil rights lawyers emphasized the inherent inequality and general destructiveness of segregated schooling rather than any particular examples of inequality in specific school districts. Had the attack emphasized particular disparities in funding and facilities, courts could have remedied those inequalities without addressing the underlying problem of de jure racial segregation. In a similar fashion, Walker and company sought to demonstrate not that the literacy test had been unjustly applied against Louise Lassiter but rather that it was intrinsically unjust and unconstitutional. As the court understood it, the "contention of counsel for plaintiffs . . . is not that the literacy test was discriminatingly applied . . . but that it is inherently void."[88]

Because *Lassiter* alleged that a state law violated the federal Constitution, it was heard by a three-judge federal court panel. (One of the three was Wilson Warlick, who, as a superior court judge, had presided over the Greenwich Village padlocking trial.) That panel found that North Carolina's *original* literacy test was indeed "violative of the . . . 14th and 15th Amendments to the Constitution of the United States." But that original literacy test no longer existed; the 1957 revision had superseded it. Was the new literacy test, like the old one, unconstitutional? The federal panel would not say. Instead, it directed Louise Lassiter to exhaust the new state-level administrative remedies that the 1957 revision had established. If still unsatisfied, she should then take her case to the North Carolina Supreme Court for an authoritative interpretation of the new law, in light of the state constitution. Only after passing through all of these state-level steps without obtaining relief, the panel said, could Lassiter return to federal court.[89]

Less than two weeks after this ruling, Louise Lassiter returned to Helen Taylor's office and sought, once again, to register to vote. Lassiter may have dreaded failing another literacy test. Walker, who accompanied his client, feared just the reverse: that the registrar would deem Lassiter literate this time and register her to vote, thereby mooting her test case. Determined to return to federal court, Walker advised his client to refuse the test.

Lassiter declined to take the literacy test, claiming that it was unconstitutional. She thereby kept her case alive, but it now was a different case. Future appeals, including the one heard by the Supreme Court of the United States, would not even mention Taylor's 1956 rejection of Lassiter for mispronouncing "indictment" and a few other words. Her case now concerned the constitutionality of the (comparatively reasonable) 1957 revision and Taylor's quite reasonable decision to reject Lassiter for declining to take a required test.

In order to return to federal court, Lassiter first had to exhaust all of the new state-level remedies. She did so, appealing in turn to the Northampton County Board of Elections, the Northampton County superior court, and the North Carolina Supreme Court.[90] Her lawyers' principal argument was that the North Carolina literacy test violated federal guarantees against discrimination and disfranchisement, especially those contained in the Fourteenth and Fifteenth Amendments.[91]

Lawyers for the Northampton County Board of Elections denied that Lassiter's case had anything to do with racial discrimination or disfranchisement. They called the suit "an action brought for the advancement of illiteracy." They argued that the 1957 revision was valid under both the U.S. and the North Carolina constitutions and that it was consummately fair. After all, Lassiter had received—but had declined—three different invitations to prove that she could read. And, in a polemical discussion of Reconstruction history, they argued that the literacy test was urgently needed. "Prior to 1900," they asserted, "the Constitution of North Carolina contained no express requirement of literacy." But the "outrages perpetrated upon the people of this State during the Tragic Era of Reconstruction" taught North Carolinians "what it means to have the power of the ballot placed in the hands of illiterate people controlled by unscrupulous men supported by the armed might of the Federal Government." Fortunately, they argued, wise North Carolinians remedied this "intolerable" situation by adopting the literacy test in order to "safeguard elections from the power of illiteracy."[92] This historical argument cast doubt on their denial that the case had anything to do with race.

The North Carolina Supreme Court ruled against Lassiter in April 1958. Chief Justice Wallace Winborne's opinion cited *Guinn v. United States*, a 1915 U.S. Supreme Court case, to support the proposition that literacy tests were constitutional. "No time need be spent on the question of the validity of the literacy test," the Court opined in *Guinn*, "since . . . its establishment was but the exercise by the state of a lawful power . . . not subject to our [federal court] supervision."[93]

Having exhausted all North Carolina appeals, Walker set his sights on the Supreme Court of the United States. In order to get there, however, he would need help. Once again, he called on his Raleigh collaborators Mitchell and Taylor. The three lawyers worked together on the U.S. Supreme Court brief; Mitchell, a more experienced lawyer than Walker, would argue the case in Washington. But Walker also needed money. His local civil rights group was no NAACP; it had neither formal membership nor dues. Financially, it was a dry well. And by the time of the *Lassiter* appeal, Walker's willingness to litigate civil rights cases *gratis*—not to mention his need to fend off personal legal attacks (and replace his slashed automobile upholstery)—had taken its toll.

Walker contacted the national office of the NAACP in the fall of 1957 and requested three thousand dollars "to make it possible . . . to continue . . . efforts to secure civil rights for the Negro people in Eastern North Carolina." The NAACP responded coolly. The group had many competing priorities. It was also understandably reluctant to fund grassroots litigators who operated independently rather than in concert with NAACP strategists. Privately dubbing Walker a "lone wolf," the group respectfully declined his funding request.[94]

Walker then looked locally. He convinced the Reverend Alexander Mosely, a black pastor in Weldon, to head what he called the Walker-Lassiter Defense Fund. (Walker believed that he "could not ethically be connected with fundraising for my own cases . . . they would take my license." He happily left the fundraising to others. "I never bothered with the money," he later quipped. "That's one reason I stayed pretty clean.") Mosely was the vice president of Walker's local civil rights group. He also chaired a local group that was affiliated with the Southern Conference Educational Fund (SCEF), an interracial civil rights organization that opposed "all forms of segregation and discrimination . . . in all southern states." Mosely persuaded SCEF's national field secretaries, the white husband-and-wife team of Carl and Anne Braden, that *Lassiter* had landmark potential. SCEF joined the Walker-Lassiter Defense Fund in an "advisory capacity for publicity and fund raising." In 1958, the organization produced and distributed a pamphlet entitled "North Carolina Mother Is Denied Right to Vote," which related the Lassiter-Walker saga and solicited financial contributions to their legal defense fund. The pamphlet elicited responses from as far away as Oklahoma and generated some much-needed funding for the appeal to the U.S. Supreme Court.[95]

That appeal failed. In June 1959, the U.S. Supreme Court unanimously rejected all of Louise Lassiter's constitutional claims. Justice William O. Douglas, writing for the Court, noted that states traditionally enjoyed broad discretion to set nondiscriminatory suffrage standards. Age, criminal records, and length of in-state residency were examples of reasonable, race-neutral factors that states could legitimately consider when determining suffrage eligibility. Literacy was another. "[I]n our society where newspapers, periodicals, books, and other printed matter . . . debate campaign issues," the Court reasoned, "a State might conclude that only those who are literate should exercise the franchise." Justice Douglas also noted that, at the time of his writing, nineteen states—spanning a cultural and geographical range from Alabama and Mississippi to Massachusetts and Oregon—used literacy tests. Expressing no opinion concerning the wisdom of such tests, Douglas held that they were not inherently unconstitutional.[96]

Lassiter was, at best, a mixed result for Walker. The case's negative consequences were conspicuous. Far from slaying the literacy test, *Lassiter* had inadvertently strengthened it by eliciting a unanimous Supreme Court seal of approval. Coming as it did from the highest court in the land—a unanimous court at that—*Lassiter* appeared to entrench literacy tests in all states that employed them, not just in North Carolina.

But the ruling also contained some subtle silver linings. Justice Douglas's opinion affirmed the Court's previously stated finding that Congress had the authority to oversee state suffrage requirements. Years later, supporters of the bill that became the Voting Rights Act of 1965 invoked this passage from *Lassiter* in defense of that far-reaching bill's constitutionality. *Lassiter* also may have persuaded civil rights activists that, as a practical matter, it was the U.S. Congress that had to destroy the literacy test, since the courts had refused to do so.[97]

Following *Lassiter*, Walker did not quit. "See, you had to keep coming back," he reasoned. "You can't stop . . . when you've [got] massive state resistance." Although he could no longer argue that North Carolina's literacy test was unconstitutional per se, he could argue that state officials enforced the literacy test unconstitutionally. Indeed, multiple passages in *Lassiter* warned that "a literacy test, fair on its face, may be employed to perpetuate that discrimination which the Fifteenth Amendment was designed to uproot." Walker read these passages as an implicit invitation to challenge unfair applications of the literacy test. He soon would do just that.[98]

In May 1960, one year after the U.S. Supreme Court decision in *Lassiter*, North Carolina's voter registration books were opened once again, for that year's primary elections. Nancy Bazemore, a forty-seven-year-old African American woman, tried to register in the Woodville precinct of Bertie County. Like other northeastern counties, Bertie County had a high percentage of nonwhite residents but a low percentage of nonwhite registered voters. Blacks outnumbered whites in Bertie County in 1960 by a 3-to-2 ratio. Among registered voters in the county that year, however, whites outnumbered blacks by almost 9 to 1, reflecting both a strikingly low percentage of nonwhite potential voters registered (11 percent), and a strikingly high percentage of white potential voters registered (104 percent), the latter figure reflecting the county's failure to remove dead or departed voters from the rolls.[99]

A particularly artful application of the literacy test helped Bertie County whites suppress nonwhite registration. Recall that Louise Lassiter, in Northampton County, had been asked to read aloud from the state's constitution. In contrast, Nancy Bazemore and others in the Woodville precinct had to take dictation as the registrar, William H. Hoggard, recited from the state's constitution. Spelling counted. Hoggard graded.

This "dictation" form of the literacy test had long rankled African Americans in northeastern North Carolina. Walker's local civil rights group had repeatedly asked the state's attorney general for "an official statement of policy on methods of administering literacy tests." In particular, the group wanted to know "whether registrars could require prospective voters to spell from dictation," as many northeastern registrars did. Early in 1960, with the primaries approaching, the group renewed its longstanding request. The attorney general finally opined in March 1960 that dictation tests in which spelling counted were "illegal" and could not be "a requirement or prerequisite for the registration of voters" in North Carolina. Bertie County, however, ignored the ruling. In May 1960, just two months after the attorney general's announcement, Nancy Bazemore and other black registrants had to take precisely the sorts of tests that the attorney general had banned.[100]

The Bertie County registrar graded the dictation test harshly. Hoggard found some misspellings in Bazemore's transcription and declared that she had failed the test and was thus ineligible to vote. Bazemore was prepared for this outcome. Quite likely, Walker had coached her on how to respond. The 1957 revision of the literacy test law, which

Walker's previous litigation had provoked, allowed registrants to appeal their rejections to local boards of elections but required that a written notice of appeal had to be filed with the rejecting registrar by 5:00 P.M. on the day following the denial. Bazemore did not wait that long. She gave Hoggard "immediate written notice of appeal . . . in her own hand writing." (The irony of someone writing well enough to file an appeal in her own hand after failing the written portion of a literacy test was surely lost on the registrar.)[101]

The following Saturday Bazemore entered the Bertie County Board of Elections to appeal her registration denial. Walker accompanied her. A member of the board sat down and took out a copy of the state's constitution. Across the table, paper and pencil in hand, Nancy Bazemore "assumed a position of readiness to try to write." The board member began to read from the constitution and "directed the applicant to write down what he read to her." Bazemore's pencil had scarcely begun to scratch when her attorney announced that his client refused to submit to such a test. Bazemore put her pencil down. The board rejected her application. Walker appealed and appealed again, until he reached the North Carolina Supreme Court.[102]

Walker's brief for the North Carolina Supreme Court, which he prepared along with Samuel S. Mitchell, attacked the literacy test *as applied* in the Woodville precinct and Bertie County. He reminded the court that the state's literacy test merely required that prospective voters be able to "read and write." It required proficiency neither in the taking of dictation nor in spelling. To allow registrars to add transcription and spelling proficiency tests to the simple reading and writing test prescribed in state law would constitute an illegitimate delegation of legislative power to local executive branch officials, Walker argued. This would violate the separation of powers mandated by the state's constitution. It would also empower local officials to act in ways that were unconstitutionally "arbitrary, discriminatory, oppressive and unreasonable."[103]

Walker also argued that Bertie County officials applied the literacy test in racially discriminatory ways. Whereas white applicants were not "required to submit to dictation," Bazemore and other African Americans had to take the dictation and spelling test "solely because of [their] race, to wit: the Negro race."[104]

Then Walker called upon his experience as an African American man in the Jim Crow South. He implicitly invited the justices to close their law books for a moment and consider the demeaning nature of a dictation test administered to a black registrant by a white registrar in Bertie County. It was "harassing" and "embarrassing," Walker contended, to have to "play 'secretary' while the elections official dictates from the Constitution." Even assuming that all registrars read fluently—an assumption that Walker was not ready to concede—inconsistent pronunciations and speech habits could complicate transcribers' tasks. With no copy to check, the registrant had "no way of knowing the correctness of the elections official's reading or calling of words." Dictation could be given "at a rate of speed to the satisfaction of the officials." Applicants with hearing impairments faced additional humiliation. When the time came to grade the test, standards of evaluation were "left entirely to the whims and caprices of the elections officials." To make matters worse, the skill evaluated in these tests—transcription—bore no reasonable relationship to the act of voting. To vote, the citizen merely had to "make a cross mark (x) in a square in the proper place on the ballot."[105]

Walker and Bazemore won. Although the North Carolina Supreme Court assumed the legitimacy of the state's literacy test, it found Bertie County's application of that test to be unreasonable. The key issue for the court was the definition of the verb "to write." By statute, registrants had to be able to "read and write." Walker's appellate brief had urged the justices to look up the word "write" in their dictionaries. They did so and found, as Walker had, that the most widely accepted meaning of the verb was "to form, as characters, or to trace the letters or words of, on paper, parchment, etc., with a pen or pencil." The court concluded that the only reasonable way in which a registrar could apply the "writing" portion of the literacy test was to ask the applicant to copy "in his own handwriting any section [of the North Carolina constitution,] with such section before him for reference." After all, the court reasoned, it was a literacy test, "not a spelling test. Furthermore," the court added, "the taking of dictation, even in longhand, requires skill, learning and practice over and beyond the ordinary process of writing." The court concluded that the literacy test, "as administered by [Bertie County officials,] is unreasonable and beyond the intent of the statute."[106]

In addition to invalidating the specific form of the literacy test employed in Bertie County, the court sought to establish uniform statewide standards for the literacy test—standards that Walker and other activists had long sought. The court decreed that, in the reading portion of the test, applicants could be asked to "utter aloud," in English, any section of the North Carolina constitution, from a legible copy furnished by the test giver. In the writing portion, applicants could be asked "to write in a reasonably legible hand any section of the Constitution put before him or her." The grading standard for these tests was to be "reasonable proficiency," not perfection. "The occasional misspelling and mispronouncing of more difficult words should not necessarily disqualify."[107]

The court went further, well beyond the issues raised by *Bazemore*. Responding to activist complaints that some registrars deliberately slowed down the registration process in order to obstruct large-scale black registration, it ruled that the "length of the [literacy] tests should not be such as to unnecessarily delay others waiting to register." Finally, the court hinted that the state's Board of Elections in Raleigh might wish to finish what the court had begun by prescribing additional statewide "rules and regulations for administering" the literacy test.[108]

Bazemore was a clear victory for Walker and voting rights. To be sure, plenty of room for discrimination remained. Perhaps most troubling was the matter of who had to take the literacy test in the first place. Many whites in the region "took it for granted" that they could register without submitting to a literacy test. The *Bazemore* ruling somewhat confirmed that assumption. "It would be unrealistic," the court wrote, "to say that the [literacy] test *must* be administered to all applicants for registration." A political science professor of "known and recognized capabilities," for instance, need not be forced to take the literacy test when registering to vote. The statute "only requires that the applicant *have* the ability" to read and write, the court noted (emphasis in original). "If the registrar in good faith knows that applicant has the requisite ability, no test is necessary." Although the court warned registrars not to abuse this discretion in discriminatory ways, racist registrars, even after *Bazemore*, still had wiggle room.[109] But that wiggle room was narrowing.

The "favorable decision" in *Bazemore,* reported the black press, struck "another blow at using the literacy test to discriminate against a registrant on the basis of color." James Walker deserved much of the credit. Reporting enthusiastically on the *Bazemore* outcome, Durham's *Carolina Times,* an African American newspaper, hoped that "Negro citizens will soon awaken to the fact that many of the freedoms they now enjoy have been secured by the determination of hard working and sacrificing Negro lawyers." Praise did not come from African Americans alone. The North Carolina Supreme Court's *Bazemore* ruling explicitly complimented Walker for having "well advised" his client.[110]

"A people who vote is a people with hope," wrote African American journalist John W. Fleming in an optimistic 1961 survey of the black "political awakening" then under way in North Carolina. Black Tar Heels were voting, running for office, and even winning local elections in numbers not seen since Reconstruction. One of the main architects of this black political renaissance, Fleming thought, was James R. Walker Jr., who had "led the fight for voting and other rights" in northeastern North Carolina since his arrival there in 1955. "Mr. Walker," Fleming wrote admiringly, "is fast becoming 'Mr. Civil Rights' in Eastern Carolina."[111]

Walker's program blended two activities that civil rights historians generally treat separately: grassroots mobilization and appellate litigation. Unlike most grassroots activists, Walker was a trained lawyer who worked within the legal system at its highest levels. Unlike most civil rights litigators, Walker operated at the grassroots level in the community that he served. This strategy enabled him to work closely with clients and add sympathetic, personal touches to his appellate advocacy.

Walker's operations were poorly funded but not unsophisticated. He consciously framed individual test cases to fit an overarching, though ever-evolving, legal strategy. Although some of his decisions can be second-guessed, he achieved impressive results. His litigation showcased the professional skills of black lawyers. It publicized voting rights abuses. It inspired civil rights supporters to continue fighting for justice. More tangibly, it prompted both the General Assembly and the Supreme Court of North Carolina to make the state's voter registration rules less discriminatory. The resulting reforms, even when discounted for unenthusiastic implementation, were substantial. They reduced registrar discretion, clarified the rules governing the literacy test's administration, and made it easier for rejected applicants to appeal. Even Walker's greatest defeat had beneficial consequences. The U.S. Supreme Court's endorsement of the literacy test in *Lassiter v. Northampton County Board of Elections* (1959) helped to spur passage of the Voting Rights Act of 1965.[112]

Indeed, pound for pound and dollar for dollar, James R. Walker Jr. may have been as effective as any civil rights lawyer in the country in expanding African American voting rights. The NAACP's legal team unquestionably produced far more, but it enjoyed obvious advantages: a comparatively huge budget, an extensive network of local affiliates, a large staff of experienced civil rights lawyers, and plenty of academic experts willing to assemble sociological arguments for forensic use. But Walker's grassroots litigation had some less obvious countervailing advantages. Some NAACP cases stumbled due to the unreliability of the local lawyers with whom the national office had to collaborate. Walker had no such worries; he *was* the local lawyer. Other NAACP cases foundered due to divisions or weaknesses within local African American communities. Walker, a leader of the local African American community, did not have this problem either. Grassroots litigation might not have been a viable stand-alone alternative to the litigation program of national civil rights groups. But, as Walker's story suggests, it was an important supplement. Scholars should take grassroots litigation more seriously. In North Carolina alone, the accomplishments of such grassroots civil rights litigators as Harry E. Groves, Samuel S. Mitchell, and Herman Taylor—all contemporaries of Walker—deserve further study.

Walker's grassroots litigation campaign won modest national recognition. Lawyers' groups as far away as California and Michigan invited him to speak about "the Negro Lawyer in the South" and similar topics. The National Lawyers Guild, a group of liberal legal activists, named him Lawyer of the Year in 1978. Even the North Carolina branch of the NAACP, the organization that dismissed Walker as a "lone wolf" during the *Lassiter* case, later honored Walker with its Distinguished Service Award.[113]

The voting rights movement that Walker helped to organize in northeastern North Carolina remained active through the mid-1960s. Walker, however, moved on to other pursuits, disillusioned by what he called the "intrusion" of too many competing civil rights organizations, groups that had funds and national profiles but little feel for local conditions and little respect for local leadership. The legal team that represented Halifax County blacks in a 1964 voting rights suit did not include Walker. It did, however, feature prominent attorneys from the North, including William Kunstler, a celebrated legal activist from New York City whose other clients included Martin Luther King Jr., Malcolm X, and the "Chicago Seven" activists arrested at the 1968 Democratic National Convention. Walker's grassroots litigation, in other words, gave way to the more traditional arrangement whereby distant civil rights lawyers provided legal representation for local civil rights activists.[114]

As for the literacy test, the federal Voting Rights Act of 1965 gravely wounded it and follow-up measures, passed by Congress in 1970 and 1975, laid it to rest. Louise Lassiter did not have to wait so long. In May 1960, four years after her first attempt, she passed the literacy test and successfully registered to vote.[115]

Chapter 8

Native Americans and School Desegregation
The Chavis *Case in Robeson County*

The post–World War II battles of African American civil rights activists such as James R. Walker Jr. inspired a host of other individuals, including many who were not African American, to resist what they viewed as oppression. Braxton Chavis, a housepainter and construction worker from Robeson County, North Carolina, is a case in point. As of mid-1978, when Robeson County education officials prepared school assignments for the next academic year, Chavis had been sending his children to Prospect School for seventeen years. He was determined to see his three youngest children continue at Prospect, where he, too, had studied. Acting under federal desegregation mandates, however, county officials reassigned the Chavis children to Oxendine School, six miles away. Chavis and his family would not be moved. When classes started, they engaged in an act of civil disobedience, defiantly returning to Prospect day after day, even though the school withheld books and instruction from them. By late September 1978, county officials could take no more. They arrested Braxton Chavis and seven other parents for "failing to cause their children to attend the school to which they were assigned."[1]

By no means were the Chavises the only opponents of school desegregation in the post–*Brown v. Board of Education* South. As historians

---

Elizabeth Halligan Black, Kate Auletta, Hank Bahr, Kelly Carraway, Andrew Devore, Maurice Falls, Laura McAlister, Lane Oatey, Emily Pesses, Mark Pustay, and Alan Williams contributed to this chapter.

have carefully documented, southern white opposition was, if not universal, certainly "massive." The historical literature is rich with images of white legislators signing segregationist manifestos, white governors standing in schoolhouse doors, white mobs engaging in "massive resistance," and white parents hustling their children off to private schools and moving to homogeneous suburbs.[2]

Not one of these stock images fits the Robeson County case. The Chavises were not white. They were Native American. A fervent sense of ethnic particularity underlay their opposition to school desegregation. It also informed their understanding of the legal issues in their case. They insisted that their ethnicity exempted them from desegregation orders.

The story of *State v. Chavis* has never been told. It deserves telling, however, for it casts new light on the social and legal history of school desegregation. *Chavis* contributes intriguing new hues to the traditionally black-and-white portrait of school desegregation. Recent studies of such groups as Mexican Americans and Chinese Americans have deepened historical understanding of civil rights and public education in the United States. The present study continues this productive scholarly trend.[3]

Chavis challenges the assumption that all nonwhites during the civil rights era supported school desegregation. Recent studies have revealed pockets of African American opposition. *Chavis* reinforces these studies' important message: that opposition to desegregation, like support for it, was multicultural.[4]

This chapter also highlights the centrality of public schools to community identity in twentieth-century America. It demonstrates again how complex and difficult it was to achieve the worthy dream of racial justice through school desegregation. It illustrates how the rise of ethnic particularism in the mid-1960s complicated the integrative ideal of the mainstream civil rights movement. It shows how elite, white sympathy for ethnic particularism during the 1970s amplified separatist voices within such marginalized communities as the Native Americans of southeastern North Carolina. It also illuminates a "testimonial-therapeutic" function of litigation, whereby courtroom protest, when received respectfully, can help reconcile protestors to unwanted policies. The willingness of North Carolina lawyers and judges to listen attentively to Native American separatist grievances enhanced the protestors' esteem for the legal system and calmed their protests.

Finally, this chapter reinforces two related points from the previous chapter. First, the federal government played a much larger local role in the post–World War II period than it did in the years covered in part I of this book. Even cases litigated in state courts, such as *State v. Chavis*, occurred in the shadow of federal law. Second, the enlarged federal presence during the decades following World War II amplified the legal voices of minority groups in the South. This was obviously true in the case of James R. Walker Jr., whose civil rights efforts accorded with trends in federal law. But even groups, such as the defendants in *Chavis*, whose legal objectives clashed with the pro-integration thrust of federal law, were able to present legal claims more assertively as a result of federal developments. Read alongside the story of James R. Walker Jr., then, the *Chavis* story suggests that "top-down," Washington-led civil rights history and "bottom-up" grassroots civil rights history were not dichotomous. They were mutually reinforcing.

Robeson County sits in southeastern North Carolina, close to the South Carolina state line. In the 1960s and 1970s, about 75 percent of Robeson County residents lived in rural areas. Farming and nondurable-goods manufacturing failed to deliver prosperity. Only 52 percent of the county's homes had flush toilets; 65 percent of its houses were rated "substandard."[5]

The county's most distinctive feature was probably its triracial composition. No racial group held a majority. Whites accounted for about 42 percent of the 1970 population; they predominated in the eastern part of Robeson County and in most sizable towns. African Americans accounted for 26 percent of the county's population but were so widely dispersed that no township had a black majority. Native Americans—whom we shall call the Lumbee, the name that most of them used for much of the twentieth century—accounted for more than 31 percent of the county's population. They were the most segregated of the three groups. Most Lumbees lived either in rural communities in the western part of the county or in the west-central town of Pembroke.[6]

Although the three groups shared the county, one group—whites—enjoyed a virtual lock on political power, at least through the early 1960s. Disfranchisement helped to perpetuate white political power.

Robeson County's distinctive mix of people produced a distinctive brand of segregation. Movie theaters reserved main floor seating for whites and divided the balconies into separate black and Indian sections.

Neither Native Americans nor blacks could sit down at soda fountains. According to a 1962 report, three-way segregation in Robeson and surrounding counties prevailed in "most tax supported institutions and public facilities," including hospitals, recreation facilities, eating places, barbershops, churches, and public schools.[7]

When contemplating Native American history, most people think of such federally recognized tribes as the Navajo, Sioux, and Cherokee; they think of headdresses and reservations, treaties and tepees. None of these images fits the twentieth-century Lumbee. The Lumbee had no traditional language, no traditional dress, and no distinguishing physical features. They never signed a treaty. They never lived on a reservation. They received no benefits from the Bureau of Indian Affairs. Nonetheless, they had no doubt that they were Native Americans. Their "Indianness" may have been, as several observers phrased it, "a state of mind, a self-concept," but this "self-concept" was universally accepted in southeastern North Carolina. All locals, regardless of race, recognized certain communities, speech patterns, and surnames as distinctly "Indian."[8]

The Lumbee are of murky descent. Some scholars consider them offshoots of the Eastern Sioux. Others propose Cherokee descent—or Iroquois. Or Algonquin. Or Waccamaw, Waxhaw, Cheraw, or Sissipahaw. Some scholars trace part of the Lumbee lineage to runaway slaves; to Spanish or Portuguese stragglers; or, most famously, to the inhabitants of the Lost Colony of Roanoke Island, an English settlement that mysteriously vanished shortly after its founding in 1587 off the coast of today's North Carolina.[9]

Unlike such southeastern tribes as the Cherokee and Choctaw, the Lumbee were not subject to forced removal in the 1830s, perhaps because they held land individually, not communally. Nonetheless, the Lumbee, like other North Carolina Indians, suffered legal disabilities, beginning in the colonial era and intensifying during the Age of Jackson, when the distinctions between whites and "people of color" intensified. By the middle of the nineteenth century, on issues ranging from suffrage to marriage to the right to bear arms, "Indians," like free blacks, were second-class citizens.[10]

Discrimination reinforced solidarity. It also generated militancy. In the 1860s and 1870s, a Lumbee named Henry Berry Lowry led a swamp-based guerrilla band on a decade-long, antiwhite thieving-and-killing spree. Lowry became—and remains—a Lumbee hero.[11]

The Lumbees' long and only partially successful struggle for tribal recognition further reinforced group identity. In 1885, North Carolina officially recognized the group as the "Croatan Indians of Robeson County." The state renamed them "Indians of Robeson County" in 1911 and "Cherokee Indians of Robeson County" in 1913. Finally, in 1953, the state's General Assembly settled on "Lumbee Indians," after the county's Lumber River.[12]

Lumbee pleas for full *federal* recognition fell short. In the Lumbee Act of 1956, Congress formally acknowledged the group's designation as the "Lumbee Indians of North Carolina" but refused to loosen the purse strings for them. "Nothing in this Act shall make such [Lumbee] Indians eligible for any services performed by the United States for Indians because of their status as Indians," the act specified, "and none of the statutes of the United States which affect Indians because of their status as Indians shall be applicable to the Lumbee Indians."[13]

Segregated schools reinforced Lumbee identity. Post–Civil War Robeson County operated separate schools for whites and nonwhites. Indians and African Americans shared the nonwhite schools. That changed in 1885, when the North Carolina General Assembly recognized Robeson County Native Americans as a distinct group and established separate schools for them. The 1885 legislative act empowered Native Americans to establish "school committees of their own race and color" and to "select teachers of their own choice." Much of the land, money, materials, and labor necessary for the construction and operation of segregated Indian schools came from Robeson County Lumbees. With every acre, dollar, and day's work contributed, the Lumbees' emotional investment in "their" schools increased.[14]

Schools were central to Lumbee identity. They provided community groups with meeting places; offered much-needed employment to Lumbee teachers, administrators, and staff; and facilitated the transmission of Lumbee culture to new generations. "It meant something having Indian teachers standing in front of Indian students," the daily *Robesonian* reported in the early 1970s. "The schools gave identity to the Lumbee Indians."[15]

Brown v. Board of Education (1954) famously held that de jure public school segregation was inherently unconstitutional. In North Carolina, however, two early post-*Brown* statutes—the Pupil Assignment Act of 1955 and the Pearsall Plan of 1956—made quick and effective desegregation impossible. These acts deliberately scattered authority for public education among the state's 140-plus school districts. They offered subtle support to anti-integrationists statewide and established complicated administrative procedures that discouraged voluntary student transfers. The legislature's clear intent was to perpetuate segregation.[16]

Inspired by *Brown*, integrationist Lumbees challenged school segregation in Robeson and surrounding counties. Lumbee activism of this sort was rare. Previously, according to a 1962 report, there had been "little or no organized activity among the Lumbees." School debates, spurred by the federal courts, awakened Lumbee activism.[17]

Lumbee attacks on school segregation in the decade following *Brown* mirrored the era's black civil rights movement. Lumbees organized sit-ins that recalled the famous Greensboro protests, both in tactics (peaceful civil disobedience) and objective (integration). Like integrationist blacks, integrationist Lumbees received extensive support from national advocacy groups, most importantly the Philadelphia-based American Friends Service Committee (AFSC) and the New York–based Association on American Indian Affairs (AAIA). Lumbee activists won support from high-profile liberals and litigated successfully in federal courts.[18]

Clearly, many Lumbees were sincere integrationists. "[T]he only way to really solve this school problem," one Lumbee father observed in 1962, "is for all the children in our community, white, Negro and Indian, to go to school together." Many other Lumbees, however, opposed desegregation. "There was some resistance on the part of some of the Indian community to these [integrationist] efforts," one lawyer privately reported in 1963. AFSC staffers similarly noted that the Lumbee "were not fully determined to seek desegregated schooling for their children. They were still thinking somewhat in terms of . . . an Indian school for their children."[19]

Although Lumbee opinion split between integrationist and segregationist during these years, only integrationist voices were heard publicly. Three factors explain this imbalance. First, the persistence of segregation for years after *Brown* nurtured integrationist outrage. Segregationist Lumbees, satisfied with the status quo, had no reason to stage sit-ins. Integrationist Lumbees, dissatisfied, had ample reason to do so. Second, the contemporary African American civil rights movement provided an influential model of protest. Through the early 1960s, this model was almost entirely integrationist. Third, both of the national organizations that supported the Lumbee school campaigns of the early 1960s—the

AFSC and the AAIA—were unwavering advocates of integration. Their participation amplified the voices of Lumbee integrationists. Through "counseling and work with the Indians," the AFSC sought to strengthen Lumbee integrationism. Similarly, the AAIA, which paid the Lumbees' legal bills, made sure that its contributions aided integration. As Richard Schifter, AAIA general counsel, explained in a 1960 letter to the local North Carolina lawyers who would handle the details of the Lumbee school litigation, "We can only support a request for full integration, not for separate but equal facilities."[20]

The AAIA's unswerving commitment to school integration is representative of a brand of civil rights liberalism—call it "mid-century liberalism"—that dominated American reform thought from World War II through the mid-1960s. In large measure, it was a principled reaction to the Nazis' "master race" ideology abroad and the mistreatment of Japanese Americans and African Americans at home during the war. Sensitized as never before to the potentially appalling consequences of racial and ethnic legal distinctions, many Americans embraced a universalized notion of humanity and a color-blind conception of the U.S. Constitution. Mid-century liberal internationalists espoused worldwide human connectedness and commonality in books such as *One World* (1943) and *The Family of Man* (1955). They cheered when the United Nations—brainchild of the United States—proposed to protect "all members of the human family" in its Universal Declaration of Human Rights (1948). Their intuition that racial identity was but skin-deep seemed confirmed when white writer John Howard Griffin, in *Black Like Me* (1961), disguised himself as an African American and experienced hateful prejudice in the Jim Crow South. In 1954, the U.S. Supreme Court gave powerful legal expression to these universalistic, color-blind ideals in *Brown*.[21]

General counsel Schifter of the AAIA epitomized mid-century civil rights liberalism. He was a Jewish émigré from Austria whose parents had perished in Nazi extermination camps. Recalling how degraded he felt as a youth when segregated classrooms and streetcars were decreed for Austrian Jews, Schifter later remarked, "Growing up Jewish in Vienna in the 1930s was like growing up black in Mississippi prior to 1954." "I know what [discrimination] is all about," he added. "I know what it means to be discriminated against on the grounds of ancestry."[22]

Schifter, like other mid-century liberals, consistently supported school integration. When disgruntled Lumbees asked him to contribute to their fight for school integration in the early 1960s, he enthusiastically volunteered. As we shall soon see, however, when different Lumbee parents later asked him to contribute to their battle *against* school integration, Schifter refused. Lumbee agitation shifted; Schifter's mid-century civil rights liberalism did not.[23]

During *Brown*'s second decade, Lumbee legal activism continued. Its emphasis, however, shifted decisively from integrationism to separatism. In part, this shift reflected the quickened pace of desegregation, which left integrationists with fewer complaints and separatists, such as the *Chavis* litigants, with more complaints. In addition, as integration advanced nationally, a countervailing ethos of ethnic particularism emerged.

The Civil Rights Act of 1964 quickened the pace of desegregation nationally. Title VI of that act threatened to withhold federal education money from school districts that failed to desegregate to the satisfaction of the U.S. Department of Health, Education, and Welfare (HEW). This financial threat was especially powerful in poor counties such as Robeson, where federal money accounted for a substantial portion of total education spending.[24]

Most North Carolina school districts, including all six of Robeson County's, responded to Title VI by adopting "freedom of choice" student-assignment plans. In theory, these plans enabled students of all races to attend schools of their choice. In practice, however, very few students crossed traditional color lines, even after the removal of explicit constraints. Schools effectively remained segregated.[25]

The U.S. Supreme Court sought to close this "freedom of choice" loophole in *Green v. School Board of New Kent County* (1968). The *Green* decision declared that "freedom of choice" student-assignment plans were unacceptable unless they created actual progress toward "unitary" systems, meaning districts containing not "white" schools and "Negro" schools, "but just schools."[26]

Robeson County failed the *Green* test. In 1970, sixteen years after *Brown*, HEW declared the county's schools in violation of Title VI. Since Robeson County received $2 million a year—more than a quarter of its education budget—from the federal government, local officials felt compelled to negotiate a desegregation plan with HEW. The resulting plan called for the county to bus students and shuffle employees as necessary to achieve "racial balance" within each of its six school districts. The plan also banned district-line crossing. No longer would the county's five white-dominated city units be allowed to bus urban Lumbee students to Indian schools in the surrounding "county" district. HEW hoped that this 1970 plan would enable Robeson County's schools to operate on a "nondiscriminatory, desegregated basis."[27]

Some Robeson County whites muttered segregationist objections. Their mumbles, however, were mild compared to the indignant protests of separatist Lumbees. National trends in liberal thought, beginning with the African American civil rights movement, help explain this Lumbee response.[28]

In the second half of the 1960s, the center of gravity within the rapidly splintering African American civil rights movement shifted from integrationist nonviolence toward separatist militancy. The African American model influenced Native American activists. Native Americans quickly translated the empowering language of "black nationalism" into their own vernacular. Native American advocate Vine Deloria described "Black Power" as a "godsend" to Native Americans, for it had validated the "concept of self-determination."[29]

In the late 1960s and early 1970s, Indian activists, including many Lumbees, sought to put Deloria's theory of self-determination into practice. They founded the militant American Indian Movement (AIM), which mounted a series of dramatic protests, including a seventeen-month takeover of Alcatraz Island in California and a week-long occupation of the Bureau of Indian Affairs in Washington, D.C. AIM selected Robeson County as its East Coast headquarters. Dean Chavers, a Lumbee, was a leader at Alcatraz. Southeastern North Carolinians were reportedly the rowdiest contingent among those participating in the occupation of the Bureau of Indian Affairs in the nation's capital.[30]

Back in Robeson County, there was considerable awakening of pan-Indianism and Native American pride. Previously, one anthropologist observed in 1971, the Lumbee tended to define themselves in negative relation to neighboring groups: "not white, not black." During the early 1970s, however, Lumbees engaged in a "deliberate and growing search for what it means to be an Indian." Although the Lumbees had "completely adopted the ways of the white man," another writer observed in 1971, they were "very proud of being Indian, probably more so now than ever before."[31]

Amid this surge of Indian pride in the early 1970s, the Lumbee identified as never before with other Native American groups. They also engaged in a "great scramble," in one reporter's phrase, to preserve and celebrate Lumbee heritage. Books on Lumbee history proliferated. *Strike at the Wind*, a long-running outdoor summer drama celebrating the nineteenth-century exploits of "Lumbee hero and outlaw" Henry Berry Lowry, debuted. Other manifestations of the new Lumbee pride included an annual Miss Lumbee pageant; a "Lumbees and Friends" musical ensemble (whose repertoire, though "not traditionally Lumbee," emphasized "authentic rhythmic chants of other tribes, principally 'war songs'"); the *Carolina Indian Voice*, a bimonthly journal; and "Lumbee Homecoming," an annual celebration of Lumbee Indianness (complete with "Indian dances," a "Pow Wow," and an "Indian rally").[32]

The cultural awakening of the early 1970s predisposed many Lumbees to oppose school desegregation. A 1970 community gathering in the auditorium of the traditionally Lumbee Prospect School illustrates the connection between Lumbee cultural nationalism and the preference for all-Lumbee schools. At this gathering, Lumbee-themed entertainment, calculated to reinforce group identity and pride, comfortably shared the spotlight with an antidesegregation protest: the reigning "Miss Lumbee," Vicky Ransom, sang; the Magnolia Indian dancers performed; Lumbee historian-activist Lew Barton played his electric guitar; and a protester lay down on a bed of nails to dramatize the suffering that school integration would inflict on the Lumbee community.[33]

Many Lumbee objections to desegregation in Robeson County were identical to those of other contemporary critics of desegregation. Lumbee activists lamented the demise of neighborhood schools and the prospect of long bus rides. They resented the power of distant bureaucrats to make local school-assignment decisions. And like racist whites, some (though not all) Lumbees reportedly objected to desegregation because they did not want to associate with blacks.[34]

Other Lumbee objections were distinctive. Robeson County Lumbees argued that segregated schooling was essential to maintaining their Native American identity. All-Indian schools were, they contended, "part of a rich cultural heritage shared by the region's Lumbee tribesmen." Ripping Lumbee children away from these schools would "provoke a cultural jolt and rob the children of their own folkways." Lumbee activists feared that their unique "racial identity might be lost in the integration process." "Keep our schools and live," one Indian dramatically declared; "leave them and die."[35]

In the early 1960s, integrationist Lumbees mounted sit-ins and lawsuits. A decade later, anti-integrationist Lumbees employed the same tactics. Sit-ins came first. Robeson County's 1970 desegregation plan required about two thousand of the system's nine thousand Lumbee students to be transferred to other schools. The families of five hundred of these students refused. Demanding that "their" schools be "left alone," they vowed to defy desegregation orders and return their children to Lumbee schools in the fall, "whatever the cost." "We will sacrifice our lives, if necessary," one firebrand declared in August 1970, "to continue to stand united for our rights and our Lumbee Indian Schools." When classes started in the fall of 1970, these students staged defiant sit-ins in their former schools.[36]

Two weeks into the sit-in campaign, the school board announced that it would "reluctantly" arrest—for trespassing—all persons not authorized to be on school property. The protest dwindled. Attention turned to litigation. Over the previous summer, protest leader Luther Oxendine had written to Richard Schifter, the Austrian-born general counsel of the Association of American Indian Affairs, the New York-based group that had financed the Lumbees' earlier litigation. "[T]he Federal Government seems determined to wrest our Robeson County schools away from us," Oxendine explained. "We protest this. We are writing to formally request your legal assistance."[37]

Schifter refused to help Lumbee separatists. He was dismayed that the Lumbees, a group that recently and heroically had championed school integration, now opposed it. "Our basic problem here," Schifter wrote to an AAIA colleague, "is that the Lumbees are opposed to integration." That was troublesome for two reasons: "(1) It is highly unlikely that the law suit will succeed; and (2) . . . the law suit has overtones of Lumbee opposition to integration with Negroes; involvement in such a suit might damage the reputation of the Association [of American Indian Affairs]." Schifter identified the bottom line: "the Association should not involve itself in the litigation."[38]

Lumbee protesters pursued litigation, even without AAIA support. They retained Tally, Tally & Bouknight, the Fayetteville firm that had handled the previous school cases. But the resulting federal lawsuit—locally known as the "Prospect Suit"—went nowhere. Filed in 1970, it languished until mid-1978, when a federal judge finally dismissed it.[39]

Native American opposition to school desegregation in Robeson County simmered throughout the 1970s. Occasionally, it came to a boil.

In the spring of 1973, for instance, representatives of the Tuscaroras, a militant offshoot of the Lumbees whose top objective, beside federal recognition, was "to get our schools back," planned protest meetings at all of Robeson County's "historical Indian schools," in order to win, as the protestors phrased it, "the return of Indian control to schools that were under Indian control before desegregation." The first protest was to take place at the Prospect School. County authorities, however, prohibited the Prospect meeting, citing construction work on campus. Howard Brooks, the Tuscarora chief, defiantly announced that the meeting would occur as planned. If necessary, he announced, he was "willing to die at the steps of the school." Brooks also warned that any law enforcement officer who tried to prevent Indians from gathering at Prospect—a public school—would be guilty of "trespassing on Indian property." The meeting occurred and resulted in fifty-eight arrests.[40]

Chief Brooks and his followers opposed desegregation with loud protests, but a greater number of Native Americans opposed desegregation through quiet defiance. Disregarding desegregation orders, they continued to send their children to their preferred schools. Under the administration of Robeson County school superintendent Young H. Allen, who was white and who served from 1965 to 1977, Indian parents had little difficulty violating desegregation orders. Parents who wished to send their children to unassigned schools within their districts did so with impunity. Those wishing to send their children across district lines, in defiance of explicit HEW mandates, simply submitted affidavits to the Robeson County Board of Education, stating that their children resided with relatives in their preferred districts. "These affidavits," the press later reported, "were never questioned and the number of children crossing district lines was astronomical."[41]

Enforcement stiffened in the second half of the 1970s. Ironically, an increase in local Indian political power facilitated the crackdown. Traditionally, Lumbees controlled individual "Indian" schools in Robeson County, but whites controlled all of the county's school boards. Whites sustained this domination because they accounted for a plurality of the county's registered voters and also because they benefited from a suspect electoral scheme known to critics as "double voting." In this practice, city residents, who were predominantly white, voted both for their city-specific school boards and for the countywide school board, even though the latter exercised no jurisdiction over the five independent "city" school districts. Rural residents, who were predominantly Indian and black, voted only for the "county" school board. In the mid-1970s, a group of Robeson County Indians challenged this arrangement's constitutionality. Their victory in federal court vanquished double voting and democratized the county's educational leadership.[42]

In 1977, a moderate Lumbee, Purnell Swett, became the Robeson County Board of Education's first Native American school superintendent. Perhaps because he was a Native American, Swett lacked his predecessor's timidity in the face of militant Indian school-assignment violators. (Superintendent Allen, Swett's white predecessor, allegedly ceased enforcing school-assignment rules following an intimidating 1973 anti-integration protest, during which militant Lumbees occupied school board offices.) The Swett administration's pathbreaking willingness to enforce federally mandated integration caused "quite a stir" in the county, according to press reports, "especially for those families where [a student] had attended a particular school all his life" and now was forced to attend a different school. Such was the case with the defendants in *State v. Chavis*.[43]

At the time of the Swett administration's crackdown in the summer of 1978, the children of Braxton Chavis had, despite their assignment elsewhere, attended the Prospect School for so many years that school administrators wrongly assumed that they belonged there. County officials charged with belatedly enforcing HEW desegregation orders discovered this irregularity just prior to the start of the 1978–1979 school year. Gently but firmly—in personal home visits, followed by certified letters—officials informed the Chavises and other similarly situated parents that their children would have to transfer from Prospect to their duly assigned schools.[44]

Officials treated parents in a gingerly fashion because they recognized the situation's political volatility. They also sympathized with the people involved. When several Indian parents pleaded for permission to continue sending their children to schools to which they were not assigned, the Robeson County Board of Education spent more than two hours "trying to find a legal way" to grant their requests. Given HEW mandates and the risk of losing federal funding, however, the school board concluded that "[t]here [was] just no legal way to do it." The press reported that "several" school board members left the meeting with "[m]isty eyes" and "lumps in the[ir] throats."[45]

Home visits failed to placate the *Chavis* parents, who continued to insist that, as parents and Native Americans, they had, in the words of

Chavis defendant Sanford Barton, "freedom of choice to send [their] children to whatever school [they] desire[d]." (In a 2003 telephone interview, Barton stood by this view: "I believed I was right [then], and I still believe I was right.") Although Swett disagreed with the parents' legal analysis, he responded sympathetically. The superintendent took the trouble to ask HEW whether or not he could grant Native Americans "special exemptions" to school-assignment rules. HEW said no and reminded Swett that federal funding could be withheld if Robeson County failed to desegregate.[46]

On the first day of the 1978–1979 school year, the Chavis children and dozens of other unassigned pupils appeared at Prospect. The school board, anticipating such defiance, had instructed Prospect principal James A. Jones to allow such students to remain on campus in order to avoid open conflict and bad press. But Jones was to provide no class materials or classroom instruction. Following orders, Jones separated the thirty "Prospect Sit-ins" from the rest of the student body and assigned a teacher's aide to sit with them. Day after day, these children reappeared, although they received neither instruction nor course credit. Some children abandoned the protest fairly quickly. Thirteen, however, remained at Prospect for the entire year.[47]

About one month into the fall term, eight parents of the thirteen persistent protesters were arrested and charged with violating compulsory school-attendance laws by failing to cause their school-age children to attend the public schools to which they had been assigned. The parents pleaded not guilty. Their cases were consolidated into *State v. Chavis et al.* for a single jury trial in Robeson County superior court.[48]

The *Chavis* defendants retained Bruce T. Cunningham Jr., a young white lawyer. Cunningham practiced law two counties away from Robeson, a major plus in the eyes of his clients. The defendants did not trust the local bar to stand up to Robeson County district attorney Joe Freeman Britt, a bulldog of a lawyer whom the *Guinness Book of World Records* had recently dubbed the "World's Deadliest Prosecutor" because of his unrivaled record of obtaining death-penalty convictions. Cunningham practiced law in Moore County, well beyond Britt's reach. He also appealed to the defendants because he was well-credentialed, liberal, and familiar with Native American issues, having represented Robeson County Indians in previous disputes.[49]

The *Chavis* case engaged Cunningham's liberalism. As an undergraduate at the University of North Carolina in the late 1960s and a law student at the University of Virginia in the early 1970s, Cunningham had absorbed the liberal values that, later in life, would inspire him to become a leading advocate for capital punishment reform. He sympathized with the *Chavis* defendants and eagerly took their case.[50]

Cunningham's enthusiasm contrasts revealingly with AAIA general counsel Richard Schifter's previous refusal to help the Lumbees fight school integration in the Prospect suit of 1970. Cunningham, like Schifter, was a civil rights liberal; he sympathized with minority groups and fought to improve their situations. Years later, when recalling the *Chavis* defendants, Cunningham voiced "mid-century" civil rights sentiments: "These [were] guys that grew up laying brick on buildings that they couldn't go into, experiencing segregation where they weren't good enough." But Cunningham, who graduated from law school in 1973, was from a later generation of civil rights liberals. Cunningham's generation was as quick as Schifter's had been to diagnose the disease of racism but was more open to race-conscious remedies of the sort sought by the *Chavis* defendants. This difference reflected broader intellectual trends.

During the 1970s, the universalism that underlay mid-century civil rights liberalism declined. Reform thought underwent a "re-tribalizing" trend. Liberals focused increasingly on what social scientists called "descent-based communities." They spoke less of "unity" and more of "diversity"; less of "melting pots," more of "mosaics." Species-centered works such as *One World* and *The Family of Man* gave way to "ethnos-centered" works, such as *The World of Our Fathers* (Irving Howe's best-selling 1976 exploration of the Jewish American experience) and *Roots* (Alex Haley's mega-best-selling 1976 exploration of the African American experience, a book that suggested, John Howard Griffin's *Black Like Me* notwithstanding, that black identity was much more than skin deep). Historical writing on immigration and ethnicity flourished; writing on American political history took an ethno-cultural turn. "Kiss me, I'm Irish"—or Italian, or Polish, etc.—buttons proliferated. Black nationalists rejected integrated schooling and embraced what later would be called "Afrocentric" education, either in all-black private schools or in newly black-controlled public schools in black communities.[51]

The ethnic turn of the 1970s helped Robeson County Native Americans find legal counsel willing to support their separatist aims. Although Cunningham personally favored integration (he later expressed happiness that his own daughters had been able to attend integrated public schools), he nonetheless sympathized with the *Chavis* defendants' argument that mandatory integration, if taken to an extreme, threatened to replace valuable diversity with, in Cunningham's phrase, "generic, homogenized people." Cunningham's late-century liberalism also predisposed him to accept the argument that the Native American tradition of elder worship gave special weight to requests that Indian children be allowed to attend their forebears' schools.[52]

As a late-century civil rights liberal, Cunningham was also more open than Schifter had been to the notion that racial distinctions could legitimately be used to compensate minority groups for past mistreatment. For centuries, the white-dominated legal system in Robeson County had used Indianness against Native Americans. It was only fair, Cunningham believed, that the legal system now enable Native Americans to use Indianness to their advantage.[53]

Years later, Cunningham told an interviewer, "What we were doing [in *Chavis*] was ... resisting desegregation to the extent that it homogenized a culture into oblivion. Democracy is a great form of government, as long as you're in the majority. But if you are a small segment ... that has [its] own sets of beliefs and priorities, democracy is not necessarily the best form of government because it tends to treat everybody the same without recognizing [differences]." Differences in mind-set—in "how you use the Earth, how you respect tradition," and so forth—*did* separate "Indians [from] white Europeans," Cunningham believed. History and justice demanded special regard for Indian concerns. "You've got to understand," Cunningham explained. "They were here first."[54]

Besides considering the Prospect suit of 1970 objectionable, Richard Schifter of the AAIA had considered it unwinnable. By the fall of 1978, however, the law had changed enough to convince Cunningham that victory was possible. The use of racial classifications to benefit previously subjugated groups was much more common in schools and elsewhere in the late 1970s than it had been at the decade's outset. In June 1978, just three months before the *Chavis* arrests, the U.S. Supreme Court ruled in its famous *Bakke* "affirmative action" decision that government-funded schools could treat minority applicants preferentially, as long as those schools did not employ numerical quotas. Robeson County took note. The *Robesonian* explained *Bakke*'s significance this way: henceforth, "minority groups are entitled to special consideration" and "reverse discrimination is legally permissible" in educational settings under some circumstances. Native American opponents of school desegregation likely took heart.[55]

To Cunningham, however, the key precedent for *Chavis* was not *Bakke*. It was *Wisconsin v. Yoder* (1972), another school-related U.S. Supreme Court case that, like *Bakke*, had been unavailable to Schifter at the time of the Prospect suit. In *Yoder*, the Supreme Court ruled that the First Amendment's free-exercise-of-religion clause exempted certain Amish children from Wisconsin's compulsory school-attendance laws. Education of the sort compelled by the state, the Amish litigants successfully argued, threatened their ability to sustain some of their community's most cherished customs and beliefs. Although *Yoder* did not concern race, it reflected the late-century liberal belief that culturally distinctive communities were valuable and deserved protection. Bruce Cunningham believed that *Yoder* applied directly to *Chavis*. "Our argument" in *Chavis*, he explained years later, "was that, under the *Wisconsin v. Yoder* case, if there are strongly held beliefs that would impact the decision of whether or not to send your kid to school [as in *Yoder*] or where to send your kid to school [as in *Chavis*], then you could be exempt" from general school-attendance laws.[56]

Braxton Chavis and the other Native American parents analyzed the law differently. To them, the key legal context was neither *Bakke* nor *Yoder* but a recent trend in American public life supporting Native American self-determination. During the 1950s, the dominant theme of U.S. Indian policy had been "termination." This policy sought the eradication of tribal identity and the assimilation of Native Americans into the mainstream. By 1970, however, termination had been soundly repudiated as being, in President Richard Nixon's words, "morally and legally unacceptable." The new polestar of federal Indian policy was "self-determination." Nowhere did this star shine more brightly than in education policy. "Education of Indians should be controlled by Indians," a federal report announced in 1970. Federal laws such as the Indian Education Act of 1972 and the Indian Self-Determination and Education Assistance Act of 1975 sought to put the theory of Indian educational self-determination into practice.[57]

The federal government's "self-determination" policy toward Native Americans during the 1970s emboldened Robeson County opponents of school integration. When urging the creation of a separate Indian school system in Robeson County in 1972, for instance, separatists paraphrased President Nixon's alleged declaration that "any Indian group that wanted to control its own schools should have the right to do so." Two years later, an HEW grant funded the establishment of three "Lumbee Longhouse Learning Centers" in Robeson County. These were half-day preschools designed to expose Native American youngsters to Indian culture and history. "We want to teach the children who they are and to be proud of their heritage," one Lumbee proponent explained. "This is an Indian education project," she added, "not just an education project." Native American parents in Robeson County may have perceived mixed messages in HEW's willingness to fund these Indian-only "Longhouse Learning Centers" for three-to-five year-olds while simultaneously enacting a countywide desegregation plan for older children.[58]

The federal government sent similarly mixed messages in 1973. In that year, Washington denied Robeson County's request for $273,000 in Emergency School Assistance Act money on the ground that some of the county's schools remained "racially identifiable." But at the same time, the federal government gave Robeson County almost $500,000 in Indian Education Act (IEA) money precisely because "[s]ome of the racially identifiable schools have a largely Indian enrollment." (By the time of the *Chavis* case, Robeson County's annual IEA take had increased to nearly $900,000. According to the *Robesonian*, only one county in the nation—Gallup County, New Mexico—received more IEA money than Robeson did.) The Prospect School's huge Indian enrollment enabled it to receive more IEA money than any other school in the county. School administrators at Prospect had little incentive to promote desegregation, since Indian enrollment declines would cause IEA funding to decrease.[59]

Federal support for Indian educational autonomy inspired the *Chavis* defendants and other separatists to argue that their Indianness entitled them to distinctive legal treatment, especially in the area of education. Throughout the 1970s, Lumbee separatists, citing the IEA and other federal measures, argued that Robeson County's Indians "should be allowed to attend the Indian schools of Robeson County." Since none of the county's schools, thanks to desegregation, remained exclusively Indian, Native Americans "should be allowed to attend the schools of their choice, regardless of present school boundaries."[60] This, in a nutshell, was the argument of the *Chavis* defendants.

In *State v. Chavis,* as in many criminal trials, jury selection was key. Defense attorney Cunningham sought to prepare prospective jurors for his *Yoder* defense. On *voir dire,* he asked potential jurors, "Do you accept that there can be a belief higher or more important to [the criminal defendants] ... than the guidelines and policies set by a school board and HEW?" Prosecutors made more productive use of their time. Wielding peremptory challenges like race-conscious chisels, they sculpted the jury to six whites, five blacks, and only one Indian. Native Americans accounted for one-third of the county's population, but just one-twelfth of the *Chavis* jury.[61]

On 21 January 1979, a large crowd gathered in the Robeson County superior court in Lumberton to witness *State v. Chavis*. "There was huge interest," presiding Judge Anthony Brannon recalled years later. "The courtroom was filled."[62]

School superintendent Purnell Swett and two school principals testified for the prosecution. They affirmed that the defendants, though clearly aware of the schools to which their children had been assigned, "were not sending their [children] to the properly assigned school[s]." "There was a ton of evidence," Judge Brannon remembered thinking, "that the defendants had in fact violated the ... law." The state rested.[63]

Prior to the trial, defense attorney Cunningham, with *Yoder* in mind, hinted to the press that he planned to emphasize religious freedom. One defendant toed this line by testifying in court that it was his "Christian belief" that parents had the right to control their children's upbringing. On the whole, however, defendants emphasized Indian rights, not religious freedom. They maintained that, as Indians, they were exempt from all desegregation orders stemming from the Civil Rights Act of 1964. "Martin Luther King's Law," they explained, applied to blacks and whites only. "I consider myself an American Indian," Bertha Oxendine testified. "The Civil Rights Act [of 1964] was not passed on an Indian. It was on the black and white. The Civil Rights Act does not apply to Indians." Braxton Chavis similarly argued that he had the right to defy desegregation orders "because I am an American Indian." "The federal law in 1964 might have fallen on the rest but it did not fall on the Indian," he explained. "It just doesn't apply to an Indian."[64]

That the *Chavis* defendants would make such arguments in court reveals a good deal about their core beliefs. That they *could* make such arguments in court reveals an equal amount about the lawyers and the judge in the case. Cunningham helped his clients to voice their unorthodox views. He interrogated with a light touch, allowing them to speak their minds. Cunningham personally would have preferred a *Yoder*-

style approach, stressing communal customs and spiritual beliefs, not a blood-based approach stressing Indian exceptionalism. In light of the jury's ethnic composition, Cunningham's preference made sense. But Cunningham respectfully deferred to his clients' preferences.

Judge Brannon also helped the defendants to air their deeply held grievances in court. Brannon, who was white, knew that centuries of legal mistreatment had alienated many Robeson County Indians. He feared that stifling the defendants' testimony, even for legally legitimate reasons, might confirm their suspicion that the white-dominated legal system was hopelessly biased against them. "It is extremely important," Brannon reasoned, explaining his decision to allow essentially unfettered Native American testimony in *Chavis*, "that . . . the Indian population understand that their case is being handled in accordance with the law—that nothing is cooked up in the back room to screw them."[65]

Brannon's decision to relax the usual rules of evidence in *Chavis* facilitated what might be termed the "testimonial-therapeutic" function of protest litigation. In politically charged cases such as *Chavis*, Brannon believed, disaffected groups, in addition to seeking legal victory, often simply want to have their say. They want powerful people to sit, listen, and take their grievances seriously. In *Chavis*, Brannon insisted that the parents have their full say—and that all others in the courtroom listen respectfully.

The parents' desire to have their say, and the bench and bar's willingness to listen, accord with the "human-potential" movement of the 1970s—a pop-psychology trend that, as one critic lamented, "invaded just about every level of society" during the decade. At the core of this movement lay "encounter groups" and "sensitivity training" sessions, during which "facilitators" urged participants to express frank emotions in a group setting. Race relations presented especially fertile ground for this movement. The federal government spent hundreds of thousands of dollars per year organizing "race awareness meetings" for its workers. Both the U.S. Army and Navy sponsored "race relations seminars" at which black and white service members of all ranks "go at each other over the emotional issue of race." By the time of the *Chavis* trial, the race awareness meeting, where (among other things) minorities were encouraged to vent and whites were encouraged to listen and learn, was a familiar institution.[66]

Race awareness meetings were designed to produce therapeutic venting of pent-up grievances. Judge Brannon hoped that the parents' testimony in *Chavis* would do so. "In large measure," he reflected years later, "what [the *Chavis* defendants] wanted, I think, was ... to tell their story and express their complaints and not be cut off." An expert on the rules of evidence, Judge Brannon knew that, in most trials, as he put it, "You can't just get up there [on the witness stand] and run your mouth." But he also knew that, as a trial judge, he had wide discretion over the implementation of these rules.[67]

Brannon allowed the *Chavis* defendants the widest possible testimonial latitude. When the parents took the witness stand, "[t]he rules of evidence went right out the window, as far as I was concerned," he recalled. "Whatever they wanted to say, they could be my guest." Lawyers on both sides agreed with this approach. "We were all trying to get this job done right," Brannon explained, "so that everybody got to sing their song."[68]

After the testimony, Assistant Attorney General Woodberry Bowen delivered closing remarks for the prosecution that invoked the story of Pandora's box. If you let one group of people pick and choose where they are going to send their children to school, Bowen warned, then you will have to let everybody do so.[69]

Cunningham, in presenting his closing remarks to the 92 percent non-Indian jury, pulled back from his clients' racial essentialism. He stressed family values, education, and the best interest of the children. He also played to antibureaucratic sentiments, which he knew crossed political and ethnic lines in Robeson County. Use your vote in this case, he urged jurors, to say that "you have had enough and you are not going to let an outside government agency tell you what to do with your family."[70]

Judge Brannon suspected that the jury would vote to convict, but he wanted to assure the Native American parents that the legal system was not deaf to their concerns. To that end, he and Cunningham agreed that the latter would distill the parents' principal contentions into a request for a jury charge, a request that Brannon would deny. Brannon's refusal to charge the jury as requested would give the defendants an automatic ground for appeal should they be convicted. "This is the way," Brannon reasoned, "for [the defendants] to put the whole theory of their case in written form and take it up to ... appellate court so that that precise question can be a question of law that will be answered one way or another." After appellate judges in Raleigh and perhaps Washington, D.C., ruled in their case, Brannon thought, the defendants, win or lose, could at least rest assured that "it wasn't someone in Robeson County putting the fix on them."[71]

As planned, Cunningham requested particular jury instructions. He asked Judge Brannon to tell jurors that they should return a verdict of not guilty if they concluded that the defendants had failed to send their children to assigned schools "because of their good faith belief that as American Indians they are exempt from school board attendance guidelines established at the direction of the Department of Health, Education and Welfare."[72] Judge Brannon refused this request. Before delivering his own jury charge, however, he asked the jury to leave the courtroom for a moment, so that he could explain his actions to the defendants and their sympathizers. He announced that he would not instruct the jury to acquit if they found that the defendants had held a good faith belief that their ethnicity exempted them from desegregation orders. "I understand your contention that it should be the law," he told the parents from the bench. "Obviously, this is an issue bigger than those of you here, whether your status as an American Indian entitles you to certain things, if you have rights outside of the general statutes." Should the jury convict them, Brannon assured them, their "test case" would not end. They could—and, he implied, should—use his refusal to instruct the jury as requested as a ground for appeal.[73]

It took the jury thirty minutes to find the defendants guilty. Although the parents received sentences of fifteen to twenty days in jail, Judge Brannon promised to suspend those sentences as long as the parents promised to send their children to assigned schools the following fall. In the meantime, Brannon declared in his February 1979 ruling, the defendants' children could remain at Prospect School for the rest of the school year, even though this would violate HEW rules. Brannon ordered school officials to provide the children with books, instruction, and academic credit.[74]

After announcing this generous sentence, Brannon assured the defendants of his belief that their case concerned a "serious principle." He hoped that an appellate court would soon resolve their case's central question. "If I am wrong in my [jury] charge, based on your status as Native American Indians," Brannon told the defendants, an appellate court would overturn their convictions and "you will not have lost but won."[75]

The North Carolina Court of Appeals heard *State v. Chavis* in the fall of 1979. The one and only issue was whether the trial court had erred in refusing the defendants' requested jury instructions. "That was the only assignment of error," Judge Brannon proudly recalled. "Folks, that's almost unique in a criminal case. . . . I let in every last thing the defense wanted . . . because it was an important case to be heard."[76]

Cunningham's appellate brief sought to distinguish *Chavis* from *In re McMillan*, a 1976 North Carolina appeal that resembled *Chavis* in many respects, including defense attorney. (Cunningham represented Indian families in both cases.) In *McMillan*, two Native American parents from Robeson County had refused to allow their children to attend school "because the children were not taught about Indians, Indian heritage and culture in the school." On appeal, Cunningham argued that the Robeson parents' "deep-rooted conviction for Indian heritage," much like the Amish parents' deep-rooted beliefs in *Wisconsin v. Yoder*, justified their refusal to send their children to school. The North Carolina Court of Appeals disagreed and upheld the parents' convictions.[77]

Three years later, Cunningham attempted to distinguish *Chavis* from *McMillan*. The *McMillan* parents had refused to send their children to any school whatsoever. In contrast, the *Chavis* parents had scrupulously sent their children to school every day. Clearly, Cunningham argued, "each parent [in *Chavis*] is concerned with his children's welfare and wants to see them get a good education. . . . [E]ach parent sent his child to a public school and continued to send his child to school for the entire year." Cunningham's elaboration on this argument emphasized "late-century" multicultural themes. "[I]n this case the parents wanted not only for their children to receive an education in the basic subjects, but also to have instilled in them a sense of history and pride that comes with being from a part of tradition," he argued. "Such feelings should not be labeled as criminal in the State of North Carolina."[78] Cunningham also contended that the *Chavis* parents held a "good faith belief" that their Indianness exempted them from school-assignment laws. This belief, Cunningham suggested, constituted "a defense to the offense charged."[79]

He lost. The North Carolina Court of Appeals' 1980 ruling rejected all of Cunningham's arguments. The court conceded that, under federal law, the legal status of Native Americans was indeed "unique." But this uniqueness applied only to "American Indian as a political classification," not "American Indian as a racial classification." Members of federally recognized tribes who lived on reservations enjoyed "political classification" as Native Americans and qualified for distinctive legal treatment in areas such as "political sovereignty and tribal self-government." As a "racial classification," however, "American Indian" warranted no special legal treatment. Native Americans such as the *Chavis* parents—who were not members of a federally recognized tribe and who did not live on a reservation—had to comply with all generally applicable laws, including desegregation orders. The HEW plan for Robeson County affected the *Chavis* parents "as it affects all other county residents," the court ruled. "The trial court properly refused to give the tendered instruction. No error."[80]

The *Chavis* parents appealed and appealed again, hoping that their voices would be heard in Raleigh and Washington, but both the North Carolina Supreme Court and the Supreme Court of the United States declined to hear their case. Attorney Cunningham speculated that the upper courts sidestepped *Chavis* because it concerned some of the most nettlesome questions in American public life: How color-blind should our government be? How can we publicly acknowledge "diversity and cultural heritage" while at the same time "not allowing things over which a person has no control to determine governmental benefits and status?" In Cunningham's view, these questions remained just as vexing at the dawn of the twenty-first century as they were at the time of the *Chavis* trial.[81]

The defendants in *State v. Chavis* failed to change the law. Their experiences in the legal system, however, appeared to change them. The respectful treatment that they encountered from sympathetic lawyers and judges took the edge off of their militancy and reduced the suspicion with which they had regarded the legal system. Although Judge Brannon had presided at the trial that resulted in the parents' criminal convictions, he won their respect. Braxton Chavis commented at proceedings' end that Brannon "was a fine judge, an honest man." When the U.S. Supreme Court ended all hope of victory by refusing to grant certiorari in the fall of 1980, the *Chavis* parents accepted their defeat. Braxton Chavis, absent any of the fire that just two years previously had inspired him to defy the law by refusing to send his children to Oxendine School, remarked, "I've got to abide with what they say. We're sending our children to Oxendine."[82]

Following *Chavis*, Robeson County's heated education debate cooled. Superintendent Swett never surrendered to those of his fellow Native Americans who opposed integration, but he "kept the dialogue going." He showed antidesegregationists that he had respect for their ideas, even though he did not necessarily agree with them. "I treated them like human beings," he recalled. As a result, "we gradually resolved that problem without any conflicts."[83]

State v. Chavis was an unusual case. It was a southern school desegregation dispute, yet Native Americans, not whites or African Americans, were the protagonists. It was a criminal case, yet the defendants, as Judge Brannon told reporters following the jury's verdict, were "concerned parents, not criminals." Perhaps most unusually, as Brannon noted, *State v. Chavis* had, "unlike a lot of school desegregation suits," "no villains. . . . I don't think a single person involved in it has anything to regret or hide. . . . That's not always true. This is an atypical case. . . . Everybody was acting in good faith."[84]

Conclusion

The preceding eight chapters challenge two common assumptions regarding the nature of American law. The first assumption—no longer widespread among scholars, perhaps, but influential nonetheless—portrays the American legal process (litigation) as an impartial and apolitical form of dispute resolution. Reassuringly, the North Carolina legal system portrayed in these pages sometimes resembled this "rule of law" ideal. Some judges *were* willing to defy popular (and personal) prejudices in order to enforce legal rules and precedents, as when the North Carolina Supreme Court in 1877 felt "compelled" to uphold the validity of Pinkney and Sarah Ross's interracial marriage, even though the justices personally claimed to find such marriages "revolting."[1]

Sometimes, however, the North Carolina legal system did not reflect the rule of law ideal. Prosecutorial enforcement of longstanding laws swung from laxness to vigilance as political winds shifted. Some judges used the judicial bench to fire subjective volleys in the culture wars of their day. Some of them bent legal rules in controversial cases so as to discourage would-be critics from attacking and perhaps weakening the state's judiciary. As one unusually candid judge acknowledged while delivering an admittedly flawed ruling, "This is a concession to the . . . prejudices of the community upon this subject."[2] Such admissions were rare; such actions were not.

The second assumption challenged in the preceding pages is the "elite dominance" model, which portrays law as a tool that privileged classes use to perpetuate their supremacy. Again, there is some truth to this notion. The law indeed reinforced social stratification, as exemplified by North Carolina's long record of legalized racial oppression, beginning with slavery. But no "one-size-fits-all" class analysis works. Throughout its history, North Carolina's legal system has been a forum in which *shifting* coalitions clashed. Chapter 3, for instance, details a Jim Crow housing segregation dispute between two interclass alliances. On the pro–Jim Crow side was a coalition of lower-middle-class whites, the Winston city government, and a technocratic solicitor who was a nationally known expert in segregation law. On the anti–Jim Crow side were a poor African American tobacco worker, a small-time white real estate agent, and two of Winston's most prestigious lawyers. The local trial court ruled in favor of the former coalition. The North Carolina Supreme Court reversed the local court's decision and sided with the latter coalition. Disputes in other chapters involved similarly jumbled alliances.

The elite dominance model falls short in at least two additional respects. It fails to capture the impressive degree of initiative that non-elite North Carolinians have displayed within their state's legal system. And it fails to predict legal outcomes with any consistency. Consider race—one of the key themes of this book and of southern history generally. Elite dominance theory would presumably envision state-court *losses* for the interracial married couple that faced criminal prosecution during the late 1870s, the black tobacco worker who challenged Jim Crow in Progressive Era Winston, and the black attorney who sought to advance African American voting rights by attacking the literacy test in the early 1960s. Yet all three won at least partial victories.

The legal system described in this book was neither an entirely neutral arbiter of social conflict nor a blunt weapon of elite dominance. It was a less predictable entity, a forum within which a wide array of North Carolinians continually renegotiated basic social values and rules, while vying for personal, group, and institutional advantage.

Many of this book's historical observations hold true to this day. North Carolina's bench and bar are still, on balance, considerably more elite than the litigants they serve. The state's legal system remains neither an entirely neutral forum for dispute resolution nor a crude cudgel of elite dominance. And state law continues to affect, in fundamental ways, innumerable aspects of North Carolina life: crime and punishment (including the death penalty), public education, voting rights, medical malpractice, agriculture, corporations, contracts, business practices, labor relations, sexual harassment, marriage, divorce, adoption, child custody, domestic violence, zoning ordinances, property rights, environmental protection, and many, many more.[3]

Similarly, many of the changes identified in the preceding chapters continue apace. The diversification of the North Carolina bar, noted above, continues. Perhaps most remarkable has been the massive entry of women into the legal profession. Nell Battle Lewis was a rarity as a female attorney in the early 1930s. Today, the state's youngest cohort of lawyers—those ages thirty and under—is about equally split between men and women. Each year, as the fifty-fifty cohort of young lawyers gradually replaces retirees from the state's oldest cohort—among whom men, as of the beginning of the twenty-first century, still accounted for 97 percent of the total—gender balance in the state bar increases.[4]

Likewise, African American lawyers are much more common today than they once were. In 1950, on the eve of desegregation, African Americans accounted for about 1 percent of North Carolina's legal professionals. Thirty years later, they accounted for more than 6 percent of the state's lawyers. The recent stagnation of this figure has frustrated concerned parties in the state. In a U.S. Supreme Court case of 2003, the UNC Law School, which had fought so hard in the mid-twentieth century for the right to exclude blacks, fought equally hard for the right to continue employing race-conscious admissions procedures in order to prevent a drop in its minority student enrollment.[5]

Changes in the state judiciary mirror those in the state bar. The North Carolina bench described in this book was entirely white and male. This is no longer true. In 2006, North Carolina Supreme Court associate justice Sarah Parker was promoted to chief justice. The most significant aspect of Parker's promotion to the state's highest judicial post may be that nobody much cared that she was female. Two other women had preceded her as chief justice. Novelty seekers were more interested in Patricia Timmons-Goodson, Parker's replacement as associate justice, who became the first black woman to serve on the North Carolina Supreme Court. (The court's first African American man, Henry Frye, became associate justice in 1983 and chief justice in 1999. In a story that recalls the career of James R. Walker Jr., Frye allegedly was inspired to become a lawyer in the mid-1950s when, although a college graduate and a U.S. Air Force captain, he was forced to submit to a degrading literacy test as a condition of North Carolina voter registration. North Carolina election officials judged Frye not to have passed the "literacy" test because he was unable name from memory the signers of the Declaration of Independence.)[6]

Another major trend identified in these histories also continues: the ever-expanding reach of federal law. This trend is unlikely to be reversed. As noted, however, state law retains jurisdiction over many vital areas of American life. Moreover, the expansion of federal law into traditionally state-controlled fields does not necessarily terminate state action in those fields. For instance, although the federal judiciary famously colonized abortion law in *Roe v. Wade* (1973), the North Carolina courts continue to decide disputes regarding abortion access, abortion funding, abortion protests, and the like. Similarly, the existence of the Environmental Protection Agency in Washington, D.C., does not preclude the parallel presence of—and the frequent state-level litigation initiated by—North Carolina's Department of Environment and Natural Resources.[7]

Indeed, more federal law sometimes begets more state law. Medicaid, a health insurance program for low-income individuals, for example, was established in 1965 by federal statute but is administered by each state individually. The state-level bureaucracies established to implement this federal initiative are prodigiously active. In 2000 alone, some 1.2 million North Carolina residents—about 15 percent of the state's total—received Medicaid benefits. Disputes over Medicaid billing, funding levels, eligibility, and the like frequently reach the North Carolina courts.[8]

Federal court decisions, like federal statutes, also can generate state law. This can be true even when federal rulings appear to limit state action. In *Lawrence v. Texas* (2003), the Supreme Court of the United States held that states could no longer criminalize homosexual acts between consenting adults. Although *Lawrence* prohibited one class of state cases (prosecutions for consensual homosexual acts), such prosecutions were actually quite rare, as Justice Anthony M. Kennedy's majority ruling noted. The loss of this class of state cases was more than offset by the creation of another class: litigation designed to determine *Lawrence*'s implications for state law. Among the North Carolina cases of this sort was one in which a lower-court judge used *Lawrence* to strike down the state's age-old "fornication and adultery" statute—the law under which Pinkney and Sarah Ross were prosecuted in the 1870s.[9]

Even in the age of federal law expansion, state law will continue to grow, change, and matter. History students generations hence who gather around a seminar table seeking insight into the past will be well advised to peer closely into the "magic mirror" of state law.

Notes

Introduction

1. Roscoe Pound, *The Formative Era of American Law* (Gloucester, Mass.: Peter Smith, 1938), 4, 30–31.
2. Bertram Wyatt-Brown, *Southern Honor: Ethics and Behavior in the Old South* (New York: Oxford Univ. Press, 1982).
3. Oliver Wendell Holmes, *Collected Legal Papers* (New York: Harcourt, Brace and Howe, 1920), 26.
4. Regarding the legal constraints facing slaves, see Thomas D. Morris, *Southern Slavery and the Law, 1619–1860* (Chapel Hill: Univ. of North Carolina Press, 1996), 228; and Ariela Gross, "Pandora's Box: Slave Character on Trial in the Antebellum Deep South," *Yale Journal of Law & the Humanities* 7 (summer 1995): 310. The "under a personal incapacity to act" quotation comes from *Robertson v. Stevens*, 36 N.C. 247 at 251 (1840).

1. White Couples and "Mulatto" Babies

The authors gratefully acknowledge the financial support that they received from the George L. Abernethy Endowment and the wise counsel that they received from Elizabeth Dale, Suzanne Cooper Guasco, Brian Luskey, Sally McMillen, and Harry Watson.

1. Petition for Divorce, *Scroggins v. Scroggins*, 6 Apr. 1830, Superior Court Records (Buncombe County), North Carolina State Division of Archives and History, Raleigh, 1 (hereafter, Scroggins Divorce Petition).
2. *Jesse Barden Divorce Petition*, Supreme Court Case Index, *Barden v. Barden*, 1830 (Petition), Case #1932, North Carolina Division of Archives and History, Raleigh, N.C. (hereafter, Barden Divorce Petition).
3. *Marville Scroggins v. Lucretia Scroggins*, 14 N.C. 535 (1832); *Jesse Barden v. Ann M. Barden*, 14 N.C. 548 (1832).
4. Martha E. Hodes, *White Women, Black Men: Illicit Sex in the Nineteenth-Century South* (New Haven: Yale Univ. Press, 1997), 75; Hendrik Hartog, *Man and Wife in America: A History* (Cambridge: Harvard Univ. Press, 2000), 338 n.9; Peter W. Bardaglio, *Reconstructing the Household: Families, Sex, and the Law*

in the Nineteenth-Century South (Chapel Hill: Univ. of North Carolina Press, 1995), 63.

5. Lawrence M. Friedman, *A History of American Law,* 2nd ed. (New York: Touchstone, 1985), 204–7.

6. Stephanie McCurry, *Masters of Small Worlds: Yeoman Households, Gender Relations, and the Political Culture of the Antebellum South Carolina Low Country* (New York: Oxford Univ. Press, 1995), 48, 58, 60, 72.

7. For information regarding the social standing of Marville Scroggins and Lucretia Brigman around the time of their marriage, see Scroggins Divorce Petition, 1; and *Heads of Families of the 1st Census of United States Taken in the Year 1790—North Carolina* (Baltimore: Genealogical Publishing, 1978), 146; U.S. Census of 1830, North Carolina, microfilm M-19, roll 118, p. 287. For Jesse Barden and Ann Bradbury, see *1830 Census Population Schedules for Wayne County, North Carolina,* microfilm M-19, roll 125, pp. 505–49; *1790 Census Population Schedules for Wayne County, North Carolina,* p. 150; *1820 Census Population Schedules for Wayne County, North Carolina,* microfilm M-33, roll 33, p. 457; Joseph W. Watson, *Kinfolks of Wayne County North Carolina, 1793–1832* (Wake Forest, N.C.: Meridional Publications, 1986), 110, 119, 138, 164–65, 207, 217, 231; Bob Johnson and Charles S. Norwood, eds., *History of Wayne County, North Carolina* (Goldsboro, N.C. : Wayne County Historical Association, 1979), 170.

8. *Scroggins v. Scroggins,* 14 N.C. 535 at 540 (1832); Scroggins Divorce Petition, 1; Barden Divorce Petition, 1–2.

9. *Barden v. Barden,* 14 N.C. 548 at 548–49 (1832).

10. The quotation about Ruffin dominating his brethren comes from Martin H. Brinkley, "Supreme Court of North Carolina: A Brief History," http://www.aoc.state.nc.us/www/copyright/sc/facts.html, accessed 17 June 2003. Additional information in this paragraph comes from Roscoe Pound, *The Formative Era of American Law* (Boston: Little, Brown, 1938), 4 n.2; Jenni Parrish, "A Guide to American Legal History Methodology with an Example of Research in Progress," *Law Library Journal* 86 (winter 1994): 123; *(Fayetteville) Carolina Observer,* 25 Dec. 1832, 3; and *Scroggins v. Scroggins,* 14 N.C. 535 at 541 (1832).

11. *Barden v. Barden,* 14 N.C. 548 at 550 (1832).

12. Hartog, *Man and Wife in America,* 338 n.9.

13. *(Fayetteville) Carolina Observer,* 2 Apr. 1833; *North Carolina Reports,* vol. 14, 535–50; *(Fayetteville) Carolina Observer,* 9 Apr. 1833, 3; *Raleigh Register and North Carolina Gazette,* 2 Apr. 1833, 3.

14. *Raleigh Register and North Carolina Gazette,* 23 Nov. 1832, 3.

15. *(Wilmington) People's Press,* which began publication during the sitting of the North Carolina Supreme Court's December 1832 term; Robert V. Remini, *Andrew Jackson and the Course of American Democracy, 1833–1845* (New York: Harper & Row, 1984), 342–43.

16. For Andrew Jackson's views on the federal judiciary, see Remini, *Andrew*

Jackson, 342. The quotation regarding state judges comes from Frederick Robinson, "A Program for Labor," in *Social Theories of Jacksonian Democracy*, ed. Joseph L. Blau (New York: Hafner, 1947), 332. For the Mississippi policy on elected judges, see Mississippi Constitution of 1832, Art. IV, Sections 2, 3, 8, 11, and 16. For information on other states, see Kermit L. Hall, "The Judiciary on Trial: State Constitutional Reform and the Rise of an Elected Judiciary, 1846–1860," *Historian* 45 (May 1983): 341.

17. The "grog shop" quotation appears in *(Fayetteville) Carolina Observer*, 4 Dec. 1832, 3. Additional information in this paragraph comes from *(Fayetteville) Carolina Observer*, 4 Dec. 1832, 2–3; "Postscript," *(Fayetteville) Carolina Observer*, 18 Dec. 1832, 3–4; *(Fayetteville) Carolina Observer*, 15 Jan. 1833, 2; *Raleigh Register and North Carolina Gazette*, 7 Dec. 1832, 3; *Raleigh Register and North Carolina Gazette*, 11 Jan. 1833, 3; "State Legislature," *Raleigh Register and North Carolina Gazette*, 25 Jan. 1833, 1; *Roanoke Advocate (Halifax, N.C.)*, 13 Dec. 1832, 2; *Roanoke Advocate*, 17 Jan. 1833, 3; *Raleigh Register and North Carolina Gazette*, 14 Dec. 1832, 3.

18. *Raleigh Register and North Carolina Gazette*, 14 Dec. 1832, 3; "Editor's Correspondence," *(Fayetteville) Carolina Observer*, 11 Dec. 1832, 3; *(Fayetteville) Carolina Observer*, 25 Dec. 1832, 3.

19. For confirmation of Ruffin's elite status, see *1840 Census Population Schedules for Orange County, North Carolina*, microfilm M-704, reel 36D; and William K. Ruffin to Hon. Thomas Ruffin, 27 June 1831, *The Papers of Thomas Ruffin*, ed. J. G. de Roulhac Hamilton, vol. 2 (Raleigh: Edwards and Broughton, 1918), 36. Regarding the comparative racial liberalism of Ruffin and his slave-owning high court brethren, see Bardaglio, *Reconstructing the Household*, 71; *State v. Negro Will*, 18 N.C. 121 (1834—slaves had the right to defend themselves against any unlawful attempt by a master, or an agent of a master, to kill them); and *State v. William Manuel* (1838—a manumitted slave was a citizen of the state and thus entitled to the guarantees of the state constitution). Both decisions came from the pen of Justice William Gaston, who owned 163 slaves at his death in 1844. William Gaston Papers Inventory (#272), Manuscripts Department, University of North Carolina at Chapel Hill.

20. The word "odious" is Ruffin's in *Scroggins v. Scroggins*, 14 N.C. 535 at 545 (1832). Regarding the situation in Virginia, see Thomas E. Buckley, *The Great Catastrophe of My Life: Divorce in the Old Dominion* (Chapel Hill: Univ. of North Carolina Press, 2002), 125.

21. *Scroggins v. Scroggins*, 14 N.C. 535 at 542 (1832). Regarding Ruffin's religious faith, see Samuel A. Ashe, Stephen B. Weeks, and Charles L. van Noppen, eds., *Biographical History of North Carolina from Colonial Times to the Present* (Greensboro: C. L. van Noppen, 1905), 356; Thomas Ruffin to Catherine Ruffin, 14 Apr. 1828, *Papers of Thomas Ruffin*, vol. 1, 444; and Thomas Ruffin to Catherine Ruffin, 19 July 1831, *Papers of Thomas Ruffin*, vol. 2, 42.

22. *State v. Mann*, 13 N.C. 263 at 267 (1829).
23. *Greensborough Patriot*, 27 June 1832.
24. *(Fayetteville) Carolina Observer*, 18 Jan. 1832, 2; *Raleigh Register and North Carolina Gazette*, 21 Dec. 1832, 3; "Amendments to the Constitution of 1876," ratified 1835, Art. I, Sec. 3, Clause three; and Art. II, Clause one; *Raleigh Register and North Carolina Gazette*, 21 Dec. 1832, 3; *Raleigh Register and North Carolina Gazette*, 18 Jan. 1833, 3.
25. "Amendments to the Constitution of 1776," ratified 1835, Art. I, Sec. 3, Clause three; and Art. II, Clause one; Harold J. Counihan, "The North Carolina Constitutional Convention of 1835: A Study in Jacksonian Democracy," *North Carolina Historical Review* 46:4 (1969): 335–64; *Raleigh Register and North Carolina Gazette*, 21 Dec. 1832, 3; North Carolina Constitutional Revision of 1854, Art. I, Sec. 3, Clause two; Second Constitution of New York, 1821, Art. II, Sec. 1.
26. Bill Cecil-Fronsman, *Common Whites: Class and Culture in Antebellum North Carolina* (Lexington: Univ. Press of Kentucky, 1992), 76.
27. *State v. Mann*, 13 N.C. 263 at 264, 268.
28. Harriet Beecher Stowe, *Key to Uncle Tom's Cabin* (Boston: J. D. Jewett, 1853), 78–79, quoted in Robert M. Cover, *Justice Accused: Antislavery and the Judicial Process* (New Haven: Yale Univ. Press, 1975), 77–78.
29. *Scroggins v. Scroggins*, 14 N.C. 535 at 540 (1832), discussing Act of 1827, c. 19.
30. Ibid., c. 17. For a discussion of Ruffin as a legal "pioneer," see *Dictionary of North Carolina Biography*, ed. William S. Powell, vol. 5 (Chapel Hill: Univ. of North Carolina Press, 1994), 267.
31. *Scroggins v. Scroggins*, 14 N.C. 535 at 541–42 (1832).
32. Ibid., at 547, 544–45.
33. Ibid., at 545; *Barden v. Barden*, 14 N.C. 548 at 548–50 (1832).
34. *Barden v. Barden*, 14 N.C. 548 at 548–49 (1832).
35. Ibid., at 549–50.
36. Ibid., at 550.
37. Ibid.
38. *Long v. Long*, 77 N.C. 304 (1877); *Moss v. Moss*, 24 N.C. 55 (1841); *Steel v. Steel*, 104 N.C. 631 (1889); Walter F. Pratt Jr., "The Struggle for Judicial Independence in Antebellum North Carolina: The Story of Two Judges," *Law and History Review* 4:1 (1986): 129–59.
39. Alabama, *Federal Census*, 1840, text fiche, roll 4, p. 286, T-5; Alabama, *Federal Census*, 1850, text fiche, p. 362, M432–6.

2. A Former Slave and His White Wife during Reconstruction

The authors gratefully acknowledge the financial support of Davidson College as well as the assistance of Paul Dellinger, Walter Edgar, Katherine Franke,

Thomas Hanchett, Martha Hodes, Vicki Howard, Brian Luskey, Sally McMillen, Pam Rasfeld, Brian Smith, Ben Smoot, Katie Smoot, Christopher Waldrep, Peter Wallenstein, Jonathan Wells, and Richard Wertheimer.

1. Regarding the intensification of white opposition to intimate relationships between black men and white women following emancipation, see Martha Hodes, *White Women, Black Men: Illicit Sex in the Nineteenth-Century South* (New Haven: Yale Univ. Press, 1997).

2. "The First Train from Charlotte to Spartanburg," *Carolina Spartan,* 3 Apr. 1873, 2; "Charlotte and Spartanburg," *Charlotte Democrat,* 8 Apr. 1873, 3.

3. On "book law," see Peter W. Bardaglio, *Reconstructing the Household: Families, Sex, and the Law in the Nineteenth-Century South* (Chapel Hill: Univ. of North Carolina Press, 1995); Mary Frances Berry, "Judging Morality: Sexual Behavior and Legal Consequences in the Late Nineteenth Century South," *Journal of American History* 78 (Dec. 1991): 835–56; Peter Wallenstein, "Law and the Boundaries of Place and Race in Interracial Marriage: Interstate Comity, Racial Identity, and Miscegenation Laws in North Carolina, South Carolina, and Virginia, 1860s–1960s," *Akron Law Review* 32 (1999): 557–76; Peter Wallenstein, "Personal Liberty and Private Law: Race, Marriage, and the Law of Freedom; Alabama and Virginia, 1860s–1960s," *Chicago-Kent Law Review* 70 (1994): 371–437; Alfred Avins, "Anti-Miscegenation Laws and the Fourteenth Amendment: The Original Intent," *Virginia Law Review* 52 (July 1966): 1224–55; Harvey M. Applebaum, "Miscegenation Statutes: A Constitutional and Social Problem," *Georgetown Law Journal* 53 (1964): 49–91; and Charles Frank Robinson II, *Dangerous Liaisons: Sex and Love in the Segregated South* (Fayetteville: Univ. of Arkansas Press, 2003), 49–59. On "mob law," see Hodes, *White Women, Black Men;* Robinson, *Dangerous Liaisons,* 75–78; Scott Nelson, "Livestock, Boundaries, and Public Space in Spartanburg: African American Men, Elite White Women, and the Spectacle of Conjugal Relations," in *Sex, Love, Race: Crossing Boundaries in North American History,* ed. Martha Hodes (New York: New York Univ. Press, 1999); Lee W. Formwalt, "Notes and Documents: A Case of Interracial Marriage during Reconstruction," *Alabama Review* 45 (July 1992): 216–24.

4. Bardaglio, *Reconstructing the Household,* 188; Wallenstein, "Law and the Boundaries," 559; Hodes, *White Women, Black Men,* 266.

5. *1850 Census Population Schedules for Cleveland County, North Carolina,* microcopy M-432, roll 625, p. 169; *1860 Census Population Schedules for Gaston County, North Carolina,* microcopy M-653, roll 898, p. 3; *1870 Census Population Schedules for Lincoln County, North Carolina,* microcopy M-593, roll 1146, p. 226.

6. Paul H. Dellinger, *The Descendants of George and Jacob Dellinger* (Lincolnton, N.C.: Reprint Publisher's Press, 1995), 67; *1860 Census Population Schedules for Gaston County, North Carolina,* microcopy M-653, roll 898, p. 3;

1870 Census Population Schedules for Lincoln County, North Carolina, microcopy M-593, roll 1146, p. 226.

7. For information on Pinkney Ross's life, see *1860 Census Population Schedules, South Carolina, Slave Schedules, Spartanburg District*, microcopy M-653, reel 1237, p. 171; *1870 Census Population Schedules, Cleveland County, North Carolina*, microcopy M-593, reel 1131, p. 128; *1880 Census Population Schedules, South Carolina, Spartanburg County*, microcopy T-9, roll 1240, p. 242; *1900 Census Population Schedules, Cherokee County, South Carolina*, microcopy T-623, roll 1522, p. 95; *1910 Census Population Schedules, South Carolina, Darlington and Cherokee Counties*, microcopy T-624, roll 1454, p. 33; *1920 Census Population Schedules, Cherokee County, South Carolina*, microcopy 1690, roll 9, p. 29; and "Certificate of Death, Pink Ross," South Carolina State Board of Health: Bureau of Vital Statistics. No. 7512 (1925). On the names used by slaves and former slaves, see Herbert G. Gutman, *The Black Family in Slavery and Freedom, 1750–1925* (New York: Pantheon Books, 1976), 250–56.

8. *1870 Census Population Schedules, Cleveland County, North Carolina*, microcopy M-593, reel 1131, p. 128.

9. Gutman, *Black Family*, 93–95, 200–204, 250–56; *1870 Census Population Schedules, Lincoln County, North Carolina*, microcopy 1148, reel 125, p. 125.

10. *1870 Census Population Schedules, Cleveland County, North Carolina*, microcopy M-593, reel 1131, p. 129.

11. Carter G. Woodson, "The Beginnings of the Miscegenation of the Whites and Blacks," *Journal of Negro History* 3 (Oct. 1918): 345–46; Joseph R. Washington Jr., *Marriage in Black and White* (Boston: Beacon Press, 1970), 45; North Carolina Rev. Code, chap. 68, §7 (1838), quoted in *State v. Hairston*, 63 N.C. 451, at 452 (1869); Peter Wallenstein, *Tell the Court I Love My Wife: Race, Marriage, and Law; An American History* (New York: Palgrave Macmillan, 2002), 45.

12. Hinton Rowan Helper, *Nojoque: A Question for a Continent* (New York: G. W. Carleton, 1867), 218; Hodes, *White Women, Black Men*, 151.

13. See *State v. Alexander Reinhardt and Alice Love*, 63 N.C. 547 (1869); *State v. Wesley Hairston and Puss Williams*, 63 N.C. 451 (1869); *State v. Isaac Kennedy and Mag Kennedy*, 76 N.C. 251 (1877).

14. Regarding the tradition that marriages occur on the bride's home turf, see Arthur H. Cole, "The Price System and the Rites of Passage," *American Quarterly* 14 (winter 1962): 527–44; Steven M. Stowe, *Intimacy and Power in the Old South* (Baltimore: Johns Hopkins Univ. Press, 1987); and Ellen K. Rothman, *Hands and Hearts: A History of Courtship in America* (New York: Basic Books, 1984). We thank Vicki Howard for her input on this point. Regarding Spartanburg's role as a place for quick and easy marriages, see "A Runaway Match," *Charlotte Observer*, 25 Dec. 1875, 1.

15. Joel Williamson, *After Slavery: The Negro in South Carolina during Recon-*

struction (New York: Norton, 1975), 295; U.S. Bureau of the Census, *Historical Statistics of the United States, Colonial Times to 1970, Bicentennial Edition, Part 1* (Washington, D.C.: U.S. Department of Commerce, 1975), 34; Walter Edgar, *South Carolina: A History* (Columbia: Univ. of South Carolina Press, 1998), 383, 388; James S. Pike, *The Prostrate State: South Carolina under Negro Government* (New York: Harper and Row, 1968), 13; "A Fearful Picture of Negro Rule in South Carolina," *Charlotte Democrat*, 16 Apr. 1872, 2; Lerone Bennett, *Black Power U.S.A.: The Human Side of Reconstruction, 1867–1877* (Chicago: Johnson Publishing, 1967), 136; Wallenstein, *Tell the Court*, 80, 103–4.

    16. Edgar, *South Carolina*, 375; Joel Williamson, *New People: Miscegenation and Mulattoes in the United States* (New York: Free Press, 1980), 89; Wallenstein, *Tell the Court*, 61–62.

    17. For Fort Mill, see *1880 Census Population Schedules, York County, South Carolina*, microcopy T-9, reel 1243, pp. 520–48. For Broad River, see *1880 Census Population Schedules, Lexington County, South Carolina*, microcopy T-9, reels 1233–34, pp. 321–47.

    18. Information on the Rosses' marriage and move comes from *State v. Ross*, 76 N.C. 242, at 243 (1877). For information on economic and social conditions in South Carolina, see Edgar, *South Carolina*, 394; and Scott R. Nelson, *Iron Confederacies: Southern Railways, Klan Violence, and Reconstruction* (Chapel Hill: Univ. of North Carolina Press, 1999), 119–20.

    19. The "'hub' of this whole region" quotation comes from "North Carolina and the Region Round Charlotte," *Southern Home*, 1 Mar. 1875, 2. The "new era has dawned" quotation comes from "What Travelers Think of Charlotte," *Charlotte Democrat*, 10 Feb. 1874, 3. Facts relating to Charlotte's growth come from Thomas W. Hanchett, *Sorting Out the New South City: Race, Class, and Urban Development in Charlotte, 1875–1975* (Chapel Hill: Univ. of North Carolina Press, 1998), 22–25, 41; and Janette Greenwood, *Bittersweet Legacy: The Black and White "Better Classes" in Charlotte, 1850–1910* (Chapel Hill: Univ. of North Carolina Press, 1994), 40–41, 56–62.

    20. Quotation from "The Canvass," *Charlotte Democrat*, 22 June 1874, 3. Additional information in the paragraph comes from J. R. Davis, "Reconstruction in Cleveland County," in *Historical Papers*, series X (Durham: Trinity College Historical Society, 1914): 23; *State v. Reinhardt and Love*, 63 N.C. 547 (1869); "The Case of Judge Logan," *Charlotte Democrat*, 9 Jan. 1872, 3.

    21. On the election of 1874 in the Ninth Judicial District, see "Judge of the 9th Judicial District," *Southern Home*, 16 Mar. 1874, 2. Regarding Schenck's "Ku Kluxing" indictment, see *Charlotte Democrat*, 9 Jan. 1872, 3. Schenck's "poor, deluded, ignorant creatures" quotation comes from the David Schenck Diary, 304, in the David Schenck Papers, University of North Carolina, Chapel Hill. The "Logan is the representative of the negro party" quotation comes

from *Charlotte Democrat*, 22 June 1874, 3; see also "Independent Candidates," *Southern Home*, 1 June 1874, 2.

22. Election results from 1874 are discussed in "List of N.C. Congressmen, Judges, and Solicitors," *Southern Home*, 17 Aug. 1874, 2. The "all white men" quotation comes from "The Election," *Charlotte Democrat*, 10 Aug. 1874, 3.

23. On the wave of constitution revising in North Carolina and other southern states at the end of Reconstruction, see William Swindler, ed., *Sources and Documents of United States Constitutions*, vol. 7 (Dobbs Ferry, N.Y.: Oceana Publications, 1973–1979), 356. Regarding the idea that the Constitution of 1868 had been "dictated" to North Carolina and was, "in many particulars, unsuited to the wants and condition of our people," see "An Act to Call a Convention of the People of North Carolina," *Southern Home*, 2 Aug. 1875, 2. Regarding the support of Charlotte Democrats for the new constitution and its interracial marriage ban, see "The New Constitution of North Carolina," *Charlotte Observer*, 9 Jan. 1876; and "The Amendments," *Charlotte Democrat*, 14 Feb. 1876, 3.

24. On North Carolina's 1876 gubernatorial election, see "Gubernatorial Candidates," *Charlotte Democrat*, 14 Feb. 1876, 3. The "[w]hile white men intend to rule" quotation comes from "The Election," *Charlotte Democrat*, 10 Aug. 1874, 3. Statements regarding Democratic views on intimate relationships between black men and white women are based in part on *Charlotte Observer*, 16 July 1876, 4; and "Eloping Party Heard From," *Charlotte Observer*, 16 July 1876, 2.

25. Information on the Mecklenburg County superior court's criminal docket in 1873 comes from Minute Book, Mecklenburg County Superior Court, 1872–1875, North Carolina State Archives, Raleigh. The following F&A cases were heard in the Mecklenburg County superior court on 28 August 1876: *State v. Ben Sharron*, *State v. Isaac Kennedy and Mag Kennedy*, *State v. L. Connor and Mary Sureeh*, *State v. Wyley Davidson and Sallie Lafevers*, *State v. Matt West and ___ West*. Cases of 29 August: *State v. Lee Henderson and Nellie Ross*. Cases of 30 August: *State v. Pink Ross and Sarah Ross*. Cases of 31 August: *State v. Joe Jackson and Jane Jackson*, *State v. Isaac Kennedy and Mag Kennedy*, *State v. Jim Jackson and Sarah Jackson*. Cases of 6 September: *State v. Isaac Kennedy*.

26. *1870 Census Population Schedules, Mecklenburg County, North Carolina*, microcopy M-593, reel 1148, p. 73.

27. The F&A cases from the August 1876 special session wherein the races of the defendants could be positively identified using court reports, census records, city directory records, and newspaper reports were as follows: *State v. Ross*, *State v. Lee Henderson and Nellie Ross*, *State v. Geo Summerville and Sallie Pharr*, *State v. Isaac Kennedy and Mag Kennedy*, *State v. Jim Jackson and Sarah*

Jackson, and *State v. Joe Jackson and Jane Jackson.* See "Superior Court," *Charlotte Democrat,* 4 Sept. 1876, 3, for listings of Henderson/Ross, Summerville/Pharr, and Kennedy/Kennedy relationships. See also *1870 Population Schedules of Mecklenburg County, North Carolina,* microcopy M-593, reel 1148, p. 261, for census listing of Jim and Sarah Jackson. See also *1880 Census Population Schedules of York County, South Carolina,* microcopy T-9, reel 1243, p. 541, for census listing of Joe and Jane Jackson.

28. *State v. Kennedy,* 76 N.C. 251 (1877); "Intermarriage between Whites and Negroes," *Charlotte Observer,* 3 Sept. 1876, 4.

29. The phrase "very interesting and novel" comes from "Intermarriage between Whites and Negroes," *Charlotte Observer,* 3 Sept. 1876, 4. Proof that lawyers for both sides agreed that the special verdict should be used in their case appears in *State v. Isaac Kennedy and Mag Kennedy,* "Transcript from Mecklenburg County" (1877), 4, North Carolina State Archives, Raleigh. Schenck's charge to the jury is reported in "Judge Schenck's Charge," *Charlotte Observer,* 30 Aug. 1876, 3. Additional information regarding the Kennedy case comes from *State v. Kennedy,* 76 N.C. 251 (1877).

30. For background information regarding court-appointed lawyers, see Reginald Smith, *Justice and the Poor* (Boston: Merrymount Press, 1919), 103. For evidence suggesting that local courts did occasionally appoint attorneys, see "Served His Time Out," *Charlotte Observer,* 5 Apr. 1876, 3. For evidence suggestive of Pinkney Ross's humble economic standing at the time, see *1870 Census Population Schedules, Cleveland and Columbus Counties, North Carolina,* microcopy M-593, roll 1131, p. 128; *Beasley & Emerson's Charlotte Directory for 1875–76* (Charlotte, N.C.: Beasley & Emerson, 1875), 73; and Thomas Hanchett to John W. Wertheimer, e-mail correspondence, 7 Mar. 2002. We thank Hanchett for his assistance. For information regarding indigent legal defense, see Smith, *Justice and the Poor,* 114. For interracial marriage appeals in which the couples apparently appeared without legal representation, see *State v. Hairston,* 63 N.C. 451 (1869); and *State v. Reinhardt and Love,* 63 N.C. 547 (1869). Criminal cases from the same year as the Rosses' legal appeal in which the defendants appear to have lacked lawyers either at trial or on appeal include the following: *State v. Hawkins,* 77 N.C. 494 (1877); *State v. Martin Liles and others,* 77 N.C. 496 (1877); *State v. Belk,* 76 N.C. 10 (1877); *State v. Carter,* 76 N.C. 20 (1877); *State v. Epps,* 76 N.C. 55 (1877); *State v. Morgan,* 77 N.C. 510 (1877); and *State v. Hovis,* 76 N.C. 117 (1877).

31. The 1875 *Charlotte City Directory* reports that the law office of Shipp & Bailey was on the corner of Trade and Church streets, just one block from the corner of Trade and Tryon. For a discussion of the significance of this address, see Hanchett, *Sorting Out the New South City,* 37–38. The description of Shipp as one of the "best-informed lawyers in the State" comes from Jerome Dowd, *Sketches of Prominent Living North Carolinians* (Raleigh: Edwards and Brough-

ton, 1888), 109. Shipp's turn as judge is reported in William S. Powell, ed., *Dictionary of North Carolina Biography*, vol. 5 (Chapel Hill: Univ. of North Carolina Press, 1994), 337.

32. For details of Bailey's career, see Powell, ed., *Dictionary of North Carolina Biography*, vol. 1, 85–86. Schenck's quotation regarding Bailey's excellence as a lawyer comes from the David Schenck Diary, 226.

33. Shipp's politics are discussed in Dowd, *Sketches of Prominent Living North Carolinians*, 108; and John Macfie, "Shipp, William Marcus," in Powell, ed., *Dictionary of North Carolina Biography*, vol. 5, 337. Judge Schenck's private remarks concerning Bailey appear in the David Schenck Diary, 226. The term "very liberal and independent" regarding Bailey is from Dowd, *Sketches of Prominent Living North Carolinians*, 138.

34. See *Mills v. the Salisbury Building and Loan Association*, 75 N.C. 292 (1876); *State v. Neely*, 74 N.C. 425 (1876); *State v. Ross*, 76 N.C. 242 (1877).

35. The quotation regarding Schenck's formidable ability to read bills of indictment comes from an undated Charlotte-area newspaper clipping found in the David Schenck Diary, 238. For the indictment itself, see "State vs. Pink Ross and Sarah Ross, Transcript from Mecklenburg Co.," filed in North Carolina Supreme Court, 22 Jan. 1877, case file #280 from Mecklenburg County, North Carolina State Archives, Raleigh, N.C. (hereafter, Ross case file).

36. Shipp and Bailey's Fourteenth Amendment argument appears in "Brief of Defendant's Counsel," Ross case file. See also *Loving v. Virginia*, 388 U.S. 1 (1967). Regarding the Fourteenth Amendment and antimiscegenation laws during this period, see Peggy Pascoe, "Miscegenation Law, Court Cases, and Ideologies of 'Race' in Twentieth-Century America," *Journal of American History* 83:1 (June 1996): 50.

37. "Brief of Defendant's Counsel," Ross case file.

38. See *1870 Census Population Schedules, Cleveland and Columbus Counties, North Carolina*, microcopy M-593, roll 1131, p. 128.

39. *State v. Ross*, 76 N.C. 242, at 243 (1877).

40. For information on the jury, which likely consisted only of whites, see Minutes of the Mecklenburg County Superior Court, 1876, August special term, Mecklenburg County Superior Court, Charlotte, N.C.; *Charlotte, N.C. City Directory, 1879–1880* ([Charlotte, N.C.?]: Chas. Emerson & Co., 1879); 1870 Census; U.S. National Archives and Records Administration, Soundex, 1880 Census.

41. *State v. Moore*, 29 N.C. 228, at 230 (1847).

42. Robert W. Winston, "A Rebel Colonel: A Strange Career," *South Atlantic Quarterly* 30:1 (Jan. 1931): 84–92; Samuel A. Ashe, ed., *Biographical History of North Carolina* (Greensboro: Charles L. Van Noppen, 1906), 250.

43. *State v. Ross*, 76 N.C. 242, at 245 (1877).

44. Rodman's statement that the court agreed with the legislature's finding that interracial marriages were immoral appears in *State v. Ross,* 76 N.C. 242, at 244 (1877). Rodman's holding that Pinkney Ross was domiciled in South Carolina as of the wedding day—and that Sarah adopted her husband's domicile immediately upon marriage—appears in ibid., at 243. The quotation "as if both parties had been domiciled" appears in ibid., at 244.

45. For Justice Rodman's quoted words, see *State v. Ross,* 76 N.C. 242, at 246 (1877). Regarding the point that miscegenation, prior to *Loving v. Virginia* (1967), was the "great" exception to the general rule that marriages conducted anywhere were valid everywhere, see Hendrik Hartog, *Man and Wife in America: A History* (Cambridge, Mass.: Harvard Univ. Press, 2000), 380 n.39.

46. For the idea that Rodman felt "compelled" to rule in favor of the Rosses, see *State v. Ross,* 76 N.C. 242, at 247 (1877). For Justice Edwin Reade's dissent, see ibid., at 248–50.

47. Information on the Rosses' whereabouts comes from Charlotte City Directory, 1875, Public Library of Charlotte, Mecklenburg County; Charlotte City Directory, 1878–1879, Public Library of Charlotte, Mecklenburg County; *1880 Census Population Schedules, Spartanburg County, South Carolina,* microcopy T-9, roll 1240, p. 242. Information on South Carolina political trends and their influence on interracial marriage law comes from George Brown Tindall, *South Carolina Negroes, 1877–1900* (Columbia: Univ. of South Carolina Press, 1952), 296–98; Wallenstein, *Tell the Court,* 103–4; and South Carolina Constitution of 1895, Article 3, Section 33.

48. *1870 Census Population Schedules, Cleveland and Columbus Counties, North Carolina,* microcopy M-593, roll 1131, p. 128; *1880 Census Population Schedules, Spartanburg County, South Carolina,* microcopy T-9, roll 1240, p. 242.

49. *1870 Census Population Schedules, Lenoir, Lincoln, and Macon Counties, North Carolina,* microcopy M-593, roll 1146, p. 226; *1880 Census Population Schedules, Spartanburg County, South Carolina,* microcopy T-9, roll 1240, p. 242.

50. *1900 Census Population Schedules, Cherokee County, South Carolina,* microcopy T-623, roll 1522, p. 95.

51. "Celebration: A Dream That Became a Reality: Mike's Creek Missionary Baptist Church," unpublished pamphlet printed in 1987 to commemorate the opening of a new church facility. Copy in author's possession. We thank the current members of Mike's Creek Baptist Church for generously providing us with a copy of this pamphlet.

52. *1910 Census Population Schedules, Darlington and Cherokee Counties, South Carolina,* microcopy T-624, roll 1454, p. 33; *1920 Census Population Schedules, Cherokee County, South Carolina,* microcopy 1690, roll 9, p. 29; "Certificate of Death, Pink Ross," South Carolina State Board of Health: Bureau of Vital Statistics. No. 7512 (1925).

3. De Jure Housing Segregation in Progressive Era Winston-Salem

The authors acknowledge the generous support of an Abernethy Research Grant from Davidson College. They also thank the following people: David Bernstein, Carolyn Daly, Edward Daly, Bobby Donaldson, Ann Douglas, Earl Edmondson, the staff of the Forsyth County Public Library, Beverly Gabard, Pam Grundy, Peter Wong, Joe Gutekanst, Brian Luskey, Sally McMillen, James Miller, Gregory Mixon, Langdon Oppermann, Malcolm Partin, Patricia Perkins, Janet Shannon, Loretta Wertheimer, and Richard Wertheimer.

1. See "William H. Donnell," Certificate of Death, no. 34–95/285, North Carolina State Board of Health, Bureau of Vital Statistics, Office of the Register of Deeds of Forsyth County, N.C.; and Winston-Salem City Directories, Forsyth County Public Library.

2. "Strange career" is a coinage from C. Vann Woodward, *The Strange Career of Jim Crow*, 3rd ed. (New York: Oxford Univ. Press, 1974).

3. The quotation is from Richard Bardolph, ed., *The Civil Rights Record: Black Americans and the Law, 1849–1970* (New York: Thomas A. Cromwell, 1970), 168. See also Woodward's *Strange Career of Jim Crow*, 124; Catherine A. Barnes, *Journey from Jim Crow: The Desegregation of Southern Transit* (New York: Columbia Univ. Press, 1983), 11; John Hope Franklin and Alfred A. Moss Jr., *From Slavery to Freedom: A History of African Americans*, 7th ed. (New York: McGraw-Hill, 1994), 352, 461; and Gunnar Myrdal, *An American Dilemma: The Negro Problem and Modern Democracy*, vol. 2 (New York: Harper Brothers, 1944), 1005.

4. The "victory for Winston-Salem blacks" quotation comes from Robert Rodgers Korstad, *Civil Rights Unionism: Tobacco Workers and the Struggle for Democracy in the Mid-Twentieth-Century South* (Chapel Hill: Univ. of North Carolina Press, 2003), 74. The "challenged Winston-Salem's housing segregation ordinance and won" quotation is from Bertha Hampton Miller, "Blacks in Winston-Salem, North Carolina: Community Development in an Era of Benevolent Paternalism" (PhD diss., Duke University, 1981), 147.

5. The "powerful American commitment" quotation comes from George Fredrickson, *White Supremacy: A Comparative Study in American and South African History* (New York: Oxford Univ. Press, 1981), 254. The "*laissez-faire* jurisprudence" quotation comes from David E. Bernstein, "Philip Sober Controlling Philip Drunk: *Buchanan v. Warley* in Historical Perspective," *Vanderbilt Law Review* 51 (May 1998): 872–73. See also "John Marshall Harlan and the Constitutional Rights of Negroes: The Transformation of a Southerner," *Yale Law Review* 66 (Apr. 1957): 695–96.

6. C. Vann Woodward, *Origins of the New South, 1877–1913* (Baton Rouge: Louisiana State Univ. Press, 1971), 469.

7. Regarding Progressive Era residential segregation measures, see Gilbert

T. Stephenson, "The Segregation of White and Negro Races in Cities," *South Atlantic Quarterly* 8 (Jan. 1914): 1–8; Garrett Power, "Apartheid Baltimore Style: The Residential Segregation Ordinances of 1910–1913," *Maryland Law Review* 42 (1983): 289; Bernstein, "Philip Sober Controlling Philip Drunk," 835–36; Roger L. Rice, "Residential Segregation by Law, 1910–1917," *Journal of Southern History* 34 (May 1968): 179–99; A. Leon Higginbotham Jr., F. Michael Higginbotham, and S. Sandile Ngcobo, "De Jure Housing Segregation in the United States and South Africa: The Difficult Pursuit for Racial Justice," *University of Illinois Law Review* 1990 (1990): 763–877. Regarding the history of Winston during this period, see Korstad, *Civil Rights Unionism*, 61–92; Mary Plegar Smith, "Municipal Development in North Carolina, 1665–1930: A History of Urbanization" (PhD diss., University of North Carolina–Chapel Hill, 1930); National Urban League, *A Study of the Economic and Cultural Activities of the Negro People of Winston-Salem (and Forsyth County), North Carolina*, Book One (New York: Urban League, 1946), 10; Davyd Foard Hood, "Winston-Salem's Suburbs: West End to Reynolds Park," in *Early Twentieth-Century Suburbs in North Carolina*, ed. Catherine W. Bishir and Lawrence S. Earley (Raleigh: Division of Archives and History, 1985), 64.

8. We thank Pamela Grundy for her insight regarding the differences between tobacco towns and textile towns. Additional information in this paragraph comes from Nannie M. Tilley, *The R. J. Reynolds Tobacco Company* (Chapel Hill: Univ. of North Carolina Press, 1985), 38; Miller, "Blacks in Winston-Salem," 9, 78; Korstad, *Civil Rights Unionism*, 61–92; Langdon E. Oppermann, "Historic and Architectural Resources of African-American Neighborhoods in Northeastern Winston-Salem, North Carolina (ca. 1900–1947)," Multiple Property Documentation Form, National Register of Historic Places, Forsyth County Joint Historic Properties Commission [no date], E9–E12 and E27–E30; Michael Shirley, *From Congregation Town to Industrial City: Culture and Change in a Southern Community* (New York: New York Univ. Press, 1994), 202; Alan Willis, "Blacks in Winston—A History Emerging from Obscurity," *Sentinel (Winston-Salem)*, 10 Feb. 1983, A13; and Langdon E. Oppermann, "Winston-Salem's African American Neighborhoods: 1870–1950," Architectural and Planning Report, 1994, Forsyth County Joint Historic Properties Commission, 43–44.

9. For evidence of the dramatic growth in numbers of local real estate agents, contractors, etc., see Winston-Salem City Directories, 1890 and 1910, North Carolina Room, Forsyth County Public Library, Winston-Salem. For a representative sampling of restrictive covenants in Winston, see Deed Book 35, pp. 281, 395; and Deed Book 38, pp. 46, 83, 325, Register of Deeds, Winston-Salem. On restrictive covenants generally, see Herman H. Long and Charles S. Johnson, *People vs. Property: Restrictive Covenants in Housing* (Nashville: Fisk Univ. Press, 1947); Mark V. Tushnet, *Making Civil Rights Law: Thurgood Mar-*

shall and the Supreme Court, 1936–1961 (New York: Oxford Univ. Press, 1994), 81–98; and Thomas W. Hanchett, *Sorting Out the New South City: Race, Class, and Urban Development in Charlotte, 1875–1975* (Chapel Hill: Univ. of North Carolina Press, 1998), 116.

10. "Colored Fair to Be Held at Rural Hall," *Twin-City Daily Sentinel (Winston-Salem)*, 29 Aug. 1912, 2; "Erection of a Colored Y.M.C.A. Building Proposed," *Twin-City Daily Sentinel*, 22 Mar. 1913, 4; "Colored Women's Civic League Organized Here," *Twin-City Daily Sentinel*, 8 Mar. 1913, 7. For separate marriage notices, see *Twin-City Daily Sentinel*, ca. Oct. 1912; for hospitals, see Miller, "Blacks in Winston-Salem," 139–41; Glenda Elizabeth Gilmore, *Gender and Jim Crow: Women and the Politics of White Supremacy in North Carolina, 1896–1920* (Chapel Hill: Univ. of North Carolina Press, 1996); Woodward, *Origins of the New South;* David S. Cecelski, *Along Freedom Road: Hyde County, North Carolina, and the Fate of Black Schools in the South* (Chapel Hill: Univ. of North Carolina Press, 1994); Korstad, *Civil Rights Unionism*, 54–60.

11. Quotation from "Winston Faces a Crisis," *(Winston-Salem) Journal*, 17 July 1912, 4. For evidence of Winston-Salem's embrace of technocratic regulations during the Progressive Era, see *Journal*, 16 July 1912; and *Twin-City Daily Sentinel*, 31 July 1912, 5.

12. For the appearance of a handful of African Americans on East Fourth Street, see Winston-Salem City Directories, 1911–1913. The "stable white residential neighborhood" quotation comes from Oppermann, "Historic and Architectural Resources," E11. Regarding the quality of the African American housing in this part of town, see Korstad, *Civil Rights Unionism*, 74.

13. "Movement to Oust Negroes," *Journal*, 14 June 1912, 1.

14. "Segregate Negroes in East Winston," *Journal*, 14 June 1912, 1; "Race Segregation Ordinance Is Enacted by Aldermen," *Twin-City Daily Sentinel*, 14 June 1912, 5; and "Race Segregation," *Union Republican (Winston-Salem)*, 20 June 1912, 6.

15. "Segregate Negroes in East Winston," *Journal*, 14 June 1912, 1.

16. The 13 June measure is reproduced in Miller, "Blacks in Winston-Salem," 273, and in "Race Segregation," *Union Republican*, 20 June 1912, 6. For an account of the discussions that led to the replacement of the first ordinance, see "Mass Meeting of Citizens," *Journal*, 19 June 1912, 1; "Mass Meeting to Be Held in East Winston," *Twin-City Daily Sentinel*, 19 June 1912, 1.

17. "Segregation in Whole City," *Journal*, 6 July 1912, 1; "General Segregation," *Union Republican*, 11 July 1912, 6.

18. Miller, "Blacks in Winston-Salem," 273–74; "Segregation in Whole City," *Journal*, 6 July 1912, 1; "General Segregation," *Union Republican*, 11 July 1912, 6.

19. See "Against Removal Depot Street School," *Twin-City Daily Sentinel*, 11 Nov. 1913, 6; "Colored Man Writes on Removal of School," *Journal*, 15

Nov. 1913, 6; "Removal Colored Graded School Discussed," *Twin-City Daily Sentinel,* 8 Nov. 1913, 3; "Removal of Depot Street School Is Abandoned," *Twin-City Daily Sentinel,* 17 Nov. 1913, 1.

20. "Segregate Negroes in East Winston," *Journal,* 14 June 1912, 1; "Negroes Fight Mr. Bennett," *Journal,* 5 Nov. 1912, 1; "Colored Voters Hold Meeting Here Tonight," *Journal,* 1 Nov. 1912, 1.

21. The "there was no opposition" quotation comes from "Segregate Negroes in East Winston," *Journal,* 14 June 1912, 1. Information on Atkins comes from Oppermann, "Historic and Architectural Resources," E13–E15; "Atkins Outlines Negroes Progress," *Journal and Sentinel (Winston-Salem),* 10 Feb. 1929, 7b; and Korstad, *Civil Rights Unionism,* 77–78.

22. "Segregation Discussed by Aldermen," *Western Sentinel (Winston-Salem),* 20 May 1913, 3; "Favor Strict Enforcement of Segregation Law," *Journal,* 17 May 1913, 1; "Segregation Law Discussed by Alderman," *Twin-City Daily Sentinel,* 17 May 1913, 8.

23. "Thinks City Should Provide Good Streets for Negroes," *Twin-City Daily Sentinel,* 9 June 1913, 8.

24. Evidence of the Darnells' movements appears in Deed Book 121, p.167; Deed Book 108, p. 374. Information on the African American community in Winston comes from Miller, "Blacks in Winston-Salem," 264; and Korstad, *Civil Rights Unionism,* 61–92.

25. Deed Book 108, p. 374. For evidence of Sledge's past as a seller of groceries and sewing machines, as well as his future as a farmer, see Winston-Salem City Directories, 1902–1913, 1916. Evidence of Sledge's business practices appears in *Journal,* 12 May 1912, 4; 7 Jan. 1912; 17 Feb. 1912; 22 Mar. 1912; and 21 June 1912; and in the *Twin-City Daily Sentinel* in 1912 on 23 Mar., 30 Mar., 30 Apr., and 18 May; *Twin-City Daily Sentinel* in 1913 on 24 May, 9 June, 23 June, 28 June, and 18 Sept.

26. A photocopy of this document, which was written on the letterhead of Sledge's real estate office, appears at page 1030 of the superior court record of the *Darnell* case. The document is also introduced into the record on page 1043. The case's superior court records can be found in *Criminal Cases Docket,* vol. 14, in room 216 of the Winston-Salem Hall of Justice. This brief entry leads to the fuller court record on microfilm 1066, pp. 1021–55 (hereafter, *Darnell* superior court record).

27. "Segregation Ordinance to Be Tested in Courts," *Twin-City Daily Sentinel,* 9 July 1913, 5; "Municipal Court Did a Rushing Business," *Union Republican,* 8 Jan. 1914.

28. *Darnell* superior court record, pp. 1027–29; North Carolina Supreme Court Original Cases, 1909–1929, February term, 1914, case 337, North Carolina State Archives, Raleigh.

29. Information on black attorneys comes from 1913 Winston-Salem City

Directory. Information on John Fitts comes from "The African-American Lawyer in Forsyth County, North Carolina: 1895–1960," 1996 calendar (Winston-Salem: Society for the Study of African-American History in Winston-Salem), North Carolina Room, Forsyth County Public Library, Winston-Salem.

30. "[O]ne of the very strongest in the state" comes from R. B. Glenn, "John Cameron Buxton," in *Biographical History of North Carolina: From Colonial Times to the Present*, ed. Samuel A. Ashe, vol. 5 (Greensboro: Charles L. Van Noppen, 1906), 49. Additional information in this paragraph comes from Jeffrey J. Crow, "'Fusion, Confusion, and Negroism': Schisms among Negro Republicans in the North Carolina Election of 1896," *North Carolina Historical Review* 53 (Oct. 1976): 381–83; Annie Lee Singletary, "Cy Watson: Builder of Winston-Salem," *Journal*, 9 Nov. 1941, 39; Thomas H. Johnson Jr., "Watson, Cyrus Barksdale," in *Dictionary of North Carolina Biography*, ed. William S. Powell, vol. 6 (Chapel Hill: Univ. of North Carolina Press, 1996), 131; and W. A. Blair and S. A. Ashe, "Cyrus Barksdale Watson," in *Biographical History of North Carolina*, vol. 4, 460–68.

31. See *Union Republican*, 15 Nov. 1900, 2; "In Memoriam: John Cameron Buxton, 1852–1917," 12 [1917], North Carolina Collection, University of North Carolina Library, Chapel Hill; R. B. Glenn, "John Cameron Buxton," in *Biographical History of North Carolina*, vol. 5, 47–49.

32. On southern paternalism, see Guion Griffis Johnson, "Southern Paternalism toward Negroes after Emancipation," *Journal of Southern History* 23 (Nov. 1957): 490. On generational difference among whites in the Jim Crow era, see Glenda Gilmore's discussion of the "New White Man" in *Gender and Jim Crow*, 61–89. Watson's anti-lynching efforts are reported in Singletary, "Cy Watson," 39. Buxton's legal work on behalf of African Americans and his reputation as a "true friend" of the "negro race" are reported in *Western Sentinel*, 22 Mar. 1910; *Twin-City Daily Sentinel*, 23 July 1912, 8; and "In Memoriam: John Cameron Buxton," 12–13. Buxton's work for George Penn is discussed in "Favor Strict Enforcement of Segregation Law," *Journal*, 17 May 1913, 1.

33. For evidence of Watson and Buxton's longstanding real estate interest in Winston, see Deed Book 35, p. 367; and General Index to Real Estate Conveyances, Register of Deeds, under "Grantor 'W,'" for Watson. For evidence of Watson, Buxton & Watson's frequent service as trustee on deeds securing mortgage loans, see General Index to Real Estate Conveyances under "Grantee 'W.'" Watson and Buxton's involvement in the loan that Sledge took out on lot 169 is evident in Deed of Trust Book 73, p. 258, Register of Deeds. Buxton's service as president of the Winston-Salem Building and Loan Association is reported in Power, "Apartheid Baltimore Style," 293.

34. Stephenson was labeled "perhaps the country's foremost" scholar of racial segregation law in Clarence Poe, "Rural Land Segregation between

Whites and Negroes: A Reply to Mr. Stephenson," *South Atlantic Quarterly* 8 (July 1914): 208. Stephenson's "welfare of both races" quotation can be found in Gilbert T. Stephenson, *Race Distinctions in American Law* (New York: D. Appleton, 1910), 361. For a rephrasing of the same argument, see Gilbert T. Stephenson, "Colored People and Law Enforcement," *Journal*, 10 May 1913, 2. Stephenson's conclusion that Winston's ordinance was a legitimate separate-but-equal race distinction appears in Gilbert T. Stephenson, "The Segregation of the White and Negro Races in Cities," *South Atlantic Quarterly* 8 (Jan. 1914): 1. See also Gilbert T. Stephenson Papers, PCMS 160, box 11, folder 126, office journal #1, pp. 213–31, Special Collections, Z. Smith Reynolds Library, Wake Forest University; and Gilbert T. Stephenson, "The Segregation of the White and Negro Races in Rural Communities of North Carolina," *South Atlantic Quarterly* 8 (Apr. 1914): 107–17.

35. *State v. Gurry*, 88 A. 546 (Md. 1913); "Segregation Case in the Superior Court," *Twin-City Daily Sentinel*, 3 Oct. 1913, 1; "Appeal to Supreme Court in the Segregation Case," *Journal*, 18 Jan. 1914, 8.

36. *Darnell* superior court record, 1036–40.

37. Ibid., 1034–35.

38. Ibid., 1034, 1036.

39. Ibid., 1037–38.

40. Ibid., 1030, 1043.

41. "Appeal to the Supreme Court in the Segregation Case," *Journal*, 18 Jan. 1914, 8; *Darnell* superior court record, 1047 and 1025.

42. "Verdict of Guilty in Segregation Case Here," *Twin-City Daily Sentinel*, 19 Jan. 1914, 5; editorial, *Journal*, 20 Jan. 1914, 4.

43. "Verdict of Guilty in Segregation Case Here," *Twin-City Daily Sentinel*, 19 Jan. 1914, 5; "Colored Doctor Appeals Case," *Journal*, 12 Aug. 1913, 5; "In Municipal Court," *Journal*, 4 Sept. 1913, 8; Deed Book 122, p. 207; Deed Book 127, p. 136.

44. The "awaited with interest" quotation comes from "Mr. Stephenson's Contentions as to Segregation of Races," *Twin-City Daily Sentinel*, 4 Apr. 1914, 9. The "general welfare" clause, section 44 of the Winston city charter, is quoted in *State v. Darnell*, 166 N.C. 300 at 301 (1914). Stephenson's "[w]herever there is indiscriminate residence" quotation comes from "City Segregation," *Union Republican*, 9 Apr. 1914, 3. See also *Twin-City Daily Sentinel*, 4 Apr. 1914, 9.

45. "Brief of Watson, Buxton & Watson, Counsel for the Defendant," 3–5, North Carolina Supreme Court Original Cases, 1909–1929, February term, 1914, case 337, North Carolina State Archives, Raleigh.

46. The quotation that freedmen could not "live among us in the present state of things" comes from Willis P. Whichard, "A Place for Walter Clark in the American Judicial Tradition" (master's thesis, University of Virginia,

1984), 23–24. Additional information in this paragraph comes from Aubrey Lee Brooks, *Walter Clark, Fighting Judge* (Chapel Hill: Univ. of North Carolina Press, 1944), 28–31, 253–54; David Blackwell, "Walter Clark—North Carolina's Foremost Liberal," in Walter Clark vertical file, North Carolina Supreme Court Library; Walter Clark, "Ballots for Both: An Address" (Raleigh: Commercial Printing Co., 1916), 10; Clark, "Votes for Women" (reprint from *Wilmington [N.C.] Dispatch*, 22 Feb. 1919), in Walter Clark vertical file, North Carolina Supreme Court Library, 2–3.

47. Bernstein, "Philip Sober Controlling Philip Drunk," 804–20; platform of Walter Clark, Candidate for U.S. Senate, North Carolina Collection, Wilson Library, University of North Carolina, Chapel Hill; *Twin-City Daily Sentinel*, 21 June 1912, 3; Walter Clark, *Address on Reform in Law and Legal Procedure, 30 June 1914* (Wilmington, N.C.: Wilmington Stamp & Printing Co.), 15; Walter Clark, "Centennial of the Supreme Court of North Carolina: Response to Addresses," 4 Jan. 1919, 4–5; Walter Clark, *Government by Judges Address delivered at Cooper Union, in New York City, on January 29, 1914* (Washington, D.C.: Government Printing Office, 1914), 1–24.

48. For evidence of Watson's friendship with Clark, see C. B. Watson to Walter Clark, 4 and 6 Sept., 4 Nov., and 9 Dec. 1901, and 19 June 1913, Walter Clark Papers, North Carolina State Archives, Raleigh; Brooks, *Walter Clark*, 72; "Chief Justice Clark to Speak Here October 26," *Twin-City Daily Sentinel*, 16 Oct. 1912, 1; "Judge Clark Is Confident," *Journal*, 27 Oct. 1912, 1; "Cyrus B. Watson for Judge Clark: Distinguished Democrat Warmly Endorses Him for United States Senate" (unidentified clipping, 1912); and "Cyrus B. Watson," *News and Observer (Raleigh)*, Nov. 1916, in North Carolina Clipping File through 1975, University of North Carolina Library, Chapel Hill, reel 39, 116–17. Regarding Clark's paternalism toward African Americans, see Walter Clark, "The Negro in North Carolina and the South," speech, 26 May 1920, in Daniel Harvey Hill Jr. Papers, North Carolina Archives, Raleigh; *State v. Michner*, 172 N.C. 895 (1916); James E. Shepard to Walter Clark, 7 Feb. 1919, Walter Clark Papers; Whichard, "Place for Walter Clark," 20–22; and Brooks, *Walter Clark*, 175.

49. The two state cases that struck down residential segregation ordinances are *State v. Gurry*, 121 Md. 534 (1913); and *Carey v. City of Atlanta*, 143 Ga. 192 (1915). The two that upheld such measures are *Hopkins v. City of Richmond*, 117 Va. 692 (1915); and *Harden v. City of Atlanta*, 147 Ga. 248 (1917), discussed in Bernstein, "Philip Sober Controlling Philip Drunk," 836 n.192.

50. *State v. Darnell*, 166 N.C. 300 at 302 (1914).

51. Regarding the strength of Dillon's Rule in the South, see Clay L. Writ, "Dillon's Rule," *Virginia Town and City* 24:8 (Aug. 1989): 4. Regarding the concept of states' rights generally, see Richard E. Ellis, *The Union at Risk* (New York: Oxford Univ. Press, 1987), ix, 1; Arthur Schlesinger, "The State Rights

Fetish," in *New Viewpoints in American History* (New York: Macmillan, 1926), 220–44; Jesse T. Carpenter, *The South as a Conscious Minority, 1789–1861* (New York: New York Univ. Press, 1930; reprint, Columbia: Univ. of South Carolina Press, 1990), 245–54; Harold Mixon, "The Rhetoric of States' Rights and White Supremacy," in *A New Diversity in Contemporary Southern Rhetoric*, ed. Calvin M. Logue and Howard Dorgan (Baton Rouge: Louisiana State Univ. Press, 1987), 166–87; Bruce Nelson, "Black Equality in Mobile during World War II," *Journal of Southern History* 80 (Dec. 1993): 984; Howard W. Allen, A. R. Clausen, and Jerome M. Clubb, "Political Reform and Negro Rights in the Senate, 1909–1915," *Journal of Southern History* 37 (May 1971); Kenneth R. Johnson, "Kate Gordon and the Woman Suffrage Movement in the South," *Journal of Southern History* 38 (Aug. 1972): 365; and Adrienne Koch and Harry Ammon, "The Virginia and Kentucky Resolutions: An Episode in Jefferson's and Madison's Defense of Civil Liberties," *William and Mary Quarterly* 5 (Apr. 1948): 145.

52. *Small v. Edenton*, 146 N.C. 527 at 528 (1908). See also *Tate v. Greensboro*, 114 N.C. 392 (1894); and, contra, *State v. Webber*, 107 N.C. 962 (1890); *State v. Thomas*, 118 N.C. 1221 (1896); and *State v. Dannenberg*, 150 N.C. 799 (1909). Information on Dillon's Rule and its application to North Carolina law comes from David W. Owens, "Local Government Authority to Implement Smart Growth Progress: Dillon's Rule, Legislative Reform, and the Current State of Affairs in North Carolina," *Wake Forest Law Review* 35 (fall 2000): 671–705; and Louis Csoka, "The Dream of Greater Municipal Autonomy: Should the Legislature or the Courts Modify Dillon's Rule, a Common Law Restraint on Municipal Power?" *North Carolina Central Law Journal* 29:2 (2007): 194–223.

53. *State v. Darnell*, 166 N.C. 300 at 302 (1914); "George Hubbard Brown," in *Dictionary of North Carolina Biography*, ed. William S. Powell, vol. 1 (Chapel Hill: Univ. of North Carolina Press, 1979), 244–45; *Buchanan v. Warley*, 245 U.S. 60 (1917); Bernstein, "Philip Sober Controlling Philip Drunk," 797–879.

54. *State v. Darnell*, 166 N.C. 300 at 302 (1914).

55. Ibid., at 304.

56. Ibid., at 304–5.

57. The phrase "anxiously awaited" comes from "Segregation Not Constitutional Declares Court," *Journal*, 9 Apr. 1914, 1. The "[w]e lament" quotation comes from "Segregation Up to the Legislature," editorial, *Journal*, 10 Apr. 1914, 12. Additional local press reaction appears in "Segregation Law," *Union Republican*, 16 Apr. 1914, 1; "Winston Segregation Ordinance Cannot Be Enforced Says Court," *Twin-City Daily Sentinel*, 9 Apr. 1914, 5; and "Segregation," *Union Republican*, 9 Apr. 1914, 2. For press response from outside Winston-Salem, see "Segregation Not Allowed by Law," *News and Observer*,

12 Apr. 1914, 11; "Cannot Enforce Segregation Law," *(Charlotte) Observer,* 9 Apr. 1914, 3.

58. *University of Pennsylvania Law Review* 63 (1914–1915): 895–98; *Virginia Law Review* 3 (Jan. 1916): 305–6. See also *Michigan Law Review* 13 (May 1915): 599.

59. "Segregation," *The Crisis* 8 (June 1914), 69–70, citing articles from the *Cleveland Plain Dealer* and *New York Evening Post.* See also *The Crisis* 4 (Aug. 1912): 177, 4 (Oct. 1912): 273, and 5 (Jan. 1913): 118; and Memo for Miss Henery from [NAACP attorney J. Chapin] Brinsmade, 11 June 1914, Papers of the NAACP, part 5, "The Campaign against Residential Segregation," ed. August Meier and John Bracey, microfilm reel one, frame 0462–0463.

60. Ed Campbell, "East Winston: New Day Dawns on a Shadowed Scene," *Twin City Sentinel,* 16 Apr. 1962, 7; Hanchett, *Sorting Out the New South City,* 262; "Atkins Outlines Negroes Progress," *Journal and Sentinel,* 10 Feb. 1929, 7B; *Clinard v. Winston-Salem,* 219 N.C. 119 (1940). Racially restrictive covenants contributed to residential segregation in many twentieth-century American cities. See Kenneth T. Jackson, *Crabgrass Frontier: The Suburbanization of the United States* (New York: Oxford Univ. Press, 1985), 208; Kevin Fox Gotham, "Urban Space, Restrictive Covenants, and the Origins of Racial Residential Segregation in a US City, 1900–50," *International Journal of Urban and Regional Research* 24:3 (2000): 616–33; Michael Jones-Correa, "The Origins and Diffusion of Racial Restrictive Covenants," *Political Science Quarterly* 115:4 (2000–2001): 541–68; and Elizabeth A. Pickard, "Opening the Gates: Segregation, Desegregation, and the Story of Lewis Place," *Gateway* 26:2 (2005): 16–27.

61. Miller, "Blacks in Winston-Salem," 147.

4. Evolution and Defamation

1. "K.K.K. Causes Stir in Church," *Charlotte Observer,* 22 Mar. 1922, 14.

2. "Jazz," *Charlotte Observer,* 2 Aug. 1922, 4.

3. *Epperson v. Arkansas,* 393 U.S. 97 (1968); *Edwards v. Aguillard,* 482 U.S. 578 (1987); *Tangipahoa Parish Board of Education v. Freiler,* 530 U.S. 1251 (2000); *Scopes v. State,* 152 Tenn. 424 (1925); *Scopes v. State,* 154 Tenn. 105 (1927); *Pentuff v. Park,* 194 N.C. 146 (1927); *Pentuff v. Park,* 195 N.C. 609 (1928). Regarding the evolution debate in North Carolina during the 1920s, see Willard B. Gatewood Jr., *Preachers, Pedagogues, and Politicians: The Evolution Debate in North Carolina, 1920–1927* (Chapel Hill: Univ. of North Carolina Press, 1966).

4. Edward J. Larson, *Summer for the Gods: The Scopes Trial and America's Continuing Debate over Science and Religion* (New York: Basic Books, 1997), 4, 83; *The World's Most Famous Court Trial: State of Tennessee v. John Thomas Scopes*

(New York: DaCapo Press, 1971), the complete stenographic report of the court testimony; L. Maren Wood, "The Monkey Trial Myth: Popular Culture Representations of the Scopes Trial," *Revue canadienne d'études américaines* 32 (2002): 147–64.

5. Randal L. Hall, *William Louis Poteat: A Leader of the Progressive-Era South* (Lexington: Univ. Press of Kentucky, 2000); Edgar W. Knight, "Monkey or Mud in North Carolina?" *Independent* 118 (14 May 1927): 516; "Can a Man Be a Christian Today?" *Raleigh Times*, 25 July 1925, 4; Gatewood, *Preachers, Pedagogues, and Politicians*, 30, 60, 76; Gerald W. Johnson, "Billy with the Red Necktie," *Virginia Quarterly Review* 30 (autumn 1943): 515–61; Suzanne Cameron Linder, "William Louis Poteat and the Evolution Controversy," *North Carolina Historical Review* 40:2 (1963): 135.

6. William Louis Poteat, *Can a Man Be a Christian To-Day?* (Chapel Hill: Univ. of North Carolina Press, 1925), 35–37.

7. Quotations are from William Louis Poteat, *The New Peace: Lectures on Science and Religion* (Boston: Richard G. Badger, 1915), 21, 10, 160, respectively.

8. Poteat, *Can a Man Be a Christian To-Day?* 21–22.

9. Ibid., 36, 75–77.

10. *James R. Pentuff v. John A. Park et al.*, Supreme Court of North Carolina, spring term, 1927, *Records & Briefs*, 1927, 15–16, Clerks, Book 14, 274, pp. 17–18 (hereafter, *Pentuff v. Park*, Records & Briefs).

11. *United States Federal Census, 1900*, Schedule No. 1—Population, Iowa, Des Moines County, Burlington Township, enumeration district 8, sheet no. 2; *United States Federal Census, 1910,* Population, Texas, McLennan County, Waco City, enumeration district 84, sheet no. 13; *United States Federal Census, 1930,* Population Schedule, North Carolina, Mecklenburg County, Sharon Township, enumeration district No. 60–48, sheet no. 14–83; *Pentuff v. Park*, Records & Briefs, 17–20.

12. James R. Pentuff, *Christian Evolutionists Answered and President W. L. Poteat's Utterances Reviewed* (n.p., 1925), 4–5.

13. Pentuff, *Christian Evolutionists Answered*, 4; "Dr. Pentuff Issues Challenge for Debate," *Charlotte Observer*, 16 Feb. 1926; James R. Pentuff, PhD, "Are North Carolina Baptists Turning from the Bible to Evolution?" *Biblical Recorder*, 19 Aug. 1925, 3; *Pentuff v. Park*, Records & Briefs, 20–21.

14. Pentuff, *Christian Evolutionists Answered*, 67.

15. Ibid., 4–5, 92, 99; Pentuff, "Are North Carolina Baptists Turning from the Bible to Evolution?" 3.

16. Pentuff, *Christian Evolutionists Answered*, 92; Pentuff, "Are North Carolina Baptists Turning from the Bible to Evolution?" 4.

17. "Dr. J. R. Pentuff to Discuss Evolution This Afternoon," *Charlotte Observer*, 1 Feb. 1925; "Organic Evolution Theory of Darwin Is Unscientific," *Charlotte Observer*, 2 Feb. 1925.

18. *Raleigh News and Observer*, Dec. 14, 1922; Gatewood, *Preachers, Pedagogues, and Politicians*, 74–75, 175–76.

19. *Raleigh Times*, 23 Feb. 1925; William Louis Poteat to J. G. Pate, 7 Sept. 1925; W. L. Poteat to J. T. Davis, 19 Sept. 1925; and W. J. McGlothlin to W. L. Poteat, 12 Oct. 1925, all in William Louis Poteat Papers, Wake Forest University Archives; Joseph Martin Dawson, *A Century with Texas Baptists* (Nashville: Broadman Press, 1947), 65; Thomas Condit Miller and Hu Maxwell, *West Virginia and Its People*, vol. 1 (New York: Lewis Historical Publishing, 1913), 579; *United States Federal Census, 1900*, Schedule No. 1—Population, Iowa, Des Moines County, Burlington Township, enumeration district 8, sheet no. 2; *United States Federal Census, 1910*, Population, Texas, McLennan County, Waco City, enumeration district 84, sheet no. 13.

20. The observation that educators were uniquely central to the evolution debate in North Carolina comes from Gatewood, *Preachers, Pedagogues, and Politicians*, vii.

21. "Kill Poole Bill on Evolution by Decisive Margin," *Raleigh News and Observer*, 20 Feb. 1925; "Monkey or Bible," *Charlotte Observer*, 19 Feb. 1925; "The Gag on Teaching" (New York: American Civil Liberties Union, 1931); Arnold H. Leibowitz, "English Literacy: Legal Sanction for Discrimination," *Notre Dame Lawyer* 45:7 (1969): 7–67; Alice R. Cotton, "Poole, David Scott," in *Dictionary of North Carolina Biography*, ed. William S. Powell, vol. 5 (Chapel Hill: Univ. of North Carolina Press, 1994), 122–23; Gatewood, *Preachers, Pedagogues, and Politicians*, 105, 122–26; Edward John Larson, *Trial and Error: The American Controversy over Creation and Evolution* (New York: Oxford Univ. Press, 2003), 26–27, 36–37; Larson, *Summer for the Gods*, 23–24, 48.

22. The language of the Poole Bill is quoted in "Kill Poole Bill on Evolution by Decisive Margin," *Raleigh News and Observer*, 20 Feb. 1925. The assertion that the Poole Bill would "prohibit the teaching of evolution in the public schools of North Carolina" appears in "Brief Observations about Activities of Legislature," *Charlotte Observer*, 3 Feb. 1925, 2. "Kill Poole Bill on Evolution by Decisive Margin," *Raleigh News and Observer*, 20 Feb. 1925; "Bill Outlawing Darwinism Fails by Only One Vote," *Raleigh News and Observer*, 11 Feb. 1925, 1.

23. Walter L. Lingle, "Outlawing Evolution," *Charlotte Observer*, 16 Mar. 1925, 4; *Raleigh News and Observer*, 20 Feb. 1925, 4; "Great Crowd Hears Educators in Sharp Debate at Public Hearing on Poole's Anti-Darwinism Measure in the House," *Charlotte Observer*, 11 Feb. 1925, 1.

24. "Bill Outlawing Darwinism Fails by Only One Vote," *Raleigh News and Observer*, 11 Feb. 1925, 1, 4; "Great Crowd Hears Educators in Sharp Debate at Public Hearing on Poole's Anti-Darwinism Measure in the House," *Charlotte Observer*, 11 Feb. 1925, 1.

25. "Piety and Patriotism Making Fight on Three Institutions," *Greens-

boro Daily News, 12 Feb. 1925, 13; "Great Crowd Hears Educators in Sharp Debate at Public Hearing on Poole's Anti-Darwinism Measure in the House," *Charlotte Observer,* 11 Feb. 1925, 1; "Bill Outlawing Darwinism Fails by Only One Vote," *Raleigh News and Observer,* 11 Feb. 1925, 4; and "Chairman Connor Breaks Tie, Saving Darwin from Defeat," *Greensboro Daily News,* 11 Feb. 1925, 5.

26. "Chairman Connor Breaks Tie, Saving Darwin from Defeat," *Greensboro Daily News,* 11 Feb. 1925, 5; "Bill Outlawing Darwinism Fails by Only One Vote," *Raleigh News and Observer,* 11 Feb. 1925, 1, 4; "Great Crowd Hears Educators in Sharp Debate at Public Hearing on Poole's Anti-Darwinism Measure in the House," *Charlotte Observer,* 11 Feb. 1925, 1; *Pentuff v. Park,* Records & Briefs, 4.

27. "Bill Outlawing Darwinism Fails by Only One Vote," *Raleigh News and Observer,* 11 Feb. 1925, 1; "Jam of People Causes House to Delay Evolution Debate," *Raleigh News and Observer,* 18 Feb. 1925; "House Declines to Table Poole Evolution Bill," *Raleigh News and Observer,* 19 Feb. 1925; "Kill Poole Bill on Evolution by Decisive Margin," *Raleigh News and Observer,* 20 Feb. 1925; Nell Battle Lewis, "Incidentally," *Raleigh News and Observer,* 22 Feb. 1925.

28. "Evolution Is Only a Theory," *Charlotte Observer,* 14 Apr. 1925, 11; "The Open Forum—Evolution Section," *Charlotte Observer,* 4 Mar. 1925, 9; *Presbyterian Standard* 66 (4 Mar. 1925): 2, quoted in Gatewood, *Preachers, Pedagogues, and Politicians,* 148.

29. Quotations come from Edgar W. Knight, "Monkey or Mud in North Carolina?" *Independent* 118 (14 May 1927): 516. Additional information in this paragraph appears in "Radical Theory Again Attacked," *Charlotte Observer,* 5 Mar. 1925, 5; "Evolution Is Only a Theory," *Charlotte Observer,* 14 Apr. 1925, 11; "County Schools Oust Evolution," *Charlotte Observer,* 3 Mar. 1925, 11; *Charlotte Observer,* 4 Mar. 1925, 8.

30. Table 32: "Members in Selected Denominations, by Counties: 1926, North Carolina," U.S. Department of Commerce, Bureau of the Census, *Religious Bodies: 1926,* vol. 1 (Washington, D.C.: Government Printing Office, 1930), 650–53.

31. "Monkey or Bible," *Charlotte Observer,* 19 Feb. 1925; *Fourteenth Census of the United States, Taken in the Year 1920* (Washington, D.C.: Government Printing Office, 1921), 120–21; "Bill Outlawing Darwinism Fails by Only One Vote," *Raleigh News and Observer,* 11 Feb. 1925, 1, 4; Gatewood, *Preachers, Pedagogues, and Politicians,* 88, 149; Aubrey Lee Brooks and Hugh Talmage Lefler, eds., *The Papers of Walter Clark, Volume Two, 1902–1924* (Chapel Hill: Univ. of North Carolina Press, 1950), 191, 218–19.

32. Gatewood, *Preachers, Pedagogues, and Politicians,* 194; "Legislature Will Not Make a Monkey of Self," *Concord (N.C.) Daily Tribune,* 25 Feb. 1926,

10; "Shall the Legislature Throttle Intellectual Freedom?" *(Wake Forest) Old Gold & Black,* 20 Mar. 1926, 2; Larson, *Trial and Error,* 83; "Committee to Fight Teaching of Anti-Bible Doctrines in Schools," *Charlotte Observer,* 17 Apr. 1926, 1.

33. "Drive for Anti-Evolution Law Started in Wake County Town," *Raleigh News and Observer,* 21 Feb. 1926, 1.

34. Quoted in ibid. See also Gatewood, *Preachers, Pedagogues, and Politicians,* 184–85.

35. John T. Kneebone, *Southern Liberal Journalists and the Issue of Race, 1920–1944* (Chapel Hill: Univ. of North Carolina Press, 1985), 21–55; "Does Not Appear to Be Klan Affair," *Raleigh Times,* 13 Feb. 1925, 4; "Sweat, Sweat, Sweat, the Boys Are Marching," *Raleigh Times,* 3 July 1925, 4; "The Man Who Prepared Way for Bishop of Raleigh," *Raleigh Times,* 2 July 1925, 4; "State Senate Has No Divorce Problem," *Raleigh Times,* 12 Feb. 1925, 4; "More Women for N.C.C.W. Board," *Raleigh Times,* 18 Feb. 1926, 4; "Will Make for Better Morals," *Raleigh Times,* 31 Mar. 1925, 4; and "Vice Tests Doubtful Aid to Morality," *Raleigh Times,* 19 Feb. 1925, 4.

36. "Tennessee Legislature Outlaws Evolution," *Raleigh Times,* 24 Mar. 1925, 4; "Not a National War but a Baptist Affair," *Raleigh Times,* 19 Feb. 1926, 4; "Legislature Refuses to Enjoin Intelligence," *Raleigh Times,* 20 Feb. 1925, 4; and "Legislature Will Not Make Monkey of Self," *Raleigh Times,* 18 Feb. 1926, 4.

37. "Seek to Reinforce Omnipotence," *Raleigh Times,* 11 Feb. 1925, 4.

38. "Pentuff Re-Enters Evolution Fight," *Raleigh Times,* 23 Feb. 1926.

39. Ibid.

40. "Complaint," in *Pentuff v. Park,* Records & Briefs, 1–7.

41. "Answer" in *Pentuff v. Park,* Records & Briefs, 7–9.

42. *Pentuff v. Park,* 194 N.C. 146 at 151–52; "To Sue or Not to Sue: Pentuff's Question," *Raleigh Times,* 24 Mar. 1926; *Pentuff v. Park,* Records & Briefs, 11–13.

43. *Pentuff v. Park,* Records & Briefs, 13–14, 21.

44. Ibid., 17–18, 22; "Dr. Pentuff Talks of Life in Trial of His Suit for Big Damages," *Concord Times,* 28 Oct. 1926, 6. For evidence that 1920s North Carolinians used the words "immigrant" and "foreigner" to refer to out-of-staters (especially northerners), see Gatewood, *Preachers, Pedagogues, and Politicians,* 110.

45. *Pentuff v. Park,* Records & Briefs, 17–21.

46. "Dr. Pentuff Talks of Life in Trial of His Suit for Big Damages," *Concord Times,* 28 Oct. 1926, 6; and "Honor Dr. and Mrs. Pentuff," *Concord Tribune,* 25 Oct. 1926.

47. *Pentuff v. Park,* Records & Briefs, 22–28; "Pentuff Suit against Paper Thrown Out of Concord Court," *Charlotte Observer,* 28 Oct. 1926; "Dr. Pentuff

Talks of Life in Trial of His Suit for Big Damages," *Concord Times*, 28 Oct. 1926, 6.

48. *Pentuff v. Park*, Records & Briefs, 25–26; "Dr. Pentuff Talks of Life in Trial of His Suit for Big Damages," *Concord Times*, 28 Oct. 1926, 6.

49. "$25,000 Libel Suit against the Raleigh Times Non-Suited," *Raleigh Times*, 27 Oct. 1926, 1; "Judge Stack Orders Non-Suit in Libel Case against Times," *Raleigh Times*, 28 Oct. 1926, 2.

50. "Supreme Court to Get Pentuff Suit," *Concord Daily Tribune*, 28 Oct. 1926, 2; "Superior Court Now in Session in City," *Concord Times*, 18 Oct. 1926; "*Raleigh Times* Being Sued in Cabarrus Court," *Charlotte Observer*, 27 Oct. 1926; and *Pentuff v. Park*, Records & Briefs, 31.

51. Martin L. Newell, *The Law of Slander and Libel in Civil and Criminal Cases*, 4th ed. by Mason H. Newell (Chicago: Callaghan and Company, 1924), 39–40.

52. *M'Millan v. Birch*, 1 Binn. 178, at 184 (Penn. 1806). The "teachers and exemplars" quotation comes from *Chaddock v. Briggs*, 13 Mass. 248 at 254 (1816). The Minnesota case is *Cole v. Millspaugh*, 111 Minn. 159 at 161 (1910). The Ohio case is *Hayner v. Cowden*, 27 Ohio St. 292 at 296 (1875). The "[w]ords are often actionable" quotation at the end of the paragraph comes from Newell, *Law of Slander and Libel*, 176.

53. *Hickerson v. Masters*, 190 Ky. 168, at 171 (1921).

54. *McDowell v. Bowles*, 53 N.C. 184 (1860).

55. Plaintiff Appellant's Brief, *Pentuff v. Park*, Supreme Court of North Carolina, spring term, 1927, no. 489, 4–6 (hereafter, Plaintiff Appellant's Brief).

56. Defendant Appellee's Brief, *Pentuff v. Park*, Supreme Court of North Carolina, spring term, 1927, no. 489, 2–3, 5–6 (hereafter, Defendant Appellee's Brief).

57. *James R. Pentuff v. John A. Park, O. J. Coffin, and Times Publishing Company*, 194 N.C. 146 at 157 (1927).

58. Ibid.; Mary Lynch Johnson and Harriet V. Holmes, "Richard Tilman Vann," in *Dictionary of North Carolina Biography*, ed. William S. Powell, vol. 6 (Chapel Hill: Univ. of North Carolina Press, 1996), 89; Randal L. Hall to John W. Wertheimer, e-mail correspondence, 10 Mar. 2005.

59. *Pentuff v. Park*, 194 N.C. 146 at 157 (1927); "To Sue or Not to Sue, Pentuff's Question," *Raleigh Times*, 24 Mar. 1926; *Pentuff v. Park*, 194 N.C. 146 at 157 (1927), citing Newell, *Slander and Libel* (4th ed.), at 286–87.

60. *Pentuff v. Park*, 194 N.C. 146 at 155 (1927).

61. Ibid.; *McDowell v. Bowles*, 53 N.C. 184 (1860); Plaintiff Appellant's Brief, 4–5.

62. The quotation is from *Pugh v. Scarboro*, 200 N.C. 59 at 64 (1930). See also *Johnson v. Board of Commissioners of Wake County*, 192 N.C. 561 at 576

(1926); *State v. Herring*, 201 N.C. 543 at 552 (1931); *Jackson v. Dairymen's Creamery*, 202 N.C. 196 at 202 (1932); *Hood ex rel. North Carolina Bank & Trust Co. v. North Carolina Bank & Trust Co.*, 209 N.C. 367 at 386 (1936); *Anderson v. Bridgers*, 209 N.C. 456 at 462 (1936); and *Baxter v. W. H. Arthur Company*, 216 N.C. 276 at 280 (1939); Heriot Clarkson, "A Charge to Keep I Have," address delivered at High Point Temperance Field Day, 8 Dec. 1940, in Heriot Clarkson Papers, folder 88, Southern Historical Collection, University of North Carolina at Chapel Hill; Johnnie Virginia Anderson, "Heriot Clarkson: A Social Engineer of North Carolina" (MA thesis, Wake Forest University, 1972), 8–9, 14, 80, 100; Carol D. Taliaferro, "Heriot Clarkson: Memorial Address, Delivered before the Supreme Court of North Carolina," Raleigh, N.C., 10 Nov. 1942, 9.

63. "Walter Parker Stacy," in *Dictionary of North Carolina Biography*, vol. 5, 418–19; "George W. Connor," in ibid., vol. 1, 416.

64. *Pentuff v. Park*, 194 N.C. 146 at 157 (1927); Paul F. Parsons, "Dangers of Libeling the Clergy," *Journalism Quarterly* 62:3 (1985): 529; "Score Pentuff Second-Round Fight for Clerical License," *Concord Daily Tribune*, 29 June 1927, 4, originally published in *Raleigh Times*.

65. Sinclair Lewis, *Elmer Gantry* (New York: Harcourt, Brace, 1927); "Daniels Spurs Clergymen to Revive Old Standards," *Charlotte Observer*, 26 June 1927, 2.

66. "Pentuff Gets New Trial of His Libel Suit," *Raleigh Times*, 25 June 1927, 1; "Score Pentuff Second-Round Fight for Clerical License," *Raleigh Times*, 27 June 1927, 4.

67. Parsons, "Dangers of Libeling the Clergy," 529.

68. "Dr. Pentuff on Stand at Trial of Libel Suits in Cabarrus Superior Court," *Concord Daily Tribune*, 26 Aug. 1927, 1; *Pentuff v. Park*, 194 N.C. 146 (1927).

69. "Dr. Pentuff on Stand at Trial of Libel Suits in Cabarrus Superior Court," *Concord Daily Tribune*, 26 Aug. 1927, 1.

70. Trial Record, *James R. Pentuff v. John A. Park, O. J. Coffin and Times Publishing Company*, Supreme Court of North Carolina, spring term, 1928, 18–19 (hereafter, Trial Record, 1928); "Dr. Pentuff Talks of Life in Trial of His Suit for Big Damages," *Concord Times*, 28 Oct. 1926, 6; "Honor Dr. and Mrs. Pentuff," *Concord Tribune*, 25 Oct. 1926; "Dr. Pentuff on Stand at Trial of Libel Suits in Cabarrus Superior Court," *Concord Daily Tribune*, 26 Aug. 1927, 1; "Pentuff Damage Suit Is Started," *Raleigh News and Observer*, 26 Aug. 1927, 4.

71. "Pentuff Loses In Suits against *Raleigh Times*," *Concord Daily Tribune*, 27 Aug. 1927, 1; "Newspaper Wins Libel Case," *Charlotte Observer*, 27 Aug. 1927, 1; "Paper Winner in Libel Action," *Raleigh News and Observer*, 27 Aug. 1927, 2. Pentuff sought Supreme Court review of his trial loss, but technical

problems thwarted his attempted appeal. *Pentuff v. Park et al.*, 195 N.C. 609 (1928).

72. Norman L. Rosenberg, *Protecting the Best Men: An Interpretive History of the Law of Libel* (Chapel Hill: Univ. of North Carolina Press, 1986).

73. "Times Beats Pentuff in Action," *Charlotte News*, 27 Aug. 1927, 7; "Immigrant Ignoramuses," *Charlotte Observer*, 28 Aug. 1927, 8; "The Indictment," *Charlotte Observer*, 21 Feb. 1925, 8.

74. "Pentuff Loses Suit before a Jury of His Own County," *Raleigh Times*, 27 Aug. 1927, 4.

75. Trial Record, 1928, 26–34.

76. "Raleigh Has Much Interest in Libel Suit in Concord," *Greensboro News*, reprinted in *Concord Daily Tribune*, 29 Aug. 1927, 1.

77. Ibid.

78. Wint Capel, *Shucks and Nubbins: The Wit and Wisdom of O. J. Skipper Coffin, First Dean, UNC School of Journalism* (Chapel Hill: Cape Corp Press, 2000).

79. Hall, *William Louis Poteat*, 157–200.

80. *Fifteenth Census of the United States: 1930, Population Schedule*, North Carolina, Mecklenburg County, Sharon Township, dwelling #256, enumeration district 60–48, supervisor's district no. 7; "James Robert Pentuff," Florida Death Index, 1942, vol. 1017, certificate 20844; *Raleigh Times*, 24 Mar. 1926, 4; Gerald Bergman, "A Short History of the Modern Creation Movement and the Continuing Modern Culture Wars," *Journal of American Culture (United Kingdom)* 26:2 (2003): 243–62; Christopher P. Toumey, "Modern Creationism and Scientific Authority," *Social Studies of Science (United Kingdom)* 21:4 (1991): 681–99; and James S. Hamre, "The Creationist-Evolutionist debate and the Public Schools," *Journal of Church and State* 33:4 (1991): 765–84.

5. "Escape of the Match-Strikers"

1. "K.K.K. Causes Stir in Church," *Charlotte Observer*, 22 Mar. 1922, 14.

2. Nell Battle Lewis, "Samarcand Arson Case" (bound booklet), Nell Battle Lewis Collection (hereafter, NBL), P.C. 255.29, North Carolina State Archives, Raleigh (hereafter, NCSA); "Rebellious Girls Set Their Bunks Afire to Get Thrill," *(Raleigh) News and Observer*, 2 May 1931.

3. Lewis, "Samarcand Arson Case" (bound booklet); "Says She Caused $200,000 Blaze," *(Raleigh) News and Observer*, 24 Mar. 1931; "Rebellious Girls Set Bunks Afire to Get Thrill," *(Raleigh) News and Observer*, 2 May 1931.

4. Discussions of the "harsh double standard" appear in Jennifer Trost, *Gateway to Justice: The Juvenile Court and Progressive Child Welfare in a Southern City* (Athens: Univ. of Georgia Press, 2005); Mary Odem, *Delinquent Daughters: Protecting and Policing Adolescent Female Sexuality in the United States,*

1885–1920 (Chapel Hill: Univ. of North Carolina Press, 1995), 4, 186, 189; Estelle Freedman, *Their Sisters' Keepers: Women's Prison Reform in America, 1830–1930* (Ann Arbor: Univ. of Michigan Press, 1981), 12–15; Robert M. Mennel, *Thorns and Thistles: Juvenile Delinquents in the United States, 1825–1940* (Hanover, N.H.: Univ. Press of New England, 1973), 172; Lawrence M. Friedman, *Crime and Punishment in American History* (New York: Basic Books, 1993), 426; Anne M. Butler, "Women's Work in Prisons of the American West, 1865–1920," *Western Legal History* 7 (1994): 201–22; Jane M. Pederson, "Gender, Justice, and a Wisconsin Lynching," *Agricultural History* 67 (1993): 81; and Kermit L. Hall, *The Magic Mirror: Law in American History* (New York: Oxford Univ. Press, 1989), 182. Regarding legal chivalry, see Elizabeth F. Moulds, "Chivalry and Paternalism: Disparities of Treatment in the Criminal Justice System," *Western Political Quarterly* 31:3 (1978): 416–30; Jacquelyn Dowd Hall, "Disorderly Women: Gender and Labor Militancy in the Appalachian South," *Journal of American History* 73:2 (Sept. 1986): 374; Lucia Zedner, *Women, Crime, and Custody in Victorian England* (Oxford: Clarendon Press, 1991), 27; Joan Sangster, "'Pardon Tales' from Magistrate's Court: Women, Crime, and the Court in Peterborough County, 1920–1950," *Canadian Historical Review* 74 (1993): 161–97; Gary R. Kremer, "Strangers to Domestic Virtues: Nineteenth-Century Women in the Missouri Prison," *Missouri Historical Review* 84 (1990): 293; Robert Waite, "Necessary to Isolate the Female Prisoners: Women Convicts and the Women's Ward at the Old Idaho Penitentiary," *Idaho Yesterdays* 29 (1985): 6; Linda S. Parker, "Murderous Women and Mild Justice: A Look at Female Violence in Pre-1910 San Diego, San Luis Obispo, and Tuolomne Counties," *Journal of San Diego History* 38 (1992): 22–49; Virginia Culin Roberts, "'The Women Was Too Tough,'" *Journal of Arizona History* 26 (1985): 395–414.

5. David S. Tanenhaus, *Juvenile Justice in the Making* (New York: Oxford Univ. Press, 2004); David Wolcott, "Juvenile Justice before Juvenile Court: Cops, Courts, and Kids in Turn-of-the-Century Detroit," *Social Science History* 27:1 (2003): 109–36; David J. Rothman, *Conscience and Convenience: The Asylum and Its Alternatives in Progressive America* (Boston: Little, Brown, 1980); Odem, *Delinquent Daughters;* Trost, *Gateway to Justice.*

6. Samuel Edwin Leonard, "The History of the Eastern Carolina Industrial Training School for Boys, Rocky Mount, North Carolina," *North Carolina Historical Review* 22 (1945): 276–77; State of North Carolina, *Public Laws of 1917,* chap. 255; State Board of Public Welfare—Institutions & Corrections, State Charitable, Penal, and Correctional Institutions, "Samarcand" folder, box 164, Old Records Center (hereafter, ORC), NCSA; Kate Ford Peele, "Samarcand Girls Not Fiends Incarnate, It Is Believed, in Spite of Recent Outbreak," *Elizabeth City (N.C.) Daily Advance,* 22 Apr. 1931, in NBL, P.C. 255.29, NCSA. Regarding disorderly southern women from farm or mill-working families, see Hall, "Disorderly Women."

7. R. Eugene Brown, "Establishment of Purpose of Samarcand Industrial Training School for Girls," 10 Jan. 1919, 36–39, State Board of Public Welfare—Institutions & Corrections, State Charitable, Penal, and Correctional Institutions, "Samarcand, 1918–1924" folder, box 164, ORC, NCSA.

8. The founding of the Stonewall Jackson Training School is reported in State of North Carolina, *Public Laws of 1907*, chap. 776. For Jackson's admissions policies, see *North Carolina Code of 1931*, §7322 and 7323; "Stonewall Jackson Training School: Study of Status of 40 Cases Discharged within Last Three Years (Reeder Report)," 1921, box 166, ORC, NCSA (hereafter, Reeder Report); "Stonewall Jackson Manual Training & Industrial School, Concord, N.C., Letter of Admittance," n.d., "Stonewall Jackson, 1917–1922" folder, box 166, ORC, NCSA; Leonard, "History of the Eastern Carolina Industrial Training School for Boys," 277, 288–89. Reports of the offenses for which Jackson boys were committed to the facility appear in Reeder Report.

9. *North Carolina Code of 1931*, §7334. The "[maybe] the girl herself hasn't done anything [wrong]" quotation appears in Peele, "Samarcand Girls Not Fiends." Mary Jones's story appears in Minute Docket of Wake County, "State and City of Raleigh v. Mary Jones, July 5, 1929," "Samarcand, 1925–1931" folder, box 164, ORC, NCSA. The story about the arson suspect committed because she would not stay home appears in Lewis, "Samarcand Arson Case" (bound booklet).

10. Lewis, "Samarcand Arson Case" (bound booklet); Peele, "Samarcand Girls Not Fiends."

11. For Jackson training, see "Trades Building," in "Stonewall Jackson Training School, 1917–1922" folder, box 166, ORC, NCSA; Edward W. Boshart to Kate Burr Johnson, 31 Oct. 1928, "Stonewall Jackson Training School, 1923–1934" folder, box 166, ORC, NCSA. Regarding Samarcand "training," see Peele, "Samarcand Girls Not Fiends"; Marjorie Ferebee to Nell Battle Lewis, 13 May 1931, NBL, P.C. 225.29, NCSA.

12. Leonard, "History of the Eastern Carolina Industrial Training School for Boys," 287; Coramae Richey Mann, *Female Crime and Delinquency* (Birmingham: Univ. of Alabama Press, 1984), 181. The "cut your hair" quotation comes from the "Margaret Abernethy" section in Lewis, "Samarcand Arson Case" (bound booklet). See also "12 Samarcand Firebugs Go to State's Prison," *Sandhill Citizen*, 23 May 1931. The "made to wear dresses" quotation comes from "Stonewall Jackson Manual Training and Industrial School," "Stonewall Jackson, 1923–1934" folder, box 166, ORC, NCSA.

13. For Jackson's discharge policies, see Charles E. Boger to R. Eugene Brown, 11 Aug. 1931, "Stonewall Jackson, 1923–1934" folder, box 166, ORC, NCSA; "Admission Form," "Stonewall Jackson Training School, 1917–1923" folder, box 166, ORC, NCSA. The "sentenced to serve sixty

days for larceny" quotation comes from "Investigation of Treatment of George White Goodman," 16 July 1934, "Investigation of Death" folder, box 166, ORC, NCSA.

14. The "[n]o commitment shall be for any definite term" quotation comes from *North Carolina Code of 1931*, §§7330, 7334. The "could not understand why some girls could come and stay only a few months" quotation comes from Marjorie Ferebee to Nell Battle Lewis, 13 May 1931, NBL, P.C. 255.29, NCSA; "Rebellious Girls Set Their Bunks Afire to Get Thrill," *(Raleigh) News and Observer*, 2 May 1931.

15. Regarding racially integrated (though not necessarily racially evenhanded) juvenile facilities in the North at that time, see Sarah Potter, "'Undesirable Relations': Same-Sex Relationships and the Meaning of Sexual Desire at a Women's Reformatory during the Progressive Era," *Feminist Studies* 30:2 (2004): 394–415; and David Tanenhaus, *Juvenile Justice in the Making* (New York: Oxford Univ. Press, 2004), 36–37.

16. Regarding the history of Efland Home, see Tanya Smith Brice, "Undermining Progress in Early 20th Century North Carolina: General Attitudes toward Delinquent African American Girls," *Journal of Sociology and Social Welfare* 34:1 (Mar. 2007): 131–53. Funding levels for North Carolina's various training schools between 1 July 1928 and 30 June 1929 are reported in State of North Carolina, *Public Laws of 1927* (Charlotte: Observer Printing House, 1927), 169. On the importance of African American women's clubs, see Odem, *Delinquent Daughters*, 5, 118–21.

17. Regarding admissions policies at Efland Home, see North Carolina State Board of Charities and Public Welfare, *North Carolina's Social Welfare Program for Negroes* (Raleigh: North Carolina State Board of Charities and Public Welfare, 1926), 38, NBL, P.C. 255.28, NCSA; "State Charitable, Correctional, and Penal Institutions"; "Want Reform School for Colored Girls," *(Raleigh) News and Observer*, 23 July 1922; "Want Reform School for Colored Girls," *(Raleigh) News and Observer*, 1 Apr. 1923, "Efland, 1919–1934" folder, box 163, ORC, NCSA; "Judgment and Commitment," "Efland, 1919–1934" folder, box 163, ORC, NCSA. Regarding race, respectability, and the "southern cult of ladyhood," see Anne Firor Scott, *The Southern Lady: From Pedestal to Politics, 1830–1930* (Chicago: Univ. of Chicago Press, 1970).

18. Old Hurrygraph, "Samarcand Place for Real Reform," *(Raleigh) News and Observer*, 11 Nov. 1924, "Samarcand, 1918–1924" folder, box 164, ORC, NCSA; "North Carolina Compares Favorably in Social Work," *Charlotte Observer*, 2 July 1922, 8.

19. For examples of former employees blaming McNaughton for Samarcand's woes, see box 29, NBL, P.C. 255.29, NCSA. The "same power [over her] inmates" quotation comes from *North Carolina Code of 1931*, §7339. The "no one ever knew when they got up in the morning" quotation comes from State-

ment of Grace Henslee (1931), NBL, P.C. 255.29, NCSA. Samarcand's turnover rates are reported in "Board of Samarcand Bans Whipping Girl Inmates," *(Raleigh) News and Observer,* 31 May 1931.

20. For the physician's quotation, see C. W. Durham to Nell Battle Lewis, 11 May 1931; for the superintendent's quotation, see W. R. Mills to Nell Battle Lewis, 21 May 1931, both in NBL, P.C. 255.29, NCSA.

21. The Margaret Pridgen dessert story and the "put water in [the beaten girls'] faces" quotation come from Lewis, "Samarcand Arson Case" (bound booklet). The hospital story appears in Statement of Bessie Bishop, R.N., 1 Apr. 1931, NBL, P.C. 255.29, NCSA. The discussion of solitary confinement is based on Marjorie Ferebee to Nell Battle Lewis, 13 May 1931, NBL, P.C. 255.29, NCSA. The North Carolina state penitentiary's 1923 banning of flogging and the dark cell is reported in A. Laurance Aydlett, "The North Carolina State Board of Public Welfare," *North Carolina Historical Review* 24 (1947): 22. Additional information appears in Lewis, "Samarcand Arson Case" (bound booklet); Viola Sistare to Nell Battle Lewis, 21 Mar. 1931; Bessie Camp to Nell Battle Lewis, 1 Apr. 1931; Bessie Bishop to Nell Battle Lewis, 1 Apr. 1931; Grace Henslee to Nell Battle Lewis, 3 Apr. 3, 1931; Roberta King to Nell Battle Lewis, 12 May 1931, all in NBL, P.C. 255.29, NCSA.

22. The phrase "totally destroyed" comes from "Accuse Girls of Burning Buildings at Samarcand," *(Raleigh) News and Observer,* 17 Mar. 1931; and "16 Girls Facing Trial for Lives," *Charlotte Observer,* 17 Mar. 1931, 3. Estimates of the cost of the damage appear in *New York Times,* 17 Mar. 1931, 22; and "Says She Caused $200,000 Blaze," *(Raleigh) News and Observer,* 24 Mar. 1931. Samarcand's total annual appropriations are reported in State of North Carolina, *Public Laws of 1931* (Charlotte: Observer Printing House, 1931), 718. Samarcand's insurance coverage is discussed in "Plan Fireproof Home for Girls," *(Raleigh) News and Observer,* 18 Mar. 1931.

23. See "Sixteen Girls Facing Trial for Lives," *Charlotte Observer,* 17 Mar. 1931, 3; "Set Reformatory Fire," *New York Times,* 17 Mar. 1931, 22; "Accuse Girls of Burning Buildings at Samarcand," *(Raleigh) News and Observer,* 17 Mar. 1931, NBL, P.C. 255.29, NCSA. For the arson penalty, see *North Carolina Code of 1931,* Article 15, §4238; and *Consolidated Statutes of North Carolina, Annotated,* vol. 1 (Raleigh: Commercial Printing Company, State Printers, 1920), 1749. For background on the roots of arson law in the slave South, see Thomas D. Morris, *Southern Slavery and the Law, 1619–1860* (Chapel Hill: Univ. of North Carolina Press, 1996), 330–36.

24. Lewis, "Samarcand Arson Case" (bound booklet).

25. "Set Reformatory Fire," *New York Times,* 17 Mar. 1931, 22; Lewis, "Samarcand Arson Case" (bound booklet); "Samarcand Girls Riot in Moore County Jail," *Moore County News,* 30 Apr. 1931.

26. "Sixteen Girls Face Trial for Lives," *Charlotte Observer*, 17 Mar. 1931, 3; "Says She Caused $200,000 Blaze," *(Raleigh) News and Observer*, 24 Mar. 1931; "Accuse Girls of Burning Buildings," *(Raleigh) News and Observer*, 17 Mar. 1931.

27. Speculation that matches came from sympathetic visitors, the "worst insurrection" quotation, and the "fatherly guidance" phrase all come from "Says She Caused $200,000 Blaze," *(Raleigh) News and Observer*, 24 Mar. 1931. The "tearing out panes of glass" and "rent the air" quotations come from "Girls Fire Jail and Attack Officers," *Charlotte Observer*, 16 Apr. 1931, 10. Additional information in this paragraph comes from *(Raleigh) News and Observer*, 2 May 1931; "Rioting Girls Change Jails after Battle," *Charlotte Observer*, 19 Apr. 1931, 2.

28. The "just how much of a rampage" quotation, the "fire-proof cell" quotation, and the appendicitis information come from "Samarcand Girls Riot in Moore County Jail," *Moore County News*, 30 Apr. 1931. The "all seemed quiet" quotation comes from "Six Girls Riot in Moore County Jail," *Charlotte Observer*, 1 May 1931, 3.

29. All quotations from "some proportions" to "mostly pretty" come from "Samarcand Girls Riot in Moore County Jail," *Moore County News*, 30 Apr. 1931. Naked romping is reported in George McNeill to Nell Battle Lewis, 30 Apr. 1931, NBL, "Correspondences 1931," NCSA. The Clint McCaskill story appears in "Samarcand Girls Riot in Moore County Jail," *Moore County News*, 30 Apr. 1931; George McNeill to Nell Battle Lewis, 30 Apr. 1931; "Rebellious Girls Set Their Bunks Afire to Get Thrill," *(Raleigh) News and Observer*, 2 May 1931, both in NBL, P.C. 255.29, NCSA; and "Six Girls Riot in Moore County Jail," *Charlotte Observer*, 1 May 1931, 3.

30. On the tradition of chivalry in the South, see Glenda Elizabeth Gilmore, *Gender and Jim Crow: Women and the Politics of White Supremacy in North Carolina, 1896–1920* (Chapel Hill: Univ. of North Carolina Press, 1996); Jacquelyn Dowd Hall, *Revolt against Chivalry: Jessie Daniel Ames and the Women's Campaign against Lynching* (New York: Columbia Univ. Press, 1974); Fred Arthur Bailey, "Mildred Lewis Rutherford and the Patrician Cult of the Old South," *Georgia Historical Quarterly* 78 (1994): 509–35; Nancy MacLean, *Behind the Mask of Chivalry: The Making of the Second Ku Klux Klan* (New York: Oxford Univ. Press, 1994); Louis D. Rubin Jr., "W. J. Cash after Fifty Years," *Virginia Quarterly Review* 67 (1991): 214–28; John Fraser, *America and the Patterns of Chivalry* (Cambridge: Cambridge Univ. Press, 1982); Scott, *Southern Lady*; and Richard M. Weaver, *The Southern Tradition at Bay: A History of Post-bellum Thought* (New Rochelle, N.Y.: Arlington House, 1968). Sheriff McDonald's quotation appears in "Samarcand Girls Go on Another Rampage," *(Raleigh) News and Observer*, 1 May 1931.

31. Pearl Stiles to Governor Max Gardner, 7 May 1931, "Samarcand, 1931" folder, box 164, ORC, NCSA.

32. On women in the legal profession, see Terence C. Halliday, "Six Score Years and Ten: Demographic Transitions in the American Legal Profession," in *Law and Society: Readings on the Social Study of Law*, ed. Stewart Macaulay, Lawrence M. Friedman, and John Stookey (New York: Norton, 1995), 795. On the relative scarcity of feminism in the South, see Clement Eaton, "Breaking a Path for the Liberation of Women in the South," *Georgia Review* 28:2 (1974): 187–99. For Lewis's involvement in the case, see Bess Davenport Thompson, "Twelve Samarcand Girls Get State Prison," *(Raleigh) News and Observer*, 21 May 1931, NBL, P.C. 255.29, NCSA; George W. McNeill to Nell Battle Lewis, 30 Apr. 1931, NBL, P.C. 255.2, "Correspondence 1931–1939" folder, NCSA; "Miss Lewis to Appear in Arson Case Here," *(Raleigh) News and Observer*, 25 Apr. 1931.

33. Regarding Nell Battle Lewis's post–World War II views, see Elizabeth Gillespie McRae, "To Save a Home: Nell Battle Lewis and the Rise of Southern Conservatism, 1941–1956," *North Carolina Historical Review* 81:3 (2004): 261–87. For evidence of Lewis's prewar interest in prison reform, see Nell Battle Lewis, "Incidentally: No Blame," NBL, NCSA; and "11 Negroes Die in Duplin Prison Fire," *Charlotte Observer*, 8 Mar. 1931, 5. For evidence of Lewis's condemnation of the sexual double standard, see Nell Battle Lewis, "Incidentally," *(Raleigh) News and Observer*, 24 May 1925, NBL, P.C. 255.27, NCSA; Lewis, "Negro Slavery Influenced the South to Oppose the Women's Movement," *(Raleigh) News and Observer*, 3 May 1925, P.C. 255.27, "Incidentally" folder, NCSA.

34. "12 Samarcand Firebugs Go to State's Prison," *Sandhill Citizen*, 23 May 1931; "Guilty Pleas Made in Court," *Charlotte Observer*, 20 May 1931.

35. "Fourteen Girls to Be Sentenced Today," *Charlotte Observer*, 20 May 1931, 3; "12 Samarcand Firebugs Go to State's Prison," *Sandhill Citizen*, 23 May 1931; "Launch Plans for Rebuilding," *(Raleigh) News and Observer*, 18 Mar. 1931.

36. "Fourteen Girls to Be Sentenced Today," *Charlotte Observer*, 20 May 1931, 3; Bess Davenport Thompson, "Defense Holds Samarcand Girls Victims of State Neglect," *(Raleigh) News and Observer*, 20 May 1931, NBL, P.C. 255.29, NCSA.

37. "Defense Holds Samarcand Girls Victims of State Neglect," *(Raleigh) News and Observer*, 20 May 1931.

38. Bess Davenport Thompson, "Twelve Samarcand Girls Get State Prison," *(Raleigh) News and Observer*, 21 May 1931, NBL, P.C. 255.29, NCSA; "Fourteen Girls to Be Sentenced Today," *Charlotte Observer*, 20 May 1931, 3; "Escape of the Match-Strikers," *Charlotte Observer*, 21 May 1931, 8.

39. "Fourteen Girls to Be Sentenced Today," *Charlotte Observer*, 20 May 1931, 3.

40. All quotations in this paragraph come from "Defense Holds Samarcand

Girls Victims of State Neglect," *(Raleigh) News and Observer,* 20 May 1931. See also "Fourteen Girls to Be Sentenced Today," *Charlotte Observer,* 20 May 1931, 3.

41. "Rioting Girls Sent to Prison," *Charlotte Observer,* 21 May 1931, 4; "Escape of the Match-Strikers," *Charlotte Observer,* 21 May 1931, 8; Bess Davenport Thompson, "Twelve Samarcand Girls Get State Prison Terms," *(Raleigh) News and Observer,* 21 May 1931.

42. "Escape of the Match-Strikers," *Charlotte Observer,* 21 May 1931, 8. The cigarette story appears in "Rioting Girls Sent to Prison," *Charlotte Observer,* 21 May 1931, 4.

43. The "leave their pasts behind" quotation comes from "Fourteen Girls to Be Sentenced Today," *Charlotte Observer,* 20 May 1931, 3.

44. "Conditions at Samarcand," *Charity and Children,* 11 June 1931; "Twelve Samarcand Girls Get State Prison" and "North Carolina Fails," *Rocky Mount Telegram,* n.d., all in "Samarcand, 1931" folder, box 164, ORC, NCSA; "The State as Defendant," *Greensboro News,* 21 May 1931. See also "Bad Conditions at Samarcand," *Chapel Hill Weekly,* 29 May 1931; "Awaiting the Facts," *Greensboro News,* n.d.; "Raised a Question about Samarcand," *High Point Enterprise,* n.d., all in NBL, P.C. 255.29, NCSA; and "The State as Defendant," *Greensboro News,* 21 May 1931.

45. The "for the past ten or fifteen years" quotation appears in Lawrence Veiller, "Prisons or Men's Clubs—Which?" *World's Work* 54 (May 1927): 86, 95. For the New York judge's views, see "Pampering Convicts a Cause of Crime, Says Judge Talley," *New York Times,* 11 Feb. 1925, 23. Charles Evans Hughes's views appear in "Hughes Laments Advance on Crime," *New York Times,* 13 Jan. 1925, 4.

46. The views of the National Committee on Prisons are discussed in "Finds Jails Swell Racketeer Army," *New York Times,* 22 May 1931, 14. On the contemporary image of juvenile offenders, see Gerald W. Johnson, "The Child Convicts," *(Baltimore) Evening Sun,* 9 July 1931, NBL, P.C. 255.28, NCSA. For the "rebuild his character" quotation, see "The American Prisoner Branded as a Criminal," *Literary Digest* 110 (8 Aug. 1931): 9.

47. "Inmates Win Prizes by Prison Criticism," *New York Times,* 15 May 1931, 14.

48. Regarding Wickersham and his commission, see "Accuses Wickersham of Prison View Shift," *New York Times,* 28 July 1931, 19. The "failure so complete" quotation appears in "Prisons of Nation Declared Failure; Outworn, Inhuman," *New York Times,* 27 July 1931, 1. The "filth and misery" quotation appears in "Young Prisoners," *New York Times,* 10 July 1931, 20.

49. For evidence of the reduced public tolerance for harsh corrections officials around the time of the Samarcand trial, see "Accused Matron Charges Legislators Hugged Girls," *Charlotte Observer,* 20 Mar. 1931, 1. For evidence

of Lewis's interest in penal reform nationally, see "Finds Statistics on Crime Needed," *(Raleigh) News and Observer,* 27 April 1931, NBL, P.C. 255.28, NCSA. Lewis's support for Governor Gardner's prison commission appears in Nell Battle Lewis, "Incidentally: No Blame," *(Raleigh) News and Observer,* 15 Mar. 1931, NBL, P.C. 255.12, NCSA.

50. See "Ohio's Prison Horror," *Literary Digest* 105 (3 May 1930): 9; "Ohio's Prison Holocaust," *World's Work* 59 (July 1930): 19; "The Fire at Columbus," *Outlook and Independent* 155 (7 May 1930): 12; Spencer Miller Jr., "Lesson of the Prison Fire," letter to editor, *New York Times,* 29 Apr. 1930, 26.

51. The "culminating answer" quotation comes from "Lays Convict Riots to Policy of Force," *New York Times,* 10 May 1930, 10. Regarding the Joliet riot, see "1,100 Rebel Felons Run Amuck at Joliet," *Charlotte Observer,* 15 Mar. 1931, 1.

52. Regarding the day's many prison films, see Andrew Bergman, *We're in the Money: Depression America and Its Films* (New York: Harper Colophon Books, 1971), 93. Regarding the National Committee on Prisons report, see "Finds Jails Swell Racketeer Army," *New York Times,* 22 May 1931, 14.

53. "Another Building at School Is Burned," *(Raleigh) News and Observer,* 13 Mar. 1931, "Stonewall Jackson, 1923–1934" folder, box 166, ORC, NCSA; "Unruly Juveniles Confess Arson," *Charlotte Observer,* 19 Mar. 1931, 2; "Arson Trials on at Concord," *Charlotte Observer,* 22 Apr. 1931, 6; "Reform School Boys Are Tried," *(Raleigh) News and Observer,* 22 Apr. 1931, 11; "Alleged Firebug Acquitted," *Charlotte Observer,* 23 Apr. 1931, 6; "Young Firebug Gets One Year," *Charlotte Observer,* 26 Apr. 1931, 6. Regarding post-fire whipping policy at Jackson and Samarcand, see, respectively, "Investigation of Treatment of George White Goodman," 16 July 1934, "Investigation of Death" folder, box 166, ORC, NCSA; and "Board of Samarcand Bans Whipping Girl Inmates," *(Raleigh) News and Observer,* 31 May 1931.

54. "Bad Conditions at Samarcand," *Chapel Hill Weekly,* 29 May 1931.

55. R. Eugene Brown, "Report on the Conditions at Samarcand," 22 Jan. 1932, "Samarcand, 1932–1943" folder, box 164, ORC, NCSA.

56. R. Eugene Brown, "Report of Department of Inspection at Samarcand Manor," 10 Jan. 1934; W. T. Bost to W. P. Kimball, 3 Apr. 1934, "Samarcand, 1932–1943" folder, box 164, ORC, NCSA.

57. The "Samarcand stands as testimony" quotation appears in *Charlotte Observer,* 17 May 1939, NBL, P.C. 255.29, NCSA. For additional evidence of improving conditions at Samarcand, see "Samarcand Manor," *Charity and Children,* 1 July 1943, "Samarcand, 1932–1943" folder, box 164, ORC, NCSA. For the "until she foamed at the mouth" quotation, see W. R. Johnson to Curtis Ezell, 16 June 1937, "Efland, 1935–1938" folder, box 163, ORC, NCSA. Regarding the fate of Efland, see Aydlett, "North Carolina State Board of Public Welfare," 24.

58. Nell Battle Lewis, "Incidentally: A Buzzard Comes Home to Roost," *(Raleigh) News and Observer,* 21 Oct. 1945, NBL, P.C. 255.12, NCSA.

59. Martha Azer, "Samarcand Girls Given Chance to Prove Worth to Society," *Charlotte News,* 11 May 1946, 12A.

6. Padlocking Greenwich Village

The authors appreciatively acknowledge the help of Pamela Grundy, Thomas Hanchett, Nancy Hewitt, Davidson College, the Davidson College History Department, and the George Lawrence Abernethy Endowment.

1. James L. Roark et al., *The American Promise: A History of the United States* (Boston: Bedford Books, 1998), 910. See also James H. Shideler, "Flappers and Philosophers, and Farmers: Rural-Urban Tensions of the Twenties," *Agricultural History* 47:4 (1973): 283–99; Robert A. Divine et al., *America: Past and Present,* 7th ed., vol. 2 (New York: Pearson-Longman, 2005), 732; John Mack Faragher et al., *Out of Many: A History of the American People,* 3rd ed., vol. 1 (Upper Saddle River, N.J.: Prentice Hall, 2000), 692; Paul S. Boyer et al., *The Enduring Vision: A History of the American People,* Essentials Edition (Boston: Houghton Mifflin, 1999), 320; and John M. Murrin et al., *Liberty Equality, Power: A History of the American People,* 2nd ed., vol. 2 (Fort Worth, Tex.: Harcourt Brace, 1999), 813–14.

2. For information regarding Boyles's family background, see Harvey Jonas to Marion Butler, 8 Sept. 1925, collection no. 114, series 1.4, folder 529, Marion Butler Papers, Southern Historical Collection, University of North Carolina at Chapel Hill. Regarding Boyles's frequent moves around the country, see *Carpenter v. Boyles,* trial transcript, case no. 521, Supreme Court of North Carolina, spring term, 1938, trial of 11 Oct. 1937, Mecklenburg Superior Court, Fourteenth District (hereafter, *Carpenter v. Boyles,* trial transcript), 33–37; City Directory for Gastonia, North Carolina, 1923–1924, not paginated, Public Library of Gaston County; *Fourteenth Census of the United States,* v. 36, ed. 79, sheet 4, line 94; Memory F. Boyles Certificate of Death, 24 Jan. 1948, North Carolina State Board of Health Bureau of Vital Statistics; 1934 Charlotte City Directory, Public Library of Charlotte and Mecklenburg County; *Charlotte Observer,* 15 Apr. 1925, 1; and Harvey A. Jonas, Lincolnton, N.C., to Marion Butler, Washington, D.C., 2 Oct. 1925, folder 529, Marion Butler Papers.

3. For evidence of Boyles's profession as a doctor, see North Carolina Medical Board, license #2848; and "Dr. Boyles Service Set," *Charlotte News,* 27 Jan. 1948, 1-B. The "Boston baked beans" quotation comes from *Charlotte News,* 15 Apr. 1935, 1, 18. The "largest importers and distributors" quotation comes from Marion Butler to Harvey A. Jonas, 11 Nov. 1925, folder 534, Marion Butler Papers. The Boyles brothers' criminal sentences are reported in "Men Higher Up in Dope Cases Sent to Prison," *Charlotte Observer,* 16 Apr. 1925,

1, 12. For additional information on Boyles's narcotics prosecution, see *United States v. Dr. M. F. Boyles,* Atlanta Historical Archives, U.S. Documents, Western District, N.C., Charlotte #4655; *United States v. Dr. A. V. Boyles,* Atlanta Regional Archives R.G. 21, U.S. Documents, Western District, N.C., Charlotte #4647. See also the following *Charlotte Observer* stories: "Narcotic Cases Now on Docket," 1 Apr. 1925, 1; "Charlotte Man Given Three Years," 17 Apr. 1925, 7; "Much Time to Be Served in Narcotic Cases," 19 Apr. 1925, 3.

4. For evidence of Boyles's Republican affiliation, see Marion Butler to the Attorney General, U.S. Department of Justice, 18 Nov. 1925, folder 535, Marion Butler Papers. Regarding Boyles's parole, see Marion Butler, telegram to Harvey A. Jonas, 22 Oct. 1925, folder 533, Marion Butler Papers.

5. For evidence of Boyles's moves within Charlotte, and the racial composition of those areas, see Charlotte City Directory, 1934–1937, North Carolina Room, Public Library of Charlotte and Mecklenburg County, Charlotte, N.C. Regarding the claim that Charlotte was one of America's most segregated cities, see Thomas W. Hanchett, *Sorting Out the New South City: Race, Class, and Urban Development in Charlotte, 1875–1975* (Chapel Hill: Univ. of North Carolina Press, 1998), 262.

6. Regarding Charlotte churches at that time, see U.S. Department of Commerce, Bureau of the Census, *Religious Bodies: 1936 Selected Statistics for the United States by Denomination and Geographic Division* (Washington, D.C.: Government Printing Office, 1941), 477–78.

7. The national average age of marriage is reported in U.S. Department of Commerce, Bureau of the Census, *Historical Statistics of the United States: Colonial Times to 1970* (Washington, D.C.: Government Printing Office, 1975), part I, series A 158–159, 19. For more on the subculture of long-term bachelorhood in these years, see Howard P. Chudacoff, *The Age of the Bachelor: Creating an American Subculture* (Princeton: Princeton Univ. Press, 1999).

8. Regarding Mary's family background, see 1920 North Carolina Census, vol. 37, E.D. 92, sheet 6, line 22. For Mary's living and working arrangements in Charlotte, see Charlotte City Directories, 1927 to 1944, Public Library of Charlotte and Mecklenburg County.

9. For the median age of women at first marriage, see U.S. Department of Commerce, Bureau of the Census, *Historical Statistics of the United States: Colonial Times to 1970* (Washington, D.C.: Government Printing Office, 1975), part I, series A 158–159, 19. For average family size in the United States in 1930, see *15th Census of the United States,* vol. 6, *Families* (Washington, D.C.: Government Printing Office, 1933), 972. Additional information in this paragraph comes from "Dr. Boyles Service Set," *Charlotte News,* 27 Jan. 1948, 1-B; and Charlotte City Directories, 1936 to 1944, Public Library of Charlotte and Mecklenburg County.

10. For evidence that at least some Greenwich Village employees had pre-

viously moved around the country, see *Carpenter v. Boyles*, trial transcript, 42; *Charlotte News*, 1 Sept. 1937. For evidence that at least some Greenwich Village employees had had previous run-ins with the law, see *Carpenter v. Boyles*, trial transcript, 37; *Mecklenburg Times*, 27 May 1937. For references to "Negroes" and so forth, at trial, see *Carpenter v. Boyles*, trial transcript, 45, 51–52; *Carpenter v. Boyles*, 213 N.C. 432 at 436–39 (1938). The phrase "you could buy whiskey from the waitresses" appears in *Carpenter v. Boyles*, trial transcript, 45.

11. *Charlotte News*, 1 Sept. 1937.

12. For evidence of M. F. Boyles's marriage to Mary Springs Harkey, see Charlotte City Directory, 1936, Public Library of Charlotte and Mecklenburg County. For evidence of M. F. Boyles's legitimate pre–Greenwich Village Charlotte pharmacy, see book 846, p. 47, Mecklenburg County Register of Deeds Office, Charlotte, N.C. The assertion that half of Mecklenburg County's roadhouses were run by women, either alone or with partners, is based on the Civil Action Papers of Mecklenburg County, series 065.325, boxes 100–115, State Archives, Raleigh.

13. The description of Greenwich Village as "one of the largest roadhouses in the county" comes from the *Charlotte News*, 16 Sept. 1937. For evidence of Boyles's land purchases, see *Carpenter v. Boyles*, trial transcript, 63, and book 873, p. 255; book 890, p. 112; book 890, p. 59; and book 1148, p. 619, Mecklenburg Register of Deeds Office.

14. *Carpenter v. Boyles*, trial transcripts 13, 31.

15. Regarding the general importance of the automobile during the 1920s, see Zane L. Miller and Patricia M. Melvin, *The Urbanization of Modern America* (San Diego: Harcourt Brace Jovanovich, 1997), 145–46. For the automobile in the South, see Blain A. Brownell, "A Symbol of Modernity: Attitudes toward the Automobile in Southern Cities in the 1920s," *American Quarterly* 24:1 (Mar. 1972): 20–44; and Howard L. Preston, *Automobile Age Atlanta: The Making of a Southern Metropolis, 1900–1935* (Athens: Univ. of Georgia Press, 1979). Regarding the automobile's importance in Charlotte, see Hanchett, *Sorting Out the New South City*, 185, 200, 316, 321; the 1935 Charlotte City Directory, 838–41, Public Library of Charlotte and Mecklenburg County; and Scott Dodd, "How 100 Years of the Automobile Shaped Charlotte's Destiny," *Charlotte Observer*, 22 July 2001.

16. Nathaniel F. Magruder, "Morrison, Cameron," in *Dictionary of North Carolina Biography*, ed. William S. Powell (Chapel Hill: Univ. of North Carolina Press, 1991), 329; *Charlotte News*, 17 Apr. 1925.

17. Thomas W. Hanchett, "When Wilkinson Made History," *Charlotte Observer*, 19 Nov. 2000; *Charlotte News*, 19 Apr. 1935, 1.

18. John J. McCarthy and Robert Littell, "Three Hundred Thousand Shacks: The Arrival of a New American Industry," *Harper's Magazine* 167 (June–Nov. 1933): 183–84; *Carpenter v. Boyles*, trial transcript, 42; E. N. Knowles, "Along

the Roadside," *Christian Science Monitor,* 31 July 1935, 5; McCarthy and Littell, "Three Hundred Thousand Shacks," 182–83; Civil Action Papers of Mecklenburg County, series 065.325, boxes 100–115.

19. McCarthy and Littell "Three Hundred Thousand Shacks," 183; *Business Week,* 12 June 1937, 54; *Business Week,* 4 Jan.–25 Apr. 1936, 31–32; J. Edgar Hoover with Courtney Ryley Cooper, "Camps of Crime," *American Magazine* 129 (Feb. 1940): 14–15; E. N. Knowles "Along the Roadside," *Christian Science Monitor* 31 July 1935, 1; *Business Week,* 15 June 1940, 19–20; *Architectural Record* 74 (Oct.–Dec. 1933): 457–62; "Many Find Life in Tourist Camps Happy," *Charlotte News,* 15 July 1937.

20. Greenwich Village's layout is discussed in *Carpenter v. Boyles,* 213 N.C. 432 at 449 (1938) and *Carpenter v. Boyles,* trial transcript, 13, 31, 41. The "camps of crime" quotation comes from Hoover with Cooper, "Camps of Crime," *American Magazine* 129 (Feb. 1940): 130–33.

21. The youthfulness of the Greenwich Village clientele is reported in *Carpenter v. Boyles,* 213 N.C. 432 at 437 (1938); *Carpenter v. Boyles,* trial transcript, 29. For the effect of cars on courtship, see Beth L. Bailey, *From Front Porch to Back Seat: Courtship in Twentieth Century America* (Baltimore: Johns Hopkins Univ. Press, 1988). The "our youth" quotation appears in "Is the Christian World Asleep?" *Mecklenburg Times,* 23 Sept. 1937, 4.

22. The "going into the cabins" quotation appears in *Carpenter v. Boyles,* 213 N.C. 432 at 437 (1938). The "I have seen drunk people" quotation appears in *Carpenter v. Boyles,* trial transcript, 25. "I have heard and seen drunk men and women" comes from *Carpenter v. Boyles,* trial transcript, 23.

23. *Carpenter v. Boyles,* trial transcript, 33.

24. For evidence of the notorious laxness of the rural police, see "Representatives in Favor of Abolishing Rural Police System," *Charlotte News,* 9 Mar. 1937, 20.

25. The dimensions of Greenwich Village and Dowd Manor appear in Mecklenburg County Register of Deeds Office map book 3, p. 201. For records of this property's transfer from the Kendrick Brick and Tile Company to W. F. Pruitt, and from W. F. Pruitt to the McNeely Land Company, see deed book 591, pp. 227–28, Charlotte-Mecklenburg Register of Deeds Office. For an example of a McNeely Land Company ad, see *Charlotte Observer,* 9 July 1925, real estate section, 21.

26. *Charlotte Observer,* 2 July 1925, real estate section, 25. Quoted property deeds can be found in Mecklenburg County Register of Deeds, book 591, p. 328; and book 591, p. 201.

27. "The Spreading Out of the City," *Charlotte News,* 2 Apr. 1925, 4. Regarding suburbanization generally during the 1920s, see Kenneth T. Jackson, *Crabgrass Frontier: The Suburbanization of the United States* (New York: Oxford Univ. Press, 1985), 175. On the rapid growth of the Charlotte area in the 1920s, see *1930 Census of the United States,* population statistics, 1201.

28. Wilkinson Boulevard subdivisions are listed in Mecklenburg County Register of Deeds Office map book 3, pp. 171, 235. For evidence of restrictive covenants in the developments near Dowd Manor, see, for example, book 690, p. 221, Charlotte Mecklenburg Register of Deeds.

29. Regarding Charlotte's turn-of-the-century suburban pioneers, see Hanchett, *Sorting Out the New South City*, 145–81. Regarding the jobs held by residents of Wilkinson Boulevard neighborhoods, see 1940 Charlotte City Directory (for Greenland Avenue, Greene Street, Greene Boulevard, Wilkinson Boulevard, Wayland Avenue, Remount Avenue, Arty Avenue, Highland Avenue, and Monument Street), Public Library of Charlotte and Mecklenburg County.

30. These figures were compiled using the 1940 Charlotte City Directory and property deeds located at the Charlotte Mecklenburg Register of Deeds. Information on this research is held by John W. Wertheimer.

31. For Greenwich Village's padlocking, see "Pressing War on Roadhouses," *Charlotte News*, 16 Sept. 1937, 22. For other nearby padlocking cases, see *Charlotte News*, 11 and 24 Oct. 1937.

32. For a discussion of the broader crackdown on roadhouses during the late 1930s, see "Regulation of Roadhouses: Experience in Goldfields City, North Carolina," *American City* 53 (Sept. 1938): 17.

33. Johnnie Anderson, *Heriot Clarkson: A Social Engineer of North Carolina* (Winston-Salem: Wake Forest Univ., 1972), 93; "Dries Will Ask New Hearing," *Charlotte News*, 4 Feb. 1937, sec. A, p. 1.

34. The "under the guise of dine-and-dance emporiums" quotation comes from "Mecklenburg Liquor Raids Help Wet Cause," *Charlotte News*, 16 Feb. 1937, sec. A, 8. The $2.5 million figure comes from *Charlotte News*, 7 Feb. 1937, 12-A. For the "wet" assertions that legalization would increase both tax revenue and control over alcohol, see "Liquor Profit to Be $75,000," *Charlotte News*, 17 Mar. 1937, 19; "Liquor Profits Bill Is Passed by Legislature," *Charlotte News*, 16 Mar. 1937, 1; "Senate Almost Sure to Pass Liquor Bill," *Charlotte News*, 5 Feb. 1937, sec. A, 17; "Favorable Report on Measure," *Charlotte News*, 3 Feb. 1937, sec. A, 3, 9.

35. Both the phrase "re-consecrate Prohibition" and the quotation about "confiscating liquor instead of selling it" appear in "Re-consecrate Prohibition," *Charlotte News*, 10 Mar. 1937, sec. A, 10. For the quotation about government's responsibility for "[t]he poverty, the drunks, the debauched," see William Brown, "Mecklenburg Exhorted to Remain Dry," *Charlotte News*, 23 Mar. 1937, 6. The quotation "we do not want whisky back" appears in "Whisky? There Ought to Be a Law Against It," *Charlotte News*, 10 Mar. 1937, 6.

36. "Drys Win Whisky Issue," *Charlotte* News, 2 June 1937, 1.

37. The "driest voting, wettest drinking" quotation comes from *Charlotte*

News, 16 Feb. 1937, 8. The phrase "see that [the prohibition] laws are enforced" comes from *Charlotte News*, 2 June 1937, 6.

38. The county's charges against the rural police are reported in "Rural Police Report to Be Ready Sunday," *Charlotte News*, 28 Mar. 1937, 14. Chief Fesperman's tearful testimony is reported in "Weeps on the Witness Stand," *Charlotte News*, 2 Mar. 1937, 1.

39. *State v. Wilson*, 93 N.C. 608 (1885).

40. "Fines Are Given in Court," *Charlotte News*, 18 Feb. 1937, 1; *Carpenter v. Boyles*, trial transcript, 36–37.

41. Public-Local Laws of North Carolina, P.L. 1913, c. 761 (1913); P.L. 1919, c. 288 (1919). Quoted passages appear at P.L. 1913, c. 761, secs. 26–29. On moral reform generally during these years, see Alan Hunt, *Governing Morals: A Social History of Moral Regulation* (Cambridge: Cambridge Univ. Press, 1999); and John C. Burnham "The Progressive Era Revolution in American Attitudes toward Sex," *Journal of American History* 59:4 (Mar. 1973): 885–908. Regarding moral reform in North Carolina, see Anastasia Sims, "'The Sword of the Spirit': The WCTU and Moral Reform in North Carolina, 1883–1933," *North Carolina Historical Review* 64:4 (1987): 395–415; and Daniel J. Whitener, *Prohibition in North Carolina, 1715–1945* (Chapel Hill: Univ. of North Carolina Press, 1946).

42. Civil Action Papers of Mecklenburg County, series 065.325, boxes 100–115.

43. All quotations and information in this paragraph come from "Solicitor Ready to Use Padlocking Proceedings," *Charlotte News*, 13 July 1937.

44. For the addresses of Randall and McGinnis, see Charlotte Mecklenburg Register of Deeds, book 930, p. 90; book 794, p. 568; and book 739, p. 64.

45. *Carpenter v. Boyles*, trial transcript, 22; "Fesperman, on Stand, Denies Liquor Charges," *Charlotte News*, 2 Mar. 1937, 18.

46. *Carpenter v. Boyles*, trial transcript, 4–7, 25.

47. "Pressing War on Roadhouses," *Charlotte News*, 16 Sept. 1937; *Carpenter v. Boyles*, trial transcript, 1–8.

48. The quotation "were the sentiment of the whole community" appears in *Carpenter v. Boyles*, trial transcript, 25. For more on communal values during the 1930s, see Richard H. Pells, *Radical Visions and American Dreams: Culture and Social Thought in the Depression Years* (New York: Harper and Row, 1973); Alan Brinkley, *Voices of Protest: Huey Long, Father Coughlin, and the Great Depression* (New York: Knopf, 1982); and George C. Waldrep, *Southern Workers and the Search for Community: Spartanburg County, South Carolina* (Urbana: Univ. of Illinois Press, 2000).

49. For discussion of the one hundred people who flooded the courtroom and the fifty volunteers willing to testify against Greenwich Village, see "Jury to Hear Padlock Case," *Charlotte News*, 28 Sept. 1937, 5. The anti–Greenwich Village petition appears in the Civil Action Papers, *Carpenter v. Boyles*.

50. For an account of Boyles's jury trail, see *Mecklenburg Times*, 23 Sept. 1937. The phrase "more than a score of witnesses" comes from "Jury Rules to Continue Greenwich Padlocking," *Charlotte News*, 14 Oct. 1937, 12. For the proximity of witnesses' houses to Greenwich Village, see *Carpenter v. Boyles*, trial transcript, 23.

51. See *Carpenter v. Boyles*, trial transcript, 25, 27, 30, 51.

52. All quotations in this paragraph come from the *Carpenter v. Boyles* trial transcript. For Clara Thompson's testimony, see p. 53. For Mason McGinnis's quoted testimony, see 24. For the continual awakening of sleeping children, see 22–24. For drunk men and women, roughness, yelling, dancing, etc., see 22–25, 59.

53. *Carpenter v. Boyles*, trial transcript, 48; *Charlotte Observer*, 1–15 Apr. 1937.

54. Judge Warlick's jury charge appears in *Carpenter v. Boyles*, trial transcript, 65. The trial's result is reported in *Charlotte News*, 14 Oct. 1937, 12.

55. For reports of padlocking warfare against roadhouses, see "Padlock Four Roadhouses in County," *Charlotte News*, 24 Oct. 1937, 1; Civil Action Papers of Mecklenburg County, series 065.325, October 1937.

56. For an example of seemingly tainted evidence admitted at trial, see *Carpenter v. Boyles*, 213 N.C. 432 (1938).

57. The "marches in morality" quotation appears in Anderson, *Heriot Clarkson*, 92. The "desire to eradicate the evils of liquor" quotation appears in Carol D. Taliaferro and Walter P. Stacy, *Memorial Address* (Raleigh, N.C.: [n.p.], 1942).

58. Anderson, *Heriot Clarkson*, 7; Anti-Saloon League of Charlotte, N.C., "It Helps Business and Is a Blessing: What Leading Business Men, Bankers, Farmers, Laborers and Others Say about Prohibition in Charlotte, N.C." (1908; electronic ed., University of North Carolina, Chapel Hill Libraries, 2001), 4.

59. Information on Clarkson's youth comes from Anderson, *Heriot Clarkson*, 8. The quoted words come from an address that Clarkson delivered at High Point Temperance Field Day, 8 Dec. 1940, entitled "A Charge to Keep I Have," folder 88, Heriot Clarkson Papers, Southern Historical Collection, University of North Carolina at Chapel Hill (hereafter, Clarkson Papers, UNC).

60. Clarkson's views on Reconstruction appear in Heriot Clarkson, letter to the *News*, July 1939, "Miscellaneous" folder, box 5, series 175, Heriot Clarkson Papers, State Archives, Raleigh (hereafter, Clarkson Papers, SA). Clarkson's contributions to the white supremacy movement are discussed in Anderson, *Heriot Clarkson*, 40. The "white supremacy" quotation appears in Anderson, *Heriot Clarkson*, 37–39. The "strongly in favor of the elimination of the Negro" quotation comes from a paper by Heriot Clarkson entitled "Important Events of My Life," undated, biographical data, folder 12, Clarkson Papers, UNC.

61. For the "my strongest ambition as a boy" quotation, see E. R. Preston, "A Short Biography of Heriot Clarkson," 10 Nov. 1923, Clarkson Papers, UNC. See also Anderson, *Heriot Clarkson*, 11. Regarding Clarkson's role in the establishment of Charlotte's Anti-Saloon League, see Heriot Clarkson, "The Drink Evil," Wilmington, N.C., 13 July 1904, folder 19, Clarkson Papers, UNC. Charlotte's successful anti-saloon vote is discussed in Anderson, *Heriot Clarkson*, 34. Clarkson's successful push for statewide prohibition is discussed in "The Drink Evil," Wilmington, N.C., 13 July 1904, folder 19, Clarkson Papers, UNC; and in Anderson, *Heriot Clarkson*, 50. The story about the governor's pen going to Clarkson appears in *Raleigh News and Observer*, 28 Jan. 1942, 2; Anderson, *Heriot Clarkson*, 56.

62. For Clarkson's role in the creation of the Turlington Act, see Anderson, *Heriot Clarkson*, 89; and folder 107, Clarkson Papers, UNC. The "outvolstead[ed]" quotation comes from *Literary Digest* 105 (3 May 1930): 48. Regarding the United Dry Forces, see Anderson, *Heriot Clarkson*, 90. The phrase "drink evil" comes from Heriot Clarkson, "The Drink Evil," Wilmington, N.C., 13 July 1904, folder 19, Clarkson Papers, UNC.

63. Regarding Clarkson's role as an active member of St. Peter's Protestant Episcopal Church and a founder of St. Andrew's Chapel, see Memorial Address by Carol D. Taliaferro, 10 Nov. 1942, 9, "Sketches of Clarkson" folder, box 5, series 175, Clarkson Papers, SA; Anderson, *Heriot Clarkson*, 14. For average marriage ages, see *Historical Statistics of the United States: Colonial Times to 1970*, series A, 158–159. Information regarding Mary Osborne Clarkson comes from "Mrs. Clarkson Passes at 89," *Charlotte Observer*, 28 Apr. 1957; folder 12, Clarkson Papers, UNC. For national family-size statistics, see Commission on Population Growth and the American Future, *Population and the American Future: The Report* (Washington, D.C.: Government Printing Office, 1972), 9–21. The Clarksons' family is discussed in Anderson, *Heriot Clarkson*, 11–14. Regarding the Clarksons' place of residence, see 1925 Charlotte City Directory, 260.

64. To determine the total number of majority opinions written by Clarkson for the North Carolina Supreme Court, we consulted a computer database at the Supreme Court Library in Raleigh. Heriot Clarkson's "fight[ing] ... the deterioration of morals" quotation appears in Anderson, *Heriot Clarkson*, 95.

65. Consolidated Statutes of North Carolina (1919), chap. 60, sec. 3181; and chap. 12, sec. 493. (Consolidated Statutes hereafter referred to as C.S.; General Statutes hereafter referred to as G.S.)

66. *Carpenter v. Boyles*, 213 N.C. 432 at 445 (1938).

67. C.S. chap. 60, sec. 3181; North Carolina Constitution, Art. I, sec. 17; and U.S. Constitution, Fourteenth Amendment.

68. *Daniels v. Homer*, 139 N.C. 219 (1905).

69. Regarding Clarkson's tendency to give his "personal feelings ... vivid

expression in his court opinions," see Anderson, *Heriot Clarkson,* 80. The long Clarkson quotation is from *Carpenter v. Boyles,* 213 N.C. 432 at 450 (1938).

70. For local reporting on Clarkson's ruling, see "Padlock Case of Greenwich Village Upheld," *Charlotte News,* 5 May 1938, 6; "Court Upholds County Action," *Charlotte Observer,* 5 May 1938, 1 (section 2).

71. For padlockings, see Civil Action Papers of Mecklenburg County, series 065.324, folders 104–118, and series 065.325, folders 115–116, State Archives, Raleigh. For the 1939 law licensing roadhouses, see Public Laws 1939, chap. 188, cited in *State v. Campbell,* 223 N.C. 828, 28 S.E. 2d 499 (1944).

72. "Nuisances," *West's North Carolina Digest,* vol. 30, 2d. (1999): 821–53. For the impact of post–World War II legal liberalism on nuisance laws, see Jeffrey S. Trachtman, "Note: Pornography, Padlocks, and Prior Restraints: The Constitutional Limits of the Nuisance Power," *New York University Law Review* 58 (Dec. 1983): 1478–529; "Regulation of Obscenity through Nuisance Statutes and Injunctive Remedies: The Prior Restraint Dilemma," *Wake Forest Law Review* 19 (Feb. 1983): 685–713; Carolin D. Bakewell, "The Constitutionality of North Carolina's Nuisance Abatement Statute: A Prior Restraint on Nonobscene Speech," *North Carolina Law Review* 61 (Apr. 1983): 685–713; and Paul A. Parker, "Survey of Developments in North Carolina Law," *North Carolina Law Review* 61 (Aug. 1983): 1952–54.

73. Telephone interview with Hubert Stone, sheriff of Robeson County, N.C., 14 Aug. 2001. Interview notes in author's possession.

74. For an example of a Clarkson speech that quoted *Boyles,* see his address before High Point Temperance Field Day, 8 Dec. 1940, folder 88, Clarkson Papers, UNC. On the Judge Heriot Clarkson Award, see http://www.bcgsearch.com/crc/book2005/northcarolina.html.

75. Mecklenburg County Superior Court order, 31 May 1938, Civil Action Papers of Mecklenburg County, 1938 folder.

7. Reading and the Right to Vote

1. "She Just Wanted to Vote," *Chicago Defender,* 24 Jan. 1959; "North Carolina Mother Is Denied Right to Vote [undated pamphlet, likely 1958–1959], folder 9, box 54, Carl and Anne Braden Papers, Wisconsin State Historical Society, Madison, Wisc. (hereafter, CABP-WSHS).

2. The phrase "view from the trenches" comes from Charles Payne's contribution to Steven Lawson and Charles Payne, *Debating the Civil Rights Movement, 1945–1968* (Lanham, Md.: Rowman & Littlefield, 1998), 99–136. A recent trickle of legal-historical scholarship has focused either directly or indirectly on what this chapter calls "grassroots litigation." Although Tomiko Brown-Nagin's "local legal history" of school desegregation litigation in Atlanta retains the traditional focus on NAACP Legal Defense Fund lawyers, it also

emphasizes the crucial contributions of local actors, including lawyers. Tomiko Brown-Nagin, "Race as Identity Caricature: A Local Legal History Lesson in the Salience of Intraracial Conflict," *University of Pennsylvania Law Review* 151 (June 2003): 1913–76. Other legal-historical works that consider the efforts of grassroots litigators, though not necessarily during the post–World War II decades, include Judith Kilpatrick, "(Extra) Ordinary Men: African-American Lawyers and Civil Rights in Arkansas before 1950," *Arkansas Law Review* 53 (2000): 299–399; Steven R. Hoffbeck, "'Victories Yet to Win': Charles W. Scrutchin, Bemidji's Black Activist Attorney," *Minnesota History* 55:2 (1996): 59–73; and Mark Curriden and Leroy Phillips Jr., *Contempt of Court: The Turn-of-the-Century Lynching That Launched 100 Years of Federalism* (New York: Faber and Faber, 1999). Forthcoming works by Kenneth Mack and others will continue this positive scholarly trend.

3. See Michael Perman, *Struggle for Mastery: Disfranchisement in the South, 1888–1908* (Chapel Hill: Univ. of North Carolina Press, 2001); J. Morgan Kousser, *The Shaping of Southern Politics: Suffrage Restriction and the Establishment of the One-Party South, 1880–1910* (New Haven: Yale Univ. Press, 1974); Darlene C. Hine, William C. Hine, and Stanley Harrold, *The African American Odyssey*, vol. 2 (Upper Saddle River, N.J.: Prentice Hall, 2003), 315; and Michael J. Klarman, *From Jim Crow to Civil Rights: The Supreme Court and the Struggle for Racial Equality* (New York: Oxford Univ. Press, 2004), 31.

4. Helen G. Edmonds, *The Negro and Fusion Politics in North Carolina, 1894–1901* (Chapel Hill: Univ. of North Carolina Press, 1951); Jeffrey J. Crow and Robert F. Durden, *Maverick Republican in the Old North State: A Political Biography of Daniel L. Russell* (Baton Rouge: Louisiana State Univ. Press, 1977); George W. Reid, "Four in Black: North Carolina's Black Congressmen, 1874–1901," *Journal of Negro History* 64:3 (summer 1979): 235; Evelyn Underwood, "The Struggle for White Supremacy in North Carolina" (MA thesis, University of North Carolina–Chapel Hill, 1943); W. A. Mabry, "Negro Suffrage and Fusion Rule in North Carolina," *North Carolina Historical Review* 12 (Apr. 1935): 79–102.

5. Underwood, "Struggle for White Supremacy in North Carolina," 32–35; Rosalie Fitzhugh McNeil, "The First Fifteen Months of Governor Daniel Lindsay Russell's Administration" (master's thesis, University of North Carolina, 1939), 128–35; "How They 'Settled' the Race Question," *(Raleigh) News and Observer*, 28 Jan. 1900, 1; David S. Cecelski and Timothy B. Tyson, *Democracy Betrayed: The Wilmington Race Riot of 1898 and Its Legacy* (Chapel Hill: Univ. of North Carolina Press, 1998); Edward L. Ayers, *The Promise of the New South: Life after Reconstruction* (New York: Oxford Univ. Press, 1992), 301–4.

6. For more on the North Carolina context, see Kent Redding, *Making Race, Making Power: North Carolina's Road to Disfranchisement* (Urbana: Univ. of Illinois Press, 2003); Glenda E. Gilmore, *Gender and Jim Crow: Women and*

the Politics of White Supremacy in North Carolina, 1896–1920 (Chapel Hill: Univ. of North Carolina Press, 1996); H. Leon Prather, *Resurgent Politics and Educational Progressivism in the New South: North Carolina, 1890–1913* (Rutherford, N.J.: Fairleigh Dickinson Univ. Press, 1979); and William Alexander Mabry, "'White Supremacy' and the North Carolina Suffrage Amendment," *North Carolina Historical Review* 13 (Jan. 1936). North Carolina abolished its poll tax in 1920. Klarman, *From Jim Crow to Civil Rights*, 142.

7. *(Raleigh) News and Observer*, 28 Jan. 1900.

8. Ibid., 4 Mar. 1900.

9. For the "practically unanimous" quotation, see *(Raleigh) News and Observer*, 3 Feb. 1899. For the "greatest folly," see *(Raleigh) News and Observer*, 28 Jan. 1900. For the "white man" quotation, see *(Raleigh) News and Observer*, 30 Jan. 1900.

10. Hine et al., *African American Odyssey*, vol. 2, 337.

11. For the grandfather clause's language, see Constitution of North Carolina, Article VI, enrolled 25 Jan. 1901, quoted in *Lassiter v. Northampton County Board of Elections*, 248 N.C. 102 at 109 (1958). The U.S. Supreme Court invalidated grandfather clauses in *Guinn v. United States*, 238 U.S. 347 (1915).

12. The quoted words come from section 163-28 of the *General Statutes of North Carolina, Laws of North Carolina* (Raleigh, N.C.: Edwards & Broughton Press, 1901), 246.

13. Information on Walker's birth and family life appears in *Statesville (N.C.) Record & Landmark*, 16 Apr. 1997, 4A. In 1920, four years before Walker's birth, Hertford County's population was 61.1 percent African American. See *1920 U.S. Census, Composition and Characteristics of the Population by States*, vol. 3 (Washington, D.C.: Government Printing Office, 1922), 739.

14. James R. Walker Jr., interviewed by Marcellus Barksdale, 7 Oct. 1976, tape 1, side 1, Duke University Oral History Program, Duke University Library (hereafter, Walker, oral interview, 1976).

15. *Statesville (N.C.) Record & Landmark*, 8 Dec. 1983; *Norfolk (Va.) Journal and Guide*, 18 Apr. 1959; Walker, oral interview, 1976, tape 1, side 1.

16. Walker, oral interview, 1976, tape 1, side 1; tape 3, side 1. The assertion that it was Reverend Dockery who urged Walker to pursue a legal career comes from Anna Lee Walker, a sister of James, in a telephone interview by James McNab, 19 Apr. 2004.

17. Sander Dockery's Statesville residence is recorded in the 1920 Census, North Carolina, Iredell County, Statesville City (sheet 6).

18. Walker, oral interview, 1976, tape 1, side 1.

19. Ibid.

20. Walker's war service is reported in *Statesville (N.C.) Record & Landmark*, 16 Apr. 1997, 4A. Walker's quotations are from Walker, oral interview, 1976, tape 1, side 1; and tape 2, side 1. The "His Big Battles Were to Come

Later" caption and photograph appear in the *Norfolk (Va.) Journal and Guide,* 18 Apr. 1959 (N), second section, 11.

21. Deborah Brandt, "Treating African Americans as the New Hutchins' Hobos," *Journal of Blacks in Higher Education* 21 (autumn 1998): 110; *Statesville (N.C.) Record & Landmark,* 16 Apr. 1997, 4A; Anna Lee Walker, telephone interview by James McNab, 19 Apr. 2004.

22. *(Durham) Carolina Times,* 29 Oct. 1949.

23. The Supreme Court decision was *Missouri ex rel. Gaines v. Canada,* 305 U.S. 337 (1938). For background on the law program at the North Carolina College for Negroes, see "So Far," published as part of the North Carolina Central University School of Law's 60th Anniversary Celebration, 1939–1999, quoted at http://www.nccu.edu/law/alumni/sofar1.html, accessed 22 Apr. 2004.

24. "So Far," http://www.nccu.edu/law/alumni/sofar1.html, accessed 22 Apr. 2004; Walker, oral interview, 1976, tape 1, side 1.

25. Walker, oral interview, 1976, tape 1, side 1; *Sweatt v. Painter,* 339 U.S. 629 (1950).

26. Maria Barnes to John W. Wertheimer, 22 Dec. 2004; Anna Lee Walker, telephone interview by James McNab, 19 Apr. 2004. On North Carolina's grudging admission of African American applicants to the UNC law school, see *McKissick v. Carmichael,* 187 F.2d 949 (1951); Peter Wallenstein, "Higher Education and the Civil Rights Movement: Desegregating the University of North Carolina," in *Warm Ashes: Issues in Southern History at the Dawn of the Twenty-first Century,* ed. Winfred B. Moore Jr., Kyle S. Sinisi, and David H. White Jr. (Columbia: Univ. of South Carolina Press, 2003), 280–300; and Charles E. Daye, "The Evolution of the Modern Law School: Crucial Trends That Bridge Past and Future," *North Carolina Law Review* (1995): 680–82. On the general trend of black admission to state universities at this time, see Hine et al., *African American Odyssey,* vol. 2, 502.

27. Walker, oral interview, 1976, tape 2, side 1.

28. *(Raleigh) News and Observer,* 27 Sept. 1951.

29. Ibid., 27 Sept. 1951, 2 Oct. 1951, and 5 Oct. 1951. The "educational services . . . and social recognition" quotation comes from the 2 Oct. 1951 issue of the *(Raleigh) News and Observer.*

30. "Five Negroes Send Telegram to Gov. Scott," source unnamed, President's Office records, Gordon Gray, box 1, #90008, University of North Carolina Archives, Chapel Hill (hereafter, UNC Archives). On the inaction of Governor Scott and the UNC prior to Walker's threatened litigation, see "UNC Negro Raises Question," *(Raleigh) News and Observer,* 27 Sept. 1951. On the outcome of the football-ticket incident, see Gordon Gray to Mrs. Creighton Lacy, 16 Oct. 1951, President's Office records, Gordon Gray, box 1, Segregation 1950–1951, UNC Archives.

31. See President's Office Records, Gordon Gray, Law School 1950–1952, UNC Archives; "Mixed Social Function Rule Bans UNC Law School Dance," *(Raleigh) News and Observer,* 16 Jan. 1952.

32. Margaret Price, *The Negro and the Ballot in the South* (Atlanta: Southern Regional Council, 1959), 70–73.

33. For more on voter registration figures, see North Carolina Advisory Committee of the U.S. Commission on Civil Rights, "Voting and Voter Registration in North Carolina, 1960," 4 June 1961; Irwin Klibaner, *Conscience of a Troubled South: The Southern Conference Educational Fund, 1946–1966* (Brooklyn, N.Y.: Carlson Publishing, 1989), 157; and Price, *The Negro and the Ballot,* 70–73.

34. United States Commission on Civil Rights, *Commission on Civil Rights Report* (Washington, D.C.: Government Printing Office, 1961), 278–82 (hereafter, CCR Report 1961); U.S. Bureau of the Census, *U.S. Census Population: 1960, Vol. I., Characteristics of the Population, Part 35, North Carolina* (Washington, D.C.: Government Printing Office, 1963), 35-285, 35-288, 35-289, 35-291; *U.S. Census Bureau—Current Population Reports, Series P-23, No. 8, Feb. 12, 1963, Estimates of Illiteracy, by States: 1960;* "425,000 Tar Heels Can't Read or Write," *(Raleigh) News and Observer,* 13 Apr. 1961, 5; *U.S. Census Bureau—Current Population Reports, Series P-20, No. 217, March 10, 1971, Illiteracy in the United States: November 1969.*

35. The "you can't get most Negroes" quotation comes from "Importance of Voting," *Norfolk (Va.) Journal and Guide,* 25 Aug. 1956, 8. Walker's quotation comes from Walker, oral interview, 1976, tape 2, side 2. The "lethargy" quotation comes from "Questions on the Poll Tax," *Norfolk (Va.) Journal and Guide,* 29 Aug. 1959, 8. Additional substantiation for this paragraph can be found in Price, *The Negro and the Ballot,* 15; and Eddie N. "Blue" Watford of Bertie County, N.C., telephone interview by James McNab, 14 Mar. 2004.

36. "Arrest Lawyer Who Tried to Help Clients Register," *Norfolk (Va.) Journal and Guide,* 19 May 1956, 2 (Carolina ed.); "Teacher Says His Voting Activity Got Him Fired," *Norfolk (Va.) Journal and Guide,* 20 Aug. 1960, 13 (N); "Carolina Vote Bars, Unfair Hiring Cited," *Norfolk (Va.) Journal and Guide,* 27 June 1959, 1; and "Voters Take Hard Body Blows—'Where It Hurts,'" *Norfolk (Va.) Journal and Guide,* 9 July 1960, 11 (N). The story about the use of dogs at the Perrytown precinct comes from Eddie N. "Blue" Watford of Bertie County, N.C., telephone interview by James McNab, 14 Mar. 2004.

37. The story of Georgia abuses comes from "Why Only Whites Vote in Newton," *Norfolk (Va.) Journal and Guide,* 3 Oct. 1959, 9 (N). The Florida story comes from Mark V. Tushnet, *Making Civil Rights Law: Thurgood Marshall and the Supreme Court, 1936–1961* (New York: Oxford Univ. Press, 1994), 115; reports on Mississippi atrocities prior to the 1950s appear in Klarman, *From Jim Crow to Civil Rights,* 383, 393.

38. CCR Report 1961, 32; Steven Lawson, *Black Ballots: Voting Rights in the South, 1944–1969* (New York: Columbia Univ. Press, 1976), 87–97; Tushnet, *Making Civil Rights Law*, 115.

39. North Carolina Advisory Committee of the U.S. Commission on Civil Rights, "Voting and Voter Registration in North Carolina, 1960," 4 June 1961, 3.

40. The phrase "to the satisfaction of the registrar" appears in *Laws of North Carolina*, 246. The phrase "good mind" comes from North Carolina Advisory Committee of the Commission on Civil Rights, "Voting and Voter Registration in North Carolina, 1960," 4 June 1961, 12, 15. For the "varying practices" quotation, see United States Commission on Civil Rights, *Report of the United States Commission on Civil Rights* (Washington, D.C.: Government Printing Office, 1959), 65 (hereafter, CCR Report 1959).

41. North Carolina Advisory Committee of the Commission on Civil Rights, "Voting and Voter Registration in North Carolina, 1960," 4 June 1961, 11, 14; CCR Report 1959, 570; *1960 Census of Population, Vol. I, Characteristics of the Population*, part 35, North Carolina, table 28: "Characteristics of the Population, for Counties: 1960" (Washington, D.C.: Government Printing Office, 1963), 35–123+.

42. North Carolina Advisory Committee of the Commission on Civil Rights, "Voting and Voter Registration in North Carolina, 1960," 4 June 1961, 3. The "it is in this section" quotation comes from the *(Durham) Carolina Times*, 7 Jan. 1950, 2, quoted in Marcellus Chandler Barksdale, "The Indigenous Civil Rights Movement and Cultural Change in North Carolina: Weldon, Chapel Hill, and Monroe: 1946–1965" (PhD diss., Duke University, 1977), 95.

43. CCR Report 1961, 278–82. The quotation calling northeastern North Carolina one of the South's most repressive areas comes from "Action Memo to SCEF Friends," 5 Mar. 1964, folder 13, box 56, CABP-WSHS. Regarding dramatic increases in nonwhite voter registration in the South between 1940 and 1960 (from about 3 percent to more than 20 percent), see North Carolina Advisory Committee to the U.S. Commission on Civil Rights, "Voting and Voter Registration in North Carolina, 1960," 4 June 1961, 5; and Klarman, *From Jim Crow to Civil Rights*, 3.

44. The Bertie County registrar's "No. I mean I didn't have any to try it" quotation comes from North Carolina Advisory Committee of the Commission on Civil Rights, "Voting and Voter Registration in North Carolina, 1960," 1961, 22; CCR Report 1959, 40; CCR Report 1961, xv. The "age-old complaint" quotation comes from "Denial of Voting Rights Again in N.C. Spotlight," *Norfolk (Va.) Journal and Guide*, 13 Apr. 1957, 8 (N).

45. The Halifax County story about the militia and the General Assembly comes from "Disfranchisement Schemes," *Norfolk (Va.) Journal and Guide*, 12 May 1956, 9 (N). The additional unfair questions appear in "A Struggle

for Rights in the Old North State," *Norfolk (Va.) Journal and Guide*, 26 May 1956, 9 (N); "Nine Accuse N.C. Vote Registrar, Seek Full Probe," *Norfolk (Va.) Journal and Guide*, 21 May 1960, 19 (N); and "Frye Makes Judicial History," *(Raleigh) News and Observer*, 3 Aug. 1999.

46. "Developments Good and Bad on Segregation Issue," *Norfolk (Va.) Journal and Guide*, 19 May 1956 (N), 9.

47. Walker, oral interview, 1976, tape 1, side 2.

48. James R. Walker, *Be Firm My Hope* (New York: Comet Press, 1955). Quoted praise of this book comes from Walter Spearman, "North Carolina Fiction, 1954–1955," *North Carolina Historical Review* 33:2 (Apr. 1956): 219. The quoted stanza beginning "May all who've in her battles fought" comes from "The Freedman's Crave," *Be Firm My Hope*, 17. The stanza beginning "It matters not about your hue" comes from a poem called "Her Sacred Ballot," *Be Firm My Hope*, 4–5. Although this poem putatively concerns women's suffrage, the quoted stanza, along with the timing (the 1950s, not the 1910s), suggests that the poem was at least indirectly aimed at the African American struggle for voting rights in the 1950s. The assertion that Walker Jr. "credit[ed] much of his devotion to action in civil rights" to his father's poetry comes from "Poem by Father Inspires Walker in Civil Rights," *Norfolk (Va.) Journal and Guide*, 18 Apr. 1959, second section, 11 (N).

49. Information about Walker Jr.'s experiences on his father's book tour leading to his relocation to northeastern North Carolina comes from *Norfolk (Va.) Journal & Guide*, 18 Apr. 1959; and *Statesville (N.C.) Record and Landmark*, 8 Dec. 1983. Quotations come from Walker, oral interview, 1976, tape 1, side 2.

50. *Census of Population: 1950*, vol. II, part 33 (Washington, D.C.: Government Printing Office, 1952), table 77, pp. 33–241; and table 14, pp. 33–37. For the phrases "so many people" and "besieged," see "North Carolina Mother Is Denied Right to Vote" [undated pamphlet, likely 1958–1959], folder 9, box 54, CABP-WSHS.

51. The assertion that Walker was the only black lawyer in a six-county area comes from "North Carolina Mother Is Denied Right to Vote," [undated pamphlet, likely 1958–1959], folder 9, box 54, CABP-WSHS. Regarding the rate of marriage among men of Walker's age (thirty-two in 1956, when he began his civil rights work in northeastern North Carolina), see *Historical Statistics of the United States: Colonial Times to 1970*, part I, series A 160–171, "Marital Status of the Population, by Age and Sex: 1890–1970," 21. Information on Walker's familial and professional life comes from Zenobia Cofield of Weldon, N.C., and Muriel Walker Ramsey Cureton, telephone interview by James McNab, 15 Apr. 2004.

52. Klarman, *From Jim Crow to Civil Rights*, 236–53, 291–92; "Register and Vote Meets Scheduled in N. Carolina," *Norfolk (Va.) Journal and Guide*, 14 Jan. 1956, 6 (Carolina ed.); "N.C. Ministers Sponsor Drive for 100,000 Vot-

ers," *Norfolk (Va.) Journal and Guide,* 22 June 1957, 4 (Carolina ed.); "Churches Urged to Give Support to Vote Drive," *Norfolk (Va.) Journal and Guide,* 7 Apr. 1956, 3; "Drive for More Negro Voters in 10 Southern States," *Norfolk (Va.) Journal and Guide,* 1 Feb. 1958, 20 (N); and "Vote Rallies Set for 21 Cities in South," *Norfolk (Va.) Journal and Guide,* 8 Feb. 1958, 2 (N); "Voters [sic] Registration Slowing Down," *Norfolk (Va.) Journal and Guide,* 5 Sept. 1959, 9 (N); "Stop Colored Voters Aim of Proposed Bill," *Norfolk (Va.) Journal and Guide,* 8 Feb. 1958, 20 (N); "Ga. Governor Asks Poll Tax to Cut Negro Voting," *Norfolk (Va.) Journal and Guide,* 15 Feb. 1958, 4 (Carolina ed.); and "Death of Democracy, II," *Norfolk (Va.) Journal and Guide,* 22 Feb. 1958.

53. *Smith v. Allwright,* 321 U.S. 649 (1944). For a discussion of anti-NAACP attacks, see Tushnet, *Making Civil Rights Law,* 99, 115, 272–300, 307. For evidence of this anti-NAACP trend in North Carolina in particular, see "NAACP Faces Fight for Survival in N. Carolina," *Norfolk (Va.) Journal and Guide,* 11 Feb. 1956, 2 (Virginia-Carolina ed.); and "Carolina Senate Sets Precedent," *Norfolk (Va.) Journal and Guide,* 15 June 1957, 2 (Virginia ed.).

54. For discussions of the litigation strategies of Thurgood Marshall and the NAACP, see Mark V. Tushnet, *The NAACP's Legal Strategy against Segregated Education, 1925–1950* (Chapel Hill: Univ. of North Carolina Press, 1987); Richard Kluger, *Simple Justice: The History of Brown v. Board of Education and Black America's Struggle for Equality* (New York: Vintage Books, 1975); Tushnet, *Making Civil Rights Law;* and Juan Williams, *Thurgood Marshall: American Revolutionary* (New York: Times Books, 1998).

55. H.B. 1082, *1955 Session Laws of North Carolina,* chap. 1104, "An Act to Amend Sections 163–175 of the General Statutes of North Carolina Providing the Manner in which Votes May Be Cast for Group Candidates in All Primaries and Elections Held in this State"; U.S. Commission on Civil Rights, *The Voting Rights Act: Ten Years After* (Washington, D.C.: Government Printing Office, 1975), 207; Peyton McCrary, "Racially Polarized Voting in the South: Quantitative Evidence from the Courtroom," *Social Science History* 14:4 (winter 1990): 509. Information on the candidacies of the three Halifax County African Americans comes from "First Negro Candidates in Halifax in 58 Years," *Norfolk (Va.) Journal and Guide,* 5 May 1956, 2 (Virginia-Carolina ed.). Walker's service as "campaign manager for three Negroes running for public office in the eastern part of the state" is reported in "A Struggle for Rights in the Old North State," *Norfolk (Va.) Journal and Guide,* 26 May 1956, 9 (N). The loss of "all of the Black candidates" in the area in the Democratic primary of May 1956 is reported in Barksdale, "Indigenous Civil Rights Movement and Cultural Change in North Carolina," 121. The assertion that voting machines were returned to factories to be "one-shotted" comes from "Columbus Adjusting Voting Machines," *(Raleigh) News and Observer,* 7 Apr. 1957, 16.

56. "Northampton Suit Is Filed," *(Raleigh) News and Observer,* 22 June 1956,

29; "Fourth Vote Suit Is Filed," *(Raleigh) News and Observer,* 23 June 1956, 8; "Voting Case Is Dismissed," *(Raleigh) News and Observer,* 2 May 1957, 38. A federal court struck down North Carolina's restriction on single-shot voting in *Dunston v. Scott,* 336 F. Supp. 206 (E.D.N.C. 1972). See McCrary, "Racially Polarized Voting in the South," 522 n. 8.

57. Walker, oral interview, 1976, tape 2, side 1.

58. Ibid., tape 1, side 1.

59. Ibid., tape 2, side 1; tape 1, side 2.

60. Ibid., tape 2, side 1; tape 2, side 2.

61. Ibid., tape 1, side 2; and tape 2, side 1. See also, Barksdale, "Indigenous Civil Rights Movement and Cultural Change in North Carolina," 110.

62. Walker, oral interview, 1976, tape 1, side 1; tape 1, side 2.

63. Ibid., 1976, tape 2, side 1.

64. Ibid.

65. "Complaint," *Ernest Ivey v. T. W. Cole,* Civil Action No. 969, filed 20 June 1956, U.S. District Court for the Eastern District of North Carolina, Raleigh Division, National Archives and Records Administration, Southeast Region. Quoted questions are numbers 3 and 9 of the ten-question test. The test is reproduced as "Plaintiff's Exhibit A" in the court record. Ibid. See also "'Civics Test' Flunks Voter," *(Raleigh) News and Observer,* 21 June 1956, 1.

66. "Complaint," *Ernest Ivey v. T. W. Cole,* Civil Action no. 969, U.S. District Court for the Eastern District of North Carolina, Raleigh Division, National Archives and Records Administration, Southeast Region; "'Civics Test' Flunks Voter," *(Raleigh) News and Observer,* 21 June 1956, 1.

67. "Segregationists Now Try to Avoid Federal Courts," *Norfolk (Va.) Journal and Guide,* 5 Jan. 1957, 1 (home ed.).

68. Walker, oral interview, 1976, tape 1, side 2; tape 2, side 1. For more on Taylor and Mitchell, see National Lawyers Guild Publication, National Lawyers Guild folder, box 3, Carl and Anne Braden Collection, Special Collections, University of Tennessee–Knoxville Library (hereafter, CABC-UTK); National Lawyers Guild Publication and SCEF press release, 6 Feb. 1963, Herman Taylor and Samuel Mitchell folder, box 5, CABC-UTK. Walker was the original attorney in *Ivey.* See James R. Walker Jr. to Roy Wilkins, 4 Oct. 1957, supplement to part 4, Voting Rights, General Office files, 1956–1965, microfilm reel 6, box A-271, Papers of the NAACP.

69. Previous litigation of this sort is discussed in Klarman, *From Jim Crow to Civil Rights,* 240. For pretrial coverage of *Ivey v. Cole* in both the African American and the white press, see "Hodges Seeks Sympathy; Preacher Sues Registrar," *Norfolk (Va.) Journal and Guide,* 30 June 1956, 9; "Carolina Voting Laws Challenged in 4 Suits," *Norfolk (Va.) Journal and Guide,* 30 June 1956, 1; "'Civics Test' Flunks Voter: Sues for $5,000," *(Raleigh) News and Observer,* 21 June 1956, 1.

70. "Order," 1 Mar. 1957, U.S. District Court for the Eastern District of North Carolina, Raleigh Division, Civil Action no. 969; James R. Walker Jr. to Hon. J. D. Larkins Jr., 2 Feb. 1963, in case file for *Ernest Ivey v. T. W. Cole,* Civil Action no. 610, U.S. District Court for the Eastern District of North Carolina, Wilson Division, National Archives and Records Administration, Southeast Region. The order dismissing the case was filed on 9 July 1963 and is available in the case file.

71. Demographic figures come from *1960 Census of Population,* vol. I, Characteristics of the Population, part 35, North Carolina, table 28: "Characteristics of the Population, for Counties: 1960" (Washington, D.C.: Government Printing Office, 1963), 35–123. Voter registration figures come from North Carolina Advisory Committee of the U.S. Commission on Civil Rights, "Voting and Voter Registration in North Carolina," 4 June 1961, 37; CCR Report 1961, 278–82.

72. "Arrest Lawyer Who Tried to Help Clients Register," *Norfolk (Va.) Journal and Guide,* 19 May 1956, 2 (Carolina ed.); "Walker Was Trespassing Judge Says," *Norfolk (Va.) Journal and Guide,* 25 May 1956, 1 (N).

73. "Walker Was Trespassing Judge Says," *Norfolk (Va.) Journal and Guide,* 25 May 1956, 1 (N).

74. "Lawyer Fined in Voting Case; 'Outsiders' Warned," *Norfolk (Va.) Journal and Guide,* 26 May 1956, 2.

75. "Lawyer White Woman Said 'Pointed' Is 'Guilty,'" *Norfolk (Va.) Journal and Guide,* 25 Aug. 1956, 2 (N); "Lawyer's Appeal in Assault Case in Northampton Dismissed," *(Raleigh) News and Observer,* 21 Mar. 1957, 36; "Lawyer Jailed," *(Raleigh) News and Observer,* 4 Apr. 1957, 1.

76. For reports of Walker's "disturbing an elections registrar" prosecution, see "Lawyer Remains in Jail," *(Raleigh) News and Observer,* 5 Apr. 1957, 7; and "Money Sought to Support N.C. Lawyer and Client," *Norfolk (Va.) Journal and Guide,* 15 Nov. 1958 (N). For the tax evasion charge, see "Attorney Says His Arrest on Tax Charge 'Reprisal,'" *Norfolk (Va.) Journal and Guide,* 8 Feb. 1958. For the car vandalism story, see "Negro in Voting Suits Says Car Slashed by Vandals," *(Raleigh) News and Observer,* 24 Apr. 1957, 2. The "don't intend to have any Negro lawyers" quotation comes from "Money Sought to Support N.C. Lawyer and Client," *Norfolk (Va.) Journal and Guide,* 15 Nov. 1958 (N). For more on North Carolina's criminal prosecution of Walker, see *State v. Walker,* 249 N.C. 35 (1958).

77. Quoted words come from Walker, oral interview, 1976, tape 2, side 1; and tape 2, side 2. Additional information in the paragraph comes from "She Just Wanted to Vote," *Chicago Defender,* 24 Jan. 1959; and "Farm Wife Carries Ballot Denial to Top U.S. Court," *Norfolk (Va.) Journal and Guide,* 18 Apr. 1959. Employment figures come from *Census of the Population: 1950,* vol. II: Characteristics of the Population, part 33, North Carolina (Washington, D.C.:

Government Printing Office, 1952), table 44, "Characteristics of the Nonwhite Population for Counties: 1950," 33–129.

78. *Louise Lassiter v. Northampton County Board of Elections*, "Fact Sheet," folder 9, box 54, CABP-WSHS; "Farm Wife Carries Ballot Denial to Top U.S. Court," *Norfolk (Va.) Journal and Guide*, 18 Apr. 1959, second section, 11 (N); "She Just Wanted to Vote," *Chicago Defender*, 24 Jan. 1959; *Census of the Population: 1950*, vol. II: Characteristics of the Population, part 33, North Carolina (Washington, D.C.: Government Printing Office, 1952), table 42, 33–110.

79. "Arrest Lawyer Who Tried to Help Clients Register," *Norfolk (Va.) Journal and Guide*, 19 May 1956, 2 (Carolina ed.); "N.C. Woman Challenges Voting Laws," *Norfolk (Va.) Journal and Guide*, 2 Mar. 1957 (Virginia-Carolina ed.), 2; "Plaintiffs Added to Suit," *(Raleigh) News and Observer*, 17 Apr. 1957, 10.

80. Walker, oral interview, 1976, tape 2, side 1.

81. "An Act to Amend Article 6, Chapter 163 of the General Statutes Relating to Registration of Voters," *Session Laws of N.C. Reg. Session, 1957* (Winston-Salem, N.C.: Winston Printing, 1957), chap. 287, 277–78.

82. For evidence that frustrated black would-be registrants could appeal successfully to their local boards of elections, see *Roanoke Rapids (N.C.) Daily Herald*, 16–17 May 1960, cited in Barksdale, "Indigenous Civil Rights Movement and Cultural Change in North Carolina," 286–87.

83. "An Act to Amend Article 6, Chapter 163 of the General Statutes Relating to Registration of Voters," *Session Laws of N.C. Reg. Session, 1957*, chap. 287, section 2, 277.

84. "Senate Group Okays Election Law Change," *(Raleigh) News and Observer*, 4 Apr. 1957, 7; Attorney General Frank Patton, quoted in "Voter Registration Bill Passes," *(Raleigh) News and Observer*, 12 Apr. 1957, 5.

85. *Lassiter v. Taylor*, 152 F. Supp. 295 (1957); "Federal Jurists Hear Evidence in Test of Literacy Vote Law," *(Raleigh) News and Observer*, 20 Apr. 1957, 1–2; "U.S. Judges Halt Action in Northampton Vote Suit," *(Raleigh) News and Observer*, 11 June 1957, 2.

86. "Federal Jurists Hear Evidence in Test of Literacy Vote Law," *(Raleigh) News and Observer*, 20 Apr. 1957, 1–2; "4 Challenge N.C. Voting Clause in Federal Court," *Norfolk (Va.) Journal and Guide*, 27 Apr. 1957, 1–2 (Virginia ed.); "U.S. Judges Halt Action in Northampton Vote Suit," *(Raleigh) News and Observer*, 11 June 1957, 2.

87. Walker, oral interview, 1976, tape 2, side 1.

88. "Federal Jurists Hear Evidence in Test of Literacy Vote Law," *(Raleigh) News and Observer*, 20 Apr. 1957, 1–2; *Lassiter v. Taylor*, 152 F. Supp. 295 at 296 (1957).

89. *Lassiter v. Taylor*, 152 F. Supp. 295 at 296 (1957); "Voting Case," *(Raleigh) News and Observer*, 19 Apr. 1957, 32; Carl E. DeVane, "Candidates

Sprouting Up; Court Hears Vote Case," *Norfolk (Va.) Journal and Guide*, 4 May 1957, 8; Carl E. DeVane, "Steel Official at Shaw; Raleigh Scheme Sets Pace," *Norfolk (Va.) Journal and Guide*, 25 May 1957, 8; "U.S. Judges Halt Action in Northampton Vote Suit," *(Raleigh) News and Observer*, 11 June 1957, 2.

90. *Louise Lassiter v. Northampton County Board of Elections*, 248 N.C. 102 (1958).

91. "Plaintiff Appellant's Brief," *Lassiter v. Northampton Board of Education*, Supreme Court of North Carolina, fall term 1957, no. 172, Sixth District.

92. "Defendant Appellee's Brief," *Lassiter v. Northampton Board of Education*, Supreme Court of North Carolina, fall term 1957, no. 172, Sixth District. Quoted passages come from pages 12–13. See also "Brief of the Attorney General of North Carolina (Amicus Curiae)," *Lassiter v. Northampton Board of Election*, Supreme Court of North Carolina, fall term 1957, no. 172, Sixth District, 32–36, 54–55.

93. *Louise Lassiter v. Northampton County Board of Elections*, 248 N.C. 102 (1958); *Guinn v. United States*, 238 U.S. 347 (1915) at 366; "Suffrage—Literacy Test," *North Carolina Law Review* 37 (1959): 396–97.

94. James Walker Jr. to Roy Wilkins, 4 Oct. 1957; James R. Walker Jr. to Roy Wilkins, 10 Feb. 1958; John A. Morsell to Thurgood Marshall, 14 Jan. 1958; John A. Morsell to James Walker, 14 Jan. 1958, all in supplement to part 4, Voting Rights, General Office files, 1956–1965, microfilm reel 6, box A-271, Papers of the NAACP.

95. Walker quotations from oral interview, 1976, tape 2, side 1; "Walker Lassiter Defense Fund Press Release," 5 Oct. 1959, folder 13, box 56, CABP-WSHS; *Southern Patriot*, 16:8 (Oct. 1958): 3; and "Field Secretaries' Report," Aug. 1958, folder 97, box 2, CABP-WSHS. The October 1958 SCEF board meeting in Atlanta had the Walker-Lassiter Defense Fund on the agenda. "SCEF Board Meeting Agenda," 4 Oct. 1958, folder 4, box 22, CABP-WSHS. For more on SCEF, see Irwin Klibaner, *Conscience of a Troubled South: The Southern Conference Educational Fund, 1946–1966* (New York: Carlson Publishing, 1989), 16; and "What Is SCEF?" SCEF Files, CABC-UTK. For SCEF actions surrounding the Lassiter case, see "North Carolina Mother Is Denied Right to Vote" [undated pamphlet, likely 1958–1959], folder 9, box 54, CABP-WSHS; *Oklahoma Eagle*, 13 Nov. 1958; *(Memphis, Tenn.) Tri-State Defender*, 15 Nov. 1958; Carl Braden to Leonard Boudin, 2 Oct. 1958; Samuel Mitchell to Leonard Boudin, 19 Dec. 1958; Cherry Clarke to Carl & Anne Braden, 26 Nov. 1958, all three letters in folder 9, box 54, CABP-WSHS.

96. *Lassiter v. Northampton County Board of Elections*, 360 U.S. 45 (1959).

97. For mentions of *Lassiter* during congressional debate on the bill that became the Voting Rights Act of 1965, see U.S. House, 89th Cong., 1st sess., *Congressional Record*, 6 Apr. 1965, vol. 111, pt. 11, 15649; 89th Cong., 1st sess. *Congressional Record*, 18 Mar. 1965, vol. 111, pt. 4, 5389. Regarding the link

between the *Lassiter* ruling and the passage of the Voting Rights Act, see Sandra Guerra, "Voting Rights and the Constitution: The Disenfranchisement of Non-English Speaking Citizens," *Yale Law Journal* 97 (June 1988): 1420; and Walker, oral interview, 1976, tape 2, side 2.

98. Walker, oral interview, 1976, tape 2, side 2. The judicial quotation comes from *Lassiter v. Northampton County Board of Elections*, 360 U.S. 45 at 53 (1959).

99. Demographic figures come from *1960 Census of Population*, vol. I, Characteristics of the Population, part 35, North Carolina, table 28: "Characteristics of the Population, for Counties: 1960" (Washington, D.C.: Government Printing Office, 1963), 35–123. Voter registration figures come from North Carolina Advisory Committee of the U.S. Commission on Civil Rights, "Voting and Voter Registration in North Carolina," 4 June 1961, 36.

100. "Tri-County Group Seeks Ruling on Literacy Tests," *Norfolk (Va.) Journal and Guide*, 27 Feb. 1960, 14 (N); "'Spelling Test' Not Legal Says N.C. Attorney General," *Norfolk (Va.) Journal and Guide*, 12 Mar. 1960, 1; "Residents of 4 Counties to Push for Registration," *Norfolk (Va.) Journal and Guide*, 15 Oct. 1960, 14 (N).

101. "Plaintiff-Appellant's Brief," *Bazemore v. Bertie County Board of Elections*, Supreme Court of North Carolina, Sixth District, no. 168, spring term, 1961, 3; "Defendant Appellees' Brief," *Bazemore v. Bertie County Board of Elections*, Supreme Court of North Carolina, Sixth District, no. 168, spring term, 1961, 2.

102. *Bazemore v. Bertie County Board of Elections*, 254 N.C. 398 (1961); "Plaintiff-Appellant's Brief," *Bazemore v. Bertie County Board of Elections*, Supreme Court of North Carolina, Sixth District, no. 168, spring term, 1961, 6; "Defendant-Appellees' Brief," *Bazemore v. Bertie County Board of Elections*, Supreme Court of North Carolina, Sixth District, no. 168, spring term, 1961, 2–3.

103. "Plaintiff-Appellant's Brief," *Bazemore v. Bertie County Board of Elections*, Supreme Court of North Carolina, Sixth District, no. 168, spring term, 1961, 7–12. Attorney Robert L. Harrell Sr. also contributed to the Bazemore brief.

104. "Plaintiff-Appellant's Brief," *Bazemore v. Bertie County Board of Elections*, Supreme Court of North Carolina, Sixth District, no. 168, spring term, 1961, 17–18.

105. Ibid., 19–20.

106. *Bazemore v. Bertie County Board of Elections*, 254 N.C. 398, at 403–4, 406 (1961).

107. Ibid., 404–5.

108. Ibid, 405.

109. Ibid., 406. The assertion that many area whites took it for granted that

they could register without submitting to the literacy test comes from Malcolm Partin of Halifax County, during an interview by John W. Wertheimer, 10 Nov. 2004, Davidson, N.C. For additional testimony on this point, see North Carolina Advisory Committee of the U.S. Commission on Civil Rights, "Voting and Voter Registration in North Carolina, 1960," 4 June 1961, 20.

110. "Favorable Decision," *Norfolk (Va.) Journal and Guide,* 22 Apr. 1961, 9 (N); *(Durham) Carolina Times,* 22 Apr. 1961, 2, quoted in Barksdale, "Indigenous Civil Rights Movement and Cultural Change in North Carolina," 289; *Bazemore v. Bertie County Board of Elections,* 254 N.C. 398 at 406 (1961).

111. John W. Fleming, "Carolina News Digest," *Norfolk (Va.) Journal and Guide,* 6 May 1961, 9 (N); John W. Fleming, "Carolina News Digest," *Norfolk (Va.) Journal and Guide,* 4 Mar. 1961, 9 (N).

112. For a broader discussion of the intangible impact of civil rights litigation, see Michael J. Klarman, "Is the Supreme Court Sometimes Irrelevant? Race and the Southern Criminal Justice System in the 1940s," *Journal of American History* 89:1 (2002): 119–53. For the contribution of Lassiter to the passage of the Voting Rights Act of 1965, see Guerra, "Voting Rights and the Constitution."

113. "N.C. Attorney to Speak at Lawyer's Convention," *Norfolk (Va.) Journal and Guide,* 30 July 1960, 14 (N); "James Robert Walker Jr.," obituary, *Statesville (N.C.) Record & Landmark,* 16 Apr. 1997, 4A.

114. Barksdale, "Indigenous Civil Rights Movement and Cultural Change in North Carolina," 306; Walker, oral interview, 1976, tape 2, side 2; and tape 3, side 1; "An Upsurge in Carolina," *Southern Patriot* 22:6 (June 1964).

115. *United States Code: Congressional and Administrative News, 91st Congress–2nd Session, Vol. 1 (Laws) 1970* (St. Paul, Minn.: West Publishing, 1970), 373–74. The congressionally imposed ban on state-level literacy tests as conditions for voting survived the judicial scrutiny of the U.S. Supreme Court in *Katzenbach v. Morgan,* 384 U.S. 641 (1966). See also *United States Code: Congressional and Administrative News, 94th Congress–1st Session, Vol. 1 (Laws) 1975,* 774 and 812; and 42 USC sec. 1973aa. Louise Lassiter's 1960 registration is reported in CCR Report 1961, 34.

8. Native Americans and School Desegregation

1. *State v. Braxton Chavis,* 45 N.C. App 438 (1980); *State v. Braxton Chavis et al.,* trial transcript, Robeson County Superior Court, 19 Feb. 1979 session, certified 22 June 1979, 21–22, in *State v. Braxton Chavis et al.,* North Carolina Court of Appeals, Sixteenth District, from Robeson, No. 7916SC602 (1979) (hereafter, *State v. Chavis,* trial transcript).

2. See, for instance, Matthew D. Lassiter and Andrew B. Lewis, eds., *The Moderates' Dilemma: Massive Resistance to School Desegregation in Virginia*

(Charlottesville: Univ. Press of Virginia, 1998); Graeme Cope, "'Honest White People of the Middle and Lower Classes?' A Profile of the Capital Citizens' Council during the Little Rock Crisis of 1957," *Arkansas Historical Quarterly* 61:1 (2002): 36–58; Kenneth T. Andrews, "Movement-Countermovement Dynamics and the Emergence of New Institutions: The Case of 'White Flight' Schools in Mississippi," *Social Forces* 80:3 (2002): 911–36; Phoebe Godfrey, "Bayonets, Brainwashing, and Bathrooms: The Discourse of Race, Gender, and Sexuality in the Desegregation of Little Rock's Central High," *Arkansas Historical Quarterly* 62:1 (2003): 42–67; Brent J. Aucoin, "The Southern Manifesto and Southern Opposition to Desegregation," *Arkansas Historical Quarterly* 55:2 (1996): 173–93; and Kevin M. Kruse, *White Flight: Atlanta and the Making of Modern Conservatism* (Princeton: Princeton Univ. Press, 2005).

3. See, generally, Scott Kurashige, "The Many Facets of Brown: Integration in a Multiracial Society," *Journal of American History* 91:1 (2004): 56–68. For Mexican Americans and school desegregation, see Guadalupe San Miguel, *Brown Not White: School Integration and the Chicano Movement in Houston* (College Station: Texas A&M Univ. Press, 2001); Steven H. Wilson, "*Brown* over 'Other White': Mexican Americans' Legal Arguments and Litigation Strategy in School Desegregation Lawsuits," *Law and History Review* 21:1 (spring 2003): 145–94; Rubén Garza, "A Reflection of the Past: Desegregation for Goliad, Texas," *American Educational History Journal* 28 (2001): 111–18; Francisco A. Rosales, *Chicano! The History of the Mexican American Civil Rights Movement* (Houston: Arte Público, 1996); and Gary Orfield, "The Growth of Segregation: African Americans, Latinos, and Unequal Education," in *Dismantling Desegregation: The Quiet Reversal of* Brown v. Board of Education, ed. Gary Orfield and Susan E. Eaton (New York: New Press, 1996). On Chinese Americans, see Bill Ong Hing, "Asians without Blacks and Latinos in San Francisco: Missed Lessons of the Common Good," *Amerasia Journal* 27:2 (2001): 19–27; and Philip A. Lum, "The Creation and Demise of San Francisco Chinatown Freedom Schools: One Response to Desegregation," *Amerasia Journal* 5:1 (1978): 57–73. On the disabled community, see Mozelle Berkowitz, "Just a Kid in Our Class: The Integration of Children with Severe Disabilities in Neighborhood Schools" (PhD diss., Boston University, 1993); Joseph P. Shapiro, *No Pity: People with Disabilities Forging a New Civil Rights Movement* (New York: Three Rivers, 1994).

4. For some examples of nonwhite opposition to desegregation, see David Cecelski, *Along Freedom Road: Hyde County, North Carolina, and the Fate of Black Schools in the South* (Chapel Hill: Univ. of North Carolina Press, 1994); Derrick A. Bell Jr., "Serving Two Masters: Integration Ideals and Client Interests in School Desegregation Litigation," *Yale Law Journal* 85 (March 1976): 470–516; and Tomiko Brown-Nagin, "Race as Identity Caricature: A Local Legal History Lesson in the Salience of Intraracial Conflict," *University of*

Pennsylvania Law Review 151 (June 2003): 1913–76. For examples of non-black support for desegregation, see Milton S. Katz and Susan B. Tucker, "A Pioneer in Civil Rights: Esther Brown and the South Park Desegregation Case of 1948," *Kansas History* 18:4 (1995–1996): 234–47; and David L. Chappell, "Diversity within a Racial Group: White People in Little Rock, 1957–1959," *Arkansas Historical Quarterly* 54:4 (1995): 444–56.

5. Karen I. Blu, *The Lumbee Problem: The Making of an American Indian People* (New York: Cambridge Univ. Press, 1980), 12; U.S. Department of Commerce, *General Population Characteristics: 1970 Census of Population*, table 122: Occupation and Earnings for Counties, 1970 (Washington, D.C.: Department of Commerce, 1973), 35–414; "'State of Robeson,'" *Robesonian (Lumberton, N.C.)*, 21 Apr. 1969, 8; John Gregory Peck, "Urban Station-Migration of the Lumbee Indians" (PhD diss., University of North Carolina at Chapel Hill, 1972), 40; Blu, *Lumbee Problem*, 16–17; and *Census of Population, 1970* (Washington, D.C.: Government Printing Office, 1972), tables 120, 124, 125, and 128.

6. Thomas E. Ross, *One Land, Three Peoples: A Geography of Robeson County, North Carolina* (Southern Pines, N.C.: Hollow Press, 1993), 67.

7. American Friends Service Committee, "School Desegregation Report: Staff Work with Lumbee Indians," 30 June 1962, folder 6, box 276, Association on American Indian Affairs, Inc., Papers, Mudd Manuscript Library, Princeton University, Princeton, N.J. (hereafter, AAIA Papers.) Information on theater and soda fountain segregation comes from Purnell Swett, Robeson County's first Native American school superintendent, telephone interview by Elizabeth Halligan Black, 23 July 2003.

8. For several variations on the "Lumbee Indianness as 'self-concept'" theme, see Adolph Dial and David K. Eliades, "The Lumbee Indians of North Carolina and Pembroke State University," *Indian Historian* 4:4 (1971): 23; Jerry Bledsoe, "The Lumbee Indians of Robeson County," *Robesonian*, 1 Aug. 1971, 4B; Adolph L. Dial, "From Adversity to Progress," *Southern Exposure* 13:6 (1985): 85; Karen I. Blu, "'We People': Understanding Lumbee Indian Identity in a Tri-Racial Situation" (PhD diss., University of Chicago, 1972), 52; Blu, *Lumbee Problem*, 134–35; Peck, "Urban Station-Migration of the Lumbee Indians," 66; and Gerald M. Sider, *Lumbee Indian Histories: Race, Ethnicity, and Indian Identity in the Southern United States* (Cambridge: Cambridge Univ. Press, 1993), 8–9, 171.

9. Dial and Eliades, "Lumbee Indians of North Carolina and Pembroke State University," 1–24; Anne Merline McCulloch and David E. Wilkins, "'Constructing' Nations within States: The Quest for Federal Recognition by the Catawba and Lumbee Tribes," *American Indian Quarterly* 19:3 (1995): 375–76; Thomas E. Ross, *American Indians in North Carolina: Geographic Interpretations* (Southern Pines, N.C.: Karo Hollow Press, 1999), 108–9; Hamilton

McMillan, *Sir Walter Raleigh's Lost Colony* (Raleigh: Edwards and Broughton, 1907), 27–40; Cindy D. Padget, "The Lost Indians of the Lost Colony: A Critical Legal Study of the Lumbee Indians of North Carolina," *American Indian Law Review* 21 (winter 1997): 391–424; Jerry Bledsoe, "'Lost' Colony—No Mystery to Lumbees," *Robesonian*, 22 Aug. 1971, 4B; Vanessa Karns, "Lumbee Indian Names Linked to Elizabethan Era England," *Robesonian*, 11 July 1978, 14; Lew Barton, "'Roanoke in Virginia': Where We Came From," *Carolina Indian Voice (Pembroke, N.C.)*, 1 Jan. 1981, 5.

10. See *State v. Chavers*, 50 N.C. 11 at 15 (1857). On the right to bear arms, see *State v. Dempsey*, 31 N.C. 384 (1849). For suffrage disabilities, see Art. I, sec. 3 of the 1854 amendments to the North Carolina constitution. For restrictions on "Indians'" rights to marry whites, see *State v. Watters*, 25 N.C. 455 (1843); and *State v. Melton & Byrd*, 44 N.C. 49 (1852). See also Dial and Eliades, "Lumbee Indians of North Carolina and Pembroke State University," 27–41; and George Lewis, "Not So Well Red: Native Americans in the Southern Civil Rights Movement Reconsidered," *Borderlines: Studies in American Culture* 3:4 (1996): 364.

11. W. McKee Evans, *To Die Game: The Story of the Lowry Band, Indian Guerrillas of Reconstruction* (Baton Rouge: Louisiana State Univ. Press, 1971); Oscar Patterson III, "The Press Held Hostage: Terrorism in a Small North Carolina Town," *American Journalism* 15:4 (fall 1998): 128–29; Gerald M. Sider, "The Political History of the Lumbee Indians of Robeson County, North Carolina: A Case Study of Ethnic Political Affiliations" (PhD diss., New School for Social Research, 1971), 60–62; "Henry Berry Lowry as a Robin Hood," *Robesonian*, 22 Aug. 1971, 4B; Ross, *American Indians in North Carolina*, 110–12.

12. "Act to Provide for Separate Schools for Croatan Indians in Robeson County," *Public Laws of North Carolina*, 1885, chap. 51, in Dial and Eliades, "Lumbee Indians of North Carolina and Pembroke State University," app. B, 182–83; McMillan, *Sir Walter Raleigh's Lost Colony*, 40–41; "An Act to Change the Name of the Indians in Robeson County and to Provide for Said Indians Separate Apartments in the State Hospital," *Public Laws of North Carolina*, 1911, chap. 215, in Dial and Eliades, "Lumbee Indians of North Carolina and Pembroke State University," app. B; "An Act to Restore to the Indians Residing in Robeson and Adjoining Counties Their Rightful and Ancestral Name," *Public Laws of North Carolina*, 1913, chap. 123, in Dial and Eliades, "Lumbee Indians of North Carolina and Pembroke State University," app. B; United States Senate, *Indians of North Carolina: Letter from the Secretary of the Interior Transmitting, in Response to a Senate Resolution of June 30, 1914, a Report on the Condition and Tribal Rights of the Indians of Robeson and Adjoining Counties of North Carolina*, 63rd Congress, 3rd Session, document no. 677, 1915; "An Act Relating to the Lumbee Indians of North Carolina," *North Carolina Session*

Laws, 1953, chap. 874; Dial and Eliades, "Lumbee Indians of North Carolina and Pembroke State University," 18–21. Also see "30,000 North Carolinians Vote Themselves a Name," *Carolina Indian Voice*, 14 Dec. 1978, 9, reprinted, according to the editor, from *The State*, a magazine about North Carolina, 26 Jan. 1952; Padget, "Lost Indians of the Lost Colony," 408–9; and McCulloch and Wilkins, "'Constructing' Nations within States," 378–80.

13. "Lumbee Act of 1956," HR 4656, "An Act Related to the Lumbee Indians of North Carolina" (1956); David E. Wilkins, "The Lumbee Tribe and Its Quest for Federal Recognition: Lumbee Centurions on the Trail of Many Years," in *A Good Cherokee, a Good Anthropologist: Papers in Honor of Robert K. Thomas*, ed. Steve Pavlik (Los Angeles: American Indian Studies Center, 1998), 157; David E. Wilkins, "Breaking into the Intergovernmental Matrix: The Lumbee Tribe's Efforts to Secure Federal Acknowledgment," *Publius* 23 (fall 2003): 126; Susan M. Presti, ed., *Public Policy and Native Americans in North Carolina: Issues for the '80s* (Raleigh: North Carolina Center for Public Policy Research, 1981): 83–84; Padget, "Lost Indians of the Lost Colony," 406–7; "An Act Relating to the Lumbee Indians of North Carolina," Public Law 84-570, chap. 375, 2nd session, printed in full in Dial and Eliades, "Lumbee Indians of North Carolina and Pembroke State University," app. B.

14. *Laws and Resolutions of the State of North Carolina, 1885*, Public Laws, chap. 51. For more on the Lumbee and segregated schools, see Adolph L. Dial, *The Lumbee* (New York: Chelsea House, 1993), 57–61; E. Dale Davis, "The Lumbee Indians of Robeson County, North Carolina, and Their Schools," paper presented at the National Conference of Christians and Jews, Pembroke, N.C., 19 Dec. 1986, 1–4; and Vernon Ray Thompson, "A History of the Education of the Lumbee Indians of Robeson County, North Carolina, 1885 to 1970" (EdD diss., University of Miami, 1973), 39–43. Regarding Lumbee contributions to schools construction and maintenance, see "Unique School Problem Found in Robeson County," *Fayetteville (N.C.) Observer*, 13 Sept. 1970, 5–6; "Lumbee Indian Exemption from HEW Order Sought," *Robesonian*, 2 Sept. 1970, 1; Dial, *Lumbee*, 58–59; and Thompson, "History of the Education of the Lumbee Indians," 42.

15. Jerry Bledsoe, "Our Schools Are Close to Us: Will Loss of Indian Schools Mean Loss of Identity?" *Robesonian*, 5 Sept. 1971, 11B.

16. "The Longest Legislature," *(Raleigh) News and Observer*, 27 May 1955, 4; Richard Schifter to LaVerne Madigan, 23 Oct. 1961, folder 6, box 276, AAIA Papers; Cecelski, *Along Freedom Road*, 26–27.

17. American Friends Service Committee, "School Desegregation Report: Staff Work with Lumbee Indians," 30 June 1962, 1, folder 6, box 276, AAIA Papers.

18. "School Desegregation Report: Staff Work with Lumbee Indians," 30 June 1962, 2, folder 6, box 276, AAIA Papers; Wil Hartzler to Barbara Mof-

fett, 12 Sept. 1960, folder 1, box 329, AAIA Papers; "State Officials to Keep Hands Off," *Raleigh Times,* 21 Sept. 1960; Oliver LaFarge to Richard Schifter, 23 Sept. 1960, folder 1, box 329, AAIA Papers; LaVerne Madigan to Richard Schifter, 4 Oct. 1960, folder 1, box 329, AAIA Papers. Lumbee sit-ins are discussed in an AAIA press release of 2 Dec. 1960, folder 6, box 276, AAIA Papers; and Bill Womble, "Harnett Board of Education Proposes School for Indians," unidentified newspaper clipping, 3 Sept. 1960, folder 6, box 276, AAIA Papers. Evidence of the supportive roles played by the AFSC and the AAIA appears throughout the material in folder 6, box 276, AAIA Papers. Attorney General Robert F. Kennedy's support for the Lumbee efforts is reported in Nelson W. Taylor to Richard S[c]hifter, 19 Apr. 1961, folder 6, box 276, AAIA Papers. Eleanor Roosevelt's involvement in the debate appears in Eleanor Roosevelt, "Justice and Prestige," *New York Post,* 3 Oct. 1960, folder 6, box 276, AAIA Papers; and LaVerne Madigan to Mrs. Franklin D. Roosevelt, 14 Nov. 1960, folder 1, box 329, AAIA Papers. For litigation, see *Chance v. Board of Education of Harnett County,* 224 F. Supp. 472 at 476 (1963); Nelson W. Taylor of Tally, Tally, Taylor & Strickland to Richard S[c]hifter, General Counsel of the Association on American Indian Affairs, 22 Mar. 1962, folder 6, box 276, AAIA Papers; "Court Suit Is Launched against County Schools," *(Clinton, N.C.) Sampsonian,* 10 Jan. 1963, folder 6, box 276, AAIA Papers; "Indian Students Enter Schools 'Peacefully,'" *Dunn (N.C.) Dispatch,* 12 Sept. 1963, in folder 6, box 276, AAIA Papers; "Minutes of the Executive Committee Meeting," 27 Sept. 1963, folder 6, box 276, AAIA Papers; *Ammons and Ammons et al. v. Board of Education of Sampson County,* No. 664—Civil, United States District Court for the Eastern District of North Carolina, Fayetteville Division (3 Sept. 1963), in folder 6, box 276, AAIA Papers; "Indians Pursue Mix in Robeson," *Fayetteville (N.C.) Observer,* 28 July 1961, in folder 1, box 329, AAIA Papers; "54 Indian Children Request Assignment to City Schools," *Robesonian,* 2 July 1962; AFSC, "School Desegregation Report: Staff Work with Lumbee Indians," 30 June 1962, 3–4, folder 6, box 276, AAIA Papers; "Indians Seek Entry to Lumberton White Schools," *Fayetteville (N.C.) Observer,* 28 June 1962, folder 6, box 276, AAIA Papers; "Indian Pupils Admitted to W. Lumberton School" [1 Sept. 1964?], folder 1, box 329, AAIA Papers.

19. For the Lumbee father's quotation, see AFSC, "School Desegregation Report: Staff Work with Lumbee Indians," 30 June 1962, 4–5, folder 6, box 276, AAIA Papers. For the lawyer's views, see Nelson W. Taylor to Richard S[c]hifter, 30 Aug. 1963, folder 6, box 276, AAIA Papers. For the AFSC observations, see AFSC, "School Desegregation Report: Staff Work with Lumbee Indians," 30 June 1962, folder 6, box 276, AAIA Papers.

20. Richard Schifter to Joseph O. Tally Jr., Esq., 15 Sept. 1960, folder 6, box 276, AAIA Papers. Additional comments to the same effect appear in Richard Schifter to Nelson W. Taylor, 29 July 1961, folder 6, box 276, AAIA Papers;

and Oliver LaFarge to Richard Schifter, 1 Aug. 1961, folder 6, box 276, AAIA Papers.

21. David A. Hollinger, "How Wide the Circle of 'We'? American Intellectuals and the Problem of the Ethnos since World War II," *American Historical Review* 98 (Apr. 1993): 317–37; Wendell L. Willkie, *One World* (New York: Simon and Schuster, 1943); Edward Steichen, *The Family of Man* (New York: Simon and Schuster, 1955); Alfred C. Kinsey et al., *Sexual Behavior in the Human Male* (Philadelphia: W. B. Saunders Co., 1948); Alfred C. Kinsey et al., *Sexual Behavior in the Human Female* (Philadelphia: W. B. Saunders Co., 1953); and John Howard Griffin, *Black Like Me* (Boston: Houghton Mifflin, 1961).

22. Quotations from "Bethesda Diplomat Beat Odds—From Nazi Persecution to County Politics to State Dept.," *Montgomery (Md.) Journal,* 19 Nov. 1985, reprinted in *Congressional Record,* vol. 131, part 23, p. 32888; and Charley Roberts, "Profile," *Los Angeles Daily Journal,* 7 Apr. 1986.

23. "Bethesda Diplomat Beat Odds—From Nazi Persecution to County Politics to State Dept.," *Montgomery (Md.) Journal,* 19 Nov. 1985, reprinted in *Congressional Record,* vol. 131, part 23, p. 32888.

24. Civil Rights Act of 1964, Title VI, section 601; Patterson, "Press Held Hostage," 124; BNA Operations Manual, *The Civil Rights Act of 1964: Text, Analysis, Legislative History* (Washington, D.C.: Bureau of National Affairs, 1974). For a discussion of Robeson County's extensive reliance on federal education aid, see "Indians Resist Integration Plan in Triracial County in Carolina," *New York Times,* 13 Sept. 1970.

25. Cecelski, *Along Freedom Road,* 32; John Egerton, "Six Districts, Three Races, and More Things," *Southern Education Report* 4 (Dec. 1968): 7; and "Here Is the Complete Text of the School Board Statement," *Robesonian,* 9 Aug. 1970, 4.

26. *Green v. School Board of New Kent County,* 391 U.S. 430 (1968).

27. On the persistence of segregation in Robeson County throughout the 1960s, see Virginia Simkins, "Study Schools as Whole, Allen Asserts," *Robesonian,* 19 Jan. 1970, 6; Sider, *Lumbee Indian Histories,* 32; and Egerton, "Six Districts, Three Races, and More Things," 7–8. The assertion that federal money accounted for more than a quarter of Robeson County's educational spending comes from "Public School System '71 Expenses Listed," *Robesonian,* 1 Apr. 1971. See also, "Indians Resist Integration Plan in Triracial County in Carolina," *New York Times,* 13 Sept. 1970; "Education Aid Funds Are Well Used in Robeson," *Robesonian,* 13 Sept. 1970, 2; and "Administrative Proceedings in the Department of Health, Education, and Welfare, National Science Foundation," Docket No. CR-577, 17 June 1970, in folder 6, box 276, AAIA Papers. Additional quotations come from: J. Stanley Pottinger of HEW to Superintendent Y. H. Allen, 24 June 1970, in folder 6, box 276, AAIA Papers. Infor-

mation on busing appears in Virginia Simkins, "Area School Boards Order Closing of District Lines," *Robesonian*, 16 Feb. 1970, 1–2; and correspondence from Zelma Locklear to Howard [*sic*] Schifter, 27 July 1970, in folder 6, box 276, AAIA Papers.

28. For white-dominated school board reaction, see "Here Is the Complete Text of School Board Statement," *Robesonian*, 9 Sept. 1970, 2. White resistance in general terms is briefly discussed in "Indians Resist Integration Plan in Triracial County in Carolina," *New York Times*, 13 Sept. 1970. For Lumbee reaction, see "Lumbee Indian Exemption from HEW Order Sought," *Robesonian*, 2 Sept. 1970, 1.

29. The Deloria quotations come from Vine Deloria Jr., *Custer Died for Your Sins: An Indian Manifesto* (New York: Macmillan, 1969), 180. See also Aileen Holmes, "Says Indians Put Up with Lesser School Facilities," *Robesonian*, 15 Nov. 1972, 4.

30. "Lumbee Indians Support Is Sought in Alcatraz Push," *Robesonian*, 10 Dec. 1969, 1–2; Lew Barton, "Lumbee Support Sought by Indians in California," *Robesonian*, 17 June 1970, 2; "Federal 'Indian Giving' Shows Up at Alcatraz," *Robesonian*, 14 July 1971, 2; Bill Price, "American Indian Group Holds Session with Local Tuscaroras," *Robesonian*, 30 Oct. 1972, 2; Bill Price, "Chief of Tuscaroras Calls for Unity in Support of Wounded Knee Indians," *Robesonian*, 8 Mar. 1973, 1–2; and "Group Plans to Form AIM Chapter in City," *Robesonian*, 14 Jan. 1973, 1. The phrase "rowdiest contingent" comes from Paul Chaat Smith and Robert Allen Warrior, *Like a Hurricane: The Indian Movement from Alcatraz to Wounded Knee* (New York: New Press, 1996), 172.

31. The quotation regarding the "awakening" of Lumbee identity comes from "Leaders Feel the Lumbees Are Awakening," *Robesonian*, 5 Sept. 1971, 13A. The "not white, not black" quotation comes from Sider, "Political History of the Lumbee Indians," 161. The "deliberate and growing search" quotation comes from J. Gregory Peck, quoted in Jerry Bledsoe, "Leaders Feel the Lumbees Are Awakening," *Robesonian*, 5 Sept. 1971, 13A. The "completely adopted" quotation comes from Jerry Bledsoe, "The Culture: Not Distinctly Indian," *Robesonian*, 8 Aug. 1971, 7A.

32. The "great scramble" quotation comes from Jerry Bledsoe, "The Culture: Not Distinctly Indian," *Robesonian*, 8 Aug. 1971, 7A. The "Lumbee hero and outlaw" quotation comes from "Willie French Lowery: Musician and Songwriter," http://www.willielowery.com/id16.html, accessed 26 May 2005. Information on *Strike at the Wind*, Lumbee Homecoming, and the Miss Lumbee pageant appears in Dial and Eliades, "Lumbee Indians of North Carolina and Pembroke State University," 171–73; and "Festival at Pembroke Set July 4," *Robesonian*, 28 June 1970, 1. Information on "Lumbees and Friends" appears in "American Indian Music Gets Boost from Lumbees," *Robesonian*, 21 June 1972, 14. The inauguration of the *Carolina Indian Voice* is reported in

"Indian Journal Begun by Group," *Robesonian*, 9 Apr. 1972, 1. The "Pow Wow" is mentioned in "Preparations Complete for Annual Lumbee Homecoming Festivities," *Robesonian*, 25 June 1976, 9.

33. "Lumbee PowWow Slated Monday on School Issue," *Robesonian*, 8 Oct. 1970, 1; "Bed of Nails," *Robesonian*, 11 Oct. 1970, 1.

34. On the widespread impulse to "save our neighborhood schools," see "Start of New School Year Will See Greatest Strides," *Robesonian*, 12 Aug. 1970, 7. On Lumbee objections to busing, see "Indian Parent Group Resolves to Return Children to Own Schools," *Robesonian*, 18 Aug. 1970, 2. The reference to "bureaucrats" appears in "Believes It to Be 'Will of God' to Protect the Indian Heritage," a letter to the editor from James W. Deese, *Robesonian*, 13 Sept. 1970. Allegations that Lumbee opposition to school desegregation had antiblack bases appear in "Indians Resist Integration Plan in Triracial County in Carolina," *New York Times*, 13 Sept. 1970.

35. The "rich cultural heritage" and "cultural jolt" quotations come from "School Officials, Lumbees Remain in Disagreement," *Robesonian*, 6 Sept. 1970. The "racial identity" quotation comes from "Lumbee Complaints Aired for State, Federal Officials," *Robesonian*, 26 Aug. 1970, 1. The "keep our schools and live" quotation comes from Critten K. Jones, letter to the editor, "Sees HEW Challenge to Indian Heritage," *Robesonian*, 21 Aug. 1970, 10.

36. The "left alone" quotation comes from "Lumbees Hold Meet[ing] on School Action," *Robesonian*, 25 Aug. 1970, 1. "Whatever the cost" comes from "Indian Parent Group Resolves to Return Children to Own Schools," *Robesonian*, 18 Aug. 1970, 1. "We will sacrifice our lives" comes from Critten K. Jones of Maxton, letter to the editor, *Robesonian*, 21 Aug. 1970, 10. See also "Unique School Problem Found in Robeson County," *Fayetteville (N.C.) Observer*, 13 Sept. 1970, 5–6; "Lumbee School Protest Aired for Commission," *Robesonian*, 9 Aug. 1970; "School Officials, Lumbees Remain in Disagreement," *Robesonian*, 6 Sept. 1970; "Indians Resist Integration Plan in Triracial County in Carolina," *New York Times*, 13 Sept. 1970.

37. For conflicting descriptions of the fate of the 1970 sit-in campaign, see "Indians Resist Integration Plan in Triracial County in Carolina," *New York Times*, 13 Sept. 1970; "Robeson Schools Return to Normal after Protests," *Robesonian*, 17 Sept. 1970, 1; and "Parents Organization Uninvolved, Says Barton," *Robesonian*, 31 Aug. 1971, 1. For communication between Lumbee protesters and the AAIA, see Luther C. Oxendine to Richard Schifter, 7 July 1970, folder 6, box 276, AAIA Papers, which contains the quoted words; Zelma Locklear to Howard [*sic*] Schifter, 27 July 1970, folder 6, box 276, AAIA Papers; and William Byler to Luther Oxendine, 1 July 1970, folder 6, box 276, AAIA Papers.

38. Richard Schifter to William S. Byler, 8 July 1970, folder 6, box 276, AAIA Papers; Richard Schifter to William S. Byler, 3 Aug. 1970, folder 6, box

276, AAIA Papers; Richard Schifter to William S. Byler, 1 Oct. 1970, folder 6, box 276, AAIA Papers.

39. Lon Bouknight to Richard Schifter, 11 Sept. 1970, folder 6, box 276, AAIA Papers; "Lumbee Fund-Raising Drive Nets $2,200 for Legal Battle," *Robesonian*, 10 Sept. 1970, 1; "Lumbees Hold Meeting on School Action," *Robesonian*, 25 Aug. 1970, 1; "Court Said Willing to Try Indian School Case," *Robesonian*, 2 Sept. 1971; "Complaint," *Locklear v. Culbreth et al.*, U.S. District Court, Eastern District of North Carolina, Fayetteville Division, 10 Sept. 1970, folder 1, box 329, AAIA Papers; "Federal Lawyer's Death Figures in Trial Delay," *Robesonian*, 7 Sept. 1971, 7; "HEW Files Answers in Robeson School Case," *Robesonian*, 19 Sept. 1971, 5B; "Prospect Suit Dismissed," *Carolina Indian Voice*, 28 Sept. 1978, 1.

40. The "to get our schools back" quotation comes from "Indian Organization in Robeson May Achieve Federal Recognition," *Robesonian*, 13 Jan. 1972, 2. Information on plans for future Tuscarora meetings appears in "Tuscaroras Set News Conference," *Robesonian*, 23 Mar. 1973, 2. The "return of Indian control" quotation comes from "Midnight Confrontation Results in Massive Tuscarora Arrests," *Robesonian*, 25 Mar. 1973. Information on the Prospect protest meeting comes from *State v. Brooks*, 24 N.C. App. 338 (1975); *State v. Brooks*, 287 N.C. 392 at 394 (1975); and Chris Boutselis, interview by Elizabeth Halligan Black, 5 Aug. 2003. For evidence of continued Native American opposition to desegregation orders in Robeson County, see "School Still Closed at Prospect in Wake of Monday Incident," *Robesonian*, 31 Aug. 1971, 1; "Parents Organization Uninvolved, Says Barton," *Robesonian*, 31 Aug. 1971, 1; "Incident at Prospect Mars School Opening," *Robesonian*, 30 Aug. 1971, 1; "Indian Vigil Ends for Negotiations," *Robesonian*, 31 Oct. 1972, 1; "Session with School Officials Termed 'Failure' by Tuscaroras," *Robesonian*, 1 Nov. 1972, 1–2; "Tuscaroras Back from Washington; Stage Night Protest in Lumberton," *Robesonian*, 10 Nov. 1972, 1–2; "Misplaced Activity," *Robesonian*, 16 Mar. 1973, 6; "Nine ECTIO Members Still in Jail After Arrest of 27 during School Board Sit-In," *Robesonian*, 18 Sept. 1973, 1–2; and "Exercise in Protest," *Robesonian*, 20 Sept. 1973, 14.

41. Quoted words come from "Indian Parents Found Guilty in Prospect Sit-in Case," *Carolina Indian Voice*, 1 Mar. 1979, 5.

42. Thompson, "History of the Education of the Lumbee Indians," 87–89; Delores Briggs, "Control County School Board: Sociologist," *Robesonian*, 1 Oct. 1972, 1–2; "Robeson Shows Gain in Voter Percentage," *Robesonian*, 14 Sept. 1978, 9; *Locklear v. N.C. State Board of Elections*, 529 F.2d 515 (1975); "Neutralized Issue," *Robesonian*, 6 May 1973, 4B, and "Minority Race Appointees Take Seats on County School Board," *Robesonian*, 11 May 1973, 1–2.

43. "Swett Chosen to Take Allen's School Post," *Robesonian*, 18 May 1977, 9; "A Closer Look. . . . Supt. Purnell Swett," *Carolina Indian Voice*, 22 Nov.

1979, 1, 4; Purnell Swett, interview by Elizabeth Halligan Black, 23 July 2003 (hereafter, Swett interview, 23 July 2003); "Board of Education Hears Complaints on Misplaced Students," *Carolina Indian Voice,* 15 Dec. 1977, 1; "Board of Education Meets," *Carolina Indian Voice,* 12 Jan. 1978, 1; "Board of Education Meets," *Carolina Indian Voice,* 16 Feb. 1978, 3; "Indian Parents Found Guilty in Prospect Sit-in Case," *Carolina Indian Voice,* 1 Mar. 1979, 5; "Nine ECTIO Members Still in Jail after Arrest of 27 during School Board Sit-In," *Robesonian,* 18 Sept. 1973, 1.

44. Former Prospect School principal James Arthur Jones, interviewed by Laura McAlister and Lane Oatey, 21 Mar. 2003; *State v. Braxton Chavis et al.,* North Carolina Court of Appeals, Sixteenth District, no. 7916SC602 (1979), "Narrative of Evidence," testimony of Pernell Sweatt [sic], 13–16 (hereafter, *State v. Chavis,* "Narrative of Evidence").

45. "Board of Education Meets," *Carolina Indian Voice,* 21 Sept. 1978, 1.

46. Testimony of Purnell Swett, *State v. Chavis,* "Narrative of Evidence," 14–15. The original Sanford Barton quotation comes from ibid, 17; the more recent Barton quotation comes from his telephone interview by Elizabeth Halligan Black, 6 Aug. 2003. Information on Swett's exchange with HEW appears in *State v. Chavis,* 45 N.C. App. 438 at 439–40.

47. Jones interview by McAlister and Oatey, 21 Mar. 2003; *State v. Chavis,* 45 N.C. App. 438 at 439–40 (1980).

48. *State v. Chavis,* 45 N.C. App. 438 (1980); *State v. Chavis,* "Narrative of Evidence," 1–22; "It's School Time Again as County Schools Opened Monday," *Carolina Indian Voice,* 31 Aug. 1978, 1.

49. On the defendants' hiring of Cunningham, see Bruce T. Cunningham, interview by Laura McAlister, 17 Mar. 2003, Southern Pines, N.C., recording in John W. Wertheimer's possession (hereafter, Cunningham interview, 17 Mar. 2003); and Judge Anthony Brannon, interview by Kate Auletta and Andrew Devore, Chapel Hill, N.C., 22 Mar. 2003 (hereafter, Brannon interview, 22 Mar. 2003). A recording of this interview is in John W. Wertheimer's possession. On Joe Freeman Britt, see "North Carolina Senate Passes Bill Suspending Executions," *Moratorium News! (Hyattsville, Md.),* summer 2003, 1; Andrea D. Walker, "'The Murderer Shall Surely Be Put to Death': The Impropriety of Biblical Arguments in the Penalty Phase of Capital Cases [*State v. Haselden,* 577 S.E. 2d 594 (N.C. 2003)]," *Washburn Law Journal* 43 (fall 2003): 197; *Newsweek,* 21 July 1975; *New York Times,* 25 Dec. 1985. For an example of Cunningham's previous work on behalf of Native American Robesonians, see *In re McMillan,* 30 N.C. App. 235 (1976).

50. On Cunningham's anti–capital punishment advocacy, see "Politics and the Death Penalty," *(Raleigh) News and Observer,* 2 Oct. 2002. He describes how he got interested in the case in Cunningham interview, 17 Mar. 2003. For his educational background, see Bruce T. Cunningham Jr., in Martindale-

Hubbell Law Directory; and *Cunningham v. Cunningham,* 345 N.C. 430 at 432 (1997).

51. Hollinger, "How Wide the Circle of the 'We'?"; David A. Hollinger, "National Culture and Communities of Descent," *Reviews in American History* 21:1 (1998): 312–28; David A. Hollinger, *Postethnic America: Beyond Multiculturalism* (New York: Basic Books, 1995); "Howe Gets History Book Award," *New York Times,* 12 Apr. 1977, 34; Matthew Frye Jacobson, "A Ghetto to Look Back To: *World of Our Fathers,* Ethnic Revival, and the Arc of Multiculturalism," *American Jewish History* 88:4 (2000): 46–74; Irving Howe, *World of Our Fathers* (New York: Harcourt Brace Jovanovich, 1976); Alex Haley, *Roots* (Garden City, N.Y.: Doubleday, 1976); Robert P. Swierenga, "Ethnicity in Historical Perspective," *Social Science* 52:1 (1977): 31–45; Rudolph J. Vecoli, "The Resurgence of American Immigration History," *American Studies International* 17:2 (1979): 46–66; Paul Kleppner, *The Cross of Culture: A Social Analysis of Midwestern Politics, 1850–1900* (New York: Free Press, 1970); Ronald P. Formisano, *The Birth of Mass Political Parties: Michigan, 1827–1861* (Princeton: Princeton Univ. Press, 1971); Richard Jenson, *The Winning of the Midwest: Social and Political Conflict, 1888–1896* (Chicago: Univ. of Chicago Press, 1971). On black nationalism and education, see Subira Kifano, "Afrocentric Education in Supplementary Schools: Paradigm and Practice at the Mary McLeod Bethune Institute," *Journal of Negro Education* 65:2 (spring 1996): 209–18; Jack Slater, "Learning Is an All-Black Thing," *Ebony* 26 (Sept. 1971): 88–92; Christopher Jenks, "Private Schools for Black Children," *New York Times,* 3 Nov. 1968, 280; Charles V. Hamilton, "The Nationalist vs. the Integrationist," *New York Times,* 1 Oct. 1972, SM36.

52. Cunningham interview, 17 Mar. 2003; Richard Schifter to William S. Byler, 1 Oct. 1970, folder 6, box 276, AAIA Papers.

53. Cunningham interview, 17 Mar. 2003.

54. Ibid.

55. Ibid.; *Regents of University of California v. Bakke,* 483 U.S. 265 (1978); "Explicity Cut," *Robesonian,* 29 June 1978.

56. *Wisconsin v. Yoder,* 406 U.S. 205 (1972); Cunningham interview, 17 Mar. 2003.

57. President Nixon's comments on the "termination" policy appear in "Excerpts from Nixon's Message on Indian Affairs," *New York Times,* 9 July 1970, 18. The quotation from the 1970 federal report appears in "Education of Indians Should Be Controlled by Indians, Three-Year Federal Study Says," *Robesonian,* 20 Dec. 1970, 1. See also "U.S. Indians Win More Self-Rule," *New York Times,* 13 Jan. 1972, 35; Guy B. Senese, *Self-Determination and the Social Education of Native Americans* (New York: Praeger Publishers, 1991); Robert J. Havighurst, "Indian Education since 1960," *Annals of the American Academy of Political and Social Science* 436 (1978): 13–26; Edmond J. Danziger Jr., "A

New Beginning of the Last Hurrah: American Indian Response to Reform Legislation of the 1970s," *American Indian Culture and Research Journal* 7:4 (1983): 69–84; Paul H. Stuart, "Financing Self-Determination: Federal Indian Expenditures, 1975–1988," *American Indian Culture and Research Journal* 14:2 (1990): 1–18; E. Fletcher McClellan, "Implementation and Policy Reformulation of Title I of the Indian Self-Determination and Education Assistance Act of 1975–80," *Wicazo Sa Review* 6:1 (1990): 45–55; and Donald D. Stull, Jerry A. Schultz, and Ken Cadue Sr., "Rights without Resources: The Rise and Fall of the Kansas Kickapoo," *American Indian Culture and Research Journal* 10:2 (1986): 41–59.

58. The Nixon paraphrase comes from "Robeson Indian Group's Hopes High for Control of Own Schools," *Robesonian*, 15 Oct. 1972, 2A. Longhouses are discussed in "Lumbee Longhouse Learning Centers to Open on Tuesday," *Robesonian*, 1 Sept. 1974, 12B.

59. "'Identifiable' Schools," *Robesonian*, 22 June 1973, 6; "Indian Education Act Monies Detailed for County School Units," *Robesonian*, 26 Oct. 1978, 1; "Robeson's School System Faces IEA Fund Reduction," *Robesonian*, 31 Jan. 1975, 1; "Prospect School to Get Largest IEA Fund Share," *Robesonian*, 12 Aug. 1973, 6A.

60. "Nine ECTIO Members Still in Jail after Arrest of 27 during School Board Sit-In," *Robesonian*, 18 Sept. 1973, 1.

61. Cunningham's question to prospective jurors is quoted in "School Attendance Testimony Starts," *Robesonian*, 21 Jan. 1979, 1. The racial composition of the jury appears in "Indian Parents Found Guilty in Prospect Sit-in Case," *Carolina Indian Voice*, 1 Mar. 1979, 5. On the prosecution's juror challenges according to race, consult Cunningham interview, 17 Mar. 2003.

62. Brannon interview, 22 Mar. 2003.

63. Testimony of Purnell Swett, superintendent of Robeson County Schools, *State v. Chavis*, "Narrative of Evidence," 14; Brannon interview, 22 Mar. 2003.

64. Testimony quoted in "Indian Parents Found Guilty in Prospect Sit-in Case," *Carolina Indian Voice*, 1 Mar. 1979, 5; testimony of Bertha Oxendine, *State v. Chavis*, "Narrative of Evidence," 20; testimony of Braxton Chavis, *State v. Chavis*, "Narrative of Evidence," 21.

65. Brannon interview, 22 Mar. 2003.

66. The "invaded just about every level of society" quotation comes from Bruce Maliver, "Encounter Groupers Up against the Wall," *New York Times*, 3 Jan. 1971, SM4. On race awareness seminars for federal workers, see "'Race Awareness' Drive Stirs Capital Dispute," *New York Times*, 29 Nov. 1971, 50. On racial seminars in the armed services, see "G.I.'s in Europe Are 'Cooler' Than Those of Vietnam Era, but Many Defy Old-Army Rules," *New York Times*, 21 Apr. 1975, 19; "Navy Base Holds Racial Seminars," *New York Times*, 26 Mar.

1973, 25. On sensitivity training and encounter group therapy generally during these years, see Kurt W. Back, *Beyond Words: The Story of Sensitivity Training and the Encounter Movement* (New York: Russell Sage Foundation, 1972); Kurt W. Back, "Encounter Groups Revisited," *Society* 26:1 (1988): 50–53; Anthony J. Vattano, "Power to the People: Self-Help Groups," *Social Work* 17:4 (1972): 7–15; Elizabeth Lasch-Quinn, *Race Experts: How Racial Etiquette, Sensitivity Training, and New Age Therapy Hijacked the Civil Rights Revolution* (New York: Norton, 2001).

67. Brannon interview, 22 Mar. 2003.
68. Ibid.
69. Cunningham interview, 17 Mar. 2003.
70. "Jury Decision Expected in School Case," *Robesonian*, 22 Feb. 1979, 1.
71. Brannon interview, 22 Mar. 2003.
72. *State v. Chavis*, 45 N.C. App. 438 at 441 (1980).
73. "Jury Decision Expected in School Case," *Robesonian*, 22 Feb. 1979, 1.
74. "Indian Parents Found Guilty in Prospect Sit-in Case," *Carolina Indian Voice*, 1 Mar. 1979, 5; "Families Lose School Attendance Fight," *Robesonian*, 23 Feb. 1979, 1.
75. "Families Lose School Attendance Fight," *Robesonian*, 23 Feb. 1979, 1.
76. Brannon interview, 22 Mar. 2003.
77. *In re McMillan*, 30 N.C. App. 235 at 235, 238 (1976).
78. *State v. Chavis*, "Defendant Appellants' Brief," North Carolina Court of Appeals, 3–5.
79. *State v. Chavis*, 45 N.C. App. 438 at 442 (1980).
80. Ibid. at 442–43.
81. *Chavis v. North Carolina*, 449 U.S. 1035 (1980); Cunningham interview, 17 Mar. 2003.
82. "Supreme Court Snubs Parents' Appeal," *Robesonian*, 9 Dec. 1980.
83. Swett interview, 23 July 2003.
84. Brannon's "concerned parents" quotation and his observation that the children were not truant appear in "Families Lose School Attendance Fight," *Robesonian*, 23 Feb. 1979, 1. Brannon's other remarks come from his interview of 22 Mar. 2003.

Conclusion

1. *State v. Ross*, 76 NC 243, at 246 (1877). See chap. 2.
2. *Barden v. Barden*, 14 N.C. 548 at 550 (1832).
3. Regarding the death penalty, see *State v. Duke*, 360 N.C. 110 (2005); *State v. Williams*, 350 N.C. 1 (1999); *State v. Stephens*, 347 N.C. 352 (1997); *State v. Garner*, 340 N.C. 573 (1995). Regarding public school funding, see

"State Now Has Money to Carry Out Leandro," editorial, *Charlotte Observer*, 30 Apr. 2006. For voting rights, see *James v. Bartlett*, 359 N.C. 260 (2005); and *Stephenson v. Bartlett*, 357 N.C. 301 (2003). On medical malpractice, see "Suit Challenges State Law on Malpractice," *(Raleigh) News and Observer*, 10 Sept. 2002, B5; LeVonda Wood, "Rule 9(j) n1—Is Requiring a Plaintiff in a Medical Malpractice Action to Certify His or Her Claim before Filing Unconstitutional? The Issue in *Anderson v. Assimos*," *Campbell Law Review* 25 (spring 2003): 219–34; J. L. Holt, "North Carolina Court Rejects 'Reform' Rule Requiring Expert Review of Med-Mal Claims," *Trial* 38:1 (Jan. 2002): 12–14; J. S. Coalter, "The Vicarious Liability of a Physician for the Negligence of Other Medical Professionals—North Carolina Charts a Middle Course—the Effect of *Harris v. Miller*," *Campbell Law Review* 17 (spring 1995): 375–94. Regarding corporations, see, prominently, *Meiselman v. Meiselman*, 309 N.C. 279 (1983). For sexual harassment cases, see *Poole v. Copland, Inc.*, 348 N.C. 260 (1998); *Coremin v. Sherrill Furniture Co.*, 614 S.E. 2d 607 (2005); and *Whitt v. Harris Teeter, Inc.*, 165 N.C. App. 32 (2004), among many others. For discussion of an adoption and child custody dispute, see "Johnston Father Fights to Raise Girl Given to California Couple," *(Raleigh) News and Observer*, 23 July 2006, A1. For zoning ordinance disputes, see *Westminster Homes, Inc., v. Town of Cary Zoning Board of Adjustment*, 354 N.C. 298 (2001); *Wise v. Harrington Grove Community Association, Inc.*, 357 N.C. 396 (2003); and *Parker v. Figure "8" Beach Homeowners' Association*, 170 N.C. App. 145 (2005). For a dispute over the power of the state to regulate private property in the name of environmental protection, see *Williams v. N.C. Dept. of Environmental and Natural Resources, Division of Coastal Management*, 144 N.C. App. 479 (2001).

4. "2002–03 State of the Profession Survey," sponsored by the North Carolina Chief Justice's Commission on Professionalism, cited in Leary Davis and Melvin F. Wright Jr., "The State of the Legal Profession in North Carolina," at http://www.nccourts.org/Courts/CRS/Councils/Professionalism/Documents/thestateofthelegal%20professioninnorthcarolina.doc, page 6, accessed 21 July 2006.

5. Figures regarding the number of blacks in North Carolina's legal profession come from United States Department of Commerce, *Census of Population: 1950*, vol. II, part 33 (Washington, D.C.: Government Printing Office, 1952), 33-241-33, table 77; U.S. Department of Commerce, *1980 Census of Population*, vol. I, Characteristics of the Population, chap. D, Detailed Population Characteristics, part 35, North Carolina, 35-267, table 218; and "EEO Residence Data Results for North Carolina," U.S. Census Bureau, Census 2000 EEO Data Tool, http://www.census.gov/cgi-bin/broker. For the UNC Law School's defense of race-conscious law school admissions procedures, see "Brief of Amicus Curiae, the School of Law of the University of North Caro-

lina, Supporting Respondent," *Bollinger v. Gruter*, in the Supreme Court of the United States, No. 02-241 (2003), 4–5.

6. Matthew Eisley, "Supreme Court Pick Breaks New Ground," *(Raleigh) News and Observer*, 20 Jan. 2006, B1; Rob Christensen, "Literacy Test Echoes Bygone Era," *(Raleigh) News and Observer*, 7 Mar. 1999, B1; Steve Tuttle, "Editorial: Chief Justice Henry Frye," *North Carolina Citizens for Business and Industry*, http://www.nccbi.org/NCMagazine/1999/mag-09–99editorial.htm, accessed 26 July 2006.

7. For a sampling of post–*Roe v. Wade* North Carolina abortion cases, see *Jackson by & Through Robinson v. A Woman's Choice, Inc.*, 130 N.C. App 590 (1998); *Phillips v. A Triangle Women's Health Clinic*, 155 N.C. App. 372 (2002); *Stam v. State*, 302 N.C. 357 (1981); *Rosie J. v. North Carolina Department of Human Resources*, 347 N.C. 247 (1997); and *Kaplan v. Prolife Action League*, 123 N.C. App. 720 (1996). For North Carolina environmental cases, see *MW Clearing & Grading, Inc., v. N.C. Dept. of Environment and Natural Resources*, 360 N.C. 392 (2006); *Williams v. N.C. Department of Environment and Natural Resources*, 359 N.C. 643 (2005); and *North Carolina Forestry Assn. v. N.C. Department of Environment and Natural Resources*, 357 N.C. 640 (2004).

8. See, for instance, *Díaz v. Division of Social Services*, 360 N.C. 384 (2006); *Luna v. Division of Social Services*, 162 N.C. App 1 (2004); *Estridge v. Housecalls Healthcare Group, Inc.*, 351 N.C. 183 (1999); *Ezell v. Grace Hosp., Inc.*, 623 S.E. 2d 79 (2005); and *Medina v. Division of Social Services*, 165 N.C. App. 502 (2004). Medicaid participation levels for North Carolina in 2000 are reported in "North Carolina's Investment in Medicaid is Critical to Residents with Mental Retardation, Cerebral Palsy, and Related Disabilities," created 8 Apr. 2003, at http://www.thearc.org/medicaid/northcarolina.doc, accessed 26 July 2006.

9. *Lawrence v. Texas*, 539 U.S. 558 at 569 (2003); *State v. Oakley*, 167 N.C. App. 318 (2004); *State v. Pope*, 168 N.C. App. 592 (2005); "Living Together No Longer Illegal," *(Greensboro, N.C.) News & Record*, 21 July 2006, A1.

Index

AAIA. *See* Association on American Indian Affairs
Abernethy, Margaret, 95, 99
abortion law, 194
affirmative action, 180
African Americans
  civil rights and, 8, 127
  disfranchisement of, 46, 119, 129–30, 137–41, 144, 155, 167
  G.I. Bill and, 134–35
  Greenwich Village roadhouse and, 109
  laissez-faire jurisprudence and, 44
  lawyers, 9, 51, 142, 162, 193
  and the legal system, 8–9
  literacy rates of, 137
  mobility, post-emancipation, 29
  northeastern North Carolina and, 132, 148
  office-holding, 129, 144, 162
  opposition to school desegregation, 166
  political apathy of, 138
  resistance to Jim Crow, 44
  response to Winston-Salem segregation ordinance, 49
  in Robeson County, 167, 169
  tobacco industry and, 45–46
  training schools for, 92–94, 105
  violence against, 138
  voter registration in North Carolina, 139–41, 143–44, 162
  voting rights of, 8, 143, 163, 192
  Winston-Salem and, 47–48, 51, 59
  World War II and, 133–34, 171

Afrocentric education, 179
AFSC (American Friends Service Committee), 9, 170–71
Ahoskie, North Carolina, 131, 133
AIM (American Indian Movement), 173
Alcatraz Island protest, 173
Algonquin, 168
Allen, Young H., 176–77
American Friends Service Committee (AFSC), 9, 170–71
American Indian Movement (AIM), 173
American Indian self-determination policy, 181–82
Amish, 181
Andrews, Brook, 27
anti-evolutionism
  cities and, 64
  Heriot Clarkson and, 82–83
  lawyers and, 5
  in Mecklenburg County, 72–73
  in the 1920s, 70
  in North Carolina, 65, 71–72
  James Pentuff and, 3, 67–68, 72–73
  Pentuff v. Park and, 86
  Poole Bill and, 69–70
  William Poteat on, 66
Anti-Saloon League, Charlotte, 120
anti-Semitism, 58
Army, U.S., 184
Association on American Indian Affairs (AAIA), 170–71, 175, 179–80
Atkins, Simon G., 49–50

Atlanta, Georgia, 110
Auletta, Kate, 165
automobiles, 110–11

Baetjer, Patrick, 13
Bahr, Hank, 165
Bailey, William, 51
  background, 35–37
  in *State v. Ross* appeal, 39–40
  in *State v. Ross* trial, 37–38
Baker, R. Stan, 43
Bakke, Regents of University of California v., 180–81
Baltimore, Maryland, 45, 53
Baptist College for Women, Missouri, 69
Baptists, 66–67, 72, 75, 85
Barbosa, Magdalena, 107
Bardaglio, Peter, 14
Barden, Ann, 15–16, 24
Barden, Jesse, 15–16, 24–25
Barden v. Barden, 24–25
  distinguished from *Scroggins v. Scroggins*, 14–18, 24–25
  effect of, 26
Barnes, V. E., 53
Barton, Lew, 174
Barton, Sanford, 178
Bates, Sanford, 103
Bazemore, Nancy, 158
Bazemore v. Bertie County Board of Elections, 159–62
Becker, Louis, 127
Be Firm My Hope (Walker), 141–42
Bell, Diana, 13
Bell, John, 43
Bennett, Joshua, 27
Bertie County, 140, 158–60
Bertie County Board of Elections, 159
Bevan, Thomas, 13
Bicket Hall, 90, 95

Black, Elizabeth Halligan, 165
Blackey, Eleanor, 127
Black Like Me (Griffin), 171, 179
black nationalism, 173, 179
Black Power, 173
blockbusting, 48, 59
Blythe, Mary, 34
Board of Elections, North Carolina, 161
Bogo, Jessica, 13
Bonapfel, Edward, 13
Boston University, 135
Bowen, Woodberry, 185
Boyles, Alphonso, 108
Boyles, Mary, 109, 120
Boyles, Memory Ford
  African Americans and, 109
  background of, 108–9
  death of, 123
  federal drug conviction of, 108
  marriage of, 109
  partisan affiliation of, 108
  public nuisance appeal, 118–22
  public nuisance trial, 116–18
  religion and, 109
Bradbury, Ann. *See* Barden, Ann
Braden, Anne, 156
Braden, Carl, 156
Brannon, Anthony, 183–88
Brigman, Lucretia. *See* Scroggins, Lucretia
Britt, Joe Freeman, 178
Broad River, South Carolina, 32
Bronson, Mary Lee, 95
Brooks, Howard, 176
Brown, Charlotte Hawkins, 93–94
Brown, George H., 57
Brown, R. Eugene, 91, 104
Brown v. Board of Education, 44, 128, 143–45, 154, 165, 169–71
Bryan, William, 34
Bryan, William Jennings, 65, 72

Index   269

Buchanan v. Warley (1917), 57
Buntin, Wilson, 43
Bureau of Indian Affairs, 173
Bureau of Mental Health and
    Hygiene, North Carolina, 99
Burke County, North Carolina, 139
bus boycotts, 128
Buxton, John C., 52, 59. *See also*
    Watson, Buxton & Watson
Byars, John, 30
Bynum, W. P., 33

Cabarrus County superior court, 78
Calvary Methodist church, 63
Camp Creek, North Carolina, 30
Camp Greene, 112
Carolina Indian Voice, 174
Carolina Military Institute, 119
Carolina Times, 161
Carpenter, John, 116–18, 121
Carpenter v. Boyles
    appeal, 121–22
    reception of, 122
    trial, 116–18, 154
Carraway, Kelly, 165
Carter, J. W., 47
Chamberlain Hall, 90, 95, 99
Chaney, James, 138
Chapel Hill, North Carolina, 135
Chapel Hill Weekly, 104
Charlotte, North Carolina
    anti-evolutionism in, 72–73, 83
    Anti-Saloon League, 120
    automobiles and, 110, 113
    Mary Boyles and, 109
    M. F. Boyles and, 108–110
    car ownership in, 110
    Heriot Clarkson and, 83, 119–20
    Greenwich Village roadhouse and,
        107–8, 123
    law enforcement in, 112
    James Pentuff and, 68–69
    prohibition in, 120
    Reconstruction-era conditions,
        32–35
    religiosity of, 109
    J. A. Sharp sermon in, 63–64, 89
    Shipp and Bailey's prominence in,
        36
    suburbanization and, 113
Charlotte Democrat, 34
Charlotte News, 85, 113, 122
Charlotte Observer, 35, 69, 85, 100,
    105, 109, 122
Chase, Harry Woodburn, 71
Chavers, Dean, 173
Chavis, Braxton, 165, 177, 181, 183,
    188
Cheraw, 168
Cherokee, 168
Cherokee Indians of Robeson
    County, 169
Chicago Seven, 163
Chinese Americans, 166
City View Heights, 113
Civil Rights Act of 1964, 172, 183
Civil War, 29, 31, 56, 107, 119
Clark, Walter, 4, 55–59
Clarkson, Heriot
    alcohol prohibition and, 82–83,
        120
    background, 82–83, 119–21
    Carpenter v. Boyles ruling, 121–22
    cultural conservatism of, 119–21
    evolution and, 83
    judicial career of, 120–21
    Pentuff v. Park ruling, 81–84
    political views of, 119–20
    post-*Pentuff* career, 87
    private life of, 120
    religious views of, 119
    style of opinion writing, 4
Cleveland County, North Carolina,
    30

Cochran, Salter J., 144
Coffin, O. J.
  background, 73–74
  James Pentuff, first editorial about, 74–76, 79–80, 82, 84
  James Pentuff, second editorial about, 76, 82, 84
  post-*Pentuff* career, 87
  religion and, 74
  sued for libel, 65
  trial victory, 85
Cole, T. W., 147
Columbia Heights, 50
Columbus, Ohio, penitentiary fire, 103
Commission on Civil Rights, U. S., 138–39
Committee of 100, 72–73
Cook, Timothy, 63
Concord, North Carolina, 74, 76, 84
Connor, George, 83
court-appointed lawyers, 203n30
court of public opinion
  interracial marriage and, 30–31
  Ruffin and, 17–18, 25–26
coverture, doctrine of, 8, 37
Crane, Harry W., 99
creationism, 68, 84, 88
Crews, George, 54
Croatan Indians of Robeson County, 169
cultural conservatism
  Heriot Clarkson and, 119–21
  law and, 7, 15, 64, 107–8
  slavery and, 15
cultural modernism
  Greenwich Village and, 108
  law and, 64
Cunningham, Bruce T., Jr., 178–81, 182–88

Daly, Michael E., 43

Daniel, Joseph, 16–17
Darnell, Lillie, 50
Darnell, William
  arrest of, 50
  background of, 44
  North Carolina Supreme Court appeal, 54–58
  result of court case, 60
  trial of, 51, 53–54
Darrow, Clarence, 65–66
Darwin, Charles, 68
Darwinism
  James R. Pentuff's views on, 67–69
  William Poteat's views on, 66–67
Dayton, Tennessee, 76
Deichert, Christian, 89
De La Beckwith, Bryon, 10
Dellinger family, 30
Deloria, Vine, 173
Democratic party
  black disfranchisement and, 130
  Heriot Clarkson and, 119
  convention of 1896, North Carolina, 119
  during the Age of Jackson, 18–19
  during Reconstruction, 28, 33–34, 36, 39–40
  Fusion as a threat to, 129
  national convention of 1968, 163
  primary elections of 1926, 73
  primary elections of 1956, 144, 149
  primary elections of 1960, 158
  State v. Darnell and, 58
  Cyrus B. Watson and, 52
  Wilmington Massacre and, 130
democratization, 18–19
Department of Environment and Natural Resources, North Carolina, 194
Department of Welfare, North Carolina, 91
Devin, W. A., 53

Devore, Andrew, 165
dictation form of literacy test, 158–60
Dillon's Rule, 56–57
disfranchisement, African American, 46, 119, 129–30, 137–41, 144, 155, 167
divorce
   North Carolina law of 1827, 22–23
   Ruffin's views of, 19–20, 23
   slavery and, 20
   yeoman farmers and, 20–21
Dockery, Sander, 133
double voting, Robeson County, 176–77
Douglas, William O., 157
Dowd Manor, 112–13, 123
Dowd Road, 110
Dulin, Mag, 35
Dupee, David, 63
Durham, North Carolina, 135

Eagle Springs, North Carolina, 91, 95
Eastern Carolina Industrial Training School, 92
Eastern Council on Community Affairs (ECCA), 146
Eastern Sioux, 168
ECCA. *See* Eastern Council on Community Affairs
Efland Home, 92, 94, 105
Eighteenth Amendment, 120
elections of 1874, North Carolina, 33
elite dominance model of law, 191–92
Elkins, Douglas, 13
Elmer Gantry (Lewis), 83
Emergency School Assistance Act, 182
encounter groups, 184
Enfield Township, 140, 146

Environmental Protection Agency, 194
ethnic particularism, 166
Evers, Medgar, 138
evidence, rules of, 184–85
evolution
   Heriot Clarkson's views on, 83
   James R. Pentuff's views on, 67–69
   William Poteat's views on, 66–67

Faison, Alexander, 151
Falls, Maurice, 165
Family of Man, The (Steichen), 171, 179
federal versus state courts during civil rights movement, 148
federal law
   increased reach of, 9, 167, 193
   versus state law, 1, 148
Federation of Colored Women's Clubs, 94
Fesperman, Vic, 115–16
Fifteenth Amendment, 129–31, 148, 155, 157
First Amendment, 181
First Baptist Church, Charlotte, 68–69
Fitts, John, 51
Fleming, Elizabeth, 27
Fleming, John W., 162
Florida, poll taxes in, 129
fornication and adultery law, 34–35, 194
Fort Mill, South Carolina, 31–32, 41
Fortune, William, 27
Four Freedoms, 134
Fourteenth Amendment, 37, 147–48, 155
freedom of choice student-assignment plans, 172
freedom of speech, 85–86
Frye, Henry, 193

272   Index

Fuquay Springs, North Carolina, 73
Furman University, 67, 69, 77
Fusion politics, 129

Gallup County, New Mexico, 182
Gardner, O. Max, 97–98, 102
Gaston, William, 1, 197
Gaston County, North Carolina, 109
Gastonia, North Carolina, 111
Gay, Ballard S., 150
G.I. Bill, 134–35
Gilreath Park, 113
Goodman, Andrew, 138
grandfather clauses, 129–31
  declared unconstitutional, 131, 152
  1957 revision and, 152
grassroots litigation, 128, 162–64, 238n2
Great Depression, 90, 101, 111, 114
Greensboro News, 101
Greensborough Patriot, 20
Green v. School Board of New Kent County, 172
Greenwich Village, New York, 107
Greenwich Village roadhouse
  construction of, 110
  contents of, 111
  employees, 109
  location of, 112
  name of, 108
  padlocking case against, 113, 116–22, 154
  post-litigation fate, 123
Griffin, John Howard, 171, 179
Guinness Book of World Records, 178
Guinn v. United States, 155

Haley, Alex, 179
Halifax County, North Carolina, 140, 142, 144, 150, 163
Halifax County Board of Elections, 144

Halligan, Elizabeth, 165
Hampton Institute, 132
Harkey, Mary Springs, 109–10
Harper, Elisabeth Summerlin, 107
Hartog, Hendrik, 14
Health, Education, and Welfare, U.S. Department of (HEW), 172–73, 176–78, 182, 186, 188
Henderson, Leonard, 1, 16–17
Herr, Scott, 43
Hertford County, North Carolina, 131–32
HEW. *See* Health, Education, and Welfare, U.S. Department of
Hodes, Martha, 14
Hoggard, William, 158–59
Holbrook, Andrew, 43
Holmes, Oliver Wendell, Jr., 3
Hoover, J. Edgar, 111
House, Robert, 136
House, Sarah, 43
Howard University Law School, 148
Howe, Irving, 179
Hughes, Charles Evans, 101
human potential movement, 184

Illinois penitentiary at Joliet, 103
illiteracy, 137
incest, 39
Indian Education Act of 1972, 181–82
Indian Self-Determination and Education Assistance Act, 181
Indian self-determination policy, 181–82
Indians of Robeson County, 169
interracial marriage
  cases involving, 34–35
  legal prohibitions against, 30–31, 39–40
  scholarly treatment of, 28
  South Carolina and, 31–32

Index   273

Irish history, 58
Iroquois, 168
Ivey, Ernest, 147–48, 153
Ivey v. Cole, 147–49, 153

Jackson, Andrew, 18
Jacksonian democracy, 18–19, 168
Japanese American internment, 171
Jazz Age, 63, 89–90, 101, 107
jazz music as defiance of law, 63–64
Jim Crow segregation
  Black Like Me and, 171
  limitations on, 44–45
  residential, 45
  University of North Carolina and, 136
  Winston-Salem and, 45–49
Jimmison, Tom, 118
Jones, Elizabeth, 22
Jones, James A. 178
Jones, Mark, 27
Jones, Mary, 92
Judge Heriot Clarkson Award, 123
judges, 4–5. *See also* Jacksonian democracy; *specific judges*
Jung, Eugene, 89

Kalett, Alison, 107
Kane, Erin, 13
Kaplan, Michael, 13
Katzenbach v. Morgan, 251n115
Kenan, Thomas, 39
Kennedy, Anthony M., 194
Kennedy, Isaac and Mag, 35, 37
Kent, James, 1
Kidd, Ralph, 116, 118
King, Martin Luther, Jr., 135, 163, 183
Kognegay, P. S., 96
Kohler, Nancy, 13
Ku Klux Klan, 32–33, 63, 73, 89, 107
Kunstler, William, 163

labor agents, 58
Ladies of the Big House (film; 1931), 103
laissez-faire jurisprudence, 44–45
Lanier, James, 115
Lanoha, Andrew, 107
Larned, Christine, 27
Lassiter, Lloyd, 151
Lassiter, Louise, 127, 150–53, 164
Lassiter v. Northampton County Board of Elections, 152–58
late-century liberalism, 178–80, 187
law
  cultural conservatism and, 15
  elite dominance model of, 191–92
  functions of, 2–3
  honor and, 3
  political functions of, 3
  politics and, 28–29, 39
  racial lines and, 5–6, 15, 191
  rule of, 29, 191
  social therapy and, 3
  values debates in, 2–3
  working class young women and, 90
Lawrence v. Texas, 194
lawyers, 5
  court-appointed, 203n30
  See also specific lawyers
legal chivalry, 90, 97, 99, 101
legal double standard, 90, 97
Lewis, Nell Battle
  background, 98
  female lawyers and, 98, 192
  Poole Bill and, 71
  prison reform and, 102
  Samarcand Manor, criticism of, 98–99, 104
  Samarcand reform and, 105
  Samarcand trial arguments, 98–100
Lewis, Sinclair, 83

274 Index

libel law, 79–83, 85–86
Lincoln County, North Carolina, 29–30, 108
literacy test (North Carolina)
  Bazemore case and, 158–62
  constitutionality, 130–31
  dictation form of, 158–60
  effect of, 131
  end of, 164
  Lassiter case and, 152–58
  1957 revision of, 152–55, 158
  origins, 129–30
  reception, 130
  scholarship on, 138
  unfair application of, 140–41
litigants, 3–4. *See also specific litigants*
litigation
  civil rights, 8, 143
  communal, 122
  cultural traditionalists and, 7
  as dispute resolution, 2, 191
  as forum for debating cultural values, 2–3, 6
  grassroots, 128, 131, 163
  honor and, 3
  minority groups and, 4
  political, 3
  public nuisance, 108, 123
  racial hierarchy and, 6
  as social therapy, 3
  testimonial-therapeutic function of, 166
  James R. Walker Jr. and, 131–32, 136–37, 143–62
Logan, George, 33, 36
Louisville, Kentucky, 57
Love, Alice, 33
Loving v. Virginia, 1967
Lowry, Henry Berry, 168, 174
Lumbee
  background, 168–69
  identity, 169, 174–75
  influenced by civil rights movement, 170
  integrationism of, 170–72
  opposition to school desegregation, 174–76, 181–82
  search for official tribal recognition, 169–70
  segregated schools and, 169–70
  separatism of, 172–75, 184
  tribal name, evolution of, 169
Lumbee Homecoming, 174
Lumbee Longhouse Learning Centers, 182
Lumbees and Friends musical group, 174
Lumber River, 169
Lumberton, North Carolina, 96
Luskey, Brian, 89

MacLean, Rebecca, 89
Macon County, North Carolina, 139
Magnolia Indian dancers, 174
Major's Place, 113
Malcolm X, 163
Mann, John, 22
marriage
  interracial, 28, 30–32
  Thomas Ruffin's views on, 19–20, 23
  yeoman farmers and, 20–21
Marriage Act of 1838, 30, 33
Marshall, John, 63
Marshall, Thurgood, 8, 135, 143, 148
Marsh Estates, 113
Martin, Andrew, 127
massive resistance, 166
master-slave relationship, 20
McAlister, Laura, 165
McCarthy, J. J., 27
McCaskill, Clint, 97
McDonald, C. J., 97
McDowell v. Bowles, 80–82

Index   275

McGill Street Baptist Church, 84
McGinnis, Mason, 116–18
McMillen, In re, 187
McMullen, Harry, 137
McNab, James, 63, 127
McNaughton, Agnes, 94–95, 99, 105
McNeely Land Company, 112
McNeill, George, 98
Mecklenburg County, North Carolina
  anti-evolutionism in, 72–73, 88
  fornication and adultery prosecutions in, 34–35
  Presbyterians in, 72
  prohibition in, 114–15
  rural police, 112, 115–16, 123
  Velma Webb in, 109
Mecklenburg County Board of Education, 72
Mecklenburg Times, 111
Medicaid, 194
Meredith College, 75, 81
Methodists, 72
Mexican Americans, 166
mid-century liberalism, 171–72, 179
Mike's Creek Baptist Church, 41
Mileham, Dunn, 89
ministers, libel law and, 79–83
minority groups, 4–5, 8–9, 167, 179–180
miscegenation, 13, 21, 30–32, 39–40
Miss Lumbee pageant, 174
Miss Twitty, 77–78
Mitchell, Samuel S., 148, 152, 156, 159, 163, 246
Mitchell and Taylor, 148, 152, 156, 163, 246
Montgomery, W. J., 33–34, 37
Moore County, North Carolina, 89, 178
Moore County Jail, 96–97

Morrison, Cameron, 110
Morrison Training School for Negro Boys, 92
Mosley, Alexander, 156
Mount Holly, North Carolina, 109

NAACP. *See* National Association for the Advancement of Colored People
National Association for the Advancement of Colored People (NAACP)
  Brown v. Board of Education and, 44, 154
  civil rights litigation and, 128
  Sander Dockery and, 133
  Legal Defense Fund, 148, 163
  literacy test question about, 141
  litigation strategies of, 143–44
  State v. Darnell, reaction to, 59
  Sweatt v. Painter and, 135–36
  voting rights and, 143
  James R. Walker and, 145–46, 156, 163
National Committee on Prisons, 102–3
National Lawyers Guild, 163
Native American pride, 173–75, 184
Native American self-determination policy, 181–82
Navy, United States, 184
Nazi ideology, 171
New York City, 102
New York Times, 95
1957 revision of North Carolina literacy test, 152–55, 158
Nixon, Richard, 181
Norris, Josh, 89
Northampton County, North Carolina, 127, 149–51
Northampton County Board of Elections, 151, 155

North Carolina
  Board of Elections, 161
  Bureau of Mental Health and Hygiene, 99
  Department of Welfare, 91
  elections of 1874 in, 33
  increasing complexity of social life in, 8
  Jacksonian democracy in, 18–19
  literacy test in, 129–30
  training schools in, 91–94
North Carolina Central University, 135
North Carolina College for Negroes, 135, 148, 151
North Carolina constitution
  disfranchisement and, 130
  of 1868, 33
  of 1876, 33–34
  Jacksonian amendments to, 21
  literacy test and, 130, 155
North Carolina Court of Appeals, 186–87
North Carolina courts
  accessibility of, 4, 14–15
  attempts to democratize, 18–19
North Carolina Department of Environment and Natural Resources, 194
North Carolina General Assembly
  anti-evolutionism in, 70–71, 73–74, 86
  county option liquor stores approved in, 114
  literacy test revision approved in, 152, 162
  Lumbee Indians recognized in, 169
North Carolina State College, 71
North Carolina Supreme Court
  Barden v. Barden appeal, 14, 16–17, 19, 25
  Bazemore appeal, 159–62
  Carpenter v. Boyles appeal, 118–19, 121–22
  Chavis case and, 188
  Darnell case, 44, 54–58, 192
  democratization and, 18–19, 26
  diversity of, 193
  Lassiter appeal, 155
  limitations on the power of, 26
  Pentuff v. Park appeal, 79–84
  proposal to abolish, 19
  public opinion and, 25
  Scroggins v. Scroggins appeal, 14, 16–17, 19, 25
  Shipp & Bailey and, 36
  special verdicts and, 38
  State v. Ross ruling, 28, 39–40, 191
  voting rights appeals, 152
  James R. Walker Jr.'s criminal case, 150
  white supremacy and, 9
northeastern North Carolina, 132, 137, 139–42, 148, 158, 162

Oatey, Lane, 165
Ohanyerenwa, Chioma, 127
One World (Willkie), 171, 179
Osborne, Mary Lloyd, 120
Osborne, Philip, 127
Oxendine, Bertha, 183
Oxendine, Luther, 175
Oxendine School, 165, 188

padlocking, 113–14, 118, 122
  women and, 123
Page, Edward, 27
Park, John A., 75
Parker, Sarah, 193
paternalism, 52, 55–56
Patterson, Ryan, 89
Pearsall Plan of 1956, 169–70
penal reform, 101–3
Penn, George W., 50, 52

Pentuff, James R.
  anti-evolutionism of, 67–69, 72–73
  background, 67
  educational credentials of, 69, 77
  financial problems of, 77
  Fuquay Springs lectures, 73
  honor and, 3
  Poole Bill and, 70
  post-*Pentuff v. Park*, 87–88
  science and, 68–69
Pentuff v. Park
  background of, 69–75
  obscurity of, 64
  first trial, 75–79
  North Carolina Supreme Court appeal, 79–84
  responses to second trial, 85–87
  second trial, 84–87
Pesses, Emily, 165
Piedmont region of North Carolina, 133, 148
Phillips, Chad, 107
Phillips, F. D., 98–100
Plessy v. Ferguson, 59
poll taxes, 129–30, 140
politics and law, 28–29, 39
polygamy, 39
Poole, David, 69, 72
Poole Bill, 69–74, 76
Populist Party, 129
Porath, Carrie, 107
Poteat, William
  background, 66
  evolution and, 66–67
  Pentuff v. Park and, 81–82
  Poole Bill debate and, 71
  post-*Pentuff* career, 87
  religion and, 66–67, 69, 74
Pound, Roscoe, 1, 16
Powell, Graham, 89
Powell, Thomas William, Jr., 63
Presbyterians, 72

Prickett, Drew, 63
Pridgen, Margaret, 90, 95–96, 100
prison reform, 101–3
Progressive Era
  Jim Crow and, 47–48
  jurisprudence, 55, 59
  North Carolina public nuisance statute created during, 115
  reformism, 46–47
  Samarcand Manor's founding and the, 91, 101
prohibition, 70, 114, 120
Prospect School, 165, 174, 176–78, 182
Prospect Suit, 175, 179–80
prostitution, 92, 95, 111–12, 115
public nuisance law, 108, 115–16
  constitutionality of, 119
  suburbia and, 123
  used against Greenwich Village roadhouse, 116–17
Pupil Assignment Act of 1955, 169–70
Pustay, Mark, 165

race awareness meetings, 184
race relations seminars, 184
racial lines
  the law and, 5–6, 15, 43, 45
  Thomas Ruffin and, 19
  yeoman farmers and, 20–21
Raleigh, North Carolina, 18, 76, 148
Raleigh News and Observer, 70, 95, 98, 130
Raleigh Times, 65, 73, 75–76, 83–87
Randall, Sallie, 116–17
Ransom, Vicky, 174
Rayburn, Charles, 13
Reconstruction, 31–36, 119, 155
Regents of University of California v. Bakke, 180–81
registrars, electoral, 138–40

278   Index

rehabilitative ideal, 91, 101
Reinhardt, Alexander, 33
religion, freedom of, 181, 183
Republican party
  M. F. Boyles and, 108
  during Reconstruction, 28, 31–33, 36, 39, 119
  fusion with North Carolina Populists, 129–30
  in *State v. Darnell,* 58
residential segregation ordinances, 43–46
  African American response to, 49–50
  beyond Winston-Salem, 45
  cases concerning, 56
  in Winston-Salem, history of, 46–48
restrictive covenants, 46–48, 108, 214n60
Reynolds, R. J., 45–46
Reynolds, Shepherd, 127
Rissing, David, 107
roadhouses, 110–11, 114–16
Roanoke Island, 168
Robeson County, North Carolina, 8, 165–67
  Croatan Indians of, 169
  desegregation plan, 172–73
  double voting in, 176–77
  general characteristics of, 167
  federal funding, reliance upon, 172
  segregation in, 167–68, 172
Robeson County Board of Education, 176–77
Robeson County Jail, 96–97
Robeson County Superior Court, 178, 183
Robesonian, 169, 180, 182
Rocky Mount Telegram, 101
Rodd, D. B., 29–30
Rodman, William, 39–40

Roe v. Wade, 194
Roots, 179
Ross, Dock and Julia Ann, 29
Ross, Pinkney and Sarah
  background of, 29–30
  legal appeal, 39–40, 191
  marriage of, 31–32
  mobility of, 27–28, 30–32, 40
  post-trial lives of, 40–42
  trial of, 37–38, 194
Ruffin, Thomas
  Barden v. Barden ruling, 14, 17–18, 24–25
  divorce, views on, 19–20, 23
  marriage, views on, 19–20, 23
  prominence of, 1
  racial views of, 19
  religious views, 20
  Scroggins v. Scroggins ruling, 14, 17–18, 86–87
  slavery and, 20
  social status of, 19–20
  State v. Mann ruling, 20, 22
  style of opinion writing, 4, 21–22, 24–26, 28
rule of law, 29, 191
rules of evidence, 184–85
rural police, 112, 115–16, 123
Russell, Daniel, 129–30
Russia, 58

Salter, John, 89
Samarcand arson trial, 91, 98–101
Samarcand Manor Industrial Training School
  admissions policies, 92
  background, 91
  burning of, 90–96
  Efland Home compared to, 93–94
  poor treatment of inmates in, 93–96, 100
  portrayal in the press, 94

reform of, 101–5
Stonewall Jackson Training School compared to, 92–93, 104
training offered in, 92–93
Samarcand Sixteen, 95–97
San Marcos Academy, 77
Schenck, David, 36
election of, 33
in *State v. Kennedy*, 35
in *State v. Ross*, 37–38, 40
Schenck, Michael, 98, 100
Schifter, Richard, 171–72, 175, 179–81
school desegregation, 3, 154, 166, 174
Schwerner, Michael, 138
Scopes, John, 76
Scopes v. State, 64–65
Scott, D. H., 68
Scott, Estelle, 99
Scott, Kerr, 136–37
Scottsboro Boys, 10
Scroggins, Lucretia, 15–16, 23, 26
Scroggins, Marville, 3, 15–16, 23–26, 86–87
Scroggins v. Scroggins
distinguished from *Barden v. Barden*, 14–18, 24–25
effect of, 26
Ruffin's ruling in, 22–24
Seaboard precinct, 149–51
sensitivity training, 184
Sharp, J. A., 63–64, 89, 107
Shaw, Lemuel, 1
Shipp, William, 51
background, 35–37
in *State v. Ross* appeal, 39–40
in *State v. Ross* trial, 37–38
"single-shot" voting law, 144–45
Sissipahaw, 168
sit-ins, 128
Lumbee participation in, 170, 175

Slater Industrial Academy, 49
slavery
and family law, 20
and the legal system, 8, 195n4
Sledge, Francis M.
background, 50–51
defiance of segregation ordinance, 51
testimony in *Darnell*, 53–54
Small v. Edenton, 57
Smith, Edward, 54, 59
Smith v. Allwright (1944), 143
South Carolina, 31–32
Southern Baptist Theological Seminary, 77
Southern Bell Telephone and Telegraph, 109
Southern Conference Educational Fund, 9, 156
Spake, Harriet, 29–30
Spake, Samuel, 29
Spartanburg County, South Carolina, 29–32, 40–41
special verdict procedure, 38–39
speech, freedom of, 85–86
Stacy, Walter, 83
Standard Oil Company, 110
state courts versus federal courts, during civil rights movement, 148
state law
functions of, 2–3
and honor, 3
political functions of, 3
reach of, 192
social therapy and, 3
values debates in, 2–3
versus federal law, 1, 148
states' rights, 56–57, 60
Statesville, North Carolina, 133
State v. Chavis, 166
appeal, 186–88

State v. Chavis (cont.)
  arguments of defendants, 182–83, 187
  as an atypical case, 189
  background, 177–78
  effect on defendants' attitudes, 188
  In re McMillan and, 187
  jury selection, 182–83
  trial, 183–86
State v. Darnell
  Dillon's Rule in, 56–57
  effects of, 59–60
  North Carolina Supreme Court appeal, 54–58, 191–92
  reaction to, 58–59
  scholarly writing about, 44
  trial, 53–54
State v. Kennedy, 35
State v. Mann, 20, 22
State v. Neely, 36
State v. Negro Will, 197n19
State v. Reinhardt and Love, 33
State v. Ross
  appeal, 39–40, 191
  scholarly writing about, 28
  trial, 37–38
State v. William Manuel, 197n19
Stephens College, 77
Stephenson, Gilbert T.
  arguments in *Darnell* appeal, 54–55
  arguments in *Darnell* trial, 53
  background, 52–53
Stiles, Pearl, 97–98
Stonewall Jackson Training School, 92–94, 104
Stowe, Harriet Beecher, 22
Strader, J. Matthew, 43
Strike at the Wind, 174
suburbs, 113
suffrage and Jacksonian democracy, 18, 21
Summerlin, Elisabeth, 107

Sunday, Billy, 72
Sweatt v. Painter, 135–36
Swett, Purnell, 177, 183, 188

Tally, Tally & Bouknight, 175
Taylor, Helen H., 127, 149–51, 154–55
Taylor, Herman, 148, 152, 156, 163, 246
Taylor, W. H., 149–50
Tedrick, Daniel, 89
Tennessee, poll taxes in, 129
termination policy, 181
testimonial-therapeutic function of litigation, 166, 184
Texas State University for Negroes, 135
Thompson, Clara, 118
Timble, James, 47
Times Publishing Company, 75
Timmons-Goodson, Patricia, 193
Title VI of the Civil Rights Act of 1964, 172
Tocqueville, Alexis de, 2
tourist camps, 110–11
training schools, 91–94
Turley, Robin, 107
Turlington Act, 120
Turner, Nat, 21
Tuscaroras, 176
Twenty-first Amendment, 120

United Daughters of the Confederacy, 120
United Dry Forces, 120
United Nations, 171
Universal Declaration of Human Rights, 171
University of North Carolina-Chapel Hill, 87, 99, 119, 179
  Jim Crow segregation at, 133–36
University of North Carolina School of Law, 135–36

University of Texas School of Law, 135
University of Virginia School of Law, 179
urbanization, Winston-Salem and, 45–46
U.S. Army, 184
U.S. Commission on Civil Rights, 138–39
U.S. Department of Health, Education, and Welfare (HEW). *See* Health, Education, and Welfare, U.S. Department of
U.S. District Court in Raleigh, 148
U.S. Indian policy, 181–82
U.S. Navy, 184
U.S. Supreme Court
  affirmative action and, 180, 193
  anti-evolution laws and, 64
  Chavis case and, 188
  grandfather clauses and, 131, 152, 155
  interracial marriage bans and, 40
  Lassiter case and, 128, 151, 154–58, 162
  literacy test and, 155–58, 162
  prominence of, 1
  religious freedom and, 181
  residential segregation ordinances, 57
  school segregation and, 171–72
  segregated public legal education and, 135
  white primaries and, 143

values, law and, 2–3
Vann, Richard, 75, 81
Virginia, divorce law in, 20
Volstead Act, 120
voter registration, African American, 139–41, 143
Voting Rights Act of 1965, 138, 157, 162, 164

Waccamaw, 168
Wake County, North Carolina, 92
Wake Forest University, 66, 69, 87
Walker, Ethel, 132
Walker, James R., Jr.
  attempts to intimidate, 150
  Nancy Bazemore and, 158–59
  Bazemore appeal and, 159–62
  criminal prosecution of, 149–50
  direct action of, 145–147
  Sander Dockery's influence on, 133
  education of, 134–37
  effectiveness of, 162–63
  family background, 131–33
  family situation, 142–43
  federal law and, 167
  G.I. Bill and, 134–35
  Ivey v. Cole case, 147–49
  Louise Lassiter and, 128, 152–58
  Lassiter v. Northampton County Board of Elections case, 152–58, 162
  law practice in Statesville, 141
  legal strategies of, 143–62
  Mitchell & Taylor collaboration, 148
  NAACP and, 144–45, 156, 163
  poetry of James R. Walker Sr. and, 141–42
  recognition of, 163
  relocation to northeastern North Carolina, 142
  UNC School of Law, experiences at, 136–37
  World War II experience, 133–34
Walker, James R., Sr., 132, 141–42
Walker-Lassiter Defense Fund, 156
Warlick, Wilson, 115, 117–18, 121, 154
Warren, Earl, 64
Warren Court, 122

Watson, Buxton & Watson
  motivations for representing Darnell, 52
  reputation, 51
  State v. Darnell appellate arguments, 55
  State v. Darnell trial arguments, 53–54
Watson, Cyrus B., 51–52, 55, 59. *See also* Watson, Buxton & Watson
Waxhaw, 168
Webb, Velma, 109–10
Welch, J. D., 53
Weldon, North Carolina, 142–43, 146, 156
Wells, Bertram, 71
West Highland, 113
West's North Carolina Digest, 122
West View, 113
White, George Henry, 129–30
White, Jamison G., 89
white primaries, 129
white supremacy
  Heriot Clarkson and, 119
  courts as a limitation upon, 10
  law and, 5–6, 13
  movement during the late 1890s, 129–30
  Thomas Ruffin and, 19–20
  states' rights and, 56–57
  women's suffrage and, 55
  yeoman farmers and, 18
white supremacy club, 119
Wick, David, 89
Wickersham, George, 102
Wickersham Commission, 102
Wilkinson, William, 111
Wilkinson Boulevard, 110–14, 116–17
Williams, Alan, 165
Williams, Perry, 29
Wilmington Massacre, 130

Wilmington People's Press, 18, 196n15
Wilson, Noah, 115
Winborne, Wallace, 155
Winston-Salem
  growth of, 45–46
  Jim Crow in, 46
  progressivism in, 46–47
  post-*Darnell* residential patterns, 59
  residential segregation ordinance in (*see* residential segregation ordinances)
  size of, 72
Winston-Salem Building and Loan Association, 52
Winston-Salem Journal, 58
Winston-Salem State University, 49
Wipfler, Michael, 27
Wisconsin v. Yoder, 181, 183, 187
women
  lawyers, 98, 192–93
  legal treatment of, 90
  participation in the legal system, 8–9
Woodville precinct, 158–59
World of Our Fathers (Howe) 179
World War I, 63, 70, 101, 107, 112, 127–28, 171
World War II, 98, 105, 133–34, 141, 143
  civil rights and, 127, 133–34, 143
  James R. Walker Jr. and, 133–34
Wright, Richard, 27

Yancey County, North Carolina, 77
yeoman farmers, 15
  marriage and, 20–21
  racial views of, 21

Zenger, John Peter, 85
Zidow, John, 107
zoning ordinances, 108, 123, 192

www.ingramcontent.com/pod-product-compliance
Lightning Source LLC
Chambersburg PA
CBHW020640230426
43665CB00008B/255